Sourcebook on Labor
includes selections by
President Lyndon B. Johnson
Senator Barry Goldwater
Secretary of Labor W. Willard Wirtz
Supreme Court Justice Arthur J. Goldberg
George Meany
Walter P. Reuther
Emil Rieve
United States Chamber of Commerce
National Association of Manufacturers
Committee on Economic Development

Sourcebook
on Labor
Neil W. Chamberlain
Revised and abridged
with the assistance of
Richard Perlman

McGraw-Hill Book Company

New York Toronto London

Preface

This book is an effort to bring together some of the raw materials of the subject of industrial relations. It includes documents, company statements of labor policy, laws and court decisions, arbitration awards, and reports of governmental inquiries. It is sprinkled with excerpts from congressional hearings. It contains portions of speeches made by labor officials and management representatives.

There are two purposes to be served by a collection of this kind. One is to provide readier access to fugitive materials which are often difficult to locate even in the best-organized and best-stocked libraries. The other is to afford greater opportunity for a person to make an informed judgment for himself on the debatable issues of labor relations and to appraise for himself the plausibility of judgments made by "experts." He can see side by side different interpretations of the same problem presented in the words of those who want to convince others of their views. He is exposed to unfiltered bias, often persuasively reasoned, of the sort to which he will continue to be exposed for the rest of his life, and is invited to examine it critically.

It has not been an easy task to compile this volume, since there is a surplus of riches as well as dross. Keeping the total length manageable has not been easy. Others would not have selected as I have, I know; I would welcome from them suggestions for exclusion, inclusion, and substitution in the event there should be another edition.

Neil W. Chamberlain

Contents

Contents

Sourcebook
on Labor

1: Unions and Union Leadership

Even a parsimonious selection of materials reflecting the efforts of workers to win the right to organize unions against the opposition of employers and courts over a span of almost 150 years would take more space than we can afford. We start right out, then, from where "modern" labor-management relations takes its point of departure—the National Labor Relations Act of 1935, popularly known as the Wagner Act. The section which is reproduced below was retained in the Taft-Hartley Act of 1947 and is still law. Other provisions of these two pieces of labor legislation are given in Chapters 4, 11, and 16.

STATEMENT OF PUBLIC POLICY

National Labor Relations Act. 1935, Sec. 1

Experience has proved that protection by law of the right of employes to organize and bargain collectively safeguards commerce from injury, impairment, or interruption, and promotes the flow of commerce by removing certain recognized sources of industrial strife and unrest, by encouraging practices fundamental to the friendly adjustment of industrial disputes arising out of differences as to wages, hours, or other working conditions, and by restoring equality of bargaining power between employers and employes.

It is hereby declared to be the policy of the United States to eliminate the causes of certain substantial obstructions to the free flow of commerce and to mitigate and eliminate these obstructions when they have occurred by encouraging the practice and procedure of collective bargaining and by protecting the exercise by workers of full freedom of association, self-organization, and designation of representatives of their own choosing, for the purpose of negotiating the terms and conditions of their employment or other mutual aid or protection.

A PAGEANT OF PROGRESS

A union official once said of his fellow unionists, with rare objectivity, "They glory in their past wars like American Legionnaires." Like American citizens recalling the events of their country's greatness or veterans remembering their campaigns, old-time union members frequently dust off reminders of the grim struggle for existence in the union's formative

1

*days, the historic strikes—won or lost—to compel some recalcitrant em-
ployer to recognize the union or concede some principle. Younger members, in these days when unionism is taken more matter-of-factly, often
imbibe the emotional fervor associated with a cause. The following
excerpt from a 20th anniversary celebration of the founding of the CIO
should convey something of that impression.*

**From Ammunition, published by the United Automobile Workers, January,
1956**

MUSIC: "We will build a new world . . ."

NARRATOR: Sidney Hillman once declared: "There is no welfare without the
social welfare." CIO has always recognized that its members could not be fully
served at the collective bargaining table alone. Economic progress, peace,
democracy in all its forms—these objectives of society were the objectives of
organizd labor. CIO has said that "what is good for America is good for the
CIO." Shortly before he died, Hillman stated, with simple eloquence . . .

VOICE: "We want a better America, an America that will give its citizens,
first of all, a higher and higher standard of living so that no child will cry for
food in the midst of plenty. We want to have an America where the inventions
of science will be at the disposal of every American family, not merely for the
few who can afford them. An America that will have no sense of insecurity and
which will make it possible for all groups, regardless of race, creed, or color to
live in friendship, to be real neighbors; an America that will carry its great
mission of helping other countries to help themselves."

NARRATOR: On many fronts, CIO has been working and fighting to create
this kind of America, this kind of world. It has provided the training grounds
for citizenship. Thousands of men and women have served . . . wherever
people are working together to further the social good. . . .

VOICE: "The fact is that the CIO was born in an atmosphere of hunger and
poverty—yes, and desperation. We organized, and we went on strike. We challenged the great corporations and we resisted the nightsticks and the tear gas
of our police. Today trade unions of America have fought their way to acceptance by the corporations and the government. But keep this in mind: no government, no administration, no group of public officials, no matter how friendly,
can hold our gains for us. It is only our unions supported by the solid determination of our members, which can insure our future."

NARRATOR: It is 20 years now since the letters CIO first made an indelible
mark upon American history. And those who have been privileged to be associated with this stirring chapter are not content merely to look back upon that
chapter with pride; they again turn their eyes to the future, a future of new
opportunities, new goals, new dreams.

VOICE: "This is the beginning of what can be the most glorious chapter in
the history of the American labor movement. . . . Let us join hands with the
men and women of good will in the AFL and together face the future with the
will, the courage, and dedication that we have demonstrated in the past. . . .

Together we can be among the important architects in the building of that better tomorrow, that better world, and we can fashion it in the image of freedom and justice and decency and human brotherhood."

NARRATOR: Those were the words of hope and confidence of the President of the CIO—the words of Walter P. Reuther when the historic merger agreement was adopted earlier this year. Hope and confidence that flow from strength, from unity, from solidarity. . . .

VOICE: "When the Union's inspiration through the worker's blood shall run,
There can be no power greater anywhere beneath the sun;
Yet what force on earth is weaker than the feeble strength of one,
But the Union makes us strong."

NARRATOR: Some have sung just the last words—words of hope, words of strength, words of brotherhood—

"Solidarity forever. Solidarity forever. Solidarity forever.
For the Union makes us strong."
(Audience joins in singing. The curtain falls.)

The popular image of a labor leader is often of a rough-spoken firebrand or agitator who stirs up discontent among workers and refuses to listen to "reason" as presented by an employer. There are such people among the officials of labor unions in the United States, but they are far less typical—particularly at the national level—than the kind of person who is described below.

A DAY IN THE LIFE OF A LABOR LEADER

From Business Week, August 18, 1951, pp. 42–50, by special permission

6:00   It isn't quite 6 a.m. in the Rogers Park section of Chicago. [A] man has just asked the operator to connect him with a West Coast representative of the Building Service Employees Int'l. Union. The man in Chicago is William L. McFetridge, [former] president of the BSEIU. He's had a restless night worrying about a strike he had authorized a West Coast local union to call.

In a moment, McFetridge will be talking to his Coast officer—pulled away from a heated 12-hour bargaining session that seems fated to end in a walkout. McFetridge is going to tell him he has thought it over: A strike now looks like bad strategy; the local should agree to arbitrate. The West Coast local will do what McFetridge suggests. McFetridge's policies prevail in the BSEIU. They have built the union into a strong, respected, and well-run organization—a far cry from what it was under his predecessor, the notorious George Scalise.

To achieve that feat, and to rise as he has in the labor movement, McFetridge has used a combination of talent, shrewdness, and energy. Without being so well-known as some of his compeers, McFetridge is in some ways the model U.S. labor leader. For the log of an average day in the union executive's work life, [we continue].

7:45   McFetridge leaves his seven-room corner house. He has read two newspapers. [He has] homework under his arm.

8:00   He unparks his Cadillac and drives to work. It's usually his only half-hour of the day free from business details.

8:20   He reaches his office, just west of the Loop. The seven-story Building Service Center is owned by BSEIU.

8:30   Mail, memos, phone calls. Most deal with new contracts, union rivalries, staff problems, employer relations.

10:30   Staff conferences begin. [On this day], one is with Martin Dwyer, of Local 66, on pay rates for elevator starters.

11:30   Meetings. [Today it is] a group of BSEIU agents. The agenda: employer relations, rank-and-file sentiment, reports.

1:00   Lunch—always business. This time it's with Frank C. Wells, president of Chicago Real Estate Board, over effect of rent control on real estate income.

2:30   McFetridge budgets two afternoons a week for civic activity. [Today] he sits as a member of the Chicago Parks Commission. His associates, business and professional men, value his judgment.

4:00   At his office in the Park District's headquarters, he goes over all building plans. He has been a member since 1943, is now chairman of the commission.

5:15   Back to his own office. If he hasn't got his second wind by this time, he'll have stopped for a single Martini.

5:30   And on until 7:30—or it may be 9, 10, or midnight—in his ceaseless battle to clear his desk before leaving.

8:30   Tonight it's a dinner on the far West Side, given by one of his locals to city bowling champions. He'll make a speech. . . . With luck, he'll be home by 1 a.m.

An opinion polling organization once asked loyal union members what they thought employers did. Some of the answers were pretty sensible, but many of them would hit the average businessman like a sharp jab in the solar plexus. Reappearing frequently were such responses as: entertains customers at fancy night clubs; clips coupons; goes to Florida; sits in his club and damns the New Deal.

Shocking as these opinions are, they nevertheless bear some resemblance to those held by some businessmen about labor leaders. The average union head has some reason to believe that he is regarded in management circles as a high-living, Florida-commuting, orating, trouble-maker.

In actual fact, job descriptions of the work of responsible union executives and business executives would have a great deal in common. And even where they would appear most divergent, there are subsurface similarities.

For example: The time spent by the labor man making speeches and talking to the press is aimed at the same general object as the businessman's time for advertising and public relations problems.

The labor man's parleys with fellow laborites are of the same stuff as the management man's activities in his trade association.

And in one area now, it's almost impossible to tell whether it's a union or a business executive doing the complaining about the increasing amount of time required. That's in dealing with lawyers. How to operate under government regulations raises questions that have appreciably lengthened the workday of both. Opposed as may be their goals, philosophy, and interests, their executive responsibilities make them cousins, if not brothers, under the skin.

WOMB TO TOMB

Although labor executive William L. McFetridge gets pictured and quoted in the newspapers less than some other union leaders who preside over large organizations, his job is pretty much the same as those who are basking in the limelight.

He runs the union of 200,000 men and women who operate the elevators, do the building and grounds maintenance, wash the windows, dispose of the garbage, and perform other services in urban life.

His Building Service Employees International Union, like so many other labor organizations, is not accurately named. It includes men and women workers having nothing at all to do with building service.

It is, among other things, the world's only womb-to-tomb union. In the bizarre jurisdictional patchquilt that is the AFL, McFetridge has managed to get BSEIU membership cards into the soft hands of nurses' aides who prepare expectant mothers for their trip to the delivery room, and into the calloused palms of men who dig graves in some of the largest cemeteries in the United States.

BSEIU has contracts with Harvard College and California Tech; with burlesque theaters and Trinity Church; with Rockefeller (for Radio City), and more John Does and Richard Roes than possibly any other labor organization. The Does and Roes are the small landlords who sometimes employ only one man, a janitor.

But McFetridge wants that one employee to be in BSEIU and has made law by getting the courts to decide one employee is "an appropriate bargaining unit" for purposes of a labor board election.

RISE OF A LEADER

McFetridge will be 58 years old his next birthday. Up to a point his biography might be that of any one of scores of well-known businessmen. He was born in a Chicago factory neighborhood and was in the sixth grade at public school when the family moved to McFarland, Wis. His father, a teamsters union member, owned and operated a small ice delivery service.

McFetridge quit school and small-town life when he was 13; he got a $20-a-month office boy job at the Milwaukee Road in Chicago. Seventeen years later, he had worked himself up to traveling claims agent. Then he thought he saw a better opportunity with American Express. It wasn't there, and he went back to the Milwaukee Road, staying until 1923.

During these years, McFetridge felt squeezed between his ambitions and his limited education. To make up what he lacked, he went to night school "for more years than I want to remember," he says. Through high school, prelaw, and law school he dogged it three hours a night, night after night, year after year. It has given him one unusual attribute: No matter how tired he is, he can't nap after dinner. "I used to hold my breath to keep awake," he says, re-calling the tedium of the grubby classrooms. "Now I couldn't fall asleep in a chair if I was drugged." It's an invaluable asset for a man who has to spend a great many of his evenings on a dais, listening to speech follow speech after a very hearty serving of roast chicken.

At the age of 30, McFetridge saw his star. He accepted a job offer from his uncle, William Quesse, who was then president of the Chicago Flat Janitors Union—Local 1 of BSEIU. The newcomer to the labor movement was employed as confidential secretary, general aide, investigator, and trouble-shooter; it was work for which his experience as claims agent was not badly suited.

On his own, the union tyro organized Chicago school maintenance workers. He became head of their new local, which affiliated with BSEIU. After that, his rise was sure, if not too rapid. By 1940 he was a national vice-president of BSEIU, an officer in both the Illinois and Chicago Federations of Labor, a well-known and important union figure in the Midwest. Having reached a secure position in the second magnitude, like so many corporation vice-presidents, it looked as though he had gone just about as far as he could go.

THE TURNING POINT

But then the lightning struck. When the storm was over, George Scalise, president of BSEIU was on his way to jail for extortion; the union had declined to fewer than 70,000 discouraged, embittered members; at least $1.5-million was missing from the union treasury; and McFetridge himself had gone through—and survived unsullied—marathon grand jury sessions where every-thing including his remote cousins' bank accounts were subpoenaed, audited, and examined.

The careful, almost-reluctant conclusion of the courts and prosecutors was that McFetridge was an honest man in a nest of thieves. It was that conclusion and his experience that made him the logical man for the job of putting the union back together after Scalise and the Capone mob had left it a shambles. Along with a few seasoned men—like David Sullivan in New York, Charles Hardy in San Francisco, and William Cooper in Milwaukee—who had been uncorrupted by the gangsters, he started the rehabilitation and rebuilding.

Under his presidency, BSEIU has become powerful, wealthy, and respected. It has achieved a record of peaceful bargaining, contract observance, and wage progress that not many other unions can equal. And rising with the union, McFetridge has now moved well into the first magnitude of labor leaders.

Today he is a member of AFL's top executive council, along with such other large men as Hutcheson of the carpenters, Tobin of the teamsters, Dubinsky of the garment workers. He is the newest member of that select group, having been elected to it only last year. But already some of the people whose ideas count are saying he might be the man to succeed Bill Green when the time comes for the federation to get a new president.

LOW-PRESSURE APPROACH

Meanwhile, McFetridge preserves a rare nonconformism for a labor leader. He doesn't mind being called a Republican and was unperturbed by the barbs tossed in his direction when he came out for Dewey in the Presidential election of 1948.

His union salary is $32,000 a year—cut back to $22,000 during the war at his request. His nonunion life centers on his wife and two now-grown daughters; on a summer home near Antioch, Ill.; on a lake where he can fish and swim; and now—like many another Chicagoan—on the ups and downs of the White Sox in the American League pennant race.

In negotiations with employers, McFetridge operates at a low pressure, is addicted to brief speaking, and is almost subdued in manner. He has a habit of looking at you, intent and unsmiling, while his fingers make and unmake a church steeple in moments of greatest concentration.

McFetridge will sometimes bowl an employer over with an observation or insight that could only come from a businessman. To the question, where did he get it, the answer is simple: He's a director of the Bank of Rogers Park and participates in the conservative management of its more than $11-million assets.

UNION POLITICS

Wherever there are organizations which offer exceptional individuals a chance to distinguish themselves from the crowd by exercising leadership functions, there must be politics. People vie for office, seek to organize followings, attempt to win the approval of the electorate. Unions inescapably have their politics, and union politics sometimes "takes it out" on management.

A reply to a question addressed to William Gomberg, then Director, Management Engineering Department, International Ladies' Garment Workers Union, in a forum of the American Management Association, reprinted from The Union's Role in Production Management, American Management Association Production Series No. 189, 1950, pp. 23–24

QUESTION: Can absolute work standards be maintained by a union suffering from internal politics?

MR. GOMBERG: To the same extent to which they can be maintained by a management suffering from internal politics. That's what I call a loaded question. The assumption is that unions are more political than they are, because union bureaucracy is relatively public. Businesses are also political, but there the bureaucracy is private.

Politics enter into a union when various people vie for the confidence of the membership. And so a scramble ensues. Politics enter into a company when the various executive heads vie for the favor of the guy whose decision is final. Union politics take place in a democratic frame of reference—business politics in an authoritarian frame of reference. And with all those limitations, both management and labor have maintained production standards.

Here is the way the problem solves itself. Sooner or later, the fellow who tries to be a demagogue by continually pressing the company for an unreasonable production standard begins to get on the nerves of the membership, because they want to work—provided that they get a decent break from management—not to be kept in a state of perpetual turmoil. In the normal course of events, a local union election is held, and the fellow who has nothing more than a neurosis to recommend him to the membership is thrown out.

Why are wildcat strikes no longer a problem? Remember when everybody was so worried about wildcats? The reason wildcats are no longer a problem is that the fellows who would militantly march the boys out on the picket line, would then have to march them back a few days later without any improvement in working conditions. The boys got sick and tired of having these fellows march them in and out, so they threw them out of office and that was the end of that. These situations stabilize themselves. That is how production standards get stabilized in a union.

Now, when union politics arise as a result of management's playing politics —whether by trying to get rid of the union or by favoring the particular faction with which it thinks it can make a deal—then management becomes a party to the mess and things never get settled. But given an ordinary relationship, where management has made up its mind that it ought to live with the union, and the union is still wild—its heritage, doubtless, of the days when the very existence of unions was challenged—certain stabilizing groups begin to assert themselves in the union.

I cannot promise you that if on Monday you make up your mind to a sound relationship with the union, on Tuesday you are going to have perfect peace and complete acceptance of reasonable standards. But I can tell you this: Over the course of two years or so, given a good relationship with management, the political situation within the union will gradually stabilize. The union man who is willing to take a stand and make it possible for these fellows to keep working and make their wages will win and the result will be that you need fear no politics in the union as far as you are concerned.

What you mean by politics, of course, is the ugly sort of politics, for the very relationship of management and workers is politics. After all, what is politics? It is the way men contest for authority, whether on the board of directors or on the executive board of the union.

UNION DEMOCRACY

Hearings before a special subcommittee of the House Committee on Education and Labor, 81st Cong., 1st and 2d Sess., 1950, pp. 468–473

In 1949 the House of Representatives Committee on Education and Labor appointed a special subcommittee to inquire into the existence or *nonexistence of undemocratic processes in labor unions. In the course of those hearings the following interchange took place between Representative Andrew Jacobs of Indiana and James M. Duffy, president of the National Brotherhood of Operative Potters. The discussion relates to the union's preceding national election, in which an opposition slate of candidates had impugned the ability and integrity of the incumbent officers. As a result, the former were charged with "malicious representations" and, by decision of the Brotherhood's national convention, ordered to pay a fine of $50 each. Those who were disciplined challenged the validity of this judgment in the Ohio courts, which ruled "that the action of the 1949 convention in fining plaintiffs because of publication or distribution of the handbills constituted an infringement of the right of free speech. . . ."*

MR. JACOBS: Mr. Duffy, I would like to ask you a few questions. This committee, of course, was not constituted for the purpose of deciding an election issue in your union. That is the function of the membership. Nor are we to sit in judgment upon the wisdom of the membership in electing or rejecting any slate of candidates.

You refer to this [opposition] group as a " disturbing element," and I suppose they were a disturbing element. Personally, I have always considered the Republican Party in my district a disturbing element. [Laughter.]

I suppose that Mr. Werdel and Mr. Morton consider the Democratic Party a disturbing element in their districts. Down where Mr. Sims comes from, I suppose there is a Democratic faction that disturbs some of the people down there once in a while.

The thing that I see in your case here is this: That here is some literature that was gotten out. And, as I view the evidence that you have given here and the evidence that the other witnesses have given, it seems to be pretty will conceded that some of these men were actually tried and penalized for circulating literature in an election. It may have been a dirty campaign. I mean I have been in dirty campaigns myself. Of course, I never participated in any dirt now; you understand that.

MR. DUFFY: We are not used to them. It is new to us. Maybe that is why we dislike it.

MR. JACOBS: But doesn't it sort of seem to you that it is just a kind of part of a political campaign for people to print their ideas and their views and what they think about the other fellow, et cetera, and circulate it? That that is just a sort of part of the American system of election, and that we just more or less take it in our stride? Don't you think that is a pretty good American custom?

MR. DUFFY: What is evidenced in those handbills in all my experience in the trade-union movement I never knew any such thing to happen. What about my family?

MR. JACOBS: Well, I know they said some—

MR. DUFFY: Why should we be subjected to such accusations and so forth without some chance to defend ourselves and get some redress from those things?

MR. JACOBS: Well, I think that is right. I think that it is a rugged game. I have been in it. I have been in politics. And it is a rugged game. I remember, notwithstanding the fact that I am a teetotaler and don't drink anything, that the rumor got around in one neighborhood in Indianapolis that I was paralyzed drunk.

MR. DUFFY: I have had the same experience.

MR. JACOBS: Well, I think I asked for it when I went in politics.

MR. DUFFY: I had the same experience, and I am the same kind of "gink" as you. I don't drink and smoke.

MR. MORTON: Somebody spread the rumor in Kentucky I was a prohibitionist. [Laughter.] That is harder on me than what they spread on you.

MR. JACOBS: Well, it seems to me—of course, we can hardly discredit all of the statements that are made. There was some controversy over salaries; and, personally, I am not questioning the justice of your salary, but the court did decide with these men. I mean we can't get away from that. And, certainly, we are not questioning whether the court was honest or not. They may have been right or wrong, but they had a right to bring out these facts, circulate the literature. You had the right to print literature and answer it.

What I am driving at is this: I would like to ask this question. Do you think that unions should operate democratically?

MR. DUFFY: We do. We do.

MR. JACOBS: You believe they should?

MR. DUFFY: I have never known any base of operation but democratically.

MR. JACOBS: That means that the membership shall vote upon who shall be the officers. Is that not right?

MR. DUFFY: No one has ever questioned that.

MR. JACOBS: Don't you think that the membership naturally must have some information about how to vote—like we get in the campaigns? Sometimes you get publicity in the newspapers. Sometimes you like it, and sometimes you do not. I have had it both ways.

MR. DUFFY: Are you assuming, may I ask, Mr. Chairman, that if there are two men contesting for public office, equally worthy and clean in every respect, that if one of those individuals by making nasty charges and calling dirty, nasty names and definite insinuations of dishonesty, can you by any moral standard that you know of condone and regard that as decent and fair?

MR. JACOBS: I am not talking so much, Mr. Duffy, about whether it is decent or not as I am the fact that no one has even been able to find the line where censorship is to be drawn. I mean in order to have a free press, in order to have free speech, in order to have free elections, we have to endure a good many things that are very distasteful and quite often very unfair. Otherwise, we do not know where to draw the line in order to make a fair rule.

I mean someone may publish something about me or you when we are seeking office, and the inference may be very bad. And yet, if you draw the line there, the censor of that must always try the case and see whether or not it is justified. And I thought that it was pretty well determined in the American way of life that we have no censorship. Of course, you can always sue for libel if it is utterly false.

But, I have read these dodgers here. I would say they are a little "salty" in places, but it seems that at least there is some basis for what they said in the court's decision. And as to whether or not you could rebut them would be a question for you to print counteracting literature.

MR. DUFFY: We don't indulge in that kind of stuff, and we never are, so far as I am concerned. The statement that we disregard, show disrespect for decisions in courts—is that serious or not? Now, maybe, Mr. Chairman, I have had the wrong kind of "fetching up," as they say, to be in this kind of lousy campaign business.

I am not interested, or I am not going to be a party to it. I am not going to participate in it. And I am going to do everything in my power to prevent it.

Mr. Finlay [opposition candidate for the president's office] is notoriously known around our neighborhood for having made the statement in barber shops —and God knows that's the place to be heard, in the barber shop—he has said on many occasions—speaking of intolerance—any laboring man who did not vote the Democratic ticket was crazy or a fool, or words to that effect.

MR. JACOBS: Well, I would say on that I don't know but what I would agree with him, but I certainly would not punish him if he didn't. I mean I would not punish him. I think he would be free.

MR. DUFFY: And how can you sit there and so facetiously and so humorously make a joke of a statement made by an individual that anyone that didn't vote a certain political way was a fool? How can you do that?

MR. JACOBS: I think that what I say is that he should not be penalized for being wrong if he wanted to be.

MR. DUFFY: He was not penalized, Mr. Chairman. But it just shows the state of mind and the inclination of the individual.

MR. JACOBS: In other words, I agree with your construction of that statement —that the man has a right to vote as he pleases. I think he has a right to argue whichever side he pleases, either verbally or in writing.

Now, let's get to the court case.

MR. DUFFY: If you give me one word—

MR. JACOBS: Sure; go ahead.

MR. DUFFY: There is nothing I would like better than everyone or anyone or all of you gentlemen to come to our convention. If I have been derelict or if I have been loose in anything in convention, it has been in my determination, as I always stated to the delegates, that no one is going to be deprived of getting up on this floor and speaking his piece. I have specifically said on many occasions that, if I must do violence to something in order to give every delegate, every individual an opportunity to speak his piece wholeheartedly and completely, I am going to do violence to parliamentary procedure and see they get on their feet and speak their piece.

Mr. Chairman, I take these things seriously, and I don't think anything in connection with a man's citizenship and his rights and privileges is anything to be making a joke over. Not one iota. I can't see that.

MR. JACOBS: Well, let's approach it in this way: I am inclined to be convinced, from what you have said here, that you have been forthright; you have been very frank. There is not any question but what these men were penalized for circulating this literature. I do not think that it is a question here of whether you are honest, but rather a question of whether you have mistaken the rights of citizenship of these men to circulate the literature.

I think you have been perfectly honest and frank about it. Well, after all, I asked you the question; you answered it. You seem to think that the union should have the right to penalize these men for circulating the literature.

MR. DUFFY: Because the constitution forbade such literature.

MR. JACOBS: I am inclined to be of the opinion that the constitution of an organization cannot forbid a member from exercising their natural rights, or, if it can, that it should be forbidden from so providing.

In other words, I have a feeling that, if your union is going to operate democratically, then the members must have a right to print and disseminate literature as they see fit—answering, of course, for libel.

MR. DUFFY: They do.

MR. JACOBS: Now, take the court case, for example. Some of them were suspended from or disfranchised, we will say, for a period of 10 years because they brought an action in court. But the court agreed with them. The court must have thought that under the law of the land they were not required to exhaust such remedies as may have been left to them. There must have been some reason, and there are many reasons, why a member of a union is not required to exhaust his remedies. Sometimes the remedies are considered inadequate.

On that I am passing no judgment. The court passed judgment on that. But doesn't it seem a good deal out of line that the union should penalize members for seeking remedy in court when the court agreed with him he was entitled to that remedy?

MR. DUFFY: In answer to that, may I state, Mr. Chairman, that I will just make use of a phrase or statement of lawyers and judges: "Coming into court with clean hands."

Now, let's assume that I have done my job conscientiously and wholeheartedly and earnestly. We have got as good increases in wages as any organization in this United States of America. We have maintained industrial peace, which means taking care of public welfare. Let's assume that I have done those things with the aid of my fellow officers. Then along comes an election. Here are men that couldn't be elected on their own ability, and so forth. Then they resort to that kind of business.

Now, listen, Chairman—Mr. Chairman—you know just as well as I do the peculiar workings of the human mind and in an eleventh-hour release what they can do by some insinuation and that sort of thing. And such things sometimes result in the more competent and better man being defeated and the lesser getting the job.

Now, surely—

MR. JACOBS: Let me ask you a question.

MR. DUFFY: Surely you are not going to give me an argument and say that is democratic procedure.

MR. JACOBS: Well, I don't believe you and I have the same comprehension of what democratic procedure is. I think you are honest. I give you credit for that. I believe that you believe that you are the best of two men in the race. And I believe that you believe that the things that were said about you in these circulars were not warranted.

MR. DUFFY: I know they were untrue.

MR. JACOBS: I think that you are honest in your views. But, on the other hand, I do not know just where you are going to draw the line on censorship. If you are going to have a censorship, you can draw the line at the wrong place as well as you can at the right place, and I do not believe that the one concerning whom the articles are being written least of all should be a censor. I mean those are my views.

But, after all, we cannot decide it here anyway, Mr. Duffy. The purpose of the hearing is not to determine whether you were right or they were right. The purpose of the hearing is to determine whether or not they were prevented from exercising democratic rights. And I do not believe you and I probably see it in the same light, so I think I have no further questions.

MR. DUFFY: Just a little comment. I disagree with you that you and I have any different comprehension as to democratic rights, and so forth. But have we not proceeded democratically? We depend on the majority.

MR. JACOBS: But curtailment of the right of free speech, free press, et cetera, those are things in our way of life that a majority cannot take away from a minority. We may be different in that.

MR. DUFFY: I agree with you in what you have said, Mr. Chairman, but surely you do not believe in compromising with falsehood and that sort of thing, and that can be involved.

MR. JACOBS: Well, my view of it is that with a good record such as you have described you should be able to meet it, and apparently you did, and that seems to me that that is the complete answer to your problem.

EXTERNAL REVIEW OF INTERNAL UNION AFFAIRS

For many years both friends and critics of the labor movement have argued that its internal governmental procedures did not adequately protect the democratic rights of its members.

In 1957 the AFL-CIO drafted a series of "ethical practice codes" one purpose of which was to encourage its constituent unions to adopt procedures where needed for ensuring individual rights of participation in union affairs. These codes set standards, but the federation had no powers of enforcing compliance. Enforceable standards have been provided through other devices: (1) a public "review board" established by a

*union itself, as in the case of the Upholsterers' and Automobile Workers'
unions, and* (2) *the Labor-Management Reporting and Disclosure Act
of 1959.*

(1) THE UAW PUBLIC REVIEW BOARD

*From A More Perfect Union . . . The UAW Public Review Board—Why,
What, How, pp. 3–7*

On April 8, 1957, the 16th constitutional convention of the United Automobile, Aircraft and Agricultural Implement Workers of America—the UAW—
took the unprecedented step of establishing a public review board of independent distinguished citizens to which members could appeal their grievances
against the union and which could act, on its own motion, as censor of the
union's moral conduct.

The board was established upon the recommendation of the UAW's international executive board. It was established in an organization whose democratic
processes, ethical standards, financial repute and existing appeals procedure
had never been seriously questioned. Indeed, the handful of convention delegates who opposed the measure did so on the grounds that the UAW's
machinery for assuring full justice for the individual member needed no improvement. . . .

The first public mention of the plan came in March 1957, in Reuther's report
to the forthcoming UAW convention.

On behalf of the UAW executive board he proposed two changes in the
union's trial machinery. The first was selection of local union trial boards by
lot, rather than by election, to prevent the administration of justice from
becoming a local political issue. The second was the public review board as
an alternative—at the member's choice—to the established procedure of an
appeal to the convention as the final step in a dispute between an individual
or a subordinate body and the international union. . . .

Under the constitutional amendment adopted by the UAW convention, the
public review board has broad powers in two major fields.

It is given the "authority and duty to make final and binding decisions" in
all cases placed before it by aggrieved members or subordinate bodies of the
UAW. Essentially these cases will involve individual members who feel they
have been unfairly disciplined by their local unions and who have failed to
obtain satisfaction upon appeal to the UAW executive board. Also included
will be local unions which feel they have been unfairly disciplined by the
international.

But in addition, the public review board has the obligation to deal with
"alleged violations of any AFL-CIO ethical practices codes, or any ethical
practices codes adopted by the international union." In such cases the chairman
of the public review board must be given copies of every complaint reaching
the UAW executive board, and must be kept advised of the progress of the
case through the executive board. Further, the public review board is author-

ized to assume jurisdiction over these cases if it is dissatisfied with the executive board's action, even if no appeal is filed.

Finally, in cases involving ethical practices, the complainant may bypass an appeal to his local union if he can convince either the public review board or the international executive board that he has valid reasons.

Other appeals begin in the same manner as previously provided by the UAW constitution. A member who has been disciplined by a trial committee of his own local must first appeal to a general membership meeting of the local union (or the delegate body of an amalgamated local union). If still dissatisfied, he must within 30 days appeal to the international executive board, with a brief written summary of the case. Should he fail to get satisfaction from the international executive board, he may, if he chooses, take his appeal to the UAW convention, as before; but he may elect, instead, to go to the public review board. He can't go to both. . . .

Obviously the personnel of the public review board is a vital element in its acceptance by the UAW membership and the general public. Reuther placed six nominees before the convention:

Rabbi Morris Adler of Detroit.

Msgr. George G. Higgins, director of the National Catholic Welfare Conference.

Dr. Clark Kerr, chancellor of the University of California.

Dr. Edwin Witte, University of Wisconsin professor.

Judge Wade H. McCree of the Michigan Circuit Court.

Bishop G. Bromley Oxnam, Methodist bishop of Washington.

Following the convention, Reuther named Magistrate J. Arthur Hanrahan of Windsor, Ont. to the seventh place. Rabbi Adler was chosen as its chairman.

From the Second Annual Report of the Public Review Board, 1959, pp. 12–13

The variety of complaints that comes to the Public Review Board is great. There are, however, certain categories in which most of them fall, and it may be of interest to set forth some of the more important. They include: claims of prejudicial handling of shop grievances; claims of political reprisals; claims of failure to abide by constitutional provisions and by-laws; claims of undue delay in processing appeals; claims of election irregularities and excesses; claims of denial of democratic rights at membership meetings and in related respects; claims of discrimination as to seniority matters; claims of union-management collusion. . . .

The typical complaint would not be confined to any one of these categories but would cut across several. For example, claims of favoritism and discrimination underlie or infiltrate, in various degrees, most of the complaints received. . . .

Early last fall, shortly after the execution of the new contracts between the Union and the large auto producers, two members of a local union came to Public Review Board headquarters. Their problem grew out of a conflict over seniority rights. Their story was one of being constantly thwarted by Local officials in their efforts to exercise certain membership rights. They said that they were not recognized at meetings, were unable to see copies of the collective bargaining agreement, were refused copies of the local by-laws, and were generally dealt with in a discriminatory fashion befitting the fact that they and the thirty-some other members in the department in which they worked were a small minority in a local of some 3,000 to 4,000 members.

Specifically, the new collective bargaining agreement covering the Local, including seniority provisions, was in the process of consideration and ratification by the Local Union membership. A series of membership meetings was accordingly being held to acquaint the membership with the various provisions of the contract and to afford them the opportunity of ratification or rejection. What the complainants wanted was an opportunity to be heard before the Local membership when the seniority question which concerned them came up for consideration.

The Office of the International President was contacted by the Public Review Board office and arrangements made for a meeting of the complainants with one of the President's administrative assistants. Thereafter, the officers of the Local Union were contacted by the International concerning the complaint. The consequence of the foregoing was that the complainants and representatives of their group were accorded a full opportunity to present their contentions when the seniority question of their concern came before the Local membership. As a result, their point of view prevailed overwhelmingly.

This experience on the part of the complainants and their colleagues in interest led to a reawakening of their interest in the political process of their local union, as evidenced by the following letter sent by the original complainants to the office of the Public Review Board several months later:

> We have taken your counsel, and got active in our local politics. We can tell you that our group was instrumental in having our opposition defeated in the primaries and finals. Mr. [name deleted], myself and all the boys in our dept. will be indebted to you and your office, for the help we have received. The boys in our dept. became more alert and active in our union, since they knew that your office is in existence, and knowing that any individual, or a minority group has a place that they can be heard and helped.
>
> We Thank You Wholeheartedly.
>
> /Signatures/

(2) BILL OF RIGHTS AND REPORTING PROVISIONS OF LABOR-MANAGEMENT RE-PORTING AND DISCLOSURE ACT OF 1959.

TITLE I—BILL OF RIGHTS OF MEMBERS OF LABOR ORGANIZATIONS

BILL OF RIGHTS

SEC. 101. (a) (1) *Equal Rights.* Every member of a labor organization shall have equal rights and privileges within such organization to nominate candidates, to vote in elections or referendums of the labor organization, to attend membership meetings, and to participate in the deliberations and voting upon the business of such meetings, subject to reasonable rules and regulations in such organization's constitution and bylaws.

(2) *Freedom of Speech and Assembly.* Every member of any labor organization shall have the right to meet and assemble freely with other members; and to express any views, arguments, or opinions; and to express at meetings of the labor organization his views, upon candidates in an election of the labor organization or upon any business properly before the meeting, subject to the organization's established and reasonable rules pertaining to the conduct of meetings: *Provided,* That nothing herein shall be construed to impair the right of a labor organization to adopt and enforce reasonable rules as to the responsibility of every member toward the organization as an institution and to his refraining from conduct that would interfere with its performance of its legal or contractual obligations.

(3) *Dues, Initiation Fees, and Assessments.* Except in the case of a federation of national or international labor organizations, the rates of dues and initiation fees payable by members of any labor organization in effect on the date of enactment of this Act shall not be increased, and no general or special assessment shall be levied upon such members, except—

(A) in the case of a local labor organization, (i) by majority vote by secret ballot of the members in good standing voting at a general or special membership meeting, after reasonable notice of the intention to vote upon such question, or (ii) by majority vote of the members in good standing voting in a membership referendum conducted by secret ballot; or

(B) in the case of a labor organization, other than a local labor organization or a federation of national or international labor organizations, (i) by majority vote of the delegates voting at a regular convention, or at a special convention of such labor organization held upon not less than thirty days' written notice to the principal office of each local or constitutent labor organization entitled to such notice, or (ii) by majority vote of the members in good standing of such labor organization voting in a membership referendum conducted by secret ballot, or (iii) by majority vote of the members of the executive board or similar governing body of such labor organization, pursuant to express authority contained in the constitution and bylaws of such labor organization: *Provided,* That such action on the part of the executive board or similar governing body shall be effective only until the next regular convention of such labor organization.

(4) *Protection of the Right To Sue.* No labor organization shall limit the right of any member thereof to institute an action in any court, or in a proceeding before any administrative agency, irrespective of whether or not the labor organization or its officers are named as defendants or respondents in such action or proceeding, or the right of any member of a labor organization to appear as a witness in any judicial, administrative, or legislative proceeding, or to petition any legislature or to communicate with any legislator: *Provided,* That any such member may be required to exhaust reasonable hearing procedures (but not to exceed a four-month lapse of time) within such organization, before instituting legal or administrative proceedings against such organizations

or any officer thereof: *And provided further,* That no interested employer or employer association shall directly or indirectly finance, encourage, or participate in, except as a party, any such action, proceeding, appearance, or petition.

(5) *Safeguards Against Improper Disciplinary Action.* No member of any labor organization may be fined, suspended, expelled, or otherwise disciplined except for nonpayment of dues by such organization or by any officer thereof unless such member has been (A) served with written specific charges; (B) given a reasonable time to prepare his defense; (C) afforded a full and fair hearing.

(b) Any provision of the constitution and bylaws of any labor organization which is inconsistent with the provisions of this section shall be of no force or effect.

CIVIL ENFORCEMENT

Sec. 102. Any person whose rights secured by the provisions of this title have been infringed by any violation of this title may bring a civil action in a district court of the United States for such relief (including injunctions) as may be appropriate. Any such action against a labor organization shall be brought in the district court of the United States for the district where the alleged violation occurred, or where the principal office of such labor organization is located.

RETENTION OF EXISTING RIGHTS

Sec. 103. Nothing contained in this title shall limit the rights and remedies of any member of a labor organization under any State or Federal law or before any court or other tribunal, or under the constitution and bylaws of any labor organization.

RIGHT TO COPIES OF COLLECTIVE BARGAINING AGREEMENTS

Sec. 104. It shall be the duty of the secretary or corresponding principal officer of each labor organization, in the case of a local labor organization, to forward a copy of each collective bargaining agreement made by such labor organization with any employer to any employee who requests such a copy and whose rights as such employee are directly affected by such agreement, and in the case of a labor organization other than a local labor organization, to forward a copy of any such agreement to each constituent unit which has members directly affected by such agreement; and such officer shall maintain at the principal office of the labor organization of which he is an officer copies of any such agreement made or received by such labor organization, which copies shall be available for inspection by any member or by any employee whose rights are affected by such agreement. The provisions of section 210 shall be applicable in the enforcement of this section.

INFORMATION AS TO ACT

Sec. 105. Every labor organization shall inform its members concerning the provisions of this Act.

TITLE II—REPORTING BY LABOR ORGANIZATIONS, OFFICERS AND EMPLOYEES OF
LABOR ORGANIZATIONS, AND EMPLOYERS

REPORT OF LABOR ORGANIZATIONS

SEC. 201. (a) Every labor organization shall adopt a constitution and bylaws
and shall file a copy thereof with the Secretary, together with a report, signed
by its president and secretary or corresponding principal officers, containing
the following information—

(1) the name of the labor organization, its mailing address, and any other
address at which it maintains its principal office or at which it keeps the
records referred to in this title;

(2) the name and title of each of its officers;

(3) the initiation fee or fees required from a new or transferred member
and fees for work permits required by the reporting labor organization;

(4) the regular dues or fees or other periodic payments required to remain
a member of the reporting labor organization; and

(5) detailed statements, or references to specific provisions of documents
filed under this subsection which contain such statements, showing the provision made and procedures followed with respect to each of the following:
(A) qualifications for or restrictions on membership, (B) levying of assessments, (C) participation in insurance or other benefit plans, (D) authorization for disbursement of funds of the labor organization, (E) audit of financial
transactions of the labor organization, (F) the calling of regular and special
meetings, (G) the selection of officers and stewards and of any representatives to other bodies composed of labor organizations' representatives, with
a specific statement of the manner in which each officer was elected, appointed, or otherwise selected, (H) discipline or removal of officers or agents
for breaches of their trust, (I) imposition of fines, suspensions, and expulsions
of members, including the grounds for such action and any provision made
for notice, hearing, judgment on the evidence, and appeal procedures, (J)
authorization for bargaining demands, (K) ratification of contract terms,
(L) authorization for strikes, and (M) issuance of work permits. Any change
in the information required by this subsection shall be reported to the Secretary at the time the reporting labor organization files with the Secretary the
annual financial report required by subsection (b).

(b) Every labor organization shall file annually with the Secretary a financial
report signed by its president and treasurer or corresponding principal officers
containing the following information in such detail as may be necessary accurately to disclose its financial condition and operations for its preceding fiscal
year—

(1) assets and liabilities at the beginning and end of the fiscal year;

(2) receipts of any kind and the sources thereof;

(3) salary, allowances, and other direct or indirect disbursements (including reimbursed expenses) to each officer and also to each employee who,
during such fiscal year, received more than $10,000 in the aggregate from

such labor organization and any other labor organization affiliated with it or with which it is affiliated, or which is affiliated with the same national or international labor organization;

(4) direct and indirect loans made to any officer, employee, or member, which aggregated more than $250 during the fiscal year, together with a statement of the purpose, security, if any, and arrangements for repayment;

(5) direct and indirect loans to any business enterprise, together with a statement of the purpose, security, if any, and arrangements for repayment; and

(6) other disbursements made by it including the purposes thereof; all in such categories as the Secretary may prescribe.

(c) Every labor organization required to submit a report under this title shall make available the information required to be contained in such report to all of its members, and every such labor organization and its officers shall be under a duty enforceable at the suit of any member of such organization in any State court of competent jurisdiction or in the district court of the United States for the district in which such labor organization maintains its principal office, to permit such member for just cause to examine any books, records, and accounts necessary to verify such report. The court in such action may, in its discretion, in addition to any judgment awarded to the plaintiff or plaintiffs, allow a reasonable attorney's fee to be paid by the defendant, and costs of the action.

(d) Subsections (f), (g), and (h) of section 9 of the National Labor Relations Act, as amended, are hereby repealed.

(e) Clause (i) of section 8 (a) (3) of the National Labor Relations Act, as amended, is amended by striking out the following: "and has at the time the agreement was made or within the preceding twelve months received from the Board a notice of compliance with sections 9 (f), (g), (h)."

REPORT OF OFFICERS AND EMPLOYEES OF LABOR ORGANIZATIONS

SEC. 202 (a) Every officer of a labor organization and every employee of a labor organization (other than an employee performing exclusively clerical or custodial services) shall file with the Secretary a signed report listing and describing for his preceding fiscal year—

(1) any stock, bond, security, or other interest, legal or equitable, which he or his spouse or minor child directly or indirectly held in, and any income or any other benefit with monetary value (including reimbursed expenses) which he or his spouse or minor child derived directly or indirectly from, an employer whose employees such labor organization represents or is actively seeking to represent, except payments and other benefits received as a bona fide employee of such employer;

(2) any transaction in which he or his spouse or minor child engaged, directly or indirectly, involving any stock, bond, security, or loan to or from, or other legal or equitable interest in the business of an employer whose employees such labor organization represents or is actively seeking to represent;

(3) any stock, bond, security, or other interest, legal or equitable, which he or his spouse or minor child directly or indirectly held in, and any income or any other benefit with monetary value (including reimbursed expenses) which he or his spouse or minor child directly or indirectly derived from, any business a substantial part of which consists of buying from, selling or leasing to, or otherwise dealing with, the business of an employer whose employees such labor organization represents or is actively seeking to represent;

(4) any stock, bond, security, or other interest, legal or equitable, which her or his spouse or minor child directly or indirectly held in, and any income or any other benefit with monetary value (including reimbursed expenses) which he or his spouse or minor child directly or indirectly derived from, a business any part of which consist of buying from, or selling or leasing directly or indirectly to, or otherwise dealing with such labor organization;

(5) any direct or indirect business transaction or arrangement between him or his spouse or minor child and any employer whose employees his organization represents or is actively seeking to represent, except work performed and payments and benefits received as a bona fide employee of such employer and except purchases and sales of goods or services in the regular course of business at prices generally available to any employee of such employer; and

(6) any payment of money or other thing of value (including reimbursed expenses) which he or his spouse or minor child received directly or indirectly from any employer or any person who acts as a labor relations consultant to an employer, except payments of the kinds referred to in section 302 (c) of the Labor Management Relations Act, 1947, as amended.

(b) The provisions of paragraphs (1), (2), (3), (4), and (5) of subsection (a) shall not be construed to require any such officer or employee to report his bona fide investments in securities traded on a securities exchange registered as a national securities exchange under the Securities Exchange Act of 1934, in shares in an investment company registered under the Investment Company Act of 1940, or in securities of a public utility holding company registered under the Public Utility Holding Company Act of 1935, or to report any income derived therefrom.

(c) Nothing contained in this section shall be construed to require any officer or employee of a labor organization to file a report under subsection (a) unless he or his spouse or minor child holds or has held an interest, has received income or any other benefit with monetary value or a loan, or has engaged in a transaction described therein.

REPORT OF EMPLOYERS

SEC. 203. (a) Every employer who in any fiscal year made—

(1) any payment or loan, direct or indirect, of money or other thing of value (including reimbursed expenses), or any promise or agreement therefor, to any labor organization or officer, agent, shop steward, or other representative of a labor organization, or employee of any labor organization, except

(A) payments or loans made by any national or State bank, credit union, insurance company, savings and loan association or other credit institution and (B) payments of the kind referred to in section 302 (c) of the Labor Management Relations Act, 1947, as amended;

(2) any payment (including reimbursed expenses) to any of his employees, or any group or committee of such employees, for the purpose of causing such employee or group or committee of employees to persuade other employees to exercise or not to exercise, or as to the manner of exercising, the right to organize and bargain collectively through representatives of their own choosing unless such payments were contemporaneously or previously disclosed to such other employees;

(3) any expenditure, during the fiscal year, where an object thereof, directly or indirectly, is to interfere with, restrain, or coerce employees in the exercise of the right to organize and bargain collectively through representatives of their own choosing, or is to obtain information concerning the activities of employees or a labor organization in connection with a labor dispute involving such employer, except for use solely in conjunction with an administrative or arbitral proceeding or a criminal or civil judicial proceeding;

(4) any agreement or arrangement with a labor relations consultant or other independent contractor or organization pursuant to which such person undertakes activities where an object thereof, directly or indirectly, is to persuade employees to exercise or not to exercise, or persuade employees as to the manner of exercising, the right to organize and bargain collectively through representatives of their own choosing, or undertakes to supply such employer with information concerning the activities of employees or a labor organization in connection with a labor dispute involving such employer, except information for use solely in conjunction with an administrative or arbitral proceeding or a criminal or civil judicial proceeding; or

(5) any payment (including reimbursed expenses) pursuant to an agreement or arrangement described in subdivision (4);

shall file with the Secretary a report, in a form prescribed by him, signed by its president and treasurer or corresponding principal officers showing in detail the date and amount of each such payment, loan, promise, agreement, or arrangement and the name, address, and position, if any, in any firm or labor organization of the person to whom it was made and a full explanation of the circumstances of all such payments, including the terms of any agreement or understanding pursuant to which they were made.

(b) Every person who pursuant to any agreement or arrangement with an employer undertakes activities where an object thereof is, directly or indirectly—

(1) to persuade employees to exercise or not to exercise, or persuade employees as to the manner of exercising, the right to organize and bargain collectively through representatives of their own choosing; or

(2) to supply an employer with information concerning the activities of employees or a labor organization in connection with a labor dispute involving such employer, except information for use solely in conjunction with an administrative or arbitral proceeding or a criminal or civil judicial proceeding;

shall file within thirty days after entering into such agreement or arrangement a report with the Secretary, signed by its president and treasurer or corresponding principal officers, containing the name under which such person is engaged in doing business and the address of its principal office, and a detailed statement of the terms and conditions of such agreement or arrangement. Every such person shall file annually, with respect to each fiscal year during which payments were made as a result of such an agreement or arrangement, a report with the Secretary, signed by its president and treasurer or corresponding principal officers, containing a statement (A) of its receipts of any kind from employers on account of labor relations advice or services, designating the sources thereof, and (B) of its disbursements of any kind, in connection with such services and the purposes thereof. In each such case such information shall be set forth in such categories as the Secretary may prescribe.

(c) Nothing in this section shall be construed to require any employer or other person to file a report covering the services of such person by reason of his giving or agreeing to give advice to such employer or representing or agreeing to represent such employer before any court, administrative agency, or tribunal of arbitration or engaging or agreeing to engage in collective bargaining on behalf of such employer with respect to wages, hours, or other terms or conditions of employment or the negotiation of an agreement or any question arising thereunder.

(d) Nothing contained in this section shall be construed to require an employer to file a report under subsection (a) unless he has made an expenditure, payment, loan, agreement, or arrangement of the kind described therein. Nothing contained in this section shall be construed to require any other person to file a report under subsection (b) unless he was a party to an agreement or arrangement of the kind described therein.

(e) Nothing contained in this section shall be construed to require any regular officer, supervisor, or employee of an employer to file a report in connection with services rendered to such employer nor shall any employer be required to file a report covering expenditures made to any regular officer, supervisor, or employee of an employer as compensation for service as a regular officer, supervisor, or employee of such employer.

(f) Nothing contained in this section shall be construed as an amendment to, or modification of the rights protected by, section 8 (c) of the National Labor Relations Act, as amended.

(g) The term "interfere with, restrain, or coerce" as used in this section means interference, restraint, and coercion which, if done with respect to the exercise of rights guaranteed in section 7 of the National Labor Relations Act, as amended, would, under section 8 (a) of such Act, constitute an unfair labor practice.

ATTORNEY-CLIENT COMMUNICATIONS EXEMPTED

SEC. 204. Nothing contained in this Act shall be construed to require an attorney who is a member in good standing of the bar of any State, to include in any report required to be filed pursuant to the provisions of this Act any information which was lawfully communicated to such attorney by any of his clients in the course of a legitimate attorney-client relationship.

REPORTS MADE PUBLIC INFORMATION

SEC. 205. (a) The contents of the reports and documents filed with the Secretary pursuant to sections 201, 202, and 203 shall be public information, and the Secretary may publish any information and data which he obtains pursuant to the provisions of this title. The Secretary may use the information and data for statistical and research purposes, and compile and publish such studies, analyses, reports, and surveys based thereon as he may deem appropriate.

(b) The Secretary shall by regulation make reasonable provision for the inspection and examination, on the request of any person, of the information and data contained in any report or other document filed with him pursuant to section 201, 202, or 203.

(c) The Secretary shall by regulation provide for the furnishing by the Department of Labor of copies of reports or other documents filed with the Secretary pursuant to this title, upon payment of a charge based upon the cost of the service. The Secretary shall make available without payment of a charge, or require any person to furnish, to such State agency as is designated by law or by the Governor of the State in which such person has his principal place of business or headquarters, upon request of the Governor of such State, copies of any reports and documents filed by such person with the Secretary pursuant to section 201, 202, or 203, or of information and data contained therein. No person shall be required by reason of any law of any State to furnish to any officer or agency of such State any information included in a report filed by such person with the Secretary pursuant to the provisions of this title, if a copy of such report, or of the portion thereof containing such information, is furnished to such officer or agency. All moneys received in payment of such charges fixed by the Secretary pursuant to this subsection shall be deposited in the general fund of the Treasury.

RETENTION OF RECORDS

SEC. 206. Every person required to file any report under this title shall maintain records on the matters required to be reported which will provide in sufficient detail the necessary basic information and data from which the documents filed with the Secretary may be verified, explained or clarified, and checked for accuracy and completeness, and shall include vouchers, worksheets, receipts, and applicable resolutions, and shall keep such records available for examination for a period of not less than five years after the filing of the documents based on the information which they contain.

EFFECTIVE DATE

SEC. 207. (a) Each labor organization shall file the initial report required under section 201 (a) within ninety days after the date on which it first becomes subject to this Act.

(b) Each person required to file a report under section 201 (b), 202, 203 (a), or the second sentence of 203 (b) shall file such report within ninety days after the end of each of its fiscal years; except that where such person is subject to section 201 (b), 202, 203 (a), or the second sentence of 203 (b), as the case may be, for only a portion of such a fiscal year (because the date of enactment of this Act occurs during such person's fiscal year or such person becomes subject to this Act during its fiscal year) such person may consider that portion as the entire fiscal year in making such report.

RULES AND REGULATIONS

SEC. 208. The Secretary shall have authority to issue, amend, and rescind rules and regulations prescribing the form and publication of reports required to be filed under this title and such other reasonable rules and regulations (including rules prescribing reports concerning trusts in which a labor organization is interested) as he may find necessary to prevent the circumvention or evasion of such reporting requirements. In exercising his power under this section the Secretary shall prescribe by general rule simplified reports for labor organizations or employers for whom he finds that by virtue of their size a detailed report would be unduly burdensome, but the Secretary may revoke such provision for simplified forms of any labor organization or employer if he determines, after such investigation as he deems proper and due notice and opportunity for a hearing, that the purposes of this section would be served thereby.

CRIMINAL PROVISIONS

SEC. 209. (a) Any person who willfully violates this title shall be fined not more than $10,000 or imprisoned for not more than one year, or both.

(b) Any person who makes a false statement or representation of a material fact, knowing it to be false, or who knowingly fails to disclose a material fact, in any document, report, or other information required under the provisions of this title shall be fined not more than $10,000 or imprisoned for not more than one year, or both.

(c) Any person who willfully makes a false entry in or willfully conceals, withholds, or destroys any books, records, reports, or statements required to be kept by any provision of this title shall be fined not more than $10,000 or imprisoned for not more than one year, or both.

(d) Each individual required to sign reports under sections 201 and 203 shall be personally responsible for the filing of such reports and for any statement contained therein which he knows to be false.

CIVIL ENFORCEMENT

SEC. 210. Whenever it shall appear that any person has violated or is about to violate any of the provisions of this title, the Secretary may bring a civil action for such relief (including injunctions) as may be appropriate. Any such action may be brought in the district court of the United States where the violation occurred or, at the option of the parties, in the United States District Court for the District of Columbia.

RACKETEERING

A perennial problem within the labor movement has been racketeering. This has taken several forms: the shake-down of employers under threat that strikes would be called against them or—when unorganized—that they would be organized and forced to pay exorbitant wage increases; violence to wrest control of a union away from another group, without respect to membership interests, for the exploitation either of union members or of employers with whom the union deals or both; kickbacks from members for special favors, such as priority in employment, or sale of membership in the union without the applicant's having to pass standard apprenticeship tests. Below, Attorney General Brownell speaks of Federal efforts to eliminate such activity.

No one knows how much labor racketeering goes on in the United States. It seems probable that it represents a rather small fraction of total union activity. The more serious consideration, however, is that such racketeering as does exist may be concentrated—in certain unions, or certain industries, or certain areas—so that its impact in particular spheres may be very considerable. It is a matter of fact that the unions most frequently mentioned as harboring such elements are the powerful Teamsters and the building trades unions.

As can readily be appreciated, racketeering within the labor movement is a source of concern to legitimate union leaders, since it colors the popular impression of unions in general and damages their acceptability in a society which has only lately come to accept them. The exposures in 1957 before the Senate Select Committee on Improper Practices in the Labor and Management Field, although largely confined to a few unions, constituted a sharp blow to the labor movement as a whole. That same year the AFL-CIO moved—many said belatedly—to deal with the problem by adopting an "ethical code" urging action on its constituent national unions to deal with the problem.

The AFL ultimatum to the International Longshoremen's Association in 1953, reprinted here, makes clear that in part the inaction of the top Federation officials has been due to the jealous regard of the national organizations for their autonomy—something only slightly less true today than at the time this ultimatum was issued.

Address delivered before the Southwestern Legal Foundation and Southern Methodist University School of Law, Dallas, Texas, April 22, 1955, by Herbert Brownell, Jr., Attornep General of the United States, pp. 2–6

THE DEPARTMENT OF JUSTICE MOVES ON LABOR RACKETEERS

During the past two years the Department of Justice has engaged in a most strenuous effort to enforce the federal criminal laws against parasitic racketeers who in many parts of the country have infested and poisoned the relations between business management and labor. . . .

There are three laws which constitute the principal weapons in the armory of the Department of Justice in combatting this kind of racketeering. Two of them apply directly; the third indirectly. The first of these is the federal Anti-Racketeering Statute, originally enacted in 1934, and often referred to as the Hobbs Act. The second is section 186 of the Labor-Management Relations Act, passed by Congress in 1947 and usually called the Taft-Hartley Act. The third, which applies indirectly, is the federal Income Tax law.

Two different types of cases are encountered so frequently as to be typical of violations of these laws. First, there is the case, covered by the Hobbs Act, where some racketeer who is in control of a labor union as an official demands a pay-off from an employer, usually in the form of cash, for his own personal enrichment under threat of damaging the employer if the pay-off is not made with strikes, slowdowns, or violent injury to his property, person or family. Such a case amounts to extortion.

The second situation, covered by section 186 of the Taft-Hartley Act, is where a crooked employer induces a union official to betray and sell out the interests of his union members in return for cash or other bribe for his personal benefit.

Both situations involve the payment of money in secret and usually when that occurs the receipt of the money is not declared for income tax purposes. That is why investigation of such cases not infrequently results in a prosecution for income tax evasion. . . .

In the little more than two years since [January 1953] there have been approximately 56 Anti-Racketeering indictments charging 126 defendants. In two other trials the jury failed to agree and the cases will have to be retried. Three indictments have been dismissed. The remaining 33 cases are on active calendar and will be tried in due course. During this same two year period there have been 14 indictments charging 23 defendants with violating section 186 of the Taft-Hartley Law. Four of them have been tried resulting in seven convictions, one has been dismissed and the remaining nine are awaiting trial.

Since January 1953, at the request of the Department, the FBI has undertaken about 1,400 investigations of possible violations of these two laws and is continuing to open new cases at the rate of approximately 50 per month. These cases have originated in such far-flung cities as St. Louis and Kansas City, Missouri; East St. Louis, Springfield and Chicago, Illinois; Detroit; St. Paul; Cleveland; New Orleans; Boston; Pittsburgh; Los Angeles; Seattle; Las Vegas; New York City; Jersey City; Providence; Louisville and Washington, D.C.

The expulsion of the International Longshoremen's Association from the AFL was preceded by the following ultimatum, issued February 3,

1953, by the executive council—the first such ultimatum issued in the Federation's history.

AFL ultimatum to ILA

To the officers and members of the International Longshoremen's Association:

The executive council of the American Federation of Labor, at its present session, has given thorough consideration to the disclosures developed by the New York State Crime Commission affecting international and local union officers of the International Longshoremen's Association.

We have followed this investigation with interest and the reported widespread alleged crime, dishonesty, racketeering and other highly irregular and objectionable practices in which it is reported that officers of your international and local unions have been and are involved.

One of the most serious features of the New York City situation as pertains to your international union and its local unions, as outlined by recent testimony before the Crime Commission, is the clear and definite indication that these workers of the Port of New York are being exploited in every possible way and that they are not receiving the protection which they have every right to expect as trade unionists and members of your organization.

We have concluded that these disclosures are of such a serious nature as to call for immediate action by us. We wish to make clear the position of the A.F.L. on crime and racketeering within your international and its local unions.

Your relationship with the A.F.L. demands that the democratic ideals, clean and wholesome free trade unionism must be immediately restored within your organization and all semblance of crime, dishonesty and racketeering be forthwith eliminated.

Reported practices of international and local union officers accepting gifts and bribes from employers and the appointment of representatives with criminal records is denounced and those persons guilty of these practices must be forthwith removed from office and eliminated from your organization.

The so-called shape-up, which encourages the kick-backs and other objectionable practices, must be supplanted by a system of regular employment and legitimate hiring methods, and we request that you immediately take vigorous and effective action to institute this reform.

Union representatives with criminal records cannot be tolerated in any official capacity and they must be immediately removed from all positions of authority within your organization.

Recognized democratic procedures of the A.F.L. must be put into operation in your local unions so that members who work on the waterfronts will be able to select true and capable trade union leaders who will serve the best interests of the A.F.L. and be free from the taint of crime and racketeering.

We deplore the reign of lawlessness and crime which has been disclosed on the New York City waterfront and we call upon those officials charged with the responsibility of law enforcement to bring to justice all those persons who may be guilty of any illegal acts.

The A.F.L. is not clothed with authority, nor is it our responsibility to do this job. We do feel, however, that your international union must forthwith take the necessary action to remove any and all of those representatives who may be participants in these unlawful activities.

The A.F.L. is, as you know, a voluntary association of free and autonomous national and international unions. The founders of the A.F.L. deliberately set up an organizational structure which would preclude the domination of our organization by any one man or group of men operating from the top.

The founders of the A.F.L. saw to it that there was no police power given to the central organization which it could use to interfere with the internal affairs of national or international unions affiliated to the A.F.L.

The executive council has no intention of changing the traditional position of the A.F.L. in regard to the freedom and autonomy of its affiliated units. We feel that the greatest factor in the strength and vigor of the A.F.L. over the years has been its adherence to the principles of freedom and voluntarism.

However, no one should make the mistake of concluding that the A.F.L. will sit by and allow abuse of autonomy on the part of any of its affiliates to bring injury to the entire movement.

The exercise of autonomy by affiliated units in an organization such as ours presupposes the maintenance of minimum standards of trade union decency. No affiliate of the A.F.L. has any right to expect to remain an affiliate "on the grounds of organizational autonomy" if its conduct, as such, is to bring the entire movement into disrepute.

Likewise, the cloak of organizational autonomy cannot be used to shield those who have forgotten that the prime purpose of a trade union is to protect and advance the welfare and interests of the individual members of that trade union.

The failure of your organization and its officers to protect your membership from exploitation and oppression by employers as well as by thugs cannot be justified or defended on the ground of autonomy.

A.F.L. affiliates have autonomy in the conduct of their affairs but it must be conceded by all that there is an unwritten law that this freedom of action must be used to advance the interests of labor and not to exploit the workers.

The executive council of the A.F.L. concludes that the I.L.A. must immediately, as a condition of continuing affiliation with the A.F.L., take such actions necessary to place the I.L.A. and its local unions above suspicion and completely free of all racketeering, crime, corruption and other irregular activities disclosed by the recent investigation of crime on the New York City waterfront, to the end that the I.L.A. will serve the legitimate social and economic needs of its members in keeping with true trade union principles traditionally established by the A.F.L.

The executive council will expect a report from you advising that the above recommendations have been and will be complied with on or before April 30, 1953.

2: Collective Bargaining

Collective bargaining is the process whereby management and union agree on the terms under which workers shall perform their duties. This includes a spelling out of management's obligations to its employees and to the union which represents them. Historically, it is this principle of agreed *and* enforceable *managerial responsibilities which has given collective bargaining its chief significance. It marked a break with a work system under which management's obligations were only self-assumed or imposed by the competitive market.*

With the growth of union power, however, collective bargaining has evolved into a system for obtaining joint agreement on reciprocal responsibilities. *Not only the obligations of management, but also the obligations of workers and unions are agreed and enforceable. Agreement on these obligations is achieved through periodical renegotiation of the collective contract.*

It is this phase to which attention is given in this chapter. Enforcement of the obligations agreed upon comes through the grievance procedure, to which the materials of Chapter 9 refer.

COLLECTIVE BARGAINING TODAY

Excerpt from an address by Paul L. Styles, member, National Labor Relations Board, before the 39th convention of the American Federation of Hosiery Workers, Philadelphia, May 7, 1951

Essentially, there are only four ways in which terms and conditions of employment can be determined: (1) They can be fixed by the employer; (2) They can be imposed by the union; (3) They can be ordered by government decree; and (4) They can be determined by collective bargaining. . . .

The fourth course—collective bargaining between the chosen representatives of management and labor—may not be the perfect system, but it is the best ever devised by free men conscious and jealous of their liberties. . . .

IN DEFENSE OF INSULTS

An editorial from Business Week, April 7, 1956, following a 150-day strike at Westinghouse by members of the International Union of Electrical Workers

James Carey, the union president who led the unconscionably long Westinghouse strike, has been severely criticized for the bad temper, rough language, and acrimonious attitude he introduced into the six months of negotiations. His uncontrolled behavior, which some believe actually protracted the strike, will not be defended here.

But abhorrence of Carey should not lead his critics to embrace an attractive fallacy. That would be the notion that collective bargaining is best conducted in an atmosphere of sweetness and light. Though reasonableness is always welcome in labor-management negotiations, affability can subvert the process and sow the seeds of trouble. If preserving the benign comity of friendliness is put above the unpleasant business of reaching precise understanding, the result may be so ambiguous and equivocal as to be the direct cause of even more bitter conflict.

Real collective bargaining is by its very nature a rough, tough undertaking. Its essence is the reluctant exchange of commitments; both parties want to yield less and get more. It is not qualitatively different from a business deal in which both negotiators have something less than 100% trust in one another. Nor is it much different from the practice of diplomacy in a mutually suspicious world. In all three forums, the calculated insult and simulated anger are familiar tactics.

In writing about Pres. Eisenhower's amiable sojourn in White Sulphur Springs with the President of Mexico and the Prime Minister of Canada, James Reston of the New York Times quoted Sir Harold Nicholson, expert on the practice of diplomacy, as follows:

"Diplomacy is the art of negotiating documents in a ratifiable and therefore dependable form. It is by no means the art of conversation. The affability inseparable from any conversation between [representatives] produces allusiveness, compromises and high intentions. Diplomacy, if it is ever to be effective, should be a disagreeable business. . . ."

That observation applies with equal cogency to collective bargaining.

COLLECTIVE BARGAINING: HOW TO MAKE IT MORE EFFECTIVE

Excerpt from a statement on national policy by the Research and Policy Committee of the Committee for Economic Development, February, 1947

VOLUNTARY PROCEDURES FOR EFFECTIVE COLLECTIVE BARGAINING

Orderly bargaining between management and union requires adequate "ground rules." While some of the rules must be established by government and should have legal status, many of the most important rules must stem from mutual agreement between management and union. Without this mutual agreement collective bargaining will not function effectively. Unless union and management bring sanity, moderation and tolerance to the bargaining table, agreement becomes difficult.

In contract making there is a mutual responsibility for establishing procedures which will permit continuity of production. Among procedures which have been found of value, and are recommended, are the following:

(*a*) Pre-negotiation exploratory discussion should be held on problems which each side feels are vital and of mutual interest. Such discussions should take place before formal contract demands and proposals are formulated by either side.

(*b*) Negotiations over contract terms should start well in advance of contract termination, where a termination date exists, with provisions for contract extension if agreement has not been reached by that date.

(*c*) Proposed contract changes should be presented in writing in advance of formal negotiations so that both sides may have ample opportunity to study the proposals.

(*d*) Prior to, or at the start of, contract negotiation meetings, the parties should specify the rules of the meetings; time and length of meetings; procedure on such matters as press releases; a list of representatives of each side and their authority; what, if any, transcript or record should be made of meetings; and like matters. All these are important in ensuring smooth and ultimately successful meetings.

THE DOLLARS AND CENTS OF INDUSTRIAL RELATIONS

Excerpt from a talk by Samuel L. H. Burk, Director, Industrial Relations Division, National Association of Manufacturers, before the Roundtable on Labor Relations, Graduate School of Business, Columbia University, February 26, 1957

The question has been asked "How can a management determine whether to settle on the union's terms or take a strike?" What actually happens when a management is faced with this issue? The cost of shutting down the plant is usually fairly well known or can be approximated with a reasonable degree of accuracy. Added to possible strike costs must be estimates of the dollars and cents impact on relations with the company's customers and suppliers. Most managements will also consider the effect of wage and salary losses on its employees and the estimated resulting cost effect of lowered production caused by reduced morale when the strike is finally settled. There will, of course, be other matters taken into consideration—such as stockholder or owner reaction to measurable as well as imponderable losses and the effect of such reaction on the tenure or progress of the members of the top management group.

From just these few sample considerations it will be evident that we progress very swiftly from hard monetary facts to matters which are pure conjecture, coupled with the dictates of experience in similar past situations. When a company is closely held or family owned, and the members of the management group are largely members of the family most directly interested financially, the decision may well be appreciably different than in the more widely held corporations. Again at the risk of oversimplification, we can define this difference as the difference between ownership management and professional management.

However, experience does not enable us to point to typical decision situations which differentiate between ownership management and professional management—again because managers of each of these general types differ widely as individuals. Generally speaking, we find that the owner-manager will tend to be somewhat more emotional than the professional manager in a potential strike situation. To the owner-manager the threat is a distinctly personal one. To the professional manager, while the threat is directed at his managerial ability, it is largely directed toward the security and profitability of money that belongs to someone else.

From the point of view of principles, there is little distinction that can be made between the owner-manager and the professional manager. We have individuals in both groups who place great weight on their philosophies with respect to the people that make up their organization. We have others who have not troubled to establish in their own minds any fundamental body of principles in these respects. But, generally speaking, professional management seems to be less governed by personal principles of individual managers than is ownership management. This is not to say that big business is "unprincipled." It merely means that the professional manager *as an individual* is more likely to subordinate both his personal principles and his personal emotions to the needs of the corporate enterprise than is the owner-manager. This, of course, is because the owner-manager has more freedom to do as he will with his own property. On the other hand, many very successful large companies, widely owned by the general public, have established organizational philosophies based on what they believe to be sound principles of human relations. Many of these companies have adhered to these principles regardless of the estimated effect upon immediate profit. It would appear that, where the principles have been sound over the long run, adherence to such principles in spite of current expedience has carried the company successfully through the crisis. On the other hand, however, where the principles have been unsound, adherence to such principles has inevitably led to deterioration of the organization in one way or another.

Therefore, at the outset management is faced with the decision as to the soundness of its principles. The soundness of such principles must be evaluated in the light of the changing economic and social atmosphere in which the organization operates. This in itself is no small assignment. Part of the management job, therefore, is to examine the fundamental principles on which it operates. In order to do so, it must do more than philosophize about the principles but must compare its principles with the principles of other well-known and successful corporations. Let us look at an actual company which we shall call Company U. For many years the company had stood firmly against compulsory unionism.* Prior to contract negotiation time, it made a complete survey of its suppliers and customers and came to the conclusion that, despite its conviction that its previous principles were morally and ethically right, it could not afford to take a strike solely on the basis of that issue because it could not get support for such a stand from its shareholders, its consumers or its suppliers. It is apparent that, although extremes of emotions were involved in arriving at this decision and although no individual member of the management was willing to change his individual conviction as to principle, some imponderable dollars and cents value was placed on stockholder, customer and supplier reaction. The dues shop clause was inserted in the contract without any argument after years of bitter holding out for the right to work. Certainly no absolute dollars and cents value could be attributed to this concession. There was no way for the management to put a dollar value on how much business would be lost or how much good or ill will would be accumulated and what the actual gain or loss to the company would be as a result of such accumulation.

On the other hand, take the case of Company S. Company S is largely a family-owner managed corporation. This company is still in the throes of a long strike. They have steadfastly held to what they consider to be a fundamental principle, namely the right to work. One would suppose that a great deal of emotion has entered into this stand. The company has lost some business to its several competitors largely because a few potential customers are uncertain of Company S's ability to meet its sales obligations. Again, however, the company has been unable to put a dollars and cents value on the amount of business lost that can be attributed solely to their having taken a strike over this one issue.

All of the above adds up to a conclusion in answer to our first question that there has been no successfully demonstrable way for a company to determine, on a purely financial basis, as to whether to settle on the union's terms or take a strike.

Let us examine another question. How far can management afford to make concessions for the sake of what it hopes will be improved morale or because of fear that failure to make concessions will adversely affect productivity in the shop? This question starts from a doubtful assumption in the first place. We have no general assurance that making concessions to union demands affects morale favorably or adversely. We have no *statistically demonstrable* broad assurance that even employee morale affects individual productivity one way or another, although isolated studies have indicated such a possibility. On the other hand, American industry has *assumed* that increased morale has a favorable effect on individual productivity, and research experiments such as those conducted by Rexford Hersey at the Pennsylvania Railroad and by the instigators of the well-known Western Electric Hawthorne experiments would indicate that there is a definite relation between productivity and certain aspects of morale but that the relationship will vary widely depending upon the individuals affected. However, for our purposes I am willing to assume with the great majority of American businessmen that good morale is good business,

* See Chapter 7.—Ed.

and that good business starts with improved individual productivity. It is not so easy for me to agree that making concessions to union demands affects morale one way or the other. One would first have to determine how basic, prevalent and widespread the desire for consummation of the demands may be among the workers affected as against the possibility that at least some of the demands may have been cooked up by union leaders at a national or international level for purposes not directly related to satisfaction of the needs of their members. All practical contract negotiators know that the union demands do not always represent either rank and file wishes or union expectation that the demands will be met. Management decision with respect to conceding to union demands is based more on its judgment as to what the union will settle for and how basic the demand itself may be to the rank and file. The increasingly prevalent practice of "organizing from the top" even indicates that employees are having less to say about organizing, let alone negotiating. The use of a man's dues money to support a political party or candidate not of his choice is not going to add to his morale, particularly if he has to pay dues to get or hold a job.

ONE COMPANY'S BARGAINING POLICY

Few company programs in personnel and industrial relations have captured so much attention as that of General Electric in the years following World War II. Popularly dubbed "Boulwareism," after Lemuel R. Boulware, formerly G. E. Vice President of Public and Employee Relations, it has been imitated by some managements, regarded dubiously by others, and criticized vigorously by unions. Below, General Electric explains the content of this program.

From General Electric Employee Relations News Letter, December 31, 1954

Skillful propaganda by certain union officials and other of our critics had filled the communication void created by the traditional reluctance of ourselves and other businessmen to speak up about our good intentions and performance.

This had prevented too many people from recognizing the growing gap between the thoroughly good theory and potentiality of unions and the too-frequently bad ideas, practices and proposals of certain individual union officials.

Regardless of how untrue it was, every improvement in employee welfare was getting to be regarded as something which we had greedily and viciously resisted, and which had had to be *forced* out of us *unwillingly*.

And certain of these union officials were too often regarded as friends of the worker and public even when sponsoring ideas and action quite contrary to the best interests of employees and public.

There was obviously wide and dangerous misinformation to combat in the balanced best interests of all.

Who had been at fault in letting this misinformation go unchallenged and grow to such proportions? The main fault was clearly ours. It seemed incredible that our intelligent employees would look right at our superior jobs and see them as bad instead of good. But even intelligent people have to have access to the facts, so we reluctantly entered upon what positive informing—and what debunking and disillusioning—was necessary to have the true facts stand out more clearly in the future.

THE PROGRAM

We resolved that our revised or broadened course of action would have our jobs measure up in every fair and feasible way not only to the material needs and desires of our employees but also to all worthy hopes and aspirations of themselves, their families and neighbors in all the human or spiritual areas over and beyond the purely financial.

We were not only going to *do right voluntarily*—we were going to have it *known* that we were.

At the same time, we realized this was no one-way street. We could not do the job alone. To supply good jobs, we would have to have the enlightened cooperation of well-informed and diligent employees and neighbors in helping us get and keep the business that brought the money and progress into the pay envelopes and the community.

As a result, we resolved to help our employees achieve the kind of jobs they said they wanted by exhausting the possibilities in these four principal areas of thought and effort:

1. *Good Pay for Good Work.* We in management wanted to do right and also knew we certainly must do right—competently and voluntarily—about pay, benefits, physical working conditions and other material aspects of jobs.

And we had to be sure our employees and neighbors *realized* we were doing our best to do right voluntarily in the balanced best interest of employees as well as all others concerned and that we did not have to be dragged *unwillingly* to do what we had learned we should from whatever sources.

We were just as anxious as anyone could be to see that each claimant got his fair share in accordance with the market value of his contribution from his own resources. In fact, we believed then as now that the good of *all*, and therefore even the jobs of *employees* themselves, depends on *each* contributor and claimant getting neither more nor less than his fair share.

But we had been drifting along with the developing fashion of the times. We had been falling into the habit of making our bargaining offers on the low side, with the full expectation that we would be "traded up" step by step to the final settlement—often to the accompaniment of much union bally-hoo while we remained silent.

For instance, if everything pointed to a 5¢ increase being about right, there was a great tendency among employers in those days to offer nothing at first. Then, under later strike-threat pressure, about half would be offered. Then, after all the union representatives had been called in from the plants and the resulting vote for a strike had been well aired in the press—management would "capitulate" by upping the offer to the full 5¢ per hour.

This was, of course, exactly what the union officials required for a conspicuous "triumph over greedy and vicious management." It could not have been carried off any more effectively if the whole thing had been rehearsed beforehand.

While all this may have been amusing amateur theatricals to the bystander who thought he was not concerned, any tendency on our part to go along further with the fashion would have seriously misled our employees and neighbors. We could not be silent about our good intentions and good deeds— nor about false charges against us. Once we began to realize the extent of the false impression the currently fashionable behavior would create, simple honesty compelled us to avoid henceforth acting out any part that might help certain union officials *look* useful in ways they were not. Otherwise, we would have been helping them fool our employees about themselves *and about us.*

We felt then and now that a union representing our employees should have every bit of credit for every good thing it does. But we believe it should certainly have a sounder and nobler function to perform than fooling its members about a particular task that is made to appear difficult but may be easy or even non-existent.

In addition, we had begun to realize we were employing here with our job customers something other than that high "single-standard" of research, preparation, value, full information and courageous public forthrightness which had been so rewarding in our relations with our product customers.

We had also begun to see that the old course was dangerous for all concerned from a *financial* as well as a relations standpoint. If, because of some difference in bargaining skills or other factors, the settlement mentioned above had been 3¢ instead of the 5¢ management privately recognized as right, it would have been unfair not only for employees *but for all concerned.* If it had been 7¢ it would still have been bad for all concerned in the end—*including the employees who got the 7¢.*

To serve the interests of employees and all others, there was nothing to do but try to arrive at what was right for all. No one should even consider *trying* to get the better of the other in such an important matter of honor affecting close associates. And we certainly were not going to go to the bargaining table and let it wrongly *appear* that we were there trying to settle for anything we could get away with. Fortunately, there was already a whole lot less actual difference between the parties than the initial demands and offers would indicate. Nevertheless, there was lots to do.

We resolved we would henceforth carry on much more intensive and continuing research in all matters affecting our employees—including those about which we bargained with our unions.

We resolved to prepare for coming negotiations by the steady accumulation of all facts available on matters likely to be discussed.

We would then add to, discard or revise these facts on the basis of any additional or different facts we learned from union or other sources *during* negotiations as well as before.

Then at the appropriate time, and when seemingly all the available significant facts were in and had been fully discussed, we would offer what the facts from all sources seemed to indicate was fully up to all that was right in the balanced best interest of all. This was to be the full truth as we saw it—with nothing held back for future jockeying.

We would stand ready and willing to alter what we had offered immediately upon our getting new or old additional facts—from union or any other source—which would indicate changes that were in the interest of all.

Incidentally, we reached agreement in a day or two without any change in one of our early national offers several years ago. But that was the first and only time, and we recall now no subsequent negotiation where such an initial offer has not been revised in some major or minor ways.

Upon questioning, we have freely admitted we do not regard the threat or the actuality of a strike as being the kind of fact that ought to change what we honestly think is right. But that opinion on our part obviously changes in no way the full right and opportunity of any union to employ the strike weapon.

We decided at the same time that we should and would publicize our offers when made. We would keep our employees and neighbors advised of the course of negotiations—including any changes in our offers in response to union representations or by reason of any other developments.

While we were spending most of our thought and action on what *we* were going to do to try to live up to doing *our* part, we had clearly in mind this was still not going to work as a one-way matter and that our individual employee had to do *his* part. We had to try to help him understand—and we hoped other economic and moral teachers would help—that he must, in his own interests, do right voluntarily about applying honestly his skill, care, and effort to giving value received through doing a full day's work by reasonable modern standards.

Here was a vast job of study and communication to enable us all to try together to develop a commonly accepted set of facts and opinions. This was needed to aid management and employees in *being* right as well as in *knowing* how and why they each were sound and right in their conclusions and actions in these material matters involving their association with each other. . . .

Thus, our bargaining has as its objective the most mature approach possible by management and union representatives: to arrive at the facts and then take the action which will be in the balanced best interest of all. We don't want any more or any less than what's right for anybody. We are seeking the facts and sound conclusions. We don't care where the facts come from, or when. We are not concerned with credit or face-saving. We just want to do right. . . .

When it comes to making offers, the only way we know to do this ably and honorably is

. . . to study all the evidence all year long as to employee compensation and benefits,

. . . to study all the applicable union statements made meanwhile,

. . . to listen to the union demands made in negotiation,

. . . to consider carefully these demands along with all other old and new information available or that may become available,

. . . to make offerings at the proper time and voluntarily include absolutely everything our research from all sources, including unions, has indicated should be included to measure up to what's fully right by every reasonable standard,

. . . to discuss fully with the unions, and

. . . to make promptly any modifications in our offers that are indicated as right by any new light on the subject from any source.

Incidentally, we are always freshly amazed when a top union official now and then will claim—despite his direct experiences with us—that this is a "take it or leave it" program and that our efforts at "doing right voluntarily" represent some sort of challenge to the whole usefulness and survival of unions. For nothing could be farther from the facts.

In the first place, this is no "take it or leave it" program as the experience of every union official with it must make him admit to himself. Every one of our offers has stated we would be glad to change on learning of any valid reason why we should—and that was the truth, as proved in practice. One of the early offers was accepted within a day or two for the surprisingly and completely acceptable offer it was. But as already indicated, in every other case we can now recall, we have made any number of modifications in our original offer—some substantial, some minor.

What one particular group of top officials is really complaining about is that we voluntarily come so close to what's obviously right that they can't make it appear that we have been dragged unwillingly to make substantial changes through pure force. Apparently they want us to adopt the outmoded "cooperating" method of making a very low offer we would know is not right and then be publicly bludgeoned up to what's right.

In the first place, we have wanted to tell the full truth in the beginning as to what our studies indicated was right. We have refused to try to fool our employees into thinking we were trying to get away with less than we thought was fairly coming to them. In the second place, where old or new facts show we ought to improve a previous offer, we are always happy to do so at once and in no sense have to be beaten into doing so. . . .

Our entire program of mutual study and public discussion of the facts—and of honest, forthright, non-artful bargaining—is intended to encourage the development and aid the influence of . . . honest, direct and responsible union leaders. In contrast, our program is bound to be somewhat discouraging to any who want to go back to the old double-standard or "fleabitten Eastern bazaar" type of bargaining.

We think this is the right basis on which to come together to settle a matter of mutual interest—since it is *not* to any one's real advantage to seek or get a temporary advantage to the unfair disadvantage of the other contributors and claimants.

We confidently expect that most of the old remaining fallacies and emotions about bargaining will soon fall of their own weight. We just as confidently anticipate that this kind of an economic and human process can only survive by "going high-grade" in the same way the older relationships in economic and human affairs had to do to survive.

It may seem naive to admit it, but we see no reason why collective bargaining cannot be conducted with both parties accepting and applying practically the same facts and standards toward a common end, and seeking at the same time to be sure emotion and misinformation do not obstruct a settlement that is fair and just for all concerned.

In such a situation, there is every reason why both parties will eventually come to the bargaining table with a fairly common set of facts about a common objective—with both sides later frankly stating publicly that they found themselves initially in such admittedly substantial agreement that they only had to work out the remaining small differences in an atmosphere of confidence and good will.

From General Electric Company and International Union of Electrical, Radio and Machine Workers, AFL-CIO (NLRB 10-CA-4682, April 2, 1963)

In 1960 the International Union of Electrical Workers (IUE) engaged General Electric in collective bargaining. The company pursued the policy described in its statement above. Under legal provisions we shall consider in Chapter 4, the union protested that the company was not bargaining "in good faith." A trial examiner for the National Labor Relations Board agreed with the union. His lengthy report contained the following assessment of the G. E. policy (footnotes omitted).

To suggest, as the Respondent's [General Electric's] declared bargaining approach appears to do, that an employer need only listen to a union's demands and supporting arguments as part of a broader research program, frame an offer on the basis of his own overall research, and then consider only such *new* information as might reveal a factual error in the offer, is to place a union in the role of an advisor rather than a participant in the determination of employment terms through the process of collective bargaining; it is to deny the Union the status to which the Act entitles it. . . .

When the Respondent formally presented its offer on August 30, it was responsive to the Union's demands only in small part. It contained features relating to benefits, employment security and even contract language that were entirely different from those that had been requested by the Union. During the earlier negotiations there had been neither mention nor discussion of them as contemplated alternatives to the Union's proposals. The Respondent explained to the Union, as it did later to the employees, that it had made its offer responsive to "employee desires" as determined by its own extensive research and surveys. The Respondent thus made it plain that it assigned the Union a subordinate or at most only a contributing role as the spokesman for employees.

The Union declared the same day that the offer was unacceptable, and that the proposals of both parties should form the basis of collective bargaining. It requested that negotiations continue for 3 days without the pressures and glare of publicity. The Respondent, however, rejected the Union's request, giving as its reason that employees should know at once what was on the table.

And the following morning, it proceeded to publicize its offer, release it to other unions, and present it directly to employees at plant meetings as well as through employee communication channels, disregarding the Union's vigorous objection that to do so would prematurely "freeze" its position and thereby interfere with good-faith negotiations.

In the particular circumstances of this case, I find that the Respondent's haste to publicize its offer reflected the want of an earnest effort on its part to seek through the processes of collective bargaining a possible basis for mutual agreement, and constituted clear evidence of bad faith.

The Union's objection that publication would operate to "freeze" the Respondent's position was well-founded. The Respondent's action must be considered, not in the abstract, but in the context of its "fair firm offer" approach to bargaining and its uniformity policy, as outlined in section C (1), above. The Respondent's "fair firm offer" approach, although assertedly leaving room for the correction of factual error disclosed by additional information from any source or a subsequent significant economic change, rejects in effect concessions, trading or compromise as a means of finding common ground. In the light of the Respondent's widely advertised bargaining philosophy, the publication of the offer was a clear indication that the Respondent as a matter of policy would not thereafter consider with an open mind proposed concessions, compromises or other suggested solutions of differences between the parties aimed at achieving through the give-and-take of collective bargaining an accommodation of conflicting positions.

DO YOU STILL HAVE THE RIGHT TO RUN YOUR PLANT?

National Association of Manufacturers

A SELF-AUDIT OF MANAGEMENT RIGHTS

Since this is a working document for the company's internal use only, it may be helpful to note such pertinent data as the following which makes provision for differing answers as between one plant location and another:

Division of Company _____

Plant _____

Name of Union _____

Date Present Agreement Expires _____

Filled Out By _____ Date _____

	Yes	No	Doubtful
Is there language in the labor contract which protects your right to:			
1. Subcontract any or all work or processes without being subject to a union veto? ...	____	____	____
Specifically, are you free to enter into contracts for:			
—— Component parts of your products? .	____	____	____

	Yes	No	Doubtful

___ The products themselves if necessary?

___ Basic raw materials and supplies? . . .

___ Maintenance and repair work? . . . . .

___ Construction of new facilities? . . . . .

___ Plant or office services? . . . .

2. Increase or reduce the size of the work force, freely, as business conditions require?

___ Can management veto union demands for a reduction in the work week in place of layoffs? . . . .

___ Can management veto union demands that a full work schedule be maintained by laying off junior employees?

___ Is management free to retain employees on a basis of needed skills rather than by strict seniority? . . . .

___ Is management free to recall employees on a basis of needed skills? . . . . .

3. Transfer work from the bargaining unit? . .

For example, when a job becomes overly technical or complex, can it be given to:

___ Management employees, technicians, specialists, or others? . . . .

___ Does this decision rest with management alone, free from veto by the union? . . . .

4. Determine the type of products to be manufactured? . . . .

___ Does this include the right to discontinue products? . . . .

___ Does this include the right to change the quality of products? . . . .

___ Can management decide the sales methods to be used and the prices to be charged? . . . .

	Yes	No	Doubtful
5. Discontinue operations in whole or in part?	___	___	___
— Permanently?	___	___	___
— Temporarily?	___	___	___
— Does this include processes which are part of particular operations?	___	___	___
6. Set efficient work schedules?	___	___	___

For example, can management fix:

	Yes	No	Doubtful
— The number of hours to be worked daily and weekly?	___	___	___
— The number and duration of lunch and rest periods?	___	___	___
— The number of shifts and their timing?	___	___	___
7. Introduce new equipment and methods of manufacturing?	___	___	___
— Free of union veto or joint committees?	___	___	___
— Does this include the right to change or eliminate existing equipment or methods?	___	___	___
— Can management drop displaced personnel from the payroll if necessary?	___	___	___
— Are matters relating to machines and methods specifically excluded from arbitration?	___	___	___
8. Determine the location, type and number of plants?	___	___	___
— Does this include the right to move a plant from one locality to another? .	___	___	___
9. Control the makeup of the work force? ...	___	___	___
— Can the work force be selected in accordance with requirements determined by management?	___	___	___
— Can management determine the number and types of workers needed in an operation?	___	___	___

	Yes	No	Doubtful

—— Can management seek needed skills outside the bargaining unit when it believes qualified employees are lacking? .... ———— ———— ————

10. Adjust the number of employees assigned to a particular job? .... ———— ———— ————

—— Can employees be dropped from a job when it is simplified? .... ———— ———— ————

—— Can union demands for "full crews" be vetoed? .... ———— ———— ————

—— Are there provisions against an employee's developing a "vested interest" working on a particular job or machine? .... ———— ———— ————

11. Deny that any category of work is the exclusive right of any employee or group of employees? .... ———— ———— ————

—— Specifically, does the recognition clause limit union representation to the employees and not the work they perform? .... ———— ———— ————

12. Require a reasonable amount of overtime work from the employee? .... ———— ———— ————

—— Does management have the right to penalize employees who refuse to work overtime without justification? . ———— ———— ————

—— Can management distribute overtime as it sees fit, unhampered by complex rules? .... ———— ———— ————

—— Can management schedule overtime while employees are on layoff? ..... ———— ———— ————

13. Require an employee to perform work outside his assigned job classification when necessary? .... ———— ———— ————

—— Regardless of whether there is available work in his regular classification? ———— ———— ————

	Yes	No	Doubtful

14. Promote the man best qualified for the job? ___ ___ ___

— Is strict seniority excluded as the controlling factor in promotions and transfers? .... ___ ___ ___

15. Adjust a job rate when the job itself is simplified? .... ___ ___ ___

— Is the possibility of a union veto of the new rate barred? .... ___ ___ ___

— Are rate settings specifically excluded from arbitration? .... ___ ___ ___

16. Decide on the nature of materials, supplies, tools and machinery to be used? .... ___ ___ ___

— And the price to be paid for them? .. ___ ___ ___

— And the right to discontinue the use of any material? .... ___ ___ ___

Does your labor contract:

17. Distinguish grievances which are arbitrable from those which are not? .... ___ ___ ___

— Is there a requirement that the grievance genuinely involve the interpretation of a *specific* provision of the contract? .... ___ ___ ___

18. Place definite limits on the powers of an arbitrator? .... ___ ___ ___

— Is his power and jurisdiction limited to deciding whether or not a specific clause of the agreement has been violated? .... ___ ___ ___

— Is there a provision to prevent him from amending, altering or ignoring the provisions of the contract? ..... ___ ___ ___

19. Make it clear that the contract alone is the sole source of arbitration claims? .... ___ ___ ___

— Are alleged practices and oral understandings barred as the basis for awards? .... ___ ___ ___

	Yes	No	Doubtful

20. Spell out that the contract embodies the sole agreement between the parties? ..... ____ ____ ____

— Is further bargaining on issues specifically barred for the duration of the contract term? .... ____ ____ ____

— Does the contract point out that all prior oral agreements and practices are superseded by the terms of the contract? .... ____ ____ ____

21. Enumerate the specific rights of management reserve and exclude discretion on subjects not listed and not covered elsewhere in the contract, any questions involving them from arbitration? .... ____ ____ ____

22. Provide for separate determination on the issue of arbitrability of a dispute? .... ____ ____ ____

— Are such issues referable to a court of law (or to a separate arbitrator) for decision? .... ____ ____ ____

23. Bar arbitration of disputes over new contract terms? .... ____ ____ ____

Does your contract empower management to:

24. Combine or consolidate jobs, free of veto by the union? .... ____ ____ ____

— Free also of such delaying devices as joint study groups, grievances and arbitration? .... ____ ____ ____

25. Demote supervisory employees back into bargaining unit jobs? .... ____ ____ ____

— Without supporting evidence to the satisfaction of the union or an arbitrator? .... ____ ____ ____

— With accrued seniority? .... ____ ____ ____

26. Prescribe job duties, content and classification? .... ____ ____ ____

	Yes	No	Doubtful

—— Free from union interference in the form of a veto power or participation by union industrial engineers? .....

—— Does this management power extend to both old and new jobs? ....

27. Determine the work pace and work performance levels? ....

28. Discharge or otherwise discipline employees for bad conduct or infractions of plant rules?

29. Make and enforce fair and reasonable rules to promote safety, efficiency, order and discipline, and the protection of personnel and the company's property and operations? ..

Are you certain that in your plant:

30. Foremen know the exact extent of their authority? ....

—— And are encouraged to exercise it? ..

—— And realize it may be lost or weakened by inaction? ....

31. Foremen understand the requirements of the labor contract? ....

—— And are able to explain the provisions to employees? ....

32. Foremen have been trained to avoid making concessions to union representatives in settling day-to-day disputes? ....

—— Oral concessions? ....

—— Concessions through lax enforcement of the contract? ....

33. Employees can be assigned to other work in the event of absenteeism, or emergency; or when they finish a job ahead of time? ..

34. Union activities on company property and time are limited? ....

	Yes	No
35. Foremen are kept abreast of changes in company policy?	—	—
— Proposed changes are discussed with foremen?	—	—
36. Cases are prepared with care before being presented to a carefully-selected arbitrator?	—	—
— Witnesses interviewed?	—	—
— Past practice analyzed?	—	—
— Graphic aids prepared?	—	—
— Arguments outlined?	—	—
37. The management rights' implications of every issue are scrutinized for opportunities for communication?	—	—

MANAGEMENT'S RIGHTS

From the report of labor members of Committee II of the President's National Labor-Management Confeernce, November 5–30, 1945

It would be extremely unwise to build a fence around the rights and responsibilities of management on the one hand and the unions on the other. The experience of many years shows that with the growth of mutual understanding the responsibilities of one of the parties today may well become the joint responsibility of both parties tomorrow.

We cannot have one sharply delimited area designated as management prerogatives and another equally sharply defined area of union prerogatives without either side constantly attempting to invade the forbidden territory, thus creating much unnecessary strife. . . .

In our American political democracy the tradition is well established that government operates best when it enjoys the confidence and consent of the governed. In the same American tradition both labor and management must come to a realization that both can function most effectively when each enjoys the confidence and has the consent of the other.

3: The Bargaining Unit

The size of the bargaining unit is a matter of concern to both union and management. Each feels that it may gain or lose depending on whether negotiations are conducted for a single plant in a multiplant corporation, or for a single employer in contrast to the whole industry. The positions which employers and unions have taken on this subject have changed over the years. Traditionally, employers have sought smaller units (single plant, single company) and unions larger units (industry-wide), but in recent years there has been some switching of attitudes, as one side or the other sees its advantage changing.

LOCAL BARGAINING

Anglo-American Council on Productivity, Industrial Engineering, London, 1954, pp. 72–73

Contrary to U.K. practice, in the U.S. collective bargaining on a national basis is rare. Wage increases are negotiated generally on a plant or, in some instances, a district basis and, moreover, by the local branch of the union concerned, whose autonomy is far greater than that of the local union branch in Britain. . . . Local negotiation of wages and conditions adds to the interest taken by employees in the activities of their own company, since their trade union's success in wage negotiation is closely related to the success of the company. This outlook is natural where one trade union includes all employees in a firm within its ranks, irrespective of their trades.

From National Association of Manufacturers, Industry Believes, New York, 1951, p. 25

RESOLUTION, CONGRESS OF AMERICAN INDUSTRY, DECEMBER, 1947

Where collective bargaining exists as the result of the voluntary and free choice of employees, the Congress of American Industry urges that, in accordance with public policy, such collective bargaining should be carried on at the plant and company level in order to assure maximum production and industrial peace.

INDUSTRY–WIDE BARGAINING

Statement of A. P. Richards, Vice President and Treasurer, The Ohio Can & Crown Co., Massillon, Ohio, in Taft-Hartley Act Revisions, hearings before the Senate Committee on Labor and Public Welfare, 83d Cong., 1st Sess., 1953, part 2, pp. 792–793

Our basic business is the can business. In the can industry upward of 75 percent of all cans are manufactured by two large corporations, and the remainder by some 50 or 60 smaller companies of varying size. We are one of the smallest. The larger can companies with unlimited financial resources are in a position to and do to a certain extent offset increased labor cost by installation of labor-saving equipment. For instance there is available, to those with the money to buy it, equipment which will save one-half the labor of printing the labels on cans. There is equipment available to cut the labor of stamping tops and bottoms of cans by more than one-half, and many other labor-saving devices available to those in our industry where money is no problem. But, those of us who do not have access to unlimited capital must live with a labor disadvantage when compared to the large corporations.

Now, it is very apparent that if through industrywide bargaining we are required to pay the industry rate, that it is only a matter of time until we must close our plant. But you say, aren't the workers in your plant entitled to make as much money as the workers in the plants of the big corporation? That seems like a reasonable question. But the real question is, Would our workers be better off at what we can afford to pay them, or being without a job? There is no doubt about how our employees would answer that.

We do not hear too much complaint from the large corporation about industrywide bargaining. I think that the reason is obvious, as it is evidently very much to their advantage to know that all companies in the industry must pay the same labor rates, giving to the large companies whatever advantage they can have and do obtain through more modern and labor-saving equipment.

There can be no question that industrywide bargaining, if allowed to continue, will eventually mean the end of all small and even medium-sized companies who do not have the unlimited capital resources possessed by dominant industry corporations.

From Federal Labor Relations Act of 1947, minority views of Senator Thomas, Senate Committee on Labor and Public Welfare, 80th Cong., 1st Sess., Report 105, 1947, part 2, pp. 6–8

INDUSTRY-WIDE COLLECTIVE BARGAINING

Provisions specifically prohibiting area-wide and industry-wide collective bargaining were rejected by the committee for inclusion in the bill as reported. We approve this action by the committee but, in view of announcements by some members of the committee that they intend to reinsert such provisions through amendments offered on the floor of the Senate, we have set forth below the considerations which motivated us in supporting the striking of such provisions from the bill.

The Bureau of Labor Statistics estimates that more than 4,000,000 workers in American industry are covered by contracts between a union and more than one employer. Some of these are industry-wide; most are regional or city-wide in character. A ban on such bargaining would disrupt existing relation-ships in these industries and make it necessary to renegotiate contracts covering 4,000,000 workers. Instead of negotiations resulting in a relative handful of agreements, which cover thousands of employers as a group, the result would be piecemeal negotiations with thousands of individual employers, over a pro-longed period of time, with thousands of individual agreements splintering the uniform standards previously achieved through industry bargaining.

Industry-wide bargaining is a logical development of present-day industrial organization. Employers are organized on an industry-wide scale; first in Nation-wide corporations, and second in trade associations. Competition is Nation-wide in character.

We should like to indicate what would be the effect of a ban on industry-wide bargaining on present-day industrial relations.

Any attempt to ban actions by employers to form voluntary associations for the purpose of collective bargaining would deny this group the protection accorded employee organizations. In many trades and industries, employers have joined together to bargain with unions representing their employees. In such industries as longshoring and building construction—where workers change employers from day to day or week to week—bargaining through employers' associations is the only practical method for establishing uniform wages and working conditions and eliminating cutthroat competition. Almon E. Roth, President of the National Federation of American Shipping, in a statement before the committee, warned that a ban against industry-wide bargaining would result in a diversity of wage rates and working conditions among ships operated from the same coast, plying between the same ports, tying at the same docks, and employing, in turn, the same men:

Such a condition leads to the playing off of one steamship company against another by the unions, to extreme labor unrest, and eventually to the disruption of steamship operation.

Many employers prefer industry-wide or association bargaining. Mr. Vincent P. Ahearn, executive secretary of the National Sand and Gravel Association, testified before the committee:

Some employers believe that if they could not bargain on an industry-wide basis, unions could simply isolate one employer after another and force capitulation to their demands.

This would create a situation where the weakest member of an industry would set the standard for the others.

Because numerous employers are covered by a single collective-bargaining agreement, less time is lost in the bargaining process. Settlements are made simultaneously for these employers rather than on an individual employer-by-employer basis. Industrial peace is achieved in one step, rather than over a prolonged period of time. Bargaining with hundreds of individual firms for the same things is both wasteful and unfair to both sides.

Many small employers lack the skill in bargaining and research facilities available to unions. A ban on association of employers combining for the purpose of pooling their knowledge and resources in collective-bargaining negotiations would impair the bargaining power of employers.

Industry-wide agreement on wages protects wage standards from being undercut by lower-wage areas and lower-wage employers. By the same token, industry-wide bargaining may save individual employers from being singled out as wage leaders in their respective industries. A ban on such agreements would result in separate agreements with individual locals. Many firms control or own subsidiary plants in districts outside an immediate geographic area. Such firms would have to negotiate agreements with numerous local unions in widely scattered localities—a task that would unavoidably become snarled up in wage differentials and eventually would revive the old cutthroat competition and the law of the jungle between company and company, between area and area.

Barring joint activities of local unions and reducing the functions of international unions to that of an advisory body should, in fairness, require the same treatment for corporations with plants scattered widely over the country.

The charge is made that industry-wide bargaining leads to industry-wide strikes which threaten the public welfare. We should like to emphasize that it is not the character of the bargaining which brings about major strikes, but the organized joint refusal of that industry's employers to meet the union's demands. Under company-by-company bargaining, employers would try to drive standards down to the level of the lowest in the industry, and unions would seek to attain the level of the highest, and the result would be an epidemic of strikes throughout the various units of the industry.

A ban on industry-wide bargaining would minimize the role of the international union and prohibit it from exercising its authority to intervene in strikes of its affiliates; and prevent it from employing its prestige in its own industry for moderation and restraining counsel. . . .

Testimony of Morton J. Baum, President, Clothing Manufacturers Association, in Taft-Hartley Revisions, hearings before the Senate Committee on Labor and Public Welfare, 83d Cong., 1st Sess., 1953, part 4, pp. 2174–2177

The Clothing Manufacturers Association of the United States of America has a membership of approximately 850 manufacturers, who produce about 90 percent of all the men's and boys' tailored clothing in this country. Our members are located in most States of the Union, from New York to California, and from Maine to the deep South. We are the national association of our industry. Local associations of clothing manufacturers that are affiliated with us are the Philadelphia Clothing Manufacturers, New York Clothing Manufacturers Exchange, Rochester Clothier's Exchange, and the New England Clothing Manufacturers Association.

Our board of directors consists of 31 manufacturers who represent all of the clothing markets, and these directors are elected by the respective markets. On our board of directors we have representatives of large firms and small firms, and various types of manufacturers, such as those who sell direct to the consumer and those who sell their product to thousands of retailers throughout the country. Therefore, it can be seen that our board is modeled after the pattern used by the Federal Government to establish industry advisory committees, and is truly representative of the entire men's and boys' clothing industry of the United States.

Prior to 1937 collective bargaining was on the regional or individual firm basis. This was highly unsatisfactory, both to the union and to the industry. We found that there was a constant shifting of factories from one locality to another in a desperate race to seek lower wage levels, with the consequent loss of job security for workers and utter chaos at the industry level. This trend encouraged competition on the basis of shaving labor costs rather than on the basis of increased efficiency and progressive methods of merchandising and selling.

It was the considered judgment of our manufacturers that industrywide bargaining was of definite advantage to the industry whose members were located in various regions of this country and were competing nationally in selling their products. It was the experience of our industry, at the time when we bargained on a regional or individual basis, that the union sought out the manufacturer or region that was most able, in the opinion of labor, to pay the highest possible wage increase, and the union then reached an agreement with that manufacturer or that region. Once a regional or individual agreement had been completed and announced, particularly if it was with a nationally known company, an industry pattern was set, and the other members of the industry found the wage demands of the union were "frozen" and further collective bargaining hampered or made impossible because of the wage increase already announced.

The position of manufacturers in the other markets thus was weakened. The union benefited considerably in regional bargaining since it could call a strike in the factory of one manufacturer or a group of manufacturers located in a market which did not grant a wage increase, and permit manufacturers located in other markets to operate. Thus great competitive pressure was exerted upon those manufacturers whose plants were closed. If the struck plants did not settle quickly, their competitors would take away the customers of the firm that was unable to deliver merchandise.

Despite this seeming advantage, the union found that regional or individual bargaining was detrimental to the functioning of orderly collective bargaining for the industry as a whole.

Recognizing that collective bargaining on a regional basis was highly unsatisfactory, both labor and management determined that industrywide bargaining was preferable. Accordingly, in 1937, the first collective bargaining contract on an industrywide basis was signed.

SENATOR TAFT: Mr. Baum, that was with the Amalgamated Clothing Workers?

MR. BAUM: That is correct, Senator Taft.

SENATOR TAFT: That is the union run by Mr. Potofsky?

MR. BAUM: By Mr. Potofsky, that is right.

Since that date, there have been periodic meetings between the national association and the union on matters subject to bargaining collectively, such as hours, wages, vacations, holidays, fringe payments, and so forth. Only recently we completed our industrywide negotiations, which had been going on for several months, granting a wage increase of 12½ cents an hour effective May 25, 1953. This is the first wage increase in our industry since November 1950, due to the fact that the industry had overproduced and was in a depressed market. Each clothing market and each type of manufacturer was represented on the association's labor committee, so that the views of all industry segments were known and fully voiced.

I wish to point out that our industrywide bargaining does not cover the problems that ordinarily arise in local markets due to local conditions and local traditions. The local member organizations that are affiliated with our association handle such matters on a day-to-day basis.

We bargain on an industrywide basis only on matters that are industrywide; we bargain locally on local labor matters.

As a result of industrywide bargaining, we find that competition which resulted from undercutting of the wage scales has practically stopped, and that greater efficiency in factory operations and progressive merchandising methods have become the important factors in determining the success of a clothing business.

I wish to stress that competition is probably stronger among the manufacturers than it has ever been. The profits of the industry are certainly no greater than they have been in the past. However, competition now is on a socially desirable level. It is not based upon lowering wages, but rather upon efficiency and merchandising skill. . . .

Now, opponents of industrywide bargaining have said, "The industry meets with the union, agrees upon a wage increase, and then manufacturers uniformly raise prices at the expense of the consumer." Obviously, such a situation is entirely fantastic as far as the clothing industry is concerned. We have about 900 manufacturers in our industry, located in all parts of the United States, and general agreement to increase prices would not merely be illegal but physically impossible. Let me stress, labor, usually representing well over 30 percent of the wholesale price, is merely one of the many components entering into the cost of the garment. In fact, the cost of the piece goods and trimmings totals over 45 percent of the wholesale price. These three are the principal items of cost. Gentlemen, I cannot emphasize too strongly that ability to purchase desirable fabric well styled and at the right price, innate skill to design a well-fitting and attractive garment, experience in producing that garment efficiently, and a lifetime knowledge of selling, promoting, and advertising the garment are the outstanding reasons for the success of any men's clothing manufacturer. Strong and active competition is the lifeblood of our industry, but not at the expense of the workers.

As a result of constructive industrywide bargaining, we have had no stoppage or strike during this period, and there has been constant recognition on the part of labor and management that it is most desirable that both cooperate so that we have a healthy industry and satisfied employees.

From Business Week, July 2, 1955

FORD SUGGESTS INDUSTRY-WIDE BARGAINING

There was some consternation in the business community at Henry Ford II's decision to give the CIO auto union a contract that Walter Reuther could hail as a great victory in his union's fight for the guaranteed annual wage. Close analysis of that contract has now convinced many in industry that the Ford Motor Co. got itself a pretty good deal and that much of what Reuther claims is a considerable exaggeration.

Now Henry Ford has jolted businessmen again. In an interview published in the Detroit News, he declared, "I am very much in favor of industry-wide bargaining." This is a shocker. For even longer than they have been attacking GAW, business spokesmen and business organizations have been inveighing against industry-wide bargaining as an unmitigated evil. As a matter of fact, employer opposition in principle to industry-wide bargaining has existed for so long that it is taken for granted to the point where the merits and demerits of the issue are rarely, if at all, discussed in business circles.

Employers formulated their position on industry-wide bargaining in a period when unions were much weaker than they are now. With only a part of an industry organized, the unions pressed for industry-wide negotiations as a device for imposing their wage bargains and contract conditions on unorganized firms. Employers resisted this successfully and adhered to a theory of bargaining under which each individual firm would be free to make the most advantageous contract it could.

When powerful unions spreadeagled the steel, auto, and other mass production industries, the situation changed. Now, the union makes a key bargain with the one company best suited to its bargaining purposes. Thus, in the steel industry, the steel union made its first pension contract with Bethlehem because, for historic reasons, that company was less resistant on the pension issue. For reasons equally cogent, it makes its key wage bargains with U.S. Steel. In every case, however, that key bargain becomes, in effect, a master contract which the rest of the industry adopts.

In autos, the situation is even bleaker. There, the union has been concerned to have the contract termination dates for GM, Ford, and Chrysler come at spaced intervals. Its standard tactic is to whipsaw one against the other; getting, for example, a package worth X from one company, then bargaining with the second, not on the basis of its expiring contract but on the new X base, to come out with X + 1. It ends up with X + 2 from the third company, then starts the round over again.

Ford has just been through a rugged experience in which the union was able to win what it did by keeping the employers separated and coolly picking

Ford as its target. Many employers, remote from the pressures that were put on Ford, complained about the result. Now Ford has a suggestion which, by making it impossible for the union to play one employer off against another might affect such results. It is not without significance that Reuther responded by stating that "the UAW is opposed to industry-wide bargaining," and by declairng that, "the UAW won't accept it."

The Ford proposal just won't make sense in many industries, and he made it clear when he offered it that he was only talking about his own. Within that context, and in other industries where the very big and powerful unions operate, it is worth more than rejection without consideration simply because it doesn't fit what may now be an obsolete business shibboleth.

From Business Week, June 16, 1956

A STEP FORWARD IN STEEL BARGAINING

Just as the auto industry resents the suggestion that its Supplementary Unemployment Benefit programs are in the genus Guaranteed Annual Wage, so the steel industry bridles when the technique it is using in current labor negotiations is described as industrywide bargaining. Yet what the steel companies are doing now is certainly a change from what they have done in the past and a change in the unmistakable direction of industrywide bargaining.

Tandem bargaining is perhaps the best quick description of how steel dealt with its union up until this month's new contract negotiations got under way. One company—U.S. Steel, except for one year when Bethlehem took the slot—did all the haggling with the union. If an agreement wasn't reached peacefully, the whole industry was struck, and it waited passively until the one company found settlement terms. Then, all the other producers signed for the identical terms that the one company had accepted. Invariably there was growling from other managements at what the "big fellows" had settled for, but the system continued year after year.

Tandem bargaining has, from the employer's point of interest, all of the major disadvantages of industrywide bargaining and none of its advantages. There is some real value to employers, if one wage contract is going to blanket them all, to have the marginal companies represented at the bargaining table. The less prosperous firms are then in a position to exercise a veto power over a bargain that is just too rich for them to take. Individual bargaining is, of course, more realistic and greatly preferable, but the steel industry has never tried it and apparently won't in the discernible future.

This year, John Stephens for U.S. Steel is only one among three equals who represent U.S., Bethlehem, and Republic in negotiating the fateful 1956 contract. It would be better, we think, if all the basic steel producers who will sign the contract ultimately written were represented at the bargaining table—that is, as long as individual bargaining isn't going to be tried. But what is happening this year makes more sense than what prevailed in the past. We hope that it augurs a peaceful, satisfactory settlement.

WHERE SHOULD BARGAINING TAKE PLACE

One industry in which the parties have been particularly contentious over the definition of the bargaining unit has been the telephone industry, or more accurately the American Telephone and Telegraph Company's portion of that industry. The A.T. and T. wholly owned operating subsidiaries historically have negotiated local agreements with their employees, but the union has maintained that this leads to "shadow" bargaining since the subsidiaries' policies are made by A.T. and T. headquarters (or by "195 Broadway," as the head office is often referred to, after its New York address), with which the union is not in a direct bargaining relationship. The company has denied that it exercises such a control.

In 1950, following several telephone strikes, a special subcommittee of the Senate Committee on Labor and Public Welfare conducted hearings on industrial relations in the Bell System, at which representatives of the parties testified. Majority and minority reports and recommendations were subsequently issued by the subcommittee. The following excerpts relate to the question of the "unit"—whether negotiations should be conducted by the individual subsidiaries or on a systemwide basis. These committee reports were reprinted in later committee hearings.

Excerpts from Taft-Hartley Act Revisions, 83d Cong., 1st Sess., 1953, part 3, pp. 1576–1577, 1599–1600

LABOR-MANAGEMENT RELATIONS IN THE BELL TELEPHONE SYSTEM

FROM THE MAJORITY REPORT

. . . Any description of the local associated Bell companies as autonomous corporations is theoretical and can only be justified in the strictest legal sense, for, as the summary of the evidence that follows will show, these companies function as parts in a closely integrated corporate system completely and directly controlled by the A.T. & T. management. This A.T. & T. control flows from its stock ownership of most of the associated companies, from license contracts which it has with all the operating associated companies in the system, and from the long, continued control which A.T. & T. executives have exercised through the years over promotions and salary increases of administrative officers in the associated companies. This latter type of control has gradually built up within the Bell System a Nation-wide administrative staff which is highly responsive to the suggestions and advice on policies and practices emanating from the A.T. & T. management staff. . . .

This controlling influence of A.T. & T., as the evidence shows, has had a direct effect upon the course of labor relations in the system. . . . Much of this effect, under present bargaining conditions, is disruptive. For instance, there have developed among the various Bell companies uniform bargaining strategies and approaches which have slowed and thwarted the collective bargaining process on the local company level, until bargaining has steadily become less and less effective, and strikes and threats of strikes, throughout the system are becoming more and more common. . . .

The integrated wage structure that has been established in the system is another factor resulting from this closely coordinated control which has complicated collective bargaining at the local company level and engendered poor labor-management relations. Management insists that Bell System wage rates are based on the prevailing wage rates in each community, and that, therefore, bargaining on wage increases is a purely local matter which must take place on the local company level. But the evidence shows that the closely woven Bell System reflects itself in a wage policy extending beyond the local labor market areas in which the telephone exchanges exist, and as a means of maintaining stability to the system's wage structure, wage differentials have been established between the various Bell companies, as well as between the different wage areas within each company. These differentials are therefore factors for consideration in any bargaining on wage changes, and this fact prompted the national telephone panel, in applying the wage-stabilization policy of World War I to the telephone industry, to conclude that "any realistic application of wage policy to the telephone industry must take into account the existence of the Bell System itself." [1]

The coordinating influence of the A.T. & T., and its concomitant effect on the collective bargaining process, is even more apparent in the case of the pension plans of the Bell companies. These plans are uniform throughout the system and provide for the interchange of benefit credits of employees transferring from company to company. The plans are merged, through this interchange arrangement, into one general system plan, which makes it impracticable for the unions to bargain with respect to changes in the plan at the local company level, because a change in any one company's plan would disrupt the general plan. The futility of bargaining on pensions under these conditions becomes even more evident when the union doing the bargaining represents the employees of only one department of a single company. The evidence shows no attempt on the part of the Bell System management to correct this situation, although the Bell companies say they recognize that pensions are a proper subject matter for bargaining. . . . In fact, the companies have refused to do any real bargaining on pensions and have made uniform unilateral changes in the plan from time to time. . . . The repeatedly unsuccessful attempt of the various unions throughout the system to bargain on pension

[1] The national telephone panel was a tripartite body established by the War Labor Board in 1944 for the purpose of settling labor disputes in the telephone industry under the national economic stabilization program. The panel was composed of six members, of whom two represented the public, two represented labor, and two represented industry, one of whom was from the Bell System (H. 313, subcommittee exhibit B, p. 4.).

changes over the last several years has materially worsened labor-management relations in the system. . . .

The basic cause for the bad labor-management relations in the Bell System revolves around the collective-bargaining process, and the inability of the unions to bargain at a level of management which possesses the responsibility and authority to make final decisions. We have seen that in this closely integrated system matters such as wages and pensions cannot be adequately dealt with at a local management level, where only a part of the problem can be considered. The subcommittee believes very definitely that A.T. & T. cannot expect to contain collective bargaining within small segments throughout the system while it makes system-wide decisions for piecemeal application to those segments. When A.T. & T. has bargained with CWA [Communications Workers of America] on system-wide issues, negotiations have been successful.

The subcommittee is not impressed with the claims of management that bargaining can be more effective on the departmental level. The Southern Co. covers 9 whole States with 11 different wage areas and 600 different communities; yet, bargaining for the whole company is done at one table where negotiations are carried on to cover the entire 9-State area. And, in the long-lines department of A.T. & T., which operates throughout 41 different States and the District of Columbia, bargaining is coordinated for all five of its major departments by only one chief negotiator.

Some of the unions in the alliance * have urged that this subcommittee find some way in which the Bell System can be required to bargain on the local associated company level. But in view of the closely integrated nature of the system itself and the controlling influence of A.T. & T., the subcommittee believes that it is utterly unrealistic to expect the parent A.T. & T. to relax the control which it has by the economic fact of stock ownership and by the political fact of the election of company boards of directors and the selection of company officers. The subcommittee strongly believes that A.T. & T. should do the bargaining with the unions on national issues such as wages and pensions which extend beyond any departmental or associated company bargaining unit. With this view, even some of the unions within the alliance appear to agree.

MINORITY VIEWS OF MR. TAFT, MR. SMITH OF NEW JERSEY, AND MR. NIXON

The majority of the committee conclude that—

The Bell System cannot expect to contain collective bargaining within small segments throughout the system while it makes system-wide decisions for piecemeal application to those segments. When A.T. & T. has bargained with CWA on systemwide issues, negotiations have been suc-

* Editor's note: The Alliance of Independent Telephone Unions, an association of small unions, represents employees in perhaps one-third of the fractionalized units of the Bell System. It is opposed by the Communications Workers of America, AFL-CIO, the largest union in the telephone industry, representing about half the bargaining units in the Bell System. CWA would prefer a system-wide unit, while most of the Alliance unions prefer the present arrangement of local departmental units.

cessful. . . . The subcommittee strongly believes that A.T. & T. should do the bargaining with the unions on national issues such as wages and pensions. . . .

We recognize that the power of the American Telephone and Telegraph Co. to control the labor policy of its affiliated companies does present a problem and some justification for requiring the company to bargain on a system-wide unit. But this condition is not unique as applied to employers. Of equal concern is the fact that international unions such as the steel workers and the auto workers and the truck drivers not only have the power to, but frequently do, dictate the terms and conditions of every collective bargaining contract entered into by their affiliated locals with many completely independent small businesses. This fact was established by abundant evidence presented to the Senate Committee on Labor and Public Welfare and other Senate committees in the Eightieth and Eighty-first Congresses. The steel workers union in particular forbade any local to settle for less than a national wage pattern decreed for the steel industry, even though the members of the local were employed in another industry having no relation to the steel industry. . . .

If CWA were to obtain the right to represent nationally in a single unit all employees in the Bell System the effect inevitably would be to freeze out all of the other unions which now represent at least 40 per cent of the employees. Employees now represented by non-CWA unions have repeatedly refused CWA affiliation in spite of extensive and costly organizing campaigns conducted among them. Furthermore, while these hearings were in progress, the National Labor Relations Board conducted an election among the traffic employees of the New England Telephone & Telegraph Co. (90 NLRB No. 102 (1950).) The CWA lost the election to an independent union by an overwhelming margin (H. 483). If a national unit were to be established, the interests of such competing unions would be sacrificed and the wishes of thousands of employees overridden. It is significant that Edward J. Moynahan, on behalf of the Alliance of Independent Telephone Unions, representing about 100,000 telephone workers in unaffiliated unions, testified (H. 257):

It is the position, too, of the Alliance that so-called *Bell System-wide bargaining would be completely improper* since the largest portion of the Bell System is not represented by any one union. In fact, any recommendation by this committee for system-wide bargaining would fly in the face of the rights that have been assured to the large number of collective bargaining agents throughout the Bell System which have been freely chosen by groups of employees outside of any national union set-up. [Italics added]

A 1949 NLRB proceeding in Ohio demonstrated in miniature what the majority recommendation would accomplish on a Nation-wide basis. The CWA desired a unit comprising all of the employees of the Ohio Bell Telephone Co. The Board ordered an election on that basis which was won by the CWA. Wiped out entirely in the process was the Southwestern Ohio Telephone Workers, which for many years had represented the employer's plant department in the southwestern part of the State and which had an unexpired contract in effect at the time of the election. This union, having no membership in other parts of the State, could not compete with the CWA in a State-wide election. (See Ohio Bell Telephone Co., 87 NLRB No. 161 (1949).)

The results of the present system of representation do not warrant the freezing out of freely chosen unions by the institution of a system of Nation-wide bargaining. Collective bargaining throughout the period of 1940–50 has resulted in substantial wage improvement for telephone workers. The CWA in 1950 issued a pamphlet entitled "Then and Now" which points to the gains made by telephone workers not only as to wages, but as to pensions, vacations, sick leave payments, etc., as a "record to be proud of." The union claims credit for the "good wages and working conditions employees enjoy today." . . .

This pamphlet is also evidence that wage and working conditions of tele-phone workers throughout the United States have not been placed in a strait jacket of uniformity. Increased living costs prevailing in large metropolitan cities are shown to be offset by wage differentials. Other regional and sectional differences are likewise revealed. The need for such variations to meet local conditions would be overlooked or become subordinated if bargaining were conducted on a national basis under the threat of Nation-wide interruption of an essential service. . . .

A Nation-wide bargaining unit, on the other hand, would give one labor organization control over all employees in this vital communications industry, a power not unlike that possessed by the United Mine Workers in the coal industry and the railroad brotherhoods in rail transportation. The United Mine Workers, by strike action almost each year since the war, has cut off or limited the national supply of coal. Railroad strikes, in recent years, prevented only by Federal seizure, have threatened economic paralysis. The demand for industry-wide bargaining in the telephone industry means entrusting to the hands of a few union leaders the power to strangle the voice communication lines of economic life in the United States.

If industrywide bargaining is extended to the telephone industry, the American people must face the prospect of frequent and paralyzing interrup-tions of service called by union leaders, who in 1949–50 advocated both strike action, against the desires of their membership, and "jamming" or other forms of sabotage to "completely choke telephone communications in this country" (H. 564). Complete cessation of telephone communications cannot be tolerated. No union today has achieved such a position of power as to enable it to bring about a complete interruption of telephone service or to risk the consequences of such an attempt. It would be shortsighted and foolish for the Government to assist the ambition of the CWA to seize such power.

NEW POWER IN TEAMSTERS' PACT COULD BOOMERANG AGAINST HOFFA

John D. Pomfret, The New York Times, January 17, 1964

CHICAGO, Jan. 16—The first national labor contract in the trucking industry was seen today as having an important long-range impact on the industry and the International Brotherhood of Teamsters—the nation's largest union.

The immediate effect of the national pact is to concentrate more power in the hands of James R. Hoffa, president of the 1.5 million-member union.

In the long run, the national bargaining that Mr. Hoffa has worked so hard to bring about may greatly increase the industry's power in relation to the union.

The union clearly was the dominant party in the negotiations here that led to agreement yesterday on the terms of the national pact and its area supplements. With insignificant exceptions, what Mr. Hoffa wanted, Mr. Hoffa got.

But, while the national pact is the symbol of his present control, it may also signal the end of it.

To understand why, it is necessary to know the nature of the industry with which Mr. Hoffa deals.

It is made up of thousands of small, fiercely competitive companies, many of which operate on the slimmest of profit margins.

POTENT THREAT

To be shut down by a strike while competitors continue to operate amounts to a death warrant for many of these concerns.

Mr. Hoffa knows this and uses it to full advantage.

To get what he wants at the bargaining table, he has only to threaten a strike against key companies while letting the rest operate.

In theory, the industry's response would be to threaten to retaliate by closing down entirely if the union strikes against any of its members. But the industry has never been able to develop the cohesion necessary to do this.

The national pact may pave the way. In the first place, it is expected to result in fewer but larger companies. The industry is already moving in this direction.

In 1950, according to Interstate Commerce Commission figures, there were 19,597 trucking concerns in the United States. By the end of 1961, the number had dropped to 15,998. In the same period, however, the number doing a gross business of $200,000 a year or more had risen from 2,053 to 2,988.

In 1957, when the I.C.C. began reporting the number of companies with gross business of $1 million or more, there were 933 such concerns. At the end of 1961, there were 1,106.

MERGERS FORESEEN

National bargaining, by pegging labor costs at a virtually uniform and relatively high level, is expected to accelerate this trend by forcing companies to merge in search of the economies of large-scale operation.

As the large concerns come to dominate the industry, they will be in a position to withstand the economic impact of strikes and to take effective action to lock out employes if the union calls selective strikes.

This would mean escalating a limited strike into a national shutdown—and a national emergency. And it could force Government intervention. This is the bargaining strategy that the nation's railroads used in their long dispute over work rules with the five operating rail unions.

Mr. Hoffa is scornful of accusations that he might want to call a national strike. He points out that it would deprive him of his key negotiating weapon —the ability to play one employer off against another.

Qualified observers do not expect the industry to develop new power overnight. But by some time in the 1970's, they expect that national bargaining and a national contract will have altered significantly the power relationships between the union and the industry.

Meanwhile, however, Mr. Hoffa and the teamsters clearly have the upper hand. And the new contract strengthens it.

For one thing, it allows the union to skirt more easily the prohibitions in the Taft-Hartley and Landrum-Griffin Acts against the use of union pressure on employers not directly involved in a labor strike.

It also allows questions involving interpretation of the master contract or, under some circumstances, of the supplemental agreements to be processed under a new national grievance procedure, which allows the union to strike to back up its position, except in the limited instance of grievances over discharges in areas that have arbitration clauses in their present contracts.

4: The National Labor Relations Board and Representation Elections

The functions of the National Labor Relations Board established by the Wagner Act of 1935 were not much modified by the Labor Management Relations (Taft-Hartley) Act of 1947, although the structure of the Board was considerably altered. As the Act itself declares, in the sections reprinted below, the Board is principally concerned with two functions: (1) the conduct of representation elections, to determine whether a majority of employees wishes to be represented by some specified union, within a bargaining unit which has been defined by the Board; and (2) the determination of whether employer or union has engaged in the "unfair labor practices" spelled out in the Act, which, on the whole, seeks to eliminate hindrances to the collective-bargaining process without intervening in the actual collective-bargaining settlement.

In this and the next two chapters the Board's role will be examined. This chapter contains the portions of the Labor Management Relations Act which relate to the Board's functions as well as materials dealing with representation elections. Chapter 5 considers unfair labor practices chargeable to employers, while Chapter 6 is concerned with union unfair labor practices, concluding with a few over-all impressions of whether the Act and the Board's administration of it have impinged adversely on the unions.

LEGAL DEFINITION OF NLRB FUNCTIONS

Portions of Labor Management Relations Act of 1947 Relating to the National Labor Relations Board, as amended by Public Law 189 of 1951 °

NATIONAL LABOR RELATIONS BOARD

Sec. 3. (a) The National Labor Relations Board (hereinafter called the "Board") created by this Act prior to its amendment by the Labor Management Relations Act, 1947, is hereby continued as an agency of the United States,

° Portions of the original act of 1947 which were eliminated by the 1951 amendment are enclosed in brackets. Provisions which were added are shown in italics.

except that the Board shall consist of five instead of three members, appointed by the President by and with the advice and consent of the Senate. Of the two additional members so provided for, one shall be appointed for a term of five years and the other for a term of two years. Their successors, and the successors of the other members, shall be appointed for terms of five years each, excepting that any individual chosen to fill a vacancy shall be appointed only for the unexpired term of the member whom he shall succeed. The President shall designate one member to serve as Chairman of the Board. Any member of the Board may be removed by the President, upon notice and hearing, for neglect of duty or malfeasance in office, but for no other cause.

(b) The Board is authorized to delegate to any group of three or more members any or all of the powers which it may itself exercise. A vacancy in the Board shall not impair the right of the remaining members to exercise all of the powers of the Board, and three members of the Board shall, at all times, constitute a quorum of the Board, except that two members shall constitute a quorum of any group designated pursuant to the first sentence hereof. The Board shall have an official seal which shall be judicially noticed.

(c) The Board shall at the close of each fiscal year make a report in writing to Congress and to the President stating in detail the cases it has heard, the decisions it has rendered, the names, salaries, and duties of all employees and officers in the employ or under the supervision of the Board, and an account of all moneys it has disbursed.

(d) There shall be a General Counsel of the Board who shall be appointed by the President, by and with the advice and consent of the Senate, for a term of four years. The General Counsel of the Board shall exercise general supervision over all attorneys employed by the Board (other than trial examiners and legal assistants to Board members) and over the officers and employees in the regional offices. He shall have final authority, on behalf of the Board, in respect of the investigation of charges and issuance of complaints under section 10, and in respect of the prosecution of such complaints before the Board, and shall have such other duties as the Board may prescribe or as may be provided by law.

Sec. 4. (a) Each member of the Board and the General Counsel of the Board shall receive a salary of $12,000 a year, shall be eligible for reappointment, and shall not engage in any other business, vocation, or employment. The Board shall appoint an executive secretary, and such attorneys, examiners, and regional directors, and such other employees as it may from time to time find necessary for the proper performance of its duties. The Board may not employ any attorneys for the purpose of reviewing transcripts of hearings or preparing drafts of opinions except that any attorney employed for assignment as a legal assistant to any Board member may for such Board member review such transcripts and prepare such drafts. No trial examiner's report shall be reviewed, either before or after its publication, by any person other than a member of the Board or his legal assistant, and no trial examiner shall advise or consult with the Board with respect to exceptions taken to his findings, rulings, or recommendations. The Board may establish or utilize such regional, local, or other agencies, and utilize such voluntary and uncompensated services, as may from time to time be needed. Attorneys appointed under this section may, at the direction of the Board, appear for and represent the Board in any case in court. Nothing in this Act shall be construed to authorize the Board to appoint individuals for the purpose of conciliation or mediation, or for economic analysis.

(b) All of the expenses of the Board, including all necessary traveling and subsistence expenses outside the District of Columbia incurred by the members or employees of the Board under its orders, shall be allowed and paid on the presentation of itemized vouchers therefor approved by the Board or by any individual it designates for that purpose.

Sec. 5. The principal office of the Board shall be in the District of Columbia, but it may meet and exercise any or all of its powers at any other place. The Board may, by one or more of its members or by such agents or agencies as it may designate, prosecute any inquiry necessary to its functions in any part of the United States. A member who participates in such an inquiry shall not be disqualified from subsequently participating in a decision of the Board in the same case.

Sec. 6. The Board shall have authority from time to time to make, amend, and rescind, in the manner prescribed by the Administrative Procedure Act, such rules and regulations as may be necessary to carry out the provisions of this Act.

RIGHTS OF EMPLOYEES

Sec. 7. Employees shall have the right to self-organization, to form, join, or assist labor organizations, to bargain collectively through representatives of their own choosing, and to engage in other concerted activities for the purpose of collective bargaining or other mutual aid or protection, and shall also have the right to refrain from any or all of such activities except to the extent that such right may be affected by an agreement requiring membership in a labor organization as a condition of employment as authorized in section 8 (a) (3).

UNFAIR LABOR PRACTICES

Sec. 8. (a) It shall be an unfair labor practice for an employer—

(1) to interfere with, restrain, or coerce employees in the exercise of the rights guaranteed in section 7;

(2) to dominate or interfere with the formation or administration of any labor organization or contribute financial or other support to it: *Provided,* That subject to rules and regulations made and published by the Board pursuant to section 6, an employer shall not be prohibited from permitting employees to confer with him during working hours without loss of time or pay;

(3) by discrimination in regard to hire or tenure of employment or any term or condition of employment to encourage or discourage membership in any labor organization: *Provided,* That nothing in this Act, or in any other statute of the United States, shall preclude an employer from making an

agreement with a labor organization (not established, maintained, or assisted by any action defined in section 8 (a) of this Act as an unfair labor practice) to require as a condition of employment membership therein on or after the thirtieth day following the beginning of such employment or the effective date of such agreement, whichever is the later, (i) if such labor organization is the representative of the employees as provided in section 9 (a), in the appropriate collective-bargaining unit covered by such agreement when made; [and (ii) if, following the most recent election held as provided in section 9 (e) the Board shall have certified that at least a majority of the employees eligible to vote in such election have voted to authorize such labor organization to make such an agreement:] *and has at the time the agreement was made or within the preceding twelve months received from the Board a notice of compliance with Sections 9 (f), (g), (h), and (ii) unless following an election held as provided in section 9 (e) within one year preceding the effective date of such agreement, the Board shall have certified that at least a majority of the employees eligible to vote in such an election have voted to rescind the authority of such labor organization to make such an agreement: Provided further,* That no employer shall justify any discrimination against an employee for nonmembership in a labor organization (A) if he has reasonable grounds for believing that such membership was not available to the employee on the same terms and conditions generally applicable to other members, or (B) if he has reasonable grounds for believing that membership was denied or terminated for reasons other than the failure of the employee to tender the periodic dues and the initiation fees uniformly required as a condition of acquiring or retaining membership;

(4) to discharge or otherwise discriminate against an employee because he has filed charges or given testimony under this Act;

(5) to refuse to bargain collectively with the representatives of his employees, subject to the provisions of section 9 (a).

(b) It shall be an unfair labor practice for a labor organization or its agents—

(1) to restrain or coerce (A) employees in the exercise of the rights guaranteed in section 7: *Provided,* That this paragraph shall not impair the right of a labor organization to prescribe its own rules with respect to the acquisition or retention of membership therein; or (B) an employer in the selection of his representatives for the purposes of collective bargaining or the adjustment of grievances;

(2) to cause or attempt to cause an employer to discriminate against an employee in violation of subsection (a) (3) or to discriminate against an employee with respect to whom membership in such organization has been denied or terminated on some ground other than his failure to tender the periodic dues and the initiation fees uniformly required as a condition of acquiring or retaining membership;

(3) to refuse to bargain collectively with an employer, provided it is the representative of his employees subject to the provisions of section 9 (a);

(4) to engage in, or to induce or encourage the employees of any em-

ployer to engage in, a strike or a concerted refusal in the course of their employment to use, manufacture, process, transport, or otherwise handle or work on any goods, articles, materials, or commodities or to perform any services, where an object thereof is: (A) forcing or requiring any employer or self-employed person to join any labor or employer organization or any employer or other person to cease using, selling, handling, transporting, or otherwise dealing in the products of any other producer, processor, or manufacturer, or to cease doing business with any other person; (B) forcing or requiring any other employer to recognize or bargain with a labor organization as the representative of his employees unless such labor organization has been certified as the representative of such employees under the provisions of section 9; (C) forcing or requiring any employer to recognize or bargain with a particular labor organization as the representative of his employees if another labor organization has been certified as the representative of such employees under the provisions of section 9; (D) forcing or requiring any employer to assign particular work to employees in a particular labor organization or in a particular trade, craft, or class rather than to employees in another labor organization or in another trade, craft, or class, unless such employer is failing to conform to an order or certification of the Board determining the bargaining representative for employees performing such work: *Provided,* That nothing contained in this subsection (*b*) shall be construed to make unlawful a refusal by any person to enter upon the premises of any employer (other than his own employer), if the employees of such employer are engaged in a strike ratified or approved by a representative of such employees whom such employer is required to recognize under this Act;

(5) to require of employees covered by an agreement authorized under subsection (*a*) (3) the payment, as a condition precedent to becoming a member of such organization, of a fee in an amount which the Board finds excessive or discriminatory under all the circumstances. In making such a finding, the Board shall consider, among other relevant factors, the practices and customs of labor organizations in the particular industry, and the wages currently paid to the employees affected; and

(6) to cause or attempt to cause an employer to pay or deliver or agree to pay or deliver any money or other thing of value, in the nature of an exaction, for services which are not performed or not to be performed.

(*c*) The expressing of any views, argument, or opinion, or the dissemination thereof, whether in written, printed, graphic, or visual form, shall not constitute or be evidence of an unfair labor practice under any of the provisions of this Act, if such expression contains no threat of reprisal or force or promise of benefit.

(*d*) For the purposes of this section, to bargain collectively is the performance of the mutual obligation of the employer and the representative of the employees to meet at reasonable times and confer in good faith with respect to wages, hours, and other terms and conditions of employment, or the negotiation of an agreement, or any question arising thereunder, and the execution of a written contract incorporating any agreement reached if requested by either party, but such obligation does not compel either party to agree to a proposal or require the making of a concession: *Provided,* That where there is in effect a collective-bargaining contract covering employees in an industry affecting commerce, the duty to bargain collectively shall also mean that no party to such contract shall terminate or modify such contract, unless the party desiring such termination or modification—

(1) serves a written notice upon the other party to the contract of the proposed termination or modification sixty days prior to the expiration date thereof, or in the event such contract contains no expiration date, sixty days prior to the time it is proposed to make such termination or modification;

(2) offers to meet and confer with the other party for the purpose of negotiating a new contract or a contract containing the proposed modifications;

(3) notifies the Federal Mediation and Conciliation Service within thirty days after such notice of the existence of a dispute, and simultaneously therewith notifies any State or Territorial agency established to mediate and conciliate disputes within the State or Territory where the dispute occurred, provided no agreement has been reached by that time; and

(4) continues in full force and effect, without resorting to strike or lockout, all the terms and conditions of the existing contract for a period of sixty days after such notice is given or until the expiration date of such contract, whichever occurs later:

The duties imposed upon employers, employees, and labor organizations by paragraphs (2), (3), and (4) shall become inapplicable upon an intervening certification of the Board, under which the labor organization or individual, which is a party to the contract, has been superseded as or ceased to be the representative of the employees subject to the provisions of section 9 (*a*), and the duties so imposed shall not be construed as requiring either party to discuss or agree to any modification of the terms and conditions contained in a contract for a fixed period, if such modification is to become effective before such terms and conditions can be reopened under the provisions of the contract. Any employee who engages in a strike within the sixty-day period specified in this subsection shall lose his status as an employee of the employer engaged in the particular labor dispute, for the purposes of sections 8, 9, and 10 of this Act, as amended, but such loss of status for such employee shall terminate if and when he is reemployed by such employer.

REPRESENTATIVES AND ELECTIONS

Sec. 9. (*a*) Representatives designated or selected for the purposes of collective bargaining by the majority of the employees in a unit appropriate for such purposes, shall be the exclusive representatives of all the employees in such unit for the purposes of collective bargaining in respect to rates of pay, wages, hours of employment, or other conditions of employment: *Provided,* That any individual employee or a group of employees shall have the right at any time to present grievances to their employer and to have such grievances adjusted, without the intervention of the bargaining representative, as long as the adjustment is not inconsistent with the terms of a collective-bargaining contract or agreement then in effect: *Provided further,* That the bargaining representative has been given opportunity to be present at such adjustment.

(*b*) The Board shall decide in each case whether, in order to assure to employees the fullest freedom in exercising the rights guaranteed by this Act, the unit appropriate for the purposes of collective bargaining shall be the employer unit, craft unit, plant unit, or subdivision thereof: *Provided,* That the Board shall not (1) decide that any unit is appropriate for such purposes if such unit includes both professional employees and employees who are not professional employees unless a majority of such professional employees vote for inclusion in such unit; or (2) decide that any craft unit is inappropriate for such purposes on the ground that a different unit has been established by a prior Board determination, unless a majority of the employees in the proposed craft unit vote against separate representation or (3) decide that any unit is appropriate for such purposes if it includes, together with other employees, any individual employed as a guard to enforce against employees and other persons rules to protect property of the employer or to protect the safety of persons on the employer's premises; but no labor organization shall be certified as the representative of employees in a bargaining unit of guards if such organization admits to membership, or is affiliated directly or indirectly with an organization which admits to membership, employees other than guards.

(*c*) (1) Whenever a petition shall have been filed, in accordance with such regulations as may be prescribed by the Board—

(*A*) by an employee or group of employees or any individual or labor organization acting in their behalf alleging that a substantial number of employees (i) wish to be represented for collective bargaining and that their employer declines to recognize their representative as the representative defined in section 9 (*a*), or (ii) assert that the individual or labor organization, which has been certified or is being currently recognized by their employer as the bargaining representative, is no longer a representative as defined in section 9 (*a*); or

(*B*) by an employer, alleging that one or more individuals or labor organizations have presented to him a claim to be recognized as the representative defined in section 9 (*a*);

the Board shall investigate such petition and if it has reasonable cause to believe that a question of representation affecting commerce exists shall provide for an appropriate hearing upon due notice. Such hearing may be conducted by an officer or employee of the regional office, who shall not make any recommendations with respect thereto. If the Board finds upon the record of such hearing that such a question of representation exists, it shall direct an election by secret ballot and shall certify the results thereof.

(2) In determining whether or not a question of representation affecting commerce exists, the same regulations and rules of decision shall apply irrespective of the identify of the persons filing the petition or the kind of relief sought

and in no case shall the Board deny a labor organization a place on the ballot by reason of an order with respect to such labor organization or its predecessor not issued in conformity with section 10 (c).

(3) No election shall be directed in any bargaining unit or any subdivision within which, in the preceding twelve-month period, a valid election shall have been held. Employees on strike who are not entitled to reinstatement shall not be eligible to vote. In any election where none of the choices on the ballot receives a majority, a run-off shall be conducted, the ballot providing for a selectiion between the two choices receiving the largest and second largest number of valid votes cast in the election.

(4) Nothing in this section shall be construed to prohibit the waiving of hearings by stipulation for the purpose of a consent election in conformity with regulations and rules of decision of the Board.

(5) In determining whether a unit is appropriate for the purposes specified in subsection (b) the extent to which the employees have organized shall not be controlling.

(d) Whenever an order of the Board made pursuant to section 10 (c) is based in whole or in part upon facts certified following an investigation pursuant to subsection (c) of this section and there is a petition for the enforcement or review of such order, such certification and the record of such investigation shall be included in the transcript of the entire record required to be filed under section 10 (e) or 10 (f), and thereupon the decree of the court enforcing, modifying, or setting aside in whole or in part the order of the Board shall be made and entered upon the pleadings, testimony, and proceedings set forth in such transcript.

(e) [(1) Upon the filing with the Board by a labor organization, which is the representative of employees as provided in section 9 (a), of a petition alleging that 30 per centum or more of the employees within a unit claimed to be appropriate for such purposes desire to authorize such labor organization to make an agreement with the employer of such employees requiring membership in such labor organization as a condition of employment in such unit, upon an appropriate showing thereof the Board shall, if no question of representation exists, take a secret ballot of such employees, and shall certify the results thereof to such labor organization and to the employer.

(2) Upon the filing with the Board, by 30 per centum or more of the employees in a bargaining unit covered by an agreement between their employer and a labor organization made pursuant to section 8 (a) (3) (ii), of a petition alleging they desire that such authority be rescinded, the Board shall take a secret ballot of the employees in such unit, and shall certify the results thereof to such labor organization and to the employer.]

(1) *Upon the filing with the Board, by 30 per centum or more of the employees in a bargaining unit covered by an agreement between their employer and a labor organization made pursuant to section 8 (a) (3), of a petition alleging they desire that such authority be rescinded, the Board shall take a secret ballot of the employees in such a unit and certify the results thereof to such labor organization and to the employer.*

[(3)] (2) No election shall be conducted pursuant to this subsection in any bargaining unit or any subdivision within which, in the preceding twelve-month period, a valid election shall have been held.

(f) No investigation shall be made by the Board of any question affecting commerce concerning the representation of employees, raised by a labor organization under subsection (c) of this section [no petition under section 9 (e) (1) shall be entertained], and no complaint shall be issued pursuant to a charge made by a labor organization under subsection (b) of section 10, unless such labor organization and any national or international labor organization of which such labor organization is an affiliate or constituent unit (A) shall have prior thereto filed with the Secretary of Labor copies of its constitution and bylaws and a report, in such form as the Secretary may prescribe, showing—

(1) the name of such labor organization and the address of its principal place of business;

(2) the names, titles, and compensation and allowances of its three principal officers and of any of its other officers or agents whose aggregate compensation and allowances for the preceding year exceeded $5,000, and the amount of the compensation and allowances paid to each such officer or agent during such year;

(3) the manner in which the officers and agents referred to in clause (2) were elected, appointed, or otherwise selected;

(4) the initiation fee or fees which new members are required to pay on becoming members of such labor organization;

(5) the regular dues or fees which members are required to pay in order to remain members in good standing of such labor organization;

(6) a detailed statement of, or reference to provisions of its constitution and bylaws showing the procedure followed with respect to, (a) qualification for or restrictions on membership, (b) election of officers and stewards, (c) calling of regular and special meetings, (d) levying of assessments, (e) imposition of fines, (f) authorization for bargaining demands, (g) ratification of contract terms, (h) authorization for strikes, (i) authorization for disbursement of union funds, (j) audit of union financial transactions, (k) participation in insurance or other benefit plans, and (l) expulsion of members and the grounds therefor;

and (B) can show that prior thereto it has—

(1) filed with the Secretary of Labor, in such form as the Secretary may prescribe, a report showing all of (a) its receipts of any kind and the sources of such receipts, (b) its total assets and liabilities as of the end of its last fiscal year, (c) the disbursements made by it during such fiscal year, including the purposes for which made; and

(2) furnished to all of the members of such labor organization copies of the financial report required by paragraph (1) hereof to be filed with the Secreteary of Labor.

(g) It shall be the obligation of all labor organizations to file annually with the Secretary of Labor, in such form as the Secretary of Labor may prescribe, reports bringing up to date the information required to be supplied in the initial filing by subsection (*f*) (*A*) of this section, and to file with the Secretary of Labor and furnish to its members annually financial reports in the form and manner prescribed in subsection (*f*) (*B*). No labor organization shall be eligible for certification under this section as the representative of any employees [no petition under section 9 (*e*) (1) shall be entertained], and no complaint shall issue under section 10 with respect to a charge filed by a labor organization unless it can show that it and any national or international labor organization of which it is an affiliate or constituent unit has complied with its obligation under this subsection.

(*h*) No investigation shall be made by the Board of any question affecting commerce concerning the representation of employees, raised by a labor organization under subsection (*c*) of this section [no petition under section 9 (*e*) (1) shall be entertained] and no complaint shall be issued pursuant to a charge made by a labor organization under subsection (*b*) of section 10, unless there is on file with the Board an affidavit executed contemporaneously or within the preceding twelve-month period by each officer of such labor organization and the officers of any national or international labor organization of which it is an affiliate or constituent unit that he is not a member of the Communist Party or affiliated with such party, and that he does not believe in, and is not a member of or supports any organization that believes in or teaches, the overthrow of the United States Government by force or by any illegal or unconstitutional methods. The provisions of section 35 *A* of the Criminal Code shall be applicable in respect to such affidavits.

PREVENTION OF UNFAIR LABOR PRACTICES

Sec. 10. (*a*) The Board is empowered, as hereinafter provided, to prevent any person from engaging in any unfair labor practice (listed in section 8) affecting commerce. This power shall not be affected by any other means of adjustment or prevention that has been or may be established by agreement, law, or otherwise: *Provided,* That the Board be empowered by agreement with any agency of any State or Territory to cede to such agency jurisdiction over any cases in any industry (other than mining, manufacturing, communications, and transportation except where predominantly local in character) even though such cases may involve labor disputes affecting commerce, unless the provision of the State or Territorial statute applicable to the determination of such cases by such agency is inconsistent with the corresponding provision of this Act or has received a construction inconsistent therewith.

(*b*) Whenever it is charged that any person has engaged in or is engaging in any such unfair labor practice, the Board, or any agent or agency designated by the Board for such purposes, shall have power to issue and cause to be served upon such person a complaint stating the charges in that respect, and containing a notice of hearing before the Board or a member thereof, or before a designated agent or agency, at a place therein fixed, not less than five days after the serving of said complaint: *Provided,* That no complaint shall issue based upon any unfair labor practice occurring more than six months prior to the filing of the charge with the Board and the service of a copy thereof upon the person against whom such charge is made, unless the person aggrieved thereby was prevented from filing such charge by reason of service in the armed forces, in which event the six-month period shall be computed from the day of his discharge. Any such complaint may be amended by the member, agent, or agency conducting the hearing or the Board in its discretion at any time prior to the issuance of an order based thereon. The person so complained of shall have the right to file an answer to the original or amended complaint and to appear in person or otherwise and give testimony at the place and time fixed in the complaint. In the discretion of the member, agent, or agency conducting the hearing of the Board, any other person may be allowed to intervene in the said proceeding and to present testimony. Any such proceeding shall, so far as practicable, be conducted in accordance with the rules of evidence applicable in the district courts of the United States under the rules of civil procedure for the district courts of the United States, adopted by the Supreme Court of the United States pursuant to the Act of June 19, 1934 (U.S.C., title 28, secs. 723–B, 723–C).

(c) The testimony taken by such member, agent, or agency or the Board shall be reduced to writing and filed with the Board. Thereafter, in its discretion, the Board upon notice may take further testimony or hear argument. If upon the preponderance of the testimony taken the Board shall be of the opinion that any person named in the complaint has engaged in or is engaging in any such unfair labor practice, then the Board shall state its findings of fact and shall issue and cause to be served on such person an order requiring such person to cease and desist from such unfair labor practice, and to take such affirmative action including reinstatement of employees with or without back pay, as will effectuate the policies of this Act: *Provided,* That where an order directs reinstatement of an employee, back pay may be required of the employer or labor organization, as the case may be, responsible for the discrimination suffered by him: *And provided further,* That in determining whether a complaint shall issue alleging a violation of section 8 (a) (1) or section 8 (a) (2), and in deciding such cases, the same regulations and rules of decision shall apply irrespective of whether or not the labor organization affected is affiliated with a labor organization national or international in scope. Such order may further require such person to make reports from time to time showing the extent to which it has complied with the order. If upon the preponderance of the testimony taken the Board shall not be of the opinion that the person named in the complaint has engaged in or is engaging in any such unfair labor practice, then the Board shall state its findings of fact and shall issue an order dismissing the said complaint. No order of the Board shall require the reinstatement of any individual as an employee who has been suspended or discharged, or the payment to him of any back pay, if such individual was suspended or discharged for cause. In case the evidence is presented before a member of the Board, or before an examiner or examiners thereof, such member, or such examiner or examiners, as the case may be, shall issue and cause to be served on the parties to the proceeding a proposed report, together with a recommended order, which shall be filed with the

Board, and if no exceptions are filed within twenty days after service thereof upon such parties, or within such further period as the Board may authorize, such recommended order shall become the order of the Board and become effective as therein prescribed.

(d) Until a transcript of the record in a case shall have been filed in a court, as hereinafter provided, the Board may at any time, upon reasonable notice and in such manner as it shall deem proper, modify or set aside, in whole or in part, any finding or order made or issued by it.

(e) The Board shall have power to petition any circuit court of appeals of the United States (including the United States Court of Appeals for the District of Columbia), or if all the circuit courts of appeals to which application may be made are in vacation, any district court of the United States (including the District Court of the United States for the District of Columbia), within any circuit or district, respectively, wherein the unfair labor practice in question occurred or wherein such person resides or transacts business, for the enforcement of such order and for appropriate temporary relief or restraining order, and shall certify and file in the court a transcript of the entire record in the proceedings, including the pleadings and testimony upon which such order was entered and the findings and order of the Board. Upon such filing, the court shall cause notice thereof to be served upon such person, and thereupon shall have jurisdiction of the proceeding and of the question determined therein, and shall have power to grant such temporary relief or restraining order as it deems just and proper, and to make and enter upon the pleadings, testimony, and proceedings set forth in such transcript a decree enforcing, modifying, and enforcing as so modified, or setting aside in whole or in part the order of the Board. No objection that has not been urged before the Board, its member, agent, or agency, shall be considered by the court, unless the failure or neglect to urge such objection shall be excused because of extraordinary circumstances. The findings of the Board with respect to questions of fact if supported by substantial evidence on the record considered as a whole shall be conclusive. If either party shall apply to the court for leave to adduce additional evidence and shall show to the satisfaction of the court that such additional evidence is material and that there were reasonable grounds for the failure to adduce such evidence in the hearing before the Board, its member, agent, or agency, the court may order such additional evidence to be taken before the Board, its members, agent, or agency, and to be made a part of the transcript. The Board may modify its findings as to the facts, or make new findings, by reason of additional evidence so taken and filed, and it shall file such modified or new findings, which findings with respect to questions of fact if supported by substantial evidence on the record considered as a whole shall be conclusive, and shall file its recommendations, if any, for the modification or setting aside of its original order. The jurisdiction of the court shall be exclusive and its judgment and decree shall be final, except that the same shall be subject to review by the appropriate circuit court of appeals if application was made to the district court as hereinabove provided, and by the Supreme Court of the United States upon writ of certiorari or certification as provided in sections 239 and 240 of the Judicial Code, as amended (U.S.C., title 28, secs. 346 and 347).

(f) Any person aggrieved by a final order of the Board granting or denying in whole or in part the relief sought may obtain a review of such order in any circuit court of appeals of the United States in the circuit wherein the unfair labor practice in question was alleged to have been engaged in or wherein such person resides or transacts business, or in the United States Court of Appeals for the District of Columbia, by filing in such court a written petition praying that the order of the Board be modified or set aside. A copy of such petition shall be forthwith served upon the Board, and thereupon the aggrieved party shall file in the court a transcript of the entire record in the proceeding, certified by the Board, including the pleading and testimony upon which the order complained of was entered, and the findings and order of the Board. Upon such filing, the court shall proceed in the same manner as in the case of an application by the Board under subsection (e), and shall have the same exclusive jurisdiction to grant to the Board such temporary relief or restraining order as it deems just and proper, and in like manner to make and enter a decree enforcing, modifying, and enforcing as so modified, or setting aside in whole or in part the order of the Board; the findings of the Board with respect to questions of fact if supported by substantial evidence on the record considered as a whole shall in like manner be conclusive.

(g) The commencement of proceedings under subsection (e) or (f) of this section shall not, unless specifically ordered by the court, operate as a stay of the Board's order.

(h) When granting appropriate temporary relief or a restraining order, or making and entering a decree enforcing, modifying and enforcing as so modified, or setting aside in whole or in part an order of the Board, as provided in this section, the jurisdiction of courts sititng in equity shall not be limited by the Act entitled 'An Act to amend the Judicial Code and to define and limit the jurisdiction of courts sitting in equity, and for other purposes', approved March 23, 1932 (U.S.C., Supp. VII, title 29, secs. 101–115).

(i) Petitions filed under this Act shall be heard expeditiously, and if possible within ten days after they have been docketed.

(j) The Board shall have power, upon issuance of a complaint as provided in subsection (b) charging that any person has engaged in or is engaging in an unfair labor practice, to petition any district court of the United States (including the District Court of the United States for the District of Columbia), within any district wherein the unfair labor practice in question is alleged to have occurred or wherein such person resides or transacts business, for appropriate temporary relief or restraining order. Upon the filing of any such petition the court shall cause notice thereof to be served upon such person, and thereupon shall have jurisdiction to grant to the Board such temporary relief or restraining order as it deems just and proper.

(k) Whenever it is charged that any person has engaged in an unfair labor practice within the meaning of paragraph (4) (D) of section 8 (b), the Board is empowered and directed to hear and determine the dispute out of which such unfair labor practice shall have arisen, unless, within ten days after notice that such charge has been filed, the parties to such dispute submit to the Board satisfactory evidence that they have adjusted, or agreed upon methods for the voluntary adjustment of, the dispute. Upon compliance by the parties to the dispute with the decision of the Board or upon such voluntary adjustment of the dispute, such charge shall be dismissed.

(*l*) Whenever it is charged that any person has engaged in an unfair labor practice within the meaning of paragraph (4) (*A*), (*B*), or (*C*) of section 8 (*b*), the preliminary investigation of such charge shall be made forthwith and given priority over all other cases except cases of like character in the office where it is filed or to which it is referred. If, after such investigation, the officer or regional attorney to whom the matter may be referred has reasonable cause to believe such charge is true and that a complaint should issue, he shall, on behalf of the Board, petition any district court of the United States (including the District Court of the United States for the District of Columbia) within any district where the unfair labor practice in question has occurred, is alleged to have occurred, or wherein such person resides or transacts business, for appropriate injunctive relief pending the final adjudication of the Board with respect to such matter. Upon the filing of any such petition the district court shall have jurisdiction to grant such injunctive relief or temporary restraining order as it deems just and proper, notwithstanding any other provision of law: *Provided further,* That no temporary restraining order shall be issued without notice unless a petition alleges that substantial and irreparable injury to the charging party will be unavoidable and such temporary restraining order shall be effective for no longer than five days and will become void at the expiration of such period. Upon filing of any such petition the courts shall cause notice thereof to be served upon any person involved in the charge and such person, including the charging party, shall be given an opportunity to appear by counsel and present any relevant testimony: *Provided further,* That for the purposes of this subsection district courts shall be deemed to have jurisdiction of a labor organization (1) in the district in which such organization maintains its pirncipal office, or (2) in any district in which its duly authorized officers or agents are engaged in promoting or protecting the interests of employee members. The service of legal process upon such officer or agent shall constitute service upon the labor organization and make such organization a party to the suit. In situations where such relief is appropriate the procedure specified herein shall apply to charges with respect to section 8 (*b*) (4) (*D*).

INVESTIGATORY POWERS

Sec. 11. For the purpose of all hearings and investigations, which, in the opinion of the Board, are necessary and proper for the exercise of the powers vested in it by section 9 and section 10—

(1) The Board, or its duly authorized agents or agencies, shall at all reasonable times have access to, for the purpose of examination, and the right to copy any evidence of any person being investigated or proceeded against that

relates to any matter under investigation or in question. The Board, or any member thereof, shall upon application of any party to such proceedings, forthwith issue to such party subpenas requiring the attendance and testimony of witnesses or the production of any evidence in such proceeding or investigation requested in such application. Within five days after the service of a subpena on any person requiring the production of any evidence in his possession or under his control, such person may petition the Board to revoke, and the Board shall revoke, such subpena if in its opinion the evidence whose production is required does not relate to any matter under investigation, or any matter in question in such proceedings, or if in its opinion such subpena does not describe with sufficient particularity the evidence whose production is required. Any member of the Board, or any agent or agency designated by the Board for such purposes, may administer oaths and affirmations, examine witnesses, and receive evidence. Such attendance of witnesses and the production of such evidence may be required from any place in the United States or any Territory or possession thereof, at any designated place of hearing.

(2) In case of contumacy or refusal to obey a subpena issued to any person, any district court of the United States or the United States courts of any Territory or possession, or the District Court of the United States for the District of Columbia, within the jurisdiction of which the inquiry is carried on or within the jurisdiction of which said person guilty of contumacy or refusal to obey is found or resides or transacts business, upon application by the Board shall have jurisdiction to issue to such person an order requiring such person to appear before the Board, its member, agent, or agency, there to produce evidence if so ordered, or there to give testimony touching the matter under investigation or in question; and any failure to obey such order of the court may be punished by said court as a contempt thereof.

(3) No person shall be excused from attending and testifying or from producing books, records, correspondence, documents, or other evidence in obedience to the subpena of the Board, on the ground that the testimony or evidence required of him may tend to incriminate him or subject him to a penalty or forfeiture; but no individual shall be prosecuted or subjected to any penalty or forfeiture for or on account of any transaction, matter, or thing concerning which he is compelled, after having claimed his privilege against self-incrimination, to testify or produce evidence, except that such individual so testifying shall not be exempt from prosecution and punishment for perjury committed in so testifying.

(4) Complaints, orders, and other process and papers of the Board, its member, agent, or agency, may be served either personally or by registered mail or by telegraph or by leaving a copy thereof at the principal office or place of business of the person required to be served. The verified return by the individual so serving the same setting forth the manner of such service shall be proof of the same, and the return post office receipt or telegraph receipt therefor when registered and mailed or telegraphed as aforesaid shall be proof of service of the same. Witnesses summoned before the Board, its member, agent, or agency, shall be paid the same fees and mileage that are paid witnesses in the courts of the United States, and witnesses whose depositions

are taken and the persons taking the same shall severally be entitled to the same fees as are paid for like services in the courts of the United States.

(5) All process of any court to which application may be made under this Act may be served in the judicial district wherein the defendant or other person required to be served resides or may be found.

(6) The several departments and agencies of the Government, when directed by the President, shall furnish the Board, upon its request, all records, papers, and information in their possession relating to any matter before the Board.

Sec. 12. Any person who shall willfully resist, prevent, impede, or interfere with any member of the Board or any of its agents or agencies in the performance of duties pursuant to this Act shall be punished by a fine of not more than $5,000 or by imprisonment for not more than one year, or both.

LIMITATIONS

Sec. 13. Nothing in this Act, except as specifically provided for herein, shall be construed so as either to interfere with or impede or diminish in any way the right to strike, or to affect the limitations or qualifications on that right.

Sec. 14. (a) Nothing herein shall prohibit any individual employed as a supervisor from becoming or remaining a member of a labor organization, but no employer subject to this Act shall be compelled to deem individuals defined herein as supervisors as employees for the purpose of any law, either national or local, relating to collective bargaining.

(b) Nothing in this Act shall be construed as authorizing the execution or application of agreements requiring membership in a labor organization as a condition of employment in any State or Territory in which such execution or application is prohibited by State or Territorial law.

Sec. 15. Wherever the application of the provisions of section 272 of chapter 10 of the Act entitled 'An Act to establish a uniform system of bankruptcy throughout the United States', approved July 1, 1898, and Acts amendatory thereof and supplementary thereto (U.S.C., title 11, sec. 672), conflicts with the application of the provisions of this Act, this Act shall prevail: Provided, That in any situation where the provisions of this Act cannot be validly enforced, the provisions of such other Acts shall remain in full force and effect.

Sec. 16. If any provision of this Act, or the application of such provision to any person or circumstances, shall be held invalid, the remainder of this Act, or the application of such provision to persons or circumstances other than those as to which it is held invalid, shall not be affected thereby.

The representation election can be an exciting contest. Although the vote is to determine whether or not the workers wish to be represented by a union, popularly such an election is viewed as a contest between union and company. If the union is rejected, it is often said that the company "wins."

Needless to say, unions enter such contests with every determination to come out ahead. In part it is a matter of prestige—the more victories it can win at the NLRB polls, the easier it is to persuade other workers that they too should join up. In part it is a matter of recovering an invest-ment—organizing can be an expensive undertaking, and the return on such an investment comes only with the per capita payments to the national office. This does not mean that unions organize workers with an eye to how much they can get back in dues on their original investment, but it does mean that unions, like other organizations, must have an in-come that balances their outgo in order to survive.

PREPARING FOR THE NLRB ELECTION

From Ernest Calloway, Some Notes for Trade Union Organizers, part 6, St. Louis Teamsters' Research Bulletin, April 15, 1955

In most cases an organizing campaign will reach its highest point of interest and intensity in an election conducted by the National Labor Relations Board to determine the legal collective bargaining agency for the employees in question.

To invoke the services of the board in a representation case, it is necessary to obtain signed authorization cards from at least 30 percent of the employees in the bargaining unit. However, an organizer should be extremely careful in invoking the board's services until he has at least 60 to 70 percent of the employees signed up. The prerogatives of management under the present administration of the Taft-Hartley law are many, and their traditional weapons of intimidation and coercion have been sanctified by a series of new adminis-trative decisions from the board. To over-come these hurdles, the organizer should only consider NLRB services after he has been successful in obtaining authorization cards from an overwhelming majority of the workers in the shop or plant. If the election is lost, it will require another year before a new one is permitted under NLRB rules.

So the first task of an organizer in invoking the services of the Board is to determine the extent and depth of union sentiment in the shop. If he is uncer-tain, it's better to wait until the situation improves. Hasty decisions in this matter of seeking the services of the board in representation cases have torpedoed far too many organizing efforts.

The representation election is the first initial test of unity among the new union members. It is also a test for the organizer and his efforts. The date has been set.

The nature of the campaign during this pre-election period is quite different from the initial and middle stages of the drive. The only thing that counts in an election is an 'X' in the square for the Union. Every move and all strategy should be in the direction of getting at least 51 percent of the employees to pencil an 'X' in the proper square. The early stages of the campaign moved at a slow pace. This phase of the campaign must move at a high intense tempo.

The primary object during this period of the campaign is that of holding together and creating a solid front among the employees who *have* signed authorization cards. While this does not exclude the task of obtaining additional authorization cards, it does mean that a great deal of attention must be given to the task of holding the *committed* group together for the election. This short campaign must be an enthusiastic, inspiring one. It is during this period that the employer will concentrate on defeating the Union, and nothing should be left un-done to over-come any and all efforts of the employer. All meetings, speeches, home calls, leaflet distributions, etc. should be planned in the direction of holding your committed group together.

THE LEAFLET CAMPAIGN

During this period leaflets should be distributed daily. A great number of the leaflets should be around the positive advantages of sticking together. How to Vote leaflets should be distributed as often as possible. Where to mark the X is one of the most practical leaflets during this period. In many cases, satire leaflets on the activities of the employer and his supervisor have been effective. It helps to wean workers away from the psychological influences of the employer.

If possible, a Leaflet Distribution Committee should be created among the members. This has certain definite advantages. Workers in the shop distributing leaflets before going to work will obtain greater reception, and more important it builds the spirit of determination and unity.

ACTIVE CARD FILE

An active card file on general attitude toward the Union should be set up for each individual employee who has signed an authorization card. If possible, non-signers of cards should also be included in this file. The card should include name, address, phone number, wage rate, department, years of employment, classification and space for organizer's notes on the individual. This file should be kept confidential and used only by the organizer. The file should be separated into three sections, namely: Weak, Strong, and Tend to Waver. This should aid the orgainzer in determining his points of concentration for additional work during the pre-election period.

HOME CALLS

If possible, a Home Call Committee should also be created among those who have signed authorization cards. Any work that can be given to the rank and file employees during the pre-election period will certainly add to the spirit to win. Cards for home calls should be broken down according to streets and neighborhoods, and each member of the committee made responsible for a particular area of the town. Reports on calls should be made as often as possible. Information from these reports should be added to the active card file.

ESTABLISHING A NEGOTIATING COMMITTEE

During the pre-election period, the organizer could very well establish a Negotiating Committee to prepare the group for the task ahead after certification has been granted by the National Labor Relations Board. This has certain psychological advantages during the pre-election period. It creates an atmosphere of eventual victory and serves as a form of positive encouragement for the group.

USING COMMUNITY LEADERS

In smaller communities, the organizer should attempt to hold a series of meetings in which pro-labor community leaders could be invited to urge the workers to vote for the Union. These leaders also could be used for special radio or television programs during this period. The key operation of this period is that of building a sustained enthusiasm and reducing the area of fear of the employer among the employees. The use of outstanding community leaders contributes a great deal to this aspect of the program.

MOCK ELECTION, THE NIGHT BEFORE

The night before the election is the big night. Every effort should be made to have maximum attendance at this meeting. If necessary, door prizes should be given. The meeting should be kept an enthusiastic one. Use rank and file members as much as possible. They should tell why they are voting for the Union. Don't leave any of the employer's arguments un-answered. In many campaigns, mock elections have been conducted on the night before. Pass out sample ballots and have each one vote. Count the ballots and announce the vote. This is good training on how to mark ballots. Finally, elect the individuals who will serve as observers for the Union.

RIVAL UNIONS

When two or more unions are contending in an NLRB election, the campaigning can get heated. In 1954 the International Union of Electrical, Radio and Machine Workers (IUE) challenged the representation rights of the independent union at the Tung-Sol Co., in New Jersey. The IUE accused the independent of intentions of affiliating with the United Electrical, Radio and Machine Workers (UE). The IUE and UE have been bitterly antagonistic since the latter was expelled from the CIO in 1950 on charges of being Communist dominated. Below are reproduced leaflets circulated to employees in the bargaining unit during the period of campaigning prior to the election.

THE MEANING OF THE SECRET BALLOT

Today we vote. The election is being held in an atmosphere of violence and coercion. Threats are the order of the day from the independent.

But we don't have to be the victims of intimidation. For we have the SECRET BALLOT—the greatest gift of our American heritage.

It was the SECRET BALLOT that defeated Boss Hague.

It was the SECRET BALLOT that defeated Boss Crump.

It was the SECRET BALLOT that defeated Boss Pendergast.

It was the SECRET BALLOT that defeated crooked Tammany Hall.

It was the SECRET BALLOT that always defeated the crooked Politicians.

Now, today, YOU can defeat the company union and outside interference in your affairs. Your weapon is the SECRET BALLOT. It protects you because nobody will ever know how you vote.

Win a clean, decent American Trade Union—the only Union on the ballot—the IUE-CIO.

VOTE IUE-CIO

	IUE-CIO
☐	☐

$15 ASSESSMENT TO PAY $25,000 DEBT

If the independent wins the election, every Tung-Sol worker will be assessed *$15 and up* to pay the $25,000 debt of the independents. And the debt is still going up as they run up bigger campaign bills.

With the independents in the saddle, Tung-Sol workers will face:

1. $15 and up out of everyone's paycheck to pay other people's bills.

2. Loss of the $30,000 in the local treasury to National UE. This is the result of the deal pulled off between the independent and National UE. But this is YOUR money. It belongs to YOU the members.

3. No right to vote on election of officers. Present officers are to be appointed to continue indefinitely.

IUE-CIO Stands for Immediate Election of all Officers by Voting Machines in the Plant

VOTE IUE-CIO

YOU'LL REGRET IT IF YOU DON'T VOTE INDEPENDENT ON TUES., NOV. 9TH

The INDEPENDENTS have presented to you, a program far superior to the IUE's or any other labor organization. It is a program for the people of Tung-Sol, a program that you MUST support because it means a victory to better all conditions for the workers of Tung-Sol.

FOR THOSE OF YOU WHO HAVE DEVOURED THE VICIOUS LIES, CHARACTER ASSASSINATIONS, FLIP-FLOPPERS, AND ACCUSATIONS OF THE IUE. YOU TOO, WILL REGRET THAT YOU DID NOT VOTE INDEPENDENT.

A malicious, whispering campaign started because you refused to take or read the IUE's leaflets. IUE has become more than desperate. They HAVE BECOME INSANE.

The organizers admit that they are just paid to give out leaflets. They cannot answer your questions so, they resort to lies and defamation of character to make you forget your program and what your officers have done and sacrificed for the workers in Tung-Sol. The IUE claims all the lies they have told come from the workers in Tung-Sol. Are you too, Liars? . . .

ALL OF THEIR BLOWS HAVE BEEN BOOSTS.

Your officers are known to you, have fought for you, have fought for trade unionism and a democratic principle. Your officers have presented the truth to you through-out this long, bitter campaign. Your officers have settled grievances for you to the best of their ability and limited circumstances—they have demonstrated their ability, capability and unity under great pressure. The only thoughts the INDEPENDENTS have had in the campaign have been a better program, better wages and better working conditions for their co-workers.

YOU'LL REGRET IT IF YOU DON'T WHOLEHEARTEDLY UNITE TO SUPPORT THE INDEPENDENTS AND THEIR PROGRAM. Without unity, you cannot have a strong union, strong contract and strong leadership.

IUE in all of their plants have portrayed a beautiful picture of disunity, deplorable working conditions, high initiations, high dues payments, assessments, poor selected leadership and STRIKE FANATICS, while at the same time no support is given to the workers. THEY want numbers in people and money from you to further their raids in peaceful plants.

The IUE will print lies about your program and working conditions but, not about your officers. Should they print falsehoods about your officers and members, naming them, they know court action can be taken. BEWARE OF THEIR (IUE) LAST MINUTE WHISPERING CAMPAIGN TO WHICH THEY WILL STOP AT NOTHING IN THEIR FINAL MOMENTS OF DESPERATION.

Have No Regrets After Election Day. Your Affiliation Will Be

WITH INDEPENDENT ONLY

VOTE INDEPENDENT, LOCAL 433 on Tuesday, November 9th

LOCAL 433

INDEPENDENT

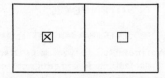

***Flash!!* IUE Monroe Settlement—**   .1¼ Cents—Lost Holiday—No Seniority

LOW TACTICS—SURE DEFEAT

The IUE has shown that it is out for personal gain and power only. They don't give a rap about the Tung-Sol workers including the people that are being fooled by their glib tongues.

It's real funny to see the holier-than-thou attitude of the IUE concerning the money spent by the Independent in this campaign. What we're wondering is—who's going to pick up the $100,000 tab the IUE spent to try to win this plant?

Don't forget they have many more raids planned for others and, more raids mean more assessments from workers.

The IUE's main objective, as stated in the papers, is to wreck the UE, not to fight for better conditions for their members. Isn't that some admission for a so-called union to make?

VOTE INDEPENDENT, LOCAL 433

Issued by Members and Workers of Local 433, Independent

CONDUCT OF REPRESENTATION ELECTIONS

From the 27th Annual Report of the National Labor Relations Board, 1962, pp. 79–86, with footnotes generally omitted

Section 9 (c) (1) provides that if a question of representation exists the Board must resolve it through an election by secret ballot. The election details are left to the Board. Such matters as voting eligibility, timing of elections, and standards of election conduct are subject to rules laid down in the Board's Rules and Regulations and in its decisions.

In fiscal 1962, the Board revised the rule concerning the cutoff date for objections in contested election cases, and revived the equal-time rule for addressing department store employees before an election. The cases involving these matters, and the more important cases decided during the year which deal with other matters relating to the conduct of representation elections, are discussed in the following sections.

a. VOTING ELIGIBILITY

An employee's voting eligibility depends generally on his status on the payroll eligibility date and on the date of the election. To be entitled to vote, an employee must have worked in the voting unit during the eligibility period and on the date of the election. However, as specified in the Board's usual direction of election, this does not apply in the case of employees who are ill or on vacation or temporarily laid off, or employees in the military service who appear in person at the polls. Other exceptions pertain to striker replacements and irregular and intermittent employees discussed below.

Laid-off employees are permitted to vote only if they have a reasonable expectancy of reemployment at the time of the election.

(1) ECONOMIC STRIKERS AND REPLACEMENTS

During fiscal 1962, the Board adhered to the principles enunciated in the *Wilton Wood* case with respect to the voting eligibility of economic strikers and permanent replacements for such strikers. Generally, the status of an economic striker for voting purposes is forfeited where the striker obtains permanent employment elsewhere before the election. But a striker's new employment must be substantially equivalent to the struck job before he can be held to such forfeit. And even a striker who secures equivalent employment may maintain his status by affirmative acts such as indicating to the new employer that he intends to return to the struck work, or that he is on strike, or that he is continuing to picket, or other credible testimony of the striker's intention to return.

(2) IRREGULAR AND INTERMITTENT EMPLOYEES

As heretofore, voting eligibility in industries where employment is intermittent or irregular has been adjusted by the use of formulas designed to enfranchise all employees with a substantial continuing interest in their employment conditions and to insure a representative vote. To this end, voting eligibility was extended to employees of a construction company who were employed during the payroll period immediately preceding the date of the direction of election, or who were employed for 30 days or more in the year immediately preceding the eligibility date for the election, or who had some employment in that year and also were employed 45 or more days in the 2 years immediately preceding the eligibility date for the election.

Generally, eligibility is determined on the basis of the employer's payroll for the period which immediately precedes the date of the direction of election. Since it is the Board's policy to make the franchise available to the largest possible number of eligible voters, elections in seasonal industries are held during peak seasons. . . .

c. STANDARDS OF ELECTION CONDUCT

Board elections are conducted in accordance with strict standards designed to assure that the participating employees have an opportunity to register a free and untrammeled choice in selecting a bargaining representative. Any party to an election who believes that the standards were not met may, within 5 days, file objections to the election with the regional director under whose supervision it was held. The regional director then may either make a report on the objections, or may issue a decision disposing of the issues raised by the objections which is subject to a limited review by the Board. In the event the regional director issues a report, any party may file exceptions to this report with the Board. The issues raised by the objections, and exceptions if any, are then finally determined by the Board.

(1) MECHANICS OF ELECTION

Election details, such as the time, place, and notice of an election, are left largely to the regional director. The Board does not interfere with the regional director's broad discretion in making arrangements for the conduct of elections except where the discretion has been abused. The test is whether the employees in fact had an adequate opportunity to cast a secret ballot. . . .

(2) INTERFERENCE WITH ELECTION

(a) ELECTION PROPAGANDA

In order to safeguard the right of employees to select or reject collective-bargaining representatives in an atmosphere which is conducive to the free expression of the employee's wishes, the Board will set aside elections which were accompanied by propaganda prejudicial to such expression. The Board adheres to its established policy of not policing or censuring the parties' election propaganda, absent coercion or fraud, unless it appears from all the circumstances that the employees could not properly evaluate the propaganda involved. In applying the evaluation test, the Board considers the total picture, including (1) whether the promulgating party had special knowledge of the facts asserted, thus making it more likely that the employees would rely on them; and (2) whether the challenging party had the opportunity to or did rebut the false assertions.

(b) NO-SOLICITATION RULES—EQUAL TIME

During the past year, the Board had occasion in *The May Co.* case to pass upon the question whether a department store unjustifiably intruded upon the free choice of its employees by using company time and property for preelection antiunion speeches, while refusing, under its broad rule forbidding solicitation in the selling areas at any time, the union's request for an equal opportunity to address the same employees. A Board majority found that the employer's conduct interfered with a free election, basing its finding on the fact that the employer's enforcement of its rule prohibiting union solicitation in the selling areas during both working and nonworking time—a rule permitted only department stores [1]—while at the same time utilizing working time and place for its antiunion campaign, created an imbalance in the opportunities for organization communication. . . .

(c) OTHER CAMPAIGN TACTICS

As in the case of prejudicial propaganda, an election will be set aside if the Board finds that campaign tactics resorted to by a party impaired the employees' free choice. . . .

In one case, an election was set aside where the employer made available to employees immediately before the election campaign badges bearing the legend "Vote on the right side—Vote No." The Board observed that because of the employer's control over the tenure and working conditions of the employees, the availability of such campaign insignia placed the employees in the position of declaring themselves as to union preference, just as if they had been interrogated.

---

[1] Department stores have long been exempted from the general ban against "no solicitation" rules for nonworking time, because the nature of the business is such that solicitation, even on nonworking time, in selling areas would unduly interfere with the retail store operations. See, e.g., *Marshall Field & Co.*, 98 NLRB 88 (1952); *Great Atlantic & Pacific Tea Co.*, 123 NLRB 747 (1959); *Walton Mfg. Co.*, 126 NLRB 697 (1960), enforced 289 F. 2d 177 (C.A. 5); Seventeenth Annual Report (1952), pp. 102–105, and 115–118.

(i) EMPLOYEE INTERVIEWS

The Board has adhered to the *General Shoe* doctrine that an election does not reflect a free choice where the employer has endeavored to influence the outcome by the device of encouraging a "no" vote while interviewing a substantial number of his employees individually or in small groups, away from their work stations and at a location the employees regard as a place of managerial authority. The Board found, in one case, that an employer's preelection notification to its employees that copies of "company policy" would be available for discussion at its offices, resulting in individual visitation by a substantial number of employees, was calculated to induce the employees to come to the various offices for the purpose of being individually propagandized.

(ii) THREATS

Preelection threats which tend to influence the employees' vote are grounds for setting aside an election. In one case, a panel majority held that the preelection statement by high-ranking supervisors to all employees that "We have been told [by customers] that we would not continue to be the sole source of supply if we become unionized, due to the ever present possibility of a work stoppage due to strikes or walkouts" constituted substantial interference with the election. Although couched in the form of a prediction, according to the majority this statement contained a clear threat of loss of employment if the employees selected the union. And in another case, a Board majority reversed the regional director's finding that an employer's preelection speech was privileged as a mere prediction of the dire consequences which would result from a union's demands and policies. The majority set aside the election because it viewed the speech as conveying to the employees the threat that the employer would go out of business if it had to deal with the union. Similarly, a Board majority held that an employer's preelection speech to his employees generated fear of economic loss if the union won the election, where the employer made unsupported assertions that a prior business decline was due to a union's organizational efforts and that business and employment conditions would improve if the union lost the election.

An election was set aside where the employer built up a pool of potential replacements before the election and emphasized to its employees the existence of this pool in campaign speeches. The Board found that such conduct could be reasonably interpreted by the employees to mean that bargaining would be futile and that a strike to enforce demands would lead only to their replacement from the pool. Such appeals to the employees' fear of loss of job opportunity, according to the Board, created an atmosphere rendering the exercise of free choice impossible.

But in one case, a panel majority overruled an objection to an election, where an employee remarked that organization could lead to shutdowns which in turn could mean cancellation of big orders that made for steady employment, and the employer avoided affirmance of the employee's remarks by stating the truism that big customers are good for business. The majority held that the employer was not obligated to disavow the employee's statement.

5: Unfair Labor Practices on the Part of Employers

The restraints on employers which were set forth in the Wagner Act have been retained in the Taft-Hartley Act. Certain labor practices are branded "unfair," and employers engaging in them may be brought before the National Labor Relations Board and ordered to "cease and desist" from such behavior. The philosophy behind this part of the law is that the decision by workers as to whether or not they wish to be represented by a union should be left to them; threats of reprisal for joining a union constitute an unwarranted denial of the worker's right to designate an agent. Moreover, refusal by an employer to recognize and bargain with a majority union is likewise viewed in the law as a denial of the worker's right to be represented by an agent. The cases below illustrate the NLRB's effort to define, through individual decisions, the line of conduct which an employer should not follow in labor matters.

SECTION 8 (a) (3) DISCRIMINATION AGAINST EMPLOYEES FOR UNION ACTIVITY

Old King Cole, Inc., and United Automobile Workers, 117 NLRB No. 48, 1957

FINDINGS OF FACT

I. THE BUSINESS OF THE RESPONDENT

The complaint alleges, the Respondent admitted, and the undersigned finds that Old King Cole, Inc., is and has been at all times material herein, a corporation duly organized under and existing by virtue of the laws of the State of Ohio. At all times material heerin, the Respondent has maintained its principal office and place of business in Louisville, Ohio, where it is now and has been continuously engaged in the design, manufacture and sale of displays and fuel cell mandrels. In the course and conduct of its business operations, the Respondent annually causes and has continuously caused its products, said products having a total value in excess of $100,000, to be sold, transported, and delivered in interstate commerce to and through States of the United States other than the State of Ohio, from its Louisville, Ohio, plant.

Respondent is, and was at all times material herein, engaged in commerce within the meaning of the Act.

II. THE LABOR ORGANIZATION INVOLVED

International Union, United Automobile, Aircraft & Agricultural Implement Workers of America, AFL-CIO, is a labor organization admitting to membership employees of the Respondent.

III. THE UNFAIR LABOR PRACTICES

A. THE FACTS

In November 1954, the Respondent opened a new plant known as Plant 3 in Louisville, Ohio, located about 1½ blocks from its Plant 1 where the Respondent manufactured displays and its main office is located. During the period in question here about 70 employees were employed manufacturing fuel cell mandrels for airplanes in Plant 3 under Paul Streby as plant superintendent, Herman Valentine as foreman of the tank building and shipping departments and Clayton Gregory as foreman of the finishing department. Neither plant was organized by any union.

For reasons only hinted at in this record, the employees of Plant 3 began thinking about joining a labor organization sometime in early June 1955.[1] At the request of some of the employees, employee Julia Capaldi through her husband, a union member employed at the Canton Ford Plant, got in touch with David Sherwood, UAW representative, who called on her at her home and explained union organization to her about June 8, 1955. Union organization had begun.

On June 16, employees Capaldi, Nettie Heddleson and Angeline Borger signed union application and authorization cards and 4 days thereafter Jack Griffiths and his mother, Beatrice, did likewise. During the period involved here approximately six union meetings were held at employee Ada Manse's house or at Eagle's Hall in Louisville which were attended by as many as 25 or 30 employees from the plant, including those mentioned above, at which time more union cards were signed. At one of these union meetings Sherwood told the employees that they should wear union buttons at the plant openly as a protection against being discharged. A number of the employees including all those aforementioned began to wear UAW and CIO buttons in the plant during working hours. These same employees and others began soliciting the other employees to attend union meetings and to join the Union. This solicitation was carried on both during working hours as well as during the rest periods and off hours. Certain of the other employees began reporting to their foremen and other supervisors about these solicitations so that the Respondent was soon aware of the union activity and convinced that some 9 employees, including Capaldi, Heddleson and the 2 Griffiths, were responsible for it.

Although Herman Valentine spent all his time among the employees of his department and Streby testified that he spent at least 7 of the 8 hours of his day among the employees of Plant 3, the testimony of these two witnesses for the Respondent indicated that during this whole period until August 8, they

[1] All dates herein are in the year 1955 unless otherwise specified.

personally heard employees talking about the Union during working hours on only one or two occasions. Nor did either of them notice any undue amount of visiting and talking among the employees during working hours until they began to receive reports from employees that they had been solicited to join the Union. Indeed, after receiving such reports, neither personally noted any unusual changes in the work habits of the employees of the plant.[2]

Perhaps this is not to be wondered at for the testimony of the Respondent's witnesses fully confirmed the evidence given by the General Counsel's witnesses that there were no plant rules against talking, chatting or visiting during working hours and that "everybody" indulged in these pastimes at will. In fact one of the Respondent's witnesses, Angeline Borger, who was prone to almost unlimited exaggeration, testified that "everybody, mostly all of the employees" took as long as "45-minute rest periods." In addition various and sundry employees, including the wife of Foreman Valentine, solicited the plant employees to purchase practically any type of merchandise one can imagine in the plant during working hours. The list of goods for sale in the plant by employees included plastics, work pants, clothes, shoes, cosmetics, shawls, household goods, linens, salt and pepper shakers, and chances on punchboards. Vice President Mike Valentine and his brother Foreman Herman Valentine sold chances for a couple of Catholic funds and athletic events in the plant. In addition there were biweekly check pools held in the plant where the money was collected and distributed during working hours to the lucky holder of the paycheck containing the best poker hand among the numbers printed on the check. Foreman Herman Valentine also participated in these.[3] Obviously

[2] Streby testified on direct examination that the only employee he ever spoke to about being away from his work was Jack Griffiths on one occasion 3 or 4 weeks before his discharge. Later, however, when asked the same question by the Trial Examiner, Streby suddenly recalled that he had warned Griffiths no less than four times about wandering around the plant too much, the last time being on the Monday before the Thursday of Griffiths' discharge. Herman Valentine, on the other hand, after testifying that he had warned Griffiths in all seven or eight times about being away from his work, suddenly testified that, as Jack Griffiths was away from his work every 5 or 10 minutes during the last 2 weeks of his employment, he had had to warn Griffiths about twice a day. However, Valentine testified further that Griffiths had not become "radical" about leaving his work until these last 2 weeks of employment. In his testimony Valentine attempted to give the impression that Jack Griffiths had no business in the shipping department or elsewhere in the plant but the facts showed that it was Griffiths' duty to pick up carts from the shipping department and materials from other parts of the plant. In other regards also the testimony of both Streby and Valentine was at least equally self-contradictory, exaggerated and unreliable. Capaldi, Heddleson and the two Griffiths all denied that either Streby or Valentine had ever warned them about spending too much time from their work or about talking about the Union on company time. In view of the unsatisfactory nature of the testimony of both Streby and Valentine, as well as the straightforward nature of the testimony of the four above-mentioned employees, the undersigned credits their denials of having received any such warnings.

[3] Herman Valentine admitted participating in these check pools only once and would only say that his wife's and his own selling activities among the employees were

the Respondent's plant was operated in a very friendly, social atmosphere without the strict adherence to rules of behavior so common in larger plants. In fact there were no posted or published rules of any kind in the plant until August 1, 1955.

As noted the Respondent was cognizant of union organizational efforts soon after its commencement.

The Respondent announced and put into effect as of July 5 a new, and presumably higher, scale of wages.

On July 5 [4] President Jackson had the employees of Plant 3 assembled about 15 minutes before the lunch hour break. After all the employees had assembled, the start of the meeting being held up for a period because some of the employees were slow arriving, Jackson made the following prepared statement:

Old King Cole has always felt that what was best for all employees was best for Old King Cole. Up to the present time it has never been necessary for Old King Cole employees to deal with management through a 3rd party in an effort to make the employees wants known. However, if the majority of the employees now feel that a third party is necessary to represent them, then Old King Cole management is willing and ready to work with the third party of the employees choice. There are several things you should know and understand before you decide.

1. Once you decide to have a third party represent you, you cannot change your mind if you don't like it. Once you're in, your're in.

2. Once you have a third party representing you, the third party and only the third party discusses and settles all questions regarding employment.

3. Wages, Old King Cole has all ways felt that we would have the best and happiest employees by paying the highest possible wages. This we have done in the past and will continue to do in the future.

4. Seniority at the present time, seniority is based on length of service to the company.

I would like to meet with a smaller representative group to discuss

---

limited to "our own time." There is credible evidence to the contrary. Due to the admitted participation of both Mike Valentine, Herman Valentine and his wife in these activities in the plant and on company time, the undersigned was not favorably impressed by the Respondent's expressed "surprise" at learning at the hearing of these things "for the first time" being "carried on behind management's back" in the plant. Nor was the undersigned impressed by the Respondent's claim that these activities were restricted to a period from November 1954 to February 1955, for the uncontradicted evidence shows that the practice was continuing as late as Christmas time 1955.

[4] Although President Jackson, Vice President Worthington, Streby and Foreman Valentine all testified that they believed this speech was made on June 20 or June 30 instead of July 5 as the witnesses for the General Counsel had testified, it was clearly established that the speech was made in fact on July 5 when Respondent's witness Menendez testified that he had gone on his vacation on July 4, had not heard the speech but had heard about it upon his return to the plant on July 11. However, the actual date of the speech is relatively unimportant.

further, any complaints you may have. Please select such a group and I will meet them on Wednesday, July 6th. In order that I may know the opinion of the majority of you, would you advise your foreman of how you feel, so that he may report to me.

Apparently while waiting for the few straggling employees to arrive, Jackson told those present that he had heard something which made him "very unhappy," i.e., that the employees were trying to organize a union, that he did not believe that the employees needed a third party to negotiate for them, but, if they thought they did, he knew a man in Akron who could get them a union.[5]

Later that same day Jackson repeated this speech almost identically to the employees of Plant 1 except that he changed the last paragraph to read:

In order that I may know the opinions of the majority, would you please take a slip of paper and mark it yes if in favor of a third party and no if not in favor.

Also later that day Foreman Valentine wtih paper and pencil took a poll of each employee in Plant 3 requiring a "yes or no" answer as to whether the individual wanted a union. Of the four employees involved here, all answered the question "yes" except Jack Griffiths who informed Valentine that after Jackson's speech he did not know how he stood on the question. When employee Mary Santee refused to vote, Valentine left but returned later to tell her that Jackson wanted the department to elect two women and a man to the committee which was to find out what it was that the employees wanted and meet with him later.

That same evening just before quitting time the employees of Plant 3 gathered at the clock preparatory to punching out and elected two women and a man to the committee. Mary Santee, Nan Kessler and Howard Adams who were elected to this committee were all wearing union buttons. Valentine was sitting at his desk 50 feet away during this so-called election.

Pursuant to instructions these three committee members conferred with their fellow employees during the lunch hour on July 6 and learned what grievances and what demands the employees had in preparation for the scheduled meeting with Jackson that day.

About 2:30 that afternoon Foreman Valentine informed Mary Santee that it was time for her to go in with the committee to see Jackson in his office. Jackson who was accompanied by Streby and Gregory at the meeting, told the committees from Plants 1 and 3 that he wanted to know what the employees wanted. He then went around the room from one committeeman to the next, having each explain what grievances or requests their fellow employees had made. After the members of the committee had each explained what their constituents wanted, Santee asked Jackson to announce which requests Respondent would grant as the employees wanted to know the results but Jackson announced that he was going on a vacation for 2 weeks but would announce his decision upon the seven requested items upon his return. During

[5] Jackson denied having made the above-found statements "in his speech" as did other of Respondent's officials and employees. With one exception he did not deny having made such statements while awaiting the arrival of the last employees.

the meeting Santee stated that the employees were not satisfied with the nonsecret poll Valentine had taken and would like to vote again at a secret election. Jackson said that the employees could have a secret vote if they wanted but "I have got the vote right here and I am satisfied." As he concluded the meeting Jackson stated: "If you went on with this union, . . . you won't meet with me again." [6]

In a speech given to the assembled employees and confirmed in an almost identical letter dated July 25 and sent to each employee, Jackson answered the requests made by the committee as follows on July 20:

On Wednesday, July 6, Mr. Streby, Mr. Gregory and myself met with a group of employees to discuss various conditions of employment which have led to some dissatisfaction in the past. These conditions as related to us by the group were as follows:

1. A dust condition in the grinding room of the finishing department.
2. Pay for 6 holidays.
3. Maintenance man for fuel cell plant.
4. A hard and fast seniority rule based on date of original employment.
5. Insurance.
6. Automatic pay increase until top pay is reached.
7. ½ days pay for employees sent home without working at least ½ day.

On July 6, we advised the group that we would report back to you in two weeks giving our answers to each of the above requests. Those answers are as follows:

1. Dust conditions: We have ordered additional equipment, the installation and proper usage of which should solve the problem.

2. Paid Holidays: We will pay 8 hours for Labor Day, Christmas Day, New Years Day, Thanksgiving Day, Decoration Day, and July 4th, provided the employee works the last scheduled 8 hours before the holiday and the first scheduled 8 hours after the holiday on his shift.

3. Maintenance: We are endeavoring to hire additional maintenance men as soon as we are able to find satisfactory men, we will assign as many as required to the fuel cell plant.

4. Seniority: We will establish at once a hard and fast seniority list based on date of original employment.

5. Insurance: For a number of months we have been investigating various kinds and costs of insurance and we will establish an insurance plan for all employees.

6. Pay Increases: We will set up a schedule of automatic pay increases until top pay is reached.

7. We will pay ½ day's pay to employees sent home without working at least ½ day.

Those are the things the group asked for, we have agreed without question to comply with all of your requests, and in addition, we are setting

---

[6] The Committee never again met with Jackson.

up for the benefit of all employees a profit sharing plan, the nature of which is still in the planning stage. We have been considering this for some time and I don't know yet just how it is going to work. I don't know any of the financial details, except this, it will be based on the profits of Old King Cole, Inc., and those figures will be taken from the financial statements which we are required by law to make each year to the Department of Internal Revenue, and which are audited by Certified Public Accountants.

At the July 6th meeting one of the group raised the question: "How do we know you will do these things if we don't have a contract?" That is a good question which I can answer in this way, we have been in business for over nine years and have provided continuous steady employment during that time. From time to time we have posted various plant rules on the bulletin boards and we have followed those rules without any contract. From time to time we have agreed to give wage increases and vacation benefits, all of these things have been done without a contract. Incidentally, wages have almost doubled in the last nine years. By the same token we will, just as soon as possible write up a detailed statement of the things which we have agreed to do in this letter and that statement will be posted on all the bulletin boards. It will be a matter of company policy and it will be followed in all respects. I should point out to you, however, that after the profit sharing is worked out it must be approved by the Department of Internal Revenue before it can go into effect. We will attempt to obtain that approval as quickly as possible after the plan is worked out.

Promptly after this speech had been given employee Angeline Borger removed the union button which she had been wearing because, as she put it, she "agreed" with everything Jackson offered. As she removed her button, Beatrice Griffiths told her not to be "a fool" and do just what Jackson wanted but to keep on wearing her union button as protection against being discharged.

Borger reported this episode to Foreman Valentine on company time along with the fact that she claimed that Beatrice Griffiths had threatened "to beat hell out of her" if she did not wear her button and that Griffiths had threatened "bloodshed" if the Union did not succeed in the plant. Herman Valentine was so unimpressed with the report that he instruced Borger: "Well, just pass it off and go back to your work." [7] Borger also reported to the Respondent that Griffiths had threatened that she, Borger, could no longer ride in their car pool if she did not wear her union button. The fact is that Borger continued in the Griffiths' car pool until the Griffiths were discharged despite the fact that

---

[7] According to Herman Valentine's testimony, he immediately went to Griffiths and "warned" her that there should be no "bloodshed" but Griffiths denied to him ever having made the remarks reported, even as she did on the witness stand. The undersigned must credit the denial. This is the only evidence of any warning being given to any employee allegedly having made a threat to be found in this report.

there is no showing that she ever wore her union button after Jackson's speech of July 20.[8]

Also after Jackson's July 20 speech shipping clerk Menendez testified that he reported during working hours in turn to Foreman Valentine, Plant Superintendent Streby and later to President Jackson that Jack Griffiths had again solicited employees Haidet, Seaman and himself in the restroom to join the Union and that, after the three shipping department employees had affirmed the fact that they were not interested in the Union as they considered Jackson's offer a very fair one, Griffiths had stated: "The hell with Mr. Jackson," that he was going to do what the Union said, that they were going to get a union in the plant or else somebody was going to get "punched in the nose."

At the hearing Menendez testified that he reported this restroom incident to Valentine and Streby the day it occurred and to Jackson "a few days" later. On July 28, however, both Menendez and employee Haidet gave signed statements to Respondent's labor relations consultant Rector in which both gave the date of the incident as July 27. Menendez was incorrect one time or the other.

Furthermore the written statement of July 28 related exclusively to Griffiths' having "solicited" Menendez and one or two other employees three times in the month of July during working hours either to join the Union or to attend union meetings. While the statement refers to the restroom incident as being "an argument about us joining the union," the statement makes no reference at all to "punching noses," "bloodshed" or "beating Menendez up" such as came out in the oral testimony of Menendez and Jackson as well as other supervisors. If Menendez' oral testimony is correct, this is a strange omission to have been made by Respondent's labor consultant who was preparing the statements for the express purpose of justifying a discharge. Especially is this so as the statement which refers to only three instances of solicitation between July 6 and July 27 contains such sentences as: "He has *continuously pressured* me, Richard Haidet and Kenneth Seaman to join the union during working hours" and "he has *continuously bothered* me at my work by arguing and coercing me in this manner" [italics added] so that it is clear that the writer of the statement was not given to understatement. On the stand Menendez testified that Jack Griffiths had approached him about the union in all "three or four times, possibly five." However, Menendez explained that he "was getting tired of [Griffiths'] getting around trying to coax me into joining the Union when I wasn't interested" and that he reiterated the same restroom incident to President Jackson because he [Menendez] "thought [Jackson] was the man

[8] As a witness Borger indicated an almost pathological determination to mouth all sorts of accusations against the dischargees in broad generalizations. She brooked no interference from the rules of evidence, the Trial Examiner, counsel, or indeed, spectators in the courtroom in carrying out her determination. She displayed an equal determination in refusing all efforts to make her become specific as to statements, times, persons and places. Her bland generalizations and obvious exaggerations were not conducive to belief in the honesty and sincerity of her testimony.

who run the company. I thought I should tell him so if Mr. Streby did not do something about it, maybe Mr. Jackson would."

About July 26, after receiving reports that the two Griffiths, Capaldi and Heddleson were continuing their activities on behalf of the Union on company time, Jackson in consultation with Streby decided to discharge all four of the aforementioned employees.

On July 28, Jackson called in his labor relations expert, Harvey B. Rector of Akron, told him of the reported incidents and that he, Jackson, thought "we should discharge the people because there was nothing we could do to change their minds and to get them back to work" and asked Rector for his advice on the situation. Rector's advice "was that we should get these people who had made complaints to me to put them in writing, which we did." Upon receipt of this advice Jackson had five employees, including Menendez, report to his office on July 28 where Rector spent the rest of the day taking statements from them regarding any union activities engaged in by the four in question here including both that engaged in on working time and on the employees' own time. The employee who gave Rector the longest statement was shipping clerk Menendez whose statement accused Griffiths of "continuously pressuring" the three shipping department employees to join the Union and "continuously bothering me at my work, by arguing and coercing me in this manner." [9]

At the end of the working day of July 28, Foreman Valentine sent Jack Griffiths to Streby's office where Streby told Griffiths that he was discharging Griffiths and handed him his paychecks and a dismissal slip stating the cause of discharge as: "Union activities on company time." When Streby could only tell Griffiths that he was being discharged for "union activities," Griffiths asked if he could go see Jackson.[10]

Following his discharge Griffiths and his car pool, including Angeline Borger, did in fact go over to Plant 1 where, on his way to Jackson's office, Griffiths met up with Menendez with the result that a fight between them ensued in the course of which Menendez was hit by Griffiths' fist in the nose and eye drawing blood and Griffiths received a bump on the head. When they

[9] It must also be noted here that, while Menendez testified that Griffiths threatened to punch somebody in the nose and while Jackson testified that he checked alleged threats by the Griffiths to "beat up" Menendez and found them to be correct from Menendez, the statement of Menendez taken by Rector on July 28 contained not one single word about any threats. Nor does this statement contain one single fact which would justify the use of the word "coerce" despite Menendez' oral testimony to the contrary. If Menendez' oral testimony was correct, it is hard to believe that a labor relations expert preparing a statement to justify the discharge of an employee would deliberately omit such facts.

[10] Streby's account of this meeting differs in that, according to Streby, after having been told that he was discharged for union activities on company time, Griffiths stated that he "knew the rat that had turned him in," "a big, one-eyed Spaniard" and that "he'd get him." The denial by Griffiths of this testimony is credited for reasons appearing throughout this report.

were separated, Griffiths continued on to Jackson's office where Jackson refused to speak with him and ordered him out of the plant.[11]

Griffiths and his car pool then repaired to the police station where Griffiths started to file a charge of assault against Menendez but was advised against it by the policeman on the desk on the ground that he would have little chance of winning if Menendez had been cut and bled. Griffiths left the station without filing the charge.

At the end of work on July 29, Foreman Valentine called Julia Capaldi to his office where he handed her a discharge notice stating the reason for the discharge to be: "Union activities on company time." Capaldi inquired if he had proof which Valentine said he had. As Capaldi stated that Valentine would have to prove it, Streby walked into the room and Capaldi asked if she was being discharged on account of her work, to which Streby answered: "No, your work is okay." [12]

Although, according to the testimony of the Respondent, it had been determined to discharge all four individuals here involved on or about July 26, Jackson explained that the discharge of Capaldi was postponed a day because he did not have "satisfactory proof of her activities" until July 29. The "proof" which Jackson secured the following day was a statement from one Mary Masterana, who did not appear as a witness at the hearing, to the effect that

[11] Jackson testified at the hearing that he called Menendez to his office at about 2:45 p.m. on July 28 and kept him there until 3:40 (10 minutes after quitting time) specifically so as to keep Menendez from harm because he, Jackson, had heard reports whose accuracy he had checked with Menendez to the effect that Jack and Beatrice Griffiths had threatened to "beat up" Menendez. As previously noted none of these alleged threats are even mentioned in the statement taken by Rector from Menendez dated July 28. If Jackson's testimony is true, this seems a strange oversight. Moreover it was on July 28, the same day as the fight, that Menendez was giving his statement to Rector in Jackson's office. It, therefore, seems more logical that Menendez happened to be in Jackson's office on the afternoon of July 28 in order to give his statement rather than for the reason advanced by Jackson.

Furthermore as Menendez was the shipping clerk stationed in Plant 3 as Griffiths well knew, it would appear more logical that Griffiths would have looked for him at his place of work in Plant 3, if he had been in fact looking for Menendez, rather than at Plant 1 for there is not one iota of testimony that Griffiths had any idea that Menendez was not at his regular place of work.

[12] Valentine's testimony differs in that he testified that he told Capaldi that he had to let her go because she was "leaving your job too much and you are throwing the burden on your partner" whereupon Capaldi swore at him saying that she ought to slap his face. On the contrary, however, Streby who spent ⅞ of the day among the employees of Plant 3 testified positively that he had never seen Capaldi, Beatrice Griffiths or Heddleson ever leave their work to go to another employee's mold during working hours. It is thus a bit difficult to accept Valentine's testimony over that of Streby—especially as it is undenied that Streby told Capaldi in Valentine's presence that her work had been "okay." Furthermore, confidence in the reliability of Herman Valentine was not enhanced by his testimony of having received reports on the union activities of the dischargees here from one Pearl Treadway who, by stipulation, was proved not even to have been employed during the period in question.

on July 6, Capaldi came to her place of work, handed her an application card and asked her to join the Union during working hours.[13]

On August 8, Streby handed Beatrice Griffiths and Nettie Heddleson their dismissal notices giving the usual reason for the discharge: "Union activities on company time." To Heddleson, Streby stated: "I don't like to fire anyone but I only work here. . . . I don't know [why Heddleson was being discharged] unless you have been talking union on company time," that her work had been good but that she would "have to let the Company and the Union fight it out." To Griffiths, Streby stated: "I don't like to do this . . . but I have to. . . . It's my orders." When Griffiths inquired if she had not been giving a good day's work, Streby answered: "It isn't that. That is not why you are being fired. I would just as leave you work for me as anyone out there." [14]

On August 1 between the two sets of discharges the Respondent posted its first and only set of plant rules which were divided into three classifications depending on the seriousness of the offense, (1) "minor," (2) "major," and (3) "intolerable." Although counsel for the Respondent disclaimed the fact that these rules played any part in the discharges of Beatrice Griffiths or Heddleson, President Jackson stated that the only rules which either of them could have broken were the following:

Major:

3. Unnecessary conversations away from respective work stations are prohibitive [sic].

6. Interfering with fellow employees on the premises at any time, such as threats, intimidation, coercion, etc. Violation of a major rule shall result in a 3-day layoff.

Despite the announced penalty, Beatrice Griffiths and Nettie Heddleson were discharged.

Either between the discharges of July 28 and 29 and those of August 8 or after all four discharges, Streby made the following announcement to the assembled employees of Plant 3:

I just called you people together to have a little talk with you. I am not a speaker so bear with me a little while will you, because what I have to say will not take long. Management and myself think we have a good group of people working in our plant, and we want to keep all of you

[13] This incident is mentioned in one of the other statements obtained by the Respondent on July 28.

[14] Streby did not deny making these statements. In fact he corroborated that opinion when he testified positively that the only one of the employees he ever spoke to about being away from work was Jack Griffiths and that he only spoke to Jack once about 3 or 4 weeks before the discharge. However, Streby was highly inconsistent in his testimony. For instance, he testified at page 304 of the record regarding the women discharges: "Well it is about the same, I mean, they were wandering back and forth from mold to mold and talking to people" whereas 4 pages later in the record, at page 308, he testified positively by the single word "no" that he had never seen any of the three women involved here go over to another employee's mold. It is difficult to put much, if any, reliance in a witness as inconsistent as that.

working for us. So I am asking you to stop union activity on company time. If you continue union activity on company time I will be forced to discharge you, as you know we have already discharged some. I don't want to do that so please don't force the issue. What you do outside of the building is up to you, so let's not have any more union activity on company time.

None of the four discharged employees have been reinstated.

B. CONCLUSIONS

1. INTERFERENCE, RESTRAINT AND COERCION

In its brief the Respondent argued that it was not guilty of interfering with, restraining, or coercing its employees in violation of Section 8 (a) (1) of the Act because: (1) Jackson's speech of July 5 [15] was a noncoercive speech and thus protected under the so-called free speech section of the Act, Section 8 (c); and (2) there was nothing "coercive" about the poll taken for the Respondent by Foreman Valentine on July 5 at which the foreman required each of the employees to vote "yes or no" on the question whether he was in favor of union representation or not.

As to Jackson's speech of July 5 it may be conceded that the speech was "noncoercive" in the sense that there were no threats of reprisal. However, Section 8 (c) of the Act protects an employer in the expression of his "views, arguments, or opinion" etc. regarding unions to his employees only so long as those expressions contain "no threats of reprisal or force or promise of benefits." The last three quoted words are important also. Speaking in the background of the new wage rates which went into effect that very same day, Jackson in effect told the employees that it was not necessary for them to be represented by a third person and suggested his meeting with a smaller representative group to discuss their complaints the next afternoon. Jackson admitted that the purpose of his making this speech was to find out what was wrong in the plant which created this desire for union representation and what the employees wanted from the Respondent. Although not spelled out in the speech placed in evidence, the committeemen and the employees were informed that it was the duty of the committeemen to find out what grievances their constituents had and what they wanted, a duty performed by their meeting with the employees at noon on July 6. Both the committeemen and the employees recognized the Respondent's implied promise of benefits to be granted to them through the suggested committee. It is significant that the

[15] Respondent's brief refers only to a single speech which from the description was that of July 5 as it was in this speech that Jackson offered to deal with "third parties" if the employees desired and also requested a smaller representative committee to meet with him the following day, July 6. The brief makes no mention of Jackson's second speech on July 20 when he announced the granting by the Respondent of all the employees' demands and, in addition, that the Respondent was instituting a profit-sharing plan. He ended this last speech by stating that these concessions would not be embodied "in a contract" but would be posted in the plant "as a matter of company policy."

committee requested an immediate answer from Jackson at the end of the meeting on the grounds that the employees would want to know the results. Jackson's promise was that implicit in the speech of July 5.

Jackson himself recognized the promise of benefit implicit in his July 5 speech by announcing on July 20 not only the granting of all the demands made on behalf of the employees by the Committee but also the granting of a new profit-sharing plan for the employees which had not even been suggested by the employees. Furthermore on July 20 Jackson made the *quid pro quo* for the benefits he had just announced crystal clear when he stated that these promised benefits would not be embodied in "a contract" but would only be "a matter of company policy" posted on the company bulletin board unilaterally by the Respondent. Hence, in order to obtain these promised benefits, the employees would have to renounce their right to union representation and their right to have their working conditions embodied in a union contract. What Jackson was stating in effect was: "These benefits the Company will unilaterally give you on condition that you employees renounce your right to union representation and to have your working conditions embodied in a union contract." Respondent's witness Borger recognized this *quid pro quo* by promptly removing her union button because, as she put it, "I thought everything he offered was all right"—and so she removed her union button in recognition of Jackson's condition. However, the two Griffiths, Capaldi and Heddleson refused to accept this illegal condition, expressed that refusal by word and deed, all of which were duly reported to the Respondent, and were discharged for their pains. It is significant that the statements taken by Rector refer exclusively to union activities occurring subsequent to the speech of July 5.

The speeches of July 5 and July 20 were integral parts of a single act: an offer of economic benefits in return for the renunciation of the right to union representation. As such these speeches do not qualify as an expression of any "views, argument, or opinion" etc. Therefore Section 8 (*c*) of the Act does not protect the Respondent in this regard either. A verbal act is not protected under Section 8 (*c*). These promised benefits conditioned as they were upon illegal restrictions on the rights of employees guaranteed by the Act amount to interference, restraint and coercion of the employees in violation of Section 8 (*a*) (1) of the Act. The undersigned so finds.[16]

Likewise in its brief the Respondent professed to see nothing "coercive" in having its Foreman Valentine require each and every employee in Plant 3 to vote "yes" or "no" on whether the individual was in favor of union representation, recording that vote (but not the name of the voter, according to the Respondent's evidence) on a pad of paper. Respondent appears to lay considerable stress upon the fact that no names were recorded by Valentine. The employees themselves protested because the poll was not taken by secret ballot. Even Foreman Valentine testified that there had been no need for

[16] The Respondent's July 5 profession of willingness to deal with "third parties" if the employees so desired, becomes pure pro forma lip service to the Act in the light of all the facts.

Jackson to tell him why he was ordered not to record names for he himself could figure out how such a vote "would be used against a person" if the names were recorded on paper.[17] If such a poll could "be used against a person" when recorded on paper, it could also "be used against a person" when recorded in the memory of a supervisor. Requiring an employee to disclose to a company supervisor a desire contrary to that just previously expressed by the employer must necessarily be coercive and an interference with the employee's freedom of choice. If the supervisor conducting the poll can recognize the danger, how much more must the employee who is required to cast the ballot. . . .

In fact in the instant case the poll was an integral part, together with Jackson's speeches of July 5 and July 20, of Respondent's offer to confer benefits on the employees in return for their repudiation of union representation. The purpose of the poll was the same as the purpose of the benefits conferred, i.e., to secure the renunciation of union representation by the employees. Thus the purpose of the poll, like the speeches and the benefits conferred, was to interfere with the right of the employees to bargain collectively through "representatives of their own choosing" and, thus, is a violation of Section 8 (a) (1) of the Act. The undersigned so finds.

2. THE DISCHARGES

The Respondent's admission, contained both on the dismissal notices and in Streby's speech, require the conclusion that each of the four dischargees was discharged by the Respondent because of its belief that each of them had been engaging in "union activities," a cause for discharge prohibited by Section 8 (a) (3) of the Act. The *Radio Officers* case [18] makes it clear that discharge for such a cause necessarily "discourages" membership in a labor organization and violates Section 8 (a) (3) of the Act. But here, due to the dismissal notices and Streby's speech, Respondent's intention to discourage union activities was made patent to all employees.

As noted, the dismissal notices state the cause of discharge in each case to be "union activities on company time." At the opening of the hearing Respondent maintained only that the stress should be laid on the phrase "on company time." During oral argument Respondent changed its position when it argued:

Now actually the union activity was more or less incidental. The important thing was that the employees were engaging in something which interfered with production and that was the reason they were discharged.

This change of position hardly jibes with Streby's speech—nor with the admitted purpose behind Jackson's two speeches which was to find out what grievances the employees had and what they wanted without even so much as mentioning any alleged decline in production in the plant. Jackson recog-

[17] Apparently the later poll in Plant 1 was taken by recording the names of the employees under headings "For" or "Against" which may well account for the fact that Jackson testified that few, if any, of the employees in Plant 1 voted in favor of union representation.

[18] 347 U.S. 17.

nized that "all was not right" in the plant and that there were existing griev- ances at the time he made his first speech. It was the union organizational drive which bothered Jackson—not the alleged decline in production which had not bothered him while it continued from late April through May nor until it became clear that the employees were organizing.

While it is quite true that an employer has a perfect right to establish reasonable rules regarding union activity on company time and property so long as such rules are not in themselves discriminatory against such activity, the Respondent's change in emphasis at the end of the hearing was necessitated by the fact, well established in the evidence, that any rule which this Respond- ent attempted to enforce against these four employees for engaging in "union activities on company time" must of necessity have been discriminatory in fact because the Respondent not only countenanced, but engaged in through its own official family, solicitations on company time and property for practically any other cause one can conceive: charities, personal merchandising, gambling, and even idle social conversation, athletics and personal pleasure. In fact the Respondent itself did not hesitate to use company time and property for antiunion solicitation. In order not to have created a discriminatory no-union- solicitation rule, the Respondent would have had to change its whole lax and friendly policy of operation in the plant. This the Respondent failed to do, except insofar as union solicitation by these four employees was concerned. None of the other activities being carried on on company time and property were stopped.[19]

As, therefore, the Respondent's making a rule against union solicitation on company time without also including in that rule all the other solicitations which were also occurring on company time and property would necessarily have been discriminatory and illegal, Respondent's position by force of those circumstances changed to the contention put forth in oral argument that the union activities on company time "interfered with production." However, Jackson as a witness testified that for some undisclosed reason these other ac- tivities occurring on company time and property somehow did not interfere with production. Jackson was unable to explain this phenomenon.

But be that as it may, in order to prove that his union solicitation inter- fered with the production of Plant 3, the Respondent produced a graph of what it called the daily "production efficiency" of Plant 3. Jackson arrived at these daily "production efficiency" figures by dividing the "market value" of the fuel cells produced at the plant during the day by the direct labor payroll of the plant for that same day. Jackson acknowledged the crudeness of this computation. An economist might well object to the very bases thereof.

According to Jackson's testimony, his long experience with this method had proved that if this problem in division resulted in a figure of 227, then produc- tion for the plant was "normal," any higher figure indicated above normal production and anything lower showed below normal production for the plant.

[19] Foreman Valentine testified that he stopped such other activities if and when he saw them. However, the evidence is undenied that such activities continued, despite Valentine's testimony, at least until Christmas 1955.

Jackson's claim of 227 as "normal production" was not substantiated by the chart in evidence which, however, commenced only as of March 1955, when the Respondent started to retain these figures as permanent records, one result of a Board field examiner's investigation of this case.

A comparison of the facts and figures for 2 individual days selected at random, one of very low "production efficiency" and the other of very high "production efficiency" when some 50-odd tanks were manufactured on the first day and only 30-odd on the second day disclosed the interesting fact that when cells for B-42 aircraft were being manufactured, "production efficiency" tended always to be higher than on those days when no B-42 mandrels were being manufactured. Thus it became apparent that "plant production efficiency" depended greatly on what orders were being filled for apparently B-42 tanks were high in "market value." One need not be a trained economist to perceive other fallacies and shortcomings in this admittedly crude yardstick on which Jackson relied in his operation of Plant 3.

However, this graph with all its obvious shortcomings would still give some indication of the production of the plant. But the graph in evidence, even if taken at full face value, fails to prove the Respondent's contention.

This graph showed "production efficiency" of Plant 3 to be:

(1) April 28–June 28 (with 2 single days excepted): below normal;

(2) June 28–July 15: approximately normal, a few days above and a few days below;

(3) July 15–August 2: steadily above normal efficiency;

(4) August 3–August 20: steadily below normal;

(5) August 21–January 19, 1956: relatively normal both above and below;

(6) January 20, 1956, and thereafter: steadily above normal.

According to the Respondent's testimony, about the last of June upon his return from his vacation, Jackson, noting the decline in production efficiency which began late in April, called in Streby and Foreman Valentine and requested them to find out the cause of this so-called decline. After checking the usual causes of such a thing, i.e., bad materials, absenteeism, etc., neither Streby nor Valentine was able to locate a cause for the phenomenon. Thereafter, according to this same testimony, Streby and Valentine began receiving reports from employees of being solicited to join the Union on company time and property.[20] Therefore, according to the Respondent's argument, there being no other discernible cause, the decline must have been, and was, therefore, caused by this union activity. Or, as stated in the Respondent's brief, "the best answer to this is that something was interfering with production efficiency and there is not even a hint of any other source of interference [other than the union solicitations reported].[21]

[20] It appears strange that these two supervisors were personally unable to discern such activities although purportedly looking for the cause of the production efficiency decline until after these reports were received if there had been any substantial amount of such solicitation.

[21] Although the Respondent professed to know of "no other cause" for this decline in production efficiency, the record here indicated an almost innumerable number of

The trouble with this argument, of course, is that the slump in production began on April 28 but union solicitation did not commence until after June 8. Chronology alone proves that the slump was not caused by union solicitations. Respondent's attorney candidly admitted at oral argument: "Now no one can say what caused it [the fall in production efficiency] in early May." Counsel is only partially correct for Jackson knew that the employees were dissatisfied with their existing working conditions but did nothing about it until he announced the new wage rates to be effective as of July 5. The responsibility for this dissatisfaction rests upon Respondent.

Despite Respondent's admission that no one could say what caused the April slump, it then went on to argue:

. . . But we do know that the production efficiency started going down in May. There could have been a dip for a while which wouldn't have been of any great consequence, but that didn't come back up. It stayed in the red. And there was absolutely no explanation of it unless it was this [union] solicitation on company time.

In addition to the speculative quality of this argument, it is also subject to two fallacies: (1) the unknown causes of the original slump still remained unresolved so that the union solicitation which began on June 8 could have been only another possible cause for the continuation of the decline; and— much more important—(2) on June 28 Respondent's graph shows that production efficiency in Plant 3 became and remained normal or above until August 2. Thus for a solid month prior to the discharges of Jack Griffiths and Capaldi allegedly for interfering with production by their union activities production was in fact normal or above for the first time since April 28, a period of 2 months. Obviously, therefore, the union activities engaged in were not interfering with production. The graph proves that Streby was correct in telling the dischargees here that they were not being discharged because of their work. Accordingly the undersigned must find that the union activities engaged in by the four involved here did not interfere with the production efficiency of Plant 3 and also that Respondent did not discharge them, or any of them, on account of any such alleged interference.

Furthermore Respondent's graph rather conclusively establishes the fact that Respondent's witnesses patently exaggerated the extent and the effect

---

other possible causes: (1) Jackson knew of the existence of a number of unresolved grievances in the plant and, indeed, had announced a pay increase effective as of July 5; (2) on July 6, Jackson discovered at least seven other instances of unsatisfactory working conditions existent in the plant; (3) according to Foreman Valentine, the plant was never busy during the first hour of the day; (4) according to the Respondent's witness, Angeline Borger, "everybody" was given to taking "45-minute rest periods"; (5) according to the testimony of other of the Respondent's witnesses, "all the employees" stood around their machines engaged in idle chatting; (6) the evidence disclosed unmistakably, albeit supposedly to the Respondent's "surprise," the existence of a number of individual enterprises being carried on during working hours having nothing to do with the Respondent's work; (7) supervisors and others were engaging even in athletic practice on company time.

of the union activities of the dischargees. It is to be recalled that Foreman Valentine testified vividly to the effect that, during his last two weeks of employment, Jack Griffiths became "radical," left his work every "five or ten minutes," could not be found "half the time" and had to be "warned" once or twice a day or more. Yet the graph proves that during this same two week period described by Valentine as Griffiths' "radical" period, production efficiency at Plant 3 was steadily above normal and climbing higher. Ironically enough July 28, the day of Jack 'Griffiths' discharge, proved to be the day of highest production efficiency with one exception until January 1956. In view of the reliance placed on the graph of Jackson in running his plant, the undersigned must accept the evidence of the graph over the oral testimony of Valentine and others. . . .

The Respondent was not excited about activities "on company time" for all the above noted extracurricular activities in the plant on company time continued unabated with the supervisors even practicing for the company horseshoe team during working hours. The social chatting at work continued. The merchandising continued. The check pools continued.

But the evidence clearly demonstrates that Jackson was worried about the threatened advent of a "third party" as exemplified by his speech of July 5. Admittedly he wanted to find out what grievances his employees had and what they wanted and thus forestall organization of the plant by granting benefits which could be posted in the plant "as a matter of company policy" but not embodied in "a union contract." The benefits granted on July 20, as recognized by Angeline Borger in removing her union button, were conditioned upon the renunciation of representation by a labor organization by the employees. Hence the benefits were granted in return for the employees' abandoning representation by a union organization.

But through reports received from employees Menendez, Isue and Borger, Jackson discovered that even after his speech of July 20, Jack Griffiths had said "to hell with Jackson's offer," he was continuing his efforts for union organization; that Beatrice Griffiths had told Borger not to be a fool and take off her union button for that was just what Jackson wanted; and that both Capaldi and Heddleson had continued their efforts to organize the Union after July 6. Thus it became clear to Jackson that his promised benefits had not succeeded in causing these four employees to renounce their efforts to obtain union representation. Hence even though Respondent's production efficiency was either normal or above for the first time in months and even though Streby found no fault with the work of any of the four, Jackson chose to discharge these four employees for continuing their activities on behalf of the Union despite the benefits he had granted them conditioned upon the abandonment of such efforts. Streby's speech confirms this finding.

Accordingly, the undersigned is convinced and, therefore, finds that the Respondent discriminatorily discharged Jack Griffiths on July 28, Julia Capaldi on July 29, and Beatrice Griffiths and Nettie Heddleson on August 8, because of their activities on behalf of the Union and in order to discourage membership therein in violation of Section 8 (a) (3) and (1) of the Act.

IV. THE EFFECT OF THE UNFAIR LABOR PRACTICES UPON COMMERCE

The activities of the Respondent set forth in Section III, above, occurring in connection with the operations of the Respondent described in Section I, have a close, intimate, and substantial relation to trade, traffic, and commerce among the several States, and tend to lead to labor disputes burdening and obstructing commerce and the free flow of commerce.

V. THE REMEDY

Having found that the Respondent has engaged in certain unfair labor practices it will be recommended that it cease and desist therefrom and that it take certain affirmative action designed to effectuate the policies of the Act.

It having been found that the Respondent discriminated in regard to the hire and tenure of employment of Jack Griffiths, Julia Capaldi, Beatrice Griffiths, and Nettie Heddleson, by discharging them, the undersigned will recommend that the Respondent offer to each of them immediate and full reinstatement to his former, or substantially equivalent positions, without prejudice to his seniority or other rights and privileges, and make each whole for any loss of pay he may have suffered by reason of said discrimination by payment to each of them of a sum of money equal to that which he would have earned as wages from the date of the discrimination against him to the date of the offer of reinstatement less his net earnings during such period, in accordance with the formula set forth in *F. W. Woolworth Company*, 90 NLRB 289.

In the opinion of the undersigned, the unfair labor practices committed by the Respondent in the instant case are such as to indicate an attitude of opposition to the purposes of the Act generally. In order, therefore, to make effective the interdependent guarantees of Section 7 of the Act, thereby minimizing industrial strife which burdens and obstructs commerce, and thus effectuate the policies of the Act, it will be recommended that the Respondent cease and desist from infringing in any manner upon the rights guaranteed in Section 7 of the Act.

Upon the basis of the foregoing findings of fact and upon the entire record, the undersigned makes the following:

CONCLUSIONS OF LAW

1. International Union, United Automobile, Aircraft & Agricultural Implement Workers of America, AFL-CIO, is a labor organization within the meaning of Section 2 (5) of the Act.

2. By discharging Jack Griffiths on July 28, 1955, Julia Capaldi on July 29, 1955, and Beatrice Griffiths and Nettie Heddleson on August 8, 1955, thus discriminating in regard to their hire and tenure of employment and thereby discouraging membership in International Union, United Automobile, Aircraft & Agricultural Implement Workers of America, AFL-CIO, the Respondent has engaged in and is engaging in unfair labor practices within the meaning of Section 8 (*a*) (3) and (1) of the Act.

3. By offering promises of benefits to employees to induce them to renounce their right to union representation and by polling their employees as to their union affiliations and sympathies; and by interfering with, restraining, and coercing its employees in the exercise of the rights guaranteed in Section 7 of the Act, the Respondent has engaged in and is engaging in unfair labor practices within the meaning of Section 8 (a) (1) of the Act.

4. The aforesaid unfair labor practices are unfair labor practices affecting commerce within the meaning of Section 2 (6) and (7) of the Act.

RECOMMENDATIONS

Upon the basis of the foregoing findings of fact and conclusions of law, and upon the entire record in the case, the undersigned recommends that Old King Cole, Inc., Louisville, Ohio, its officers, agents, successors, and assigns, shall:

1. Cease and desist from:

a. Discouraging membership in International Union, United Automobile, Aircraft & Agricultural Implement Workers of America, AFL-CIO, or any other labor organization, by discriminating in regard to their hire and tenure of employment or any term or condition of employment or in any other manner;

b. Polling its employees concerning their union affiliations and sympathies; promising employees benefits in order to induce them to renounce their right to union representation;

c. In any other manner interfering with, restraining, or coercing its employees in the exercise of their right to self-organization, to form labor organizations, or to join or assist International Union, United Automobile, Aircraft & Agricultural Implement Workers of America, AFL-CIO, or any other labor organization, to bargain collectively through representatives of their own choosing, and to engage in concerted activities for the purpose of collective bargaining or other mutual aid or protection, or to refrain from any such activities except to the extent that such right may be affected by an agreement requiring membership in a labor organization as a condition of employment as authorized in Section 8 (a) (3) of the Act.

2. Take the following affirmative which the undersigned finds necessary to effectuate the policies of the Act:

a. Offer to Jack Griffiths, Julia Capaldi, Beatrice Griffiths, and Nettie Heddleson immediate and full reinstatement to his former or substantially equivalent position, without prejudice to his seniority or other rights and privileges and make each whole, in the manner set forth in the section above entitled "The remedy," for any loss of pay each may have suffered by reason of the Respondent's discrimination against him;

b. Preserve and make available to the Board or its agents upon request, for examination and copying, all payroll records, social-security payment records, time cards, personnel records and reports, and all other records necessary to analyze the amount of back pay due and the rights of employment under the terms of this recommendation;

c. Post in conspicuous places at the Respondent's Plants 1 and 3 in Louisville, Ohio, including all places where notices to employees are customarily posted, copies of the notice attached hereto as Appendix A. Copies of said notice to be furnished by the Regional Director for the Eighth Region, shall, upon being duly signed by the Respondent's representatives, be posted by it, as aforesaid, immediately upon receipt thereof, and maintained for at least sixty (60) consecutive days thereafter. Reasonable steps shall be taken by the Respondent to insure that said notices are not altered, defaced, or covered by any other material;

d. File with the Regional Director for the Eighth Region, within twenty (20) days from the receipt of this Intermediate Report, a report in writing setting forth in detail the steps which the Respondent has taken to comply herewith.

The Board adopted the trial examiner's report and recommendations.

THE FREE SPEECH ISSUE

One issue which has excited controversy has been the extent to which employers are free to fight attempted organization by counterpropaganda. In the early days of the Board, under the Wagner Act, an employer's expressed opposition to unionization or to a particular union attempting organization might, in the context of a program of antiunion conduct, be viewed as interference with the employees' right to organize. In a context of antiunionism, an employer's statements opposing unionization were construed as carrying a threat.

This interpretation was bitterly opposed by employers, who contended that it deprived them of their constitutional right to freedom of speech. In the Taft-Hartley Act, Section 8 (c) was designed to answer their objections. It declared that any employer statement respecting unionization was privileged providing it did not carry any threat of penalty to employees if they did not conform to the views expressed, or promise of reward on condition that they did conform.

The preceding case contains actions which relate to this issue. For example, the July 5 and 20 speeches of President Jackson in the Old King Cole *case were found to contain promise of benefits if employees rejected the union, hence violative of Section 8 (a) (1) and unprotected by Section 8 (c).*

Union officials have quite generally maintained, however, that the NLRB's application of Section 8 (c) has allowed employers to make statements during organizational campaigns which, while free of threat or promise on their face, contain such threat or promise by virtue of the authority of those who make them. The decision below was one of the early decisions on this issue made by the Board following passage of the Taft-Hartley Act. In it the trial examiner found that statements of an employer were coercive in the context of his antiunion conduct, carrying an implicit threat to employees who supported the union. The Board,

*however, overruled the trial examiner's findings, holding that there was
no actual threat contained in the employer's remarks, hence they were
protected by Section 8 (c).*

*Mylan-Sparta Co. and United Construction Workers, UMW 78 NLRB No. 161,
1948, from the intermediate report of the trial examiner*

FINDINGS OF FACT

I. THE BUSINESS OF THE RESPONDENT

Mylan-Sparta Company, Inc., is a Tennessee corporation with its manufacturing plant, office and place of business at Sparta, Tennessee,[1] where it is engaged in the manufacture, sale, and distribution of men's and boys' shirts. It annually purchases and causes to be transported in interstate commerce to its plant at Sparta in excess of $1,000,000 in materials, and annually sells and causes to be transported in interstate commerce in excess of $1,000,000 in finished products.[2]

II. THE ORGANIZATION INVOLVED

United Construction Workers, UMWA, A.F. of L., is a labor organization admitting to membership employees of the Respondent.

III. THE UNFAIR LABOR PRACTICES

A. BACKGROUND AND SEQUENCE

In early March 1946, a hearing was held in Sparta, Tennessee, before a Trial Examiner of the National Labor Relations Board upon a complaint (based upon a charge filed by the Union) issued against Charles C. Bassine and certain other individuals and trustees doing business under the name of Mylan Manufacturing Company, Mylan Manufacturing Co., Inc., and Mylan-Sparta Co., Inc. (the present Respondent),[3] the Sparta-White County Chamber of Commerce, and certain Sparta citizens, alleging violation of Section 8 (1) and (3) of the Act. On April 5, 1946, the Trial Examiner issued his Intermediate Report in the above proceeding, finding that all the parties named as respondent in said complaint had engaged in and were engaging in certain unfair labor practices and recommending that they cease and desist therefrom and take certain affirmative action including the publishing of a cease and desist notice in the local newspaper, the Sparta Expositor. On August 26, 1946, the Board sustained the Trial Examiner's findings in part as to unfair labor practices committed by the respondent partnership, above described Mylan-Sparta Co., Inc.,

---

[1] The main business office is located in Nashville, Tennessee.

[2] Findings based on the pleadings and a stipulation on commerce in the record.

[3] Although Mylan-Sparta Co., Inc., is the title used in the previous case it is obvious and the undersigned finds that the Mylan-Sparta Co., Inc., and the Mylan-Sparta Company, Inc., has reference to the identical corporation.

Mylan Manufacturing Co., Inc.,[4] and M. C. Wallace, but dismissed as to the local chamber of commerce and certain other individual respondents. The Board's decision provided for the conventional posting of a cease and desist notice, but did not require that said notice be published in the local newspaper. On September 12, 1946, the Union filed a petition for certification of representatives in a unit consisting of the maintenance and production employees of the Respondent, excluding office workers and supervisory employees, and the Board ordered a pre-hearing election which was set for November 1, 1946. However, prior to the election date and on October 28, 1946, the Board granted the Union's request for leave to withdraw the petition for certification and no election has been held.

The allegations of unfair labor practices in the present complaint cover a period beginning in March after the conclusion of the previous hearing and continuing on and until the withdrawal of the representation proceeding in late October 1946. . . .

B. ACTIVITIES DURING THE REPRESENTATION PROCEEDING

As heretofore found, the Union on September 12, 1946, filed a representation petition covering the maintenance and production employees, and as a result the Board ordered a pre-hearing election to be held among such employees on November 1. Toward the end of the election campaign, on October 24, the Respondent caused to be published in the Sparta Expositor a full page advertisement entitled "Just Facts." [5] The first sentence of this published statement, in bold type was as follows:

The United Mine Workers Union is again in Sparta to try to collect yearly dues of about $15,000 from our employees. That money is the beginning and the end of what they are after and they will promise anything to get it.

The article then continued:

This is the same union that came up to the mines on the mountain several years ago [and] promised the miners the whole world . . . , nobody believed it but the mines closed up and they have stayed closed to this day . . . honest men were out of work . . . families went hungry and where was the union? The union packed up its wonderful promises and went away but left behind a ruined business and a ruined people. THE UNION WAS GONE!

It next stated:

A few years later another union came by to show the silk mill [6] how to run their business. . . . Again a business was closed down and again people were out of work. After that Sparta was left without any industry. Condi-

[4] Mylan Manufacturing Co., Inc., apparently is no longer functioning as one of the successors to the partnership and as indicated in the previous Board decision.

[5] As heretofore found, this as well as other published statements of the Respondent and Bassine, its president, were also mailed by the Respondent to all persons whose names appeared in the White County telephone directory.

[6] Welwood Sparta Silk Mill which occupied part of the Respondent's present site. See previous Board's decision [70 NLRB 592].

tions became very bad. The railroad was about to pull its tracks out of the County—and not a single union organizer was in sight with even the smallest kind of a little promise. THE UNION WAS GONE!

The statement proceeded,

Now once more the unions are back with us. They weren't here when we built our business; they weren't here when we worked day and night, borrowing money, selling goods or getting 1000 people jobs. They weren't here when we started shipping car loads over the railroads and kept the tracks running into our town. They weren't here to build our town, help our poor and give our good citizens jobs. No sir, they are here now with those same old promises all shined up to look like new. The union wants to get paid for those promises and the price is about $15,000 a year. Our employees are the people who are asked to do the paying and it is up to our employees to say whether they will or not.

TO OUR EMPLOYEES

Our relations have always been most pleasant. Sure, we've had our ups and downs but we always were able to straighten them out to every one's complete satisfaction, weren't we? Things haven't changed. We're the same happy family, all striving to contribute our part—management by every possible benefit to you—you by your good production effort. No outside element is necessary for the continued happiness and security of our employees, town and county. A union can't help! It can only hurt!

MYLAN-SPARTA CO., INC.[7]

On October 28, 1946, the Respondent caused to be published in the local newspaper another full page statement headed "UNIONS ARE OBJECTIONABLE." Excerpts from the article follow:

Unions cause . . . strikes . . . when unions cause slow downs, wages go down. When unions strike, wages disappear. . . . Unions never gave anyone in White County a job. Our history shows that unions caused our people to lose jobs. . . . The union is telling you that if you don't join the union you won't have a job. That is not true. Our history shows just the opposite. When our people joined unions in the past that is when there were no jobs. . . . the union is telling you that no matter what may happen we cannot close our factory—that is not true. We have the right for good business reasons to close . . . entirely or in part at any time. It's just the same as if we were running a farm or a grocery store or a gasoline station. Ask any of them if they can close. Ask the mines if they could close. Ask the silk mill if they could close.

TO OUR EMPLOYEES

You will shortly be asked to vote by secret ballot for or against the union. You may have already signed a union card. THIS DOES NOT LEGALLY REQUIRE YOU TO VOTE FOR THE UNION, YOU CAN CHANGE YOUR MIND, THE

[7] Full text of the article is attached as Appendix B. [Here omitted.]

BALLOT IS WHAT COUNTS AND THAT BALLOT IS SECRET. NO ONE WILL EVER KNOW HOW YOU VOTED. The Company wishes to impress upon you the importance of voting at the proper time. Every one is urged to vote. The Company has every confidence in your intelligence and good will. We look forward to many happy years of future benefits and accomplishments together.

MYLAN-SPARTA CO., INC.[8]

On October 28, as heretofore found, the Union's request was granted for leave to withdraw the representation petition. On October 31, Respondent published another full-page statement in the local newspaper wherein it congratulated its employees because the "Union and the National Labor Relations Board have called off the election." [9]

CONCLUSIONS AS TO INTERFERENCE, RESTRAINT, AND COERCION

The Respondent's acts and statements during the employees' organizational activities of 1946 must be viewed against the background of unfair labor practices heretofore found by the Board during the union activities of 1945, particularly the condoning by the Respondent's predecessors (including President Bassine) of a speech by a local business man in a mill meeting that the coal mines and the silk mill had been closed because they were organized by a union and warning the employees that the Mylan plant would also close in the event that the Union organized it. The published statement of the Respondent issued in April 1946, shortly after the receipt of the Trial Examiner's Intermediate Report in the previous case to the effect that the Respondent had the "right" among other things "for business reasons . . . to expand operations, to reduce operations, or to cease operations altogether and we fully intend to exercise that right," was certainly not compliance with the recommendations in the previous case. Standing alone, it could be construed as a statement on the part of Bassine and the Respondent that they disagreed with the finidngs in that Report, as they certainly had a perfect right to do. However, the use of the language above quoted, that the Respondent had a right to cease operations, and that it fully intended to exercise that right, publicly announced during the revival of the union campaign and when employees were being told that President Bassine and Plant Manager Feinstein would close the plant if the Union came in had the effect of confirming, instead of repudiating, in the minds of the employees the rumors spread by Floorlady Qualls that the mill would close in Sparta if the employees organized.

If there was any doubt in the minds of the employees or the townspeople in the spring of 1946 that the Respondent was threatening to remove the mill if

---

[8] Full text of the statement is attached to Appendix C. [Here omitted.]

[9] On another full-page of the same issue of the Expositor, the Respondent published a speech President Bassine had delivered before the local Rotary club on October 28 and before the local Civitan club on October 29. The speech so published was a diatribe against the Act, the Board, and the Board's personnel, as well as against "aggressive union organization." It stated flatly, "We will not abide by its [the Board's] decision."

the employees organized, that doubt must have been removed (after the Union had filed a petition seeking representation and a date had been set to permit the employees by an election to decide for themselves whether they wanted collective bargaining representation by the Union), when the Respondent published its "Just Facts" statement of October 24 wherein it stated, "This is the same Union" that organized the mines a few years ago and "the mines closed . . . a union tried to show the silk mills how to run their business . . . again a business was closed down and again people were out of work." "Now once more the Unions are back with us . . . with the same old promises . . ."; and when it published "Unions are Objectionable" on October 28, wherein Respondent said, "Unions never gave anyone in White County a job. Our history shows that Unions caused our people to lose jobs. When people joined unions in the past that is when there were no jobs." "The Union is telling you that no matter what may happen we cannot close our factory . . . that is not true. We have the right for good business reasons to close . . . at any time." "Ask the mines if they could close. Ask the silk mill if they could close." . . .

DECISION OF THE BOARD, PASSING ON THE TRIAL EXAMINER'S REPORT (ABOVE)

. . . (a) The published statements of the Respondent, in substance, recited the history of a local mill and a mine, each of which had closed after being organized, and declared that the Respondent could close its plant at any time for good business reasons despite assertions to the contrary by the Union. The Trial Examiner found these statements coercive when viewed against a background of previous unfair labor practices.[10] The statements, however, contain no threat of coercion, and they do not acquire a coercive character because the Respondent had on another occasion committed unfair labor practices.[11] A prophecy that unionization will ultimately lead to loss of employment is not coercive where there is no threat that the Respondent will use its economic power to make its prophecy come true.[12] Furthermore, the Employer's statements were apparently factually correct, and the remarks about the closing the plant were made in reply to allegations by the Union that the Employer could not close its plant without violating the Act. . . .[13]

Accordingly we find that the Respondent has not interfered with, restrained,

[10] Matter of Mylan Manufacturing Company, 70 N.L.R.B. 574, enf'd. as mod., Feb. 10, 1948 (C.C.A. 6), 21 L.R.R.M. 2368.

[11] Matter of Tygart Sportswear Company, 77 N.L.R.B. No. 98.

[12] Matter of Electric Steel Foundry, 74 N.L.R.B. 129.

[13] This case is distinguishable from Matter of Lafayette National Bank of Brooklyn, 77 N.L.R.B., No. 195, where the Board majority found that the employer's statements contained a clearly implied threat to blacklist union members. In the present case, the Respondent refers to undesirable results which have followed union organization in certain instances, but does not suggest that such results will be brought about through the exercise of the Employer's influence. Member Murdock does not concur in distinguishing the instant case from the Lafayette case, having dissented in that case because of his view that there as here, the employer's remarks did not suggest that the employer's own influence would be used to bring about detrimental results to those who joined the Union.

or coerced its employees in the exercise of the rights guaranteed in the Act. The complaint will therefore be dismissed in its entirety.

Testimony of Joseph A. Beirne, President, Communications Workers of America, CIO, in Taft-Hartley Act Revisions, hearings before the Senate Committee on Labor and Public Welfare, 83d Cong., 1st Sess., 1953, part 3, pp. 1552–1553

I cannot do a legal analysis of the section of the act, 8 (c), which deals with the so-called free-speech provision. However, I can express a fundamental with relation to this provision—as Americans we unionists believe as staunchly as any group in the right of free expression. The Bill of Rights lives as vividly with union people as it does with all other segments of our people.

We are also believers in fair play and it is on that aspect of this provision of Taft-Hartley that we draw back to gain our perspective. Our experience with this provision has given us definite proof that some management has believed in and practiced the art of stretching the free-speech provision far beyond anything contemplated by Congress. Too many employers consider that section 8 (c) grants them the right to make anti-union statements. They do not differentiate between unfair labor practices and representation cases. They only understand that their expression should not contain "threat of reprisal or force or promise of benefit" whatever the occasion might be.

The phrase free speech is a misnomer when it is used to describe a right or permission under law for an employer to use his power as an employer to influence the thinking and action of his employees on matters affecting unions and their activities.

It is a coined phrase which misleads. Such free speech is a license for employers to use the privilege of their position and their economic strength to influence and to control activities of their employees and the unions to which they belong.

This is not free speech in the traditional sense, but rather it is the use of full economic weight and position to influence and affect the rights and privileges of employees.

Rights guaranteed to employees under section 7 of the act—those rights of self-organization and concerted activities for purposes of collective bargaining, and other mutual aid or protection—were sired in the conditions which were found to exist as a burden upon interstate commerce at the time of enactment of the Wagner Act. These conditions were restated in part as the basis for the Taft-Hartley Act. They are well known and need not be repeated at this time.

The point is simply this—the use of a catch phrase such as free speech should not be the basis for causing a return to conditions which existed prior to the Wagner Act.

For example: Employers should be neutral at a time when collective bargaining representatives are being chosen. They should not be allowed to use either dominant position as employers to influence—on company premises and during work hours—the choice by employees of their collective bargaining representatives.

There should be no limitation on the use of speech as evidence of an unfair labor practice simply because such speech does not express or imply any threat or reprisal or promise of benefit, as such. Any expression, whether written or oral, whose purpose is to influence employees should be considered, especially where it involves company premises, time, and money.

Where does free speech stop and "threat of reprisal or force or promise of benefit" begin when job threats are made to people whose occupations give them particular skills which cannot be used in other industries?

We in CWA are faced with such occupational problems because it is a well-known fact that work in the telephone industry builds skills but not the kind that can be utilized in other fields.

We can cite cases in which the free speech provision has been abused without conscience in captive audiences where employees have been directly threatened with their jobs if they observe picket lines and in other instances where there has been play on sectionalism and suggestions against minorities.

Employers, through the write-in of the so-called free speech provision, have been led to believe they are free to express themselves in any manner to their employees.

Employers, under the guise of free speech should not be allowed to use their positions as employers, their economic strength, and their control of employees during working time to release a flood of communications to such employees designed to interfere with the choice of collective bargaining representatives or to restrain, coerce, or interfere with lawful activities of their employees and their union.

8 (a) (5) REFUSAL TO BARGAIN

The Taft-Hartley Act, carrying over provisions from the Wagner Act. requires employers to bargain with the union concerning wages, hours, and conditions of employment. At times, however, employers have refused to negotiate with unions concerning some matter which, it is claimed, falls outside these boundaries and involves a management right. If the union alleges a refusal to bargain, it is then up to the Board to determine —subject to court review—whether the employer must bargain on the issue. That is to say, the Board must decide whether the subject is an appropriate one for collective bargaining. The materials below all deal with this matter.

NLRB v. Phoenix Mutual Life Insurance Company, 167 F. 2d 983 (C.A. 7), May 7, 1948, certiorari denied 335 U.S. 845–73 NLRB 1463

ON PETITION TO ENFORCE BOARD ORDER

BEFORE MAJOR AND MINTON, CIRCUIT JUDGES, AND DUFFY, DISTRICT JUDGE

. . . About September 1, 1944, Mr. Herbig, the manager of the Chicago-LaSalle Office, called a meeting of the salesmen and announced the resignation of the cashier, telling them selection of a successor was under consideration by the home office and that the new appointee probably would be transferred from another branch office. The impending change loomed important to the salesmen by reason of their dependence upon the cashier's department for information and assistance affecting their earnings. During the two weeks after the announcement the salesmen discussed the matter of the cashier's successor at some length.

On the morning of September 11, and again at lunch on that day, the salesmen met and expressed their dissatisfaction with the fact that they had suffered inconvenience and loss of time due to the "breaking in" of four different cashiers during the last few years. The salesmen discussed the advisability of making a recommendation to respondent and all of them agreed that the assistant cashier was well qualified to fill the vacancy, and that they would prefer her to an outsider; but as to whether the salesmen should recommend the appointment of any specific person there was some disagreement. Salesman Davis was designated by the group to write a letter which, if approved and signed by all ten of the salesmen, was to be sent to the home office. Davis, with the assistance of Johnson and Goldberg, prepared a tentative draft of such a letter, which was discussed and revised at a subsequent luncheon meeting of the salesmen.

Before the final draft had been agreed upon the manager learned of the proposed letter and questioned salesman Goldberg, who explained that the final draft had not been completed and that he therefore did not know just what the contents would be. The manager thereupon advised him not to sign it.

On September 15, before Davis had an opportunity to put the letter in final form, he and Johnson received notices from the respondent terminating their agency contracts. The letters were almost identical. Each stated:

> Your recent action and involvement in the resignations and new appointment affecting our Cashier's Department have been so far beyond the premise of your responsibility, and so completely unpleasant that in full agreement with the Home Office we are cancelling your Agent's Contract, effective thirty days from today.

The letters further instructed Davis and Johnson to turn in their supplies and rate books, to have their desks cleaned out, and their agency affairs closed by noon of the following day.

Section 7 of the act provides that "employees shall have the right . . . to engage in . . . concerted activities, for the purpose of collective bargaining *or* other mutual aid or protection." By incorporating this language, Congress must have intended to include within the act what the usual meaning of these unambiguous words conveys. A proper construction is that the employees shall have the right to engage in concerted activities for their mutual aid or protection even though no union activity be involved, or collective bargaining be contemplated. Here Davis and Johnson and other salesmen were properly concerned with the identity and capability of the new cashier. Conceding they had no authority to appoint a new cashier or even recommend anyone for the appointment, they had a legitimate interest in acting concertedly in making known their views to management without being discharged for that interest. The moderate conduct of Davis and Johnson and the others bore a reasonable relation to conditions of their employment. It was, therefore, an unfair labor practice for respondent to interfere with the exercise of the right of Davis and Johnson and the other salesmen to engage in concerted activities for their mutual aid or protection. The findings of the Board that Davis and Johnson were discharged because they engaged in concerted activities for their mutual aid or protection is supported by substantial evidence on the record as a whole. . . .

MAJOR, CIRCUIT JUDGE, DISSENTING

I would deny enforcement of the Board's order for the reason that the "concerted activities" in which respondent's insurance salesmen engaged, as found by the Board, were not for their "mutual aid or protection," as contemplated by Sec. 7 of the Act. In my judgment, both the stated purposes of the Act and a reasonable interpretation thereof required a holding that it was never contemplated by Congress that such activities should form the basis for an unfair labor practice. It must be remembered that no labor dispute or labor union, or the right to form, join or assist a labor organization, or any right on the part of the salesmen, or refusal on the part of the respondent to bargain collectively, as those terms are defined by the Act and many times construed by the courts, are involved. Neither is there any grievance concerning wages, rates of pay, hours of employment or conditions of work. In fact, the grievance is not only petty but personal and private in nature.

The grievance concerns the selection by respondent of a cashier, which was wholly the prerogative of management. To put it bluntly, their grievance was directed at a matter which was none of their business or concern. The opinion of the majority on this aspect of the case has the effect of enlarging the jurisdiction of the Board beyond all intendments and penalizes an employer for discharging an employee who busies himself in concert with fellow employees about matters which are none of their concern, all under the guise that it is for their "mutual aid or protection." I would suppose under the holding of the majority that the salesmen would also be protected if they engaged in "concerted activities" regarding respondent's president, its board of directors, its attorneys, the location of its office, or the form and contents of the policies issued by respondent which the salesmen are authorized to sell, this notwithstanding that respondent would be under no obligation to bargain with them concerning these and other matters wholly within the realm of the managerial orbit, all under the pretext that they had a "legitimate interest" in such matters.

Inland Steel Company v. NLRB; United Steel Workers of America, CIO et al. v. NLRB; 170 F. 2d 247 (C.A. 7), September 23, 1948, certiorari granted 335 U.S. 910 (United Steel Workers), certiorari denied 336 U.S. 960 (Inland Steel Company)—77 NLRB 1

BARGAINING ON PENSIONS

The Company's refusal to bargain concerning a retirement and pension plan is based solely on its contention that it is not required to do so under the terms of the Act. . . .

The Company relates in lengthy detail the complicated nature of its retirement and pension plan, for the purpose, as we understand, of showing that it is impossible, or at any rate highly impractical, for it to bargain relative thereto with the multiplicity of bargaining units which the Board has established in its plant. It states in its brief:

Retirement and pension plans such as the petitioner's cannot be dealt with through the processes of compulsory collective bargaining required by the National Labor Relations Act, which entail bargaining within the units of the character established by Section 9 (a) and (b) of that Act.

The Company concedes that "Congress could have established a requirement of compulsory collective bargaining upon any subject which a representative of the employees chose to present for that purpose," and we understand from some parts of its argument that it tacitly concedes that some retirement and pension plans may be within the scope of the bargaining requirement. However, we find in the Company's reply brief, in response to the Board's argument, what appears to be the inconsistent statement that "Congress intended to exclude from the compulsory bargaining requirement of the Act all industrial retirement and pension plans. The law is a law for all and it is the same law." We agree, of course, with the last sentence of this quotation. We also are of the view that the bargaining requirements of the Act include all retirement and pension plans or none. Otherwise, as the Board points out "some employers would have to bargain about pensions and some would not, depending entirely upon the unit structure in the plant and the nature of the pension plan the employer has established or desires to establish." Such a holding as the Act's requirements would supply the incentive for an employer to devise a plan or system which would be sufficiently comprehensive and difficult to remove it from the ambit of the statute, and success of such an effort would depend upon the ingenuity of the formulator of the plan. We are satisfied no such construction of the Act can reasonably be made.

It is, therefore, our view that the Company's retirement and pension plan, complicated as it is asserted to be, must be treated and considered the same as any other such plan. It follows that the issue for decision is, as the Board asserts, whether pension and retirement plans are part of the subject matter of compulsory collective bargaining within the meaning of the Act. The contention which we have just discussed has been treated first, and perhaps somewhat out of order, so as to obviate the necessity for a lengthy and detailed statement of the Company's plan.

Briefly, the plan as originally initiated on January 1, 1936, provided for the establishment of a contributory plan for the payment of retirement annuities pursuant to a contract between the Company and the Equitable Life Assurance Society. Only employees with earnings of $250.00 or more per month were eligible to participate. Effective December 31, 1943, the plan was extended to cover all employees regardless of the amount of their earnings, provided they had attained the age of 30 and had five years of service. The plan from the beginning was optional with the employee, who could drop out at any time, with rights upon retirement fixed as of that date. On December 28, 1945, the Company entered into an agreement with the First National Bank of Chicago, wherein the Company established a pension trust, the purpose of which was to augment the Company's pension program by making annuities available to employees whose period of service had occurred largely during years prior to the time when participation in the retirement plan was available to them. These were employees whose retirement date would occur so soon after the establishment of the plan that it would not afford them adequate retirement annuity benefits. The employees eligible to participate in the pension trust were not required to contribute thereto, but such fund was created by the Company's contributions.

An integral and it is asserted an essential part of the plan from the beginning was that employees be compulsorily retired at the age of 65. (There are some exceptions to this requirement which are not material here.)

The Company's plan had been in effect for five and one-half years when, because of the increased demands for production and with a shortage of manpower occasioned by the war, it was compelled to suspend the retirement of its employees as provided by its established program. In consequence there were no retirements for age at either of the plants involved in the instant proceeding from August 26, 1941 to April 1, 1946. This temporary suspension of the compulsory retirement rule was abrogated, and it was determined by the Company that no retirements should be deferred beyond June 30, 1946. By April 1, 1946, all of the Company's employees, some 224 in number, who had reached the age of 65, had been retired. Thereupon, the Union filed with the Company a grievance protesting its action in the automatic retirement of employees at the age of 65. The Company refused to discuss this grievance with the Union, taking the position that it was not required under the Act to do so or to bargain concerning its retirement and pension plan, and particularly concerning the compulsory retirement feature thereof. Whereupon, the instant proceeding was instituted before the Board, with the result already noted.

This brings us to the particular language in controversy. Sec. 8 (5) of the Act requires an employer "to bargain collectively with the representative of his employees, subject to the provisions of Sec. 9 (a)," and the latter section provides that the duly selected representative of the employees in an appropriate unit shall be their exclusive representative "for the purposes of collective bargaining *in respect to rates of pay, wages, hours of employment, or other conditions of employment. . . .*" [Italics supplied.] The instant controversy has to do with the construction to be given or the meaning to be attached to the italicized words; in fact, the controversy is narrowed to the meaning to be attached to the term "wages" or "other conditions of employment."

The Board found and concluded that the benefits accruing to an employee by reason of a retirement or pension plan are encompassed in both categories. As to the former it stated in its decision:

> With due regard for the aims and purposes of the Act and the evils which it sought to correct, we are convinced and find that the term 'wages' as used in Section 9 (a) must be construed to include emoluments of

value, like pension and insurance benefits, which may accrue to employees out of their employment relationship. . . . Realistically viewed, this type of wage enhancement or increase, no less than any other, becomes an integral part of the entire wage structure, and the character of the employee representative's interest in it, and the terms of its grant, is no different than in any other case where a change in the wage structure is effected.

The Board also found and concluded that in any event a retirement and pension plan is included in "conditions of employment" and is a matter for collective bargaining. After a careful study of the well written briefs with which we have been favored, we find ourselves in agreement with the Board's conclusion. In fact, we are convinced that the language employed by Congress, considered in connection with the purpose of the Act, so clearly includes a retirement and pension plan as to leave little, if any, room for construction. While, as the Company has demonstrated, a reasonable argument can be made that the benefits flowing from such a plan are not "wages," we think the better and more logical argument is on the other side, and certainly there is, in our opinion, no sound basis for an argument that such a plan is not clearly included in the phrase, "other conditions of employment." The language employed, when viewed in connection with the stated purpose of the Act, leads irresistably to such a conclusion. And we find nothing in the numerous authorities called to our attention or in the legislative history so strongly relied upon which demonstrates a contrary intent and purpose on the part of Congress.

The opening sentence in the Company's argument is as follows: "Section 8 (5) and 9 (a) of the Act do not refer to industrial retirement and pension plans, such as that of the petitioner, *in haec verba*." Of course not, and this is equally true as to the myriad matters arising from the employer-employee relationship which are recognized as included in the bargaining requirements of the Act but which are not specifically referred to. Illustrative are the numerous matters concerning which the Company and the Union have bargained and agreed, as embodied in their contract of April 30, 1945. A few of such matters are: a provision agreeing to bargain concerning nondiscriminatory discharges; a provision concerning seniority rights, with its far reaching effect upon promotions and demotions; a provision for the benefit of employees inducted into the military service; a provision determining vacation periods with pay; a provision concerning the safety and health of employees, including clinic facilities; a provision for in-plant feeding, and a provision binding the Company and the Union to bargain, in conformity with a Directive Order of the National War Labor Board concerning dismissal or severance pay for employees displaced as the result of the closing of plants or the reductions in the working force following the termination of the war. None of these matters and many others which could be mentioned are referred to in the Act "*in haec verba*," yet we think they are recognized generally, and they have been specifically recognized by the Company in the instant case as proper matters for bargaining and, as a result, have been included in a contract with the Union. Some of the benefits thus conferred could properly be designated as "wages," and they are all "conditions of employment." We think no common sense view would permit a distinction to be made as to the benefits inuring to the employees by reason of a retirement and pension plan.

EFFECTIVENESS OF LEGAL PROTECTION

Emil Rieve, President, Textile Workers of America, CIO, April, 1953, in Taft-Hartley Act Revisions, hearings before the Senate Committee on Labor and Public Welfare, 83d Cong., 1st Sess., 1953, part 3, pp. 1523–1529, 1536–1537

Let me describe, in a general way, the course of a typical organizing campaign at a typical textile mill in the South.

In the first place, let me say that we do not pick the name of a mill out of a hat, and open up a campaign. In every case we have reason to believe that the workers want and need a union. Most of the time they have told us so themselves. Once in a great while we act only on the knowledge that wages and working conditions are so far below standard that there must be a desire among the workers for a remedy.

I am making this point because it has been said by Senator Taft, among others, that we have failed in the South because the workers do not want a union. I assure you that we do not start a campaign unless we are reasonably certain of a good reception from the workers.

A campaign begins with the assignment of a single staff member—an organizer—to the project. He gets in touch with the workers who have already indicated their interest in the union. They bring him up to date on conditions in the mill; they supply him with additional names and addresses; they agree to help spread the union message to other workers.

This preliminary work is carried on, as much as possible, in secret. We all know the law forbids an employer to discharge workers for union activity. Probably the southern mill owners know it, too, but they do not let their knowledge bother them. In many mills, saying a good word for the CIO is a sure way to be fired.

If these preliminary activities indicate there is a real interest among the workers, an open campaign is begun. Additional organizers are assigned to the campaign. Leaflets are prepared and distributed at the gates. Committees of workers are organized, even though there is still a risk that they will lose their jobs.

During this period, as often as not, the employer is quiet. Of course, on some occasions the union organizers have been run out of town as soon as they appeared, by self-appointed vigilantes or even by local police. At other times union representatives have been refused accommodations at local hotels or rooming houses, and have been denied the right to rent a place for union meetings. And as I have indicated now and then there have been dismissals of pro-union workers even this early in the campaign.

But these are not typical, and it is a typical campaign I am attempting to describe. Usually the employer waits until the union asks for recognition, and files a petition for an election with the National Labor Relations Board. A union is permitted to file for an election by showing that 30 percent of the eligible workers have signed cards. But as a matter of practice our union never files for an election until more than 50 percent have signed.

As soon as a petition is filed the fun begins.

Leaders of the union movement may be fired out of hand, and if the company has a mill village, they may be evicted from their homes. . . .

Union organizers and prounion workers may be followed day and night by local police, mill supervisors, or both. . . .

SENATOR PURTELL: May I ask a question, Mr. Chairman?

THE CHAIRMAN: Senator Purtell.

SENATOR PURTELL: I noticed that when you were describing some conditions here, you said these are not typical, and it is a typical campaign that you are going to describe now. Are you now describing a typical campaign and not an unusual one?

MR. RIEVE: That is correct, Senator.

The union may be refused the right to buy advertising space in the local newspaper, or time on the local radio station. As far as the newspapers are concerned, there is no remedy at all; as for radio, the Federal Communications Commission cannot or does not provide a swift or complete remedy. . . .

Agents of the employer—agents in every sense but the terms of the Taft-Hartley Act—may conduct a violent antiunion drive, using tactics which would be illegal for the employer himself, even under the present law, and using to the fullest extent the press and radio facilities which have been denied to the union. These agents may be the chamber of commerce, or a so-called citizens' committee or even clergymen. This development is almost routine; we are surprised when it does not happen. . . .

The employer himself is sure to send out at least one antiunion letter—playing on fear, prejudice and in general the baser instincts of man. The employer may also conduct "captive audience" meetings of workers in the mill on company time. We have, over the years, presented so many cases of this kind that I will not belabor the point. I think you all know these things happen. Actually, I think it is fair to say that under the Taft-Hartley Act they are supposed to happen. At least they are encouraged to happen by the so-called free speech provision.

The result of all of these activities, in a large number of cases, is that the union withdraws its petition for an election. As you have seen when we do feel able to go through with a vote, we lose more often than we win. A majority of the workers have been convinced that it just is not healthy to vote for the union.

Several questions may have occurred to you while I have been describing this typical organizing campaign. You may be thinking that some of these employer activities are illegal, even under the Taft-Hartley Act—in particular, the firing of prounion workers. That is true. But the law has little effect, since the only penalty for such a violation is a slap on the wrist. Since the NLRB simply says, in effect, "go and sin no more," I must repeat what I have said before: The penalty for firing prounion workers is nothing more than a license fee for union-haters. . . .

You may also have in mind the fact that the final step in any organizing campaign is a secret ballot election, and therefore the workers cannot really be prevented from expressing their true feelings. Unfortunately the single safeguard of a secret vote is not enough to make up for all these antiunion activities. For one thing, we cannot convince workers we cannot reach; and in addition, the Government's guarantee of a free choice looks very weak compared to what is happening right on the scene.

Another question you may be considering is that many of these antiunion activities were also carried on under the Wagner Act. That is correct, though they were not so numerous, and the chances of obtaining a remedy from the NLRB were much better. . . .

Let us suppose that in spite of all the opposition I have described, the workers in a southern mill do in fact vote for a union. The figures I gave you at the beginning of my testimony showed that more than half the time they cannot get what they voted for.

A number of the cases in our brief, and a number of others we presented in 1950, will tell you the reasons. I will give you a summary of only one of them —the story of Aldora Mills in Barnesville, Ga. . . . This mill, I might say, is a subsidiary of the General Tire & Rubber Co.

We won an election in this mill on April 8, 1946. About a week later we wrote to the company asking for a conference. As you will see from the full record, union representatives made at least 10 efforts to arrange a meeting, using letters, telegrams, and telephone calls. But the first face-to-face contact of any kind did not take place until July 17, more than 3 months later, and this was only a meeting with the plant manager on grievances.

The first actual negotiations took place on August 27. In the next 5 months, 9 other meetings were held. The employer spokesmen spent most of their time telling the union representatives that they did not really represent the workers. This was after an election had been held.

At this point a Federal conciliator entered the case. From January 29 to March 20 there were seven more conferences. No progress was made. On March 24 and 25, a NLRB hearing was held on the union's charge of refusal to bargain. On August 23, 1948—2 years, 4 months, and 15 days after the election—the Labor Board issued an order directing the employer to bargain, and to reinstate 4 workers who had been fired for union activity.

But did this bring justice to the workers or to their union? Look at the rest of the story.

The company appealed the Board's decision to the courts. One year, 8 months, and 6 days later—April 29, 1950—the Fifth Circuit Court of Appeals upheld the Board.

SENATOR DOUGLAS: That was about 4 years after the election.

MR. RIEVE: That is right.

Even then the company found excuses not to meet until June 25. Two months elapsed until the second meeting, held August 25. The succeeding dates were September 27, October 31, November 14, and December 13. This was the final meeting; the company refused to meet again.

Since the company's refusal to obey either the Board or the court was so flagrant, one more legal weapon remained—contempt of court. The union urged the Board to undertake such a case in July 1951, when it became apparent that the company would not sit down with us at all.

A contempt action was filed by the Board in January 1952. But on June 6, 1952, the Fifth Circuit Court refused to consider the action because a decertification petition had been filed, and therefore, according to the court, the employer had "reasonable" grounds for refusing to meet with the union.

SENATOR DOUGLAS: That was over 6 years after the original election?

MR. RIEVE: That is correct. But that is not the full story yet, Senator.

The Board has refused to act on the petition, on the grounds—the very sound grounds—that if the union could be decertified, the cause was the employer's illegal refusal to recognize the union as bargaining agent. And there the matter rests, apparently forever. The court refuses to act, because there is a decertification election pending, and the Board refuses to act because it takes the position that the union should not be decertified after the company refused to deal with it.

This is not an unusual case. I am just citing it as an example.

There, gentleman, you have these "powerful unions" you have been hearing about. As I said 3 years ago, the NLRB does not give decisions in these cases —it performs autopsies.

True, we have a second alternative. We do not have to seek justice through the NLRB. If the workers are aroused, and if they insist, they can also go out on strike.

I want to take note, at this point, of the fact that in our union, as in other democratic unions, strikes are not "called"—they are voted by the workers who are going to do the striking. We who have been given the responsibilities of leadership are not very enthusiastic about strikes unless they are unavoidable. Strikes are always a risk; and they are always expensive.

But suppose the workers, in a case such as I have described, insisted upon a strike?

The company would immediately obtain from the State courts an injunction placing severe limitation on all strike activities. These injunctions usually are so broad and so vague that the strikers often cannot tell what is legal and what is not—until they are arrested. Meanwhile, company supervisors are under no restriction whatever in their efforts to threaten or bribe the strikers, or bring strikebreakers into the plant.

Whether the strikebreakers who soon appear—mostly at wages and working conditions much better than the employer had offered before—actually produce any cloth is not important. The fact that they go in and out every day, and draw regular wages, has a very discouraging effect on the strikers. . . .

Let us look briefly at what is happening to the strikers who have not been arrested for violating the injunction. I am not speaking of those who have been arrested.

They soon find they no longer have credit anywhere in the community—not even with their landlords. They may have been carried for months during a layoff, but as strikers they have suddenly become outcasts. If the plant is in a mill village, they may be evicted from their homes. They must put cash on the line for everything they need—food, rent, utilities, car payments, even hospital care. And in addition, of course, they are abused in the press and over the radio, they are snubbed on the streets, they are threatened and cursed and arrested. Is it any wonder that southern strikes are often lost?

And even if the strikers give up, if they vote to go back, they often fail to regain their old status. The leaders of the union movement are told that they have been "replaced"; and they find a cold reception elsewhere. If any of you think the blacklist has gone from American industry, I advise you to talk to some of these former strikers. . . .

6: Unfair Labor Practices on the Part of Unions

In the period of the Wagner Act, 1935–1947, Federal law imposed no proscriptions on labor unions in their dealings with their members or with employers. The National Labor Relations Board, it is true, by administrative interpretation gradually moved toward establishing certain "good faith" obligations on the unions if they were to gain admittance to the Board's processes. A union seeking representation rights on behalf of a body of employees could not (at least openly) discriminate against certain of them by denying membership on grounds of color, for example. A union not itself bargaining in good faith could not press charges that an employer refused to bargain. These somewhat uncertain and occasional constraints on union behavior were expanded and made uniform on all unions operating in interstate commerce by provisions of the Taft-Hartley Act. Behavior which deprived workers of free determination of whether or not they wished a union to represent them, and which coerced employers into conforming to union wishes by tactics defined as unfair, came under the same ban as employer unfair labor practices. The cases that follow are examples of the Board's efforts to interpret what union conduct is proscribed under the law.

COERCION OF EMPLOYEES

National Labor Relations Board, release for morning papers, Thursday, April 14, 1949

N.L.R.B. HOLDS UNION ORGANIZER VIOLATED L.M.R.A. BY THREATS IN SPEECH

In a case involving consolidated charges of unfair labor practice against both a union and an employer, the National Labor Relations Board today found a labor union organizer guilty of coercion against employees in violation of the Labor Management Relations Act when she told a meeting of employees that "those who do not join the union will eventually lose their jobs."

A majority of the Board also ruled that it was a violation of the Act when she told an employee member of the audience that "we have ways of handling people like you that argue against the Union."

The statements were made by Mavis Lane, organizer for the International

Ladies Garment Workers Union (A.F.L.), at a meeting held in McAlester, Oklahoma, December 6, 1947, for the purpose of organizing employees of Seamprufe, Inc., lingerie manufacturer. . . .

In today's decision, the majority found that both of Miss Lane's statements exceeded the bounds permitted by the "free speech" provision of the Act. About 30 Seamprufe employees were at the meeting.

Of Miss Lane's statements, the Board said:

> Both statements, taken together, give an impression of a fixed determina-
> tion by an organized group, represented by Lane, to take punitive action
> against anyone who opposed, or did not support, its program. Such state-
> ments would in our opinion be reasonably calculated to coerce anti-union
> or non-union members of Lane's audience in the exercise of their right,
> under the amended Act, to refrain from joining the Union. Accordingly,
> we find, contrary to the Trial Examiner, that both the statements quoted
> above from Lane's speech violated Section 8 (b) (1) (A) of the Act.

(Section 8 (b) (1) (A) prohibits a labor organization or its agents from restraining or coercing employees in the exercise of their rights to self-organization as guaranteed by the Act.)

RECOGNITIONAL AND ORGANIZATIONAL PICKETING

From the 27th Annual Report of the NLRB, pp. 246–248

Section 8 (b) (7) declares that in certain circumstances picketing by a union which is not currently certified as the representative of the employees involved to force an employer to recognize or bargain with it, or to organize the employees, is an unfair labor practice. Subparagraph (A) of the section prohibits such picketing when another union has been lawfully recognized by the employer as the representative of the employees and a question of representation cannot currently be raised. Subparagraph (B) provides that such picketing is unlawful during the 12 months following a valid Board-conducted election. Subparagraph (C), which would apply in those situations where an election may be conducted, provides that after a reasonable period of picketing not to exceed 30 days, further picketing is prohibited unless a representation petition has been filed with the Board before the expiration of the reasonable period. A proviso, however, exempts from the proscription of this subparagraph picketing "for the purpose of truthfully advising the public" that the employer does not employ members of or have a contract with the union, unless an effect of such picketing is to cause employees of other employers to refuse to make pickups or deliveries or perform other services. . . .

b. PICKETING WITHIN 12 MONTHS OF ELECTION

Subparagraph (B) of section 8 (b) (7) bans recognitional or organizational picketing within the 12 months following a validly conducted Board election. In *Ames IGA Foodliner, Inc.*, when the employer rejected the union's demand for recognition, the union placed him on a "We Do Not Patronize" list because of his refusal to grant recognition, and began picketing with signs which read

"IGA is on We Do Not Patronize List. Retail Clerks Union Local No. 1439." A Board election was conducted, which the union lost. The picketing then ceased. However, on July 1, 1961, within 12 months of the certification of the results of the election, the union commenced picketing again with substantially the same sign. Several days later, the union wrote the employer that it was not picketing for recognitional or organizational purposes, but merely for purposes of inducing a consumer boycott and to advertise that the employer was on the "We Do Not Patronize" list. At the hearing in the district court, the union admitted that the employer was still on the "We Do Not Patronize" list for the reason he had initially been placed on the list, i.e., his failure to grant recognition. Nonetheless, the union contended that its picketing was for consumer boycott purposes and not to secure recognition. Refusing "to accept at face value the self serving statements made by either side," and noting that the previous picketing admittedly had been for recognition, the court concluded "from those prior objectives and from the totality of the Union's conduct" that the union still was picketing for recognition. The court, therefore, issued an injunction.

In another case, *Buy Low Supermarkets, Inc.*, the union picketed within 12 months of a valid Board election with signs reading "Grocery Employees of this Store are not Union members and do not deserve the patronage of Organized Labor. Please patronize Union Stores. . . ." The union contended that the purpose of the picketing was informational. Holding that the union had a recognitional or organizational objective in view of the language of the picket sign, the court granted petitioner's motion for judgment on the pleadings, and issued an injunction.

CAUSING OR ATTEMPTING TO CAUSE DISCRIMINATION

From the 27th Annual Report of the NLRB, pp. 146–147

The cases under section 8 (b) (2) have continued to present both individual instances of unlawful union conduct directed against employees because of their lack of union membership or their failure to observe union rules, as well as instances of union agreements or arrangements with employers unlawfully conditioning employment on union membership or performance of union obligations. . . .

The Board has consistently held that to find that a union caused prohibited employer discrimination, it is not necessary that an express demand for discrimination be made. Thus, in *St. Joe Paper Co.*, the Board held that a union violated section 8 (b) (2) by causing two different employers to discharge an employee because he was not a member in good standing in the union, having been previously expelled, although no direct request for discharge was made. In finding that the union had "caused" one of the discharges, the Board relied upon the union president's statements to the employer's general manager that the discriminatee was "a troublemaker," "a bad actor," "a problem," one who "had to be watched," and that "he was always running to the Labor Board."

JURISDICTIONAL DISPUTES

From the 27th Annual Report of the NLRB, pp. 175, 178–179

Section 8 (b) (4) (D) forbids a labor organization engaging in or inducing strike action for the purpose of forcing any employer to assign particular work to "employees in a particular labor organization or in a particular trade, craft, or class rather than to employees in another labor organization or in another trade, craft, or class, unless such employer is failing to conform to an order or certification of the Board determining the bargaining representative for employees performing such work."

An unfair labor practice charge under this section, however, must be handled differently from a charge alleging any other type of unfair labor practice. Section 10 (k) requires that parties to a jurisdictional dispute be given 10 days, after notice of the filing of the charges with the Board, to adjust their dispute. If at the end of that time they are unable to "submit to the Board satisfactory evidence that they have adjusted, or agreed upon methods for the voluntary adjustment of, the dispute," the Board is empowered to hear the dispute and make an affirmative assignment of the disputed work. . . .

During the fiscal year, the Board issued three "affirmative" work assignment determinations . . .

The Board will consider all relevant factors in determining who is entitled to the work in dispute, e.g., the skills and work involved, certifications by the Board, company and industry practice, agreements between unions and between employers and unions, awards of arbitrators, joint boards and the AFL-CIO in the same or related cases, the assignment made by the employer, and the efficient operation of the employer's business. This list of factors is not meant to be exclusive, but is by way of illustration. The Board cannot at this time establish the weight to be given the various factors. Every decision will have to be an act of judgment based on common sense and experience rather than on precedent. It may be that later, with more experience in concrete cases, a measure of weight can be accorded the earlier decisions.

It then assigned the job of operating electric overhead cranes in a machine shop to electricians, rather than to machinists, giving substantial weight to the longstanding rulings by the parent federation of both disputing unions, particularly since the employer made its work assignment on the basis of the same rulings. In the *Badolato* case, which stemmed from technological changes in the plastering industry, the Board assigned the work of operating plaster mixers and applicators to hod carriers, rather than to operating engineers. In so doing the Board relied on the fact that the work could be performed as an incident to the work traditionally performed by the hod carriers, the employer and other employers in the industry traditionally assigned such work to hod carriers, and there was no contract, Board certifications, or relevant jurisdictional awards compelling the assignment to the operating engineers. And in the *Lorillard* case, the Board's assignment of "fixing" work on new cigarette boxing machines to "fixers" in the production unit, rather than to machinists, was based upon past practices in the plant, practices in the industry, the fact that the fixers were capable of performing such work and that their work was more closely related to the production process, and "fixing" work underutilized the skills of the machinists.

In each of these cases, the Board emphasized that it awarded the work assignment to a *group of employees* performing a particular type of work rather than to *members of a particular union* which represented them. And in the *Lorillard* case, the machinist union was excluded from representing the fixers by virtue of its Board certification which had excluded fixers from its bargaining unit.

EXCESSIVE OR DISCRIMINATORY MEMBERSHIP FEES

From the 27th Annual Report of the NLRB, pp. 180–181

Section 8 (*b*) (5) makes it an unfair labor practice for a labor organization to charge employees subject to a valid union-security agreement a membership fee "in an amount which the Board finds excessive or discriminatory under all the circumstances." The section further provides, "In making such a finding, the Board shall consider, among other relevant factors, the practices and customs of labor organizations in the particular industry, and the wages currently paid to the employees affected."

In *Triangle Publications,* a union was held to have violated section 8 (*b*) (5) by increasing the initiation fee for an employer's new employees, under a valid union-security clause,[1] from $50 to $500, while requiring new members of newly organized employers to pay an initiation fee of only $25. The increased fee was deemed discriminatory since it was designed to restrain the employer from hiring part-time and temporary employees who were not union members, and they, in turn, would be discouraged from accepting such employment by the size of the fee. Further, it was deemed excessive since the starting salary of new employees ranged between $90 to $95 per week; part-time employees had no guarantee of such earnings; temporary employees had no guarantee of continued employment; no other union in the area, representing the same classification of employees, charged comparable fees; and the increase in fees for employees of this employer was tenfold.

REFUSAL TO BARGAIN IN GOOD FAITH

From the 27th Annual Report of the NLRB, pp. 155–156

The statutory representative of an appropriate employee unit—as in the case of the employer—must bargain as to all matters pertaining to "wages, hours, and other terms and conditions of employment." In other matters which

[1] In this case, the Board majority found a union-security clause, which required all present employees to become members of the union and all future employees to become members within 30 days after employment, to be valid.

are lawful, bargaining is permissible though not mandatory. But insistence on inclusion in a contract of clauses dealing with matters outside the category of bargaining subjects specified in the Act, as a condition of bargaining on mandatory matters, constitutes an unlawful refusal to bargain.

In the *Mill Floor Covering* case, the question of participation in an industry promotion fund was held to be a permissive, rather than a mandatory, subject of bargaining, because it concerned neither wages, hours, nor a term or condition of employment. The Board, therefore, held that a union's insistence on bargaining with respect to the employer's participation in such a fund was violative of section 8 (*b*) (3). The Board held that an industry promotion fund is outside the employment relationship, since it concerns itself with the relationship of employers to one another or, like advertising, with the relationship of an employer to the consuming public. The Board pointed out that while it intends to keep pace with changing conditions "to insure that bargaining for new forms of 'wages' or for hitherto undeveloped terms or conditions of employment is not restricted," it is not empowered "to lend its sanctions of enforcement either to encourage or to discourage experimentation, through the bargaining process, in areas which are outside the employment relationship altogether, or which, at best, touch it only peripherally." It also emphasized that its finding here does not imply that parties are not free to include provisions of this type in collective-bargaining agreements—only that there is no obligation that either party bargain thereon.

SECONDARY BOYCOTTS

National Labor Relations Board, release for afternoon papers, Tuesday, March 29, 1949

N.L.R.B. RULES "PRODUCT" PICKETING VIOLATES BOYCOTT BAN

The National Labor Relations Board today ruled unanimously that a union violated the secondary-boycott ban of the Labor Management Relations Act by having its pickets "follow the products" of a struck employer to the premises of other employers.

The ruling was made in a case involving the Printing Specialties and Paper Converters Union, Local 388, A.F.L. Charges against the union were brought by Sealright Pacific, Ltd., Los Angeles, a manufacturer of paper food containers and milk bottle caps.

In "following" Sealright goods, union pickets followed trucks bearing Sealright merchandise to the loading platforms of Los Angeles Seattle Motor Express, Inc., a truck line, and picketed the trucks there. They also picketed the docks of West Coast Terminals Company, where paper for Sealright was being unloaded from a steamship.

The Board held that this picketing violated the secondary-boycott ban, on the ground that it constituted inducement and encouragement of employees of the two shipping concerns to refuse to handle Sealright goods with an object of compelling their employers to cease doing business with Sealright. . . .

The Board ordered the union to cease encouraging employees of the two firms "or any other employer, by picketing or by related conduct" to engage in a strike or concerted refusal to perform services with an object of compelling their employers to cease doing business with Sealright. It also ordered the union to post a notice announcing that it will cease its unlawful activities. The Board's decision said in part:

It is clear from the record in the instant case that the pickets were authorized by the Respondent [Union] to follow trucks carrying Sealright products to other plants. Indeed, as the Trial Examiner found, the Respondent regarded such conduct as an extension of its primary picket line at the Sealright plant.

Moreover, it is established by the testimony of both Walter J. Turner, secretary-treasurer, and Patrick J. Morgan, business representative of the Respondent, that these officials knew of and took an active part in all picketing operations relating to Sealright products. Turner himself warned R. C. Lacey, president of Los Angeles Motor Express, Inc., that his business would be picketed unless Lacey declined to handle Sealright products. On several occasions Morgan accompanied the pickets and spoke to employees on the Los Angeles Seattle docks. The evidence in the record is persuasive that the Respondent and its pickets were in full agreement that products destined to and from the Sealright plant should be picketed, wherever found. We find therefore that the pickets were acting within the scope of their authority as agents of the Respondent in establishing a picket line on the docks of the West Coast Terminals Co. and Los Angeles Seattle Motor Express, Inc. . . .

The union called the strike at Sealright October 27, 1947, after the parties had been unable to reach agreement on terms of a new contract. Approximately 78 production employees were involved.

International Brotherhood of Teamsters and Sterling Beverages, 90 NLRB No. 75, 1950

DECISION AND ORDER

In the recent *Schultz* case,[1] we had occasion to consider whether a labor organization had violated Section 8 (*b*) (4) (*A*) of the Act by picketing the trucks upon which its members were employed at the situs of a labor dispute with an employer, who was engaged in the business of transportation. As the Trial Examiner in the instant case observed, the dividing line between primary and secondary picketing is not susceptible of the application of a rigid formula, but must turn upon a careful analysis of the relevant facts in each case. In the *Schultz* case a majority of the Board found that the picketing complained of was primary picketing and therefore not violative of the Act. It was particularly important in that case, as here, to examine the means whereby the respondent union sought to bring pressure against the primary employer Schultz, because in both cases the picketing occurred in front of the premises of a secondary em-

[1] *Schultz Refrigerated Service, Inc.*, 87 NLRB No. 82.

ployer, who was a neutral party to the labor dispute. Under the circumstances of the *Schultz* case, the majority was persuaded that the respondent had clearly identified its picketing with the actual functioning of the primary employer's business at the scene of their labor dispute. The record in that case disclosed that the pickets had paraded in a U-shaped manner around Schultz' trucks. Pointing to this fact as evidence of the primary nature of the union's conduct, the majority's decision emphasized "that Respondent's picketing was limited strictly in time and area to *Schultz' trucks.*" In a *caveat* to its decision the Board elsewhere stated: "A different case would be presented had Respondent failed to confine its picketing to Schultz' trucks or had it otherwise employed secondary pressure against Schultz' customers."

The record in the instant case reveals that on at least two occasions the Respondent Union placed pickets at the entrance to Ruppert's brewery in anticipation of the arrival and during and after the presence inside the plant of trucks belonging to Sterling, the primary Employer with whom the Respondent Union had a labor dispute. Because the loading platforms here were located inside the plant area, rather than abutting on a public street as in the *Schultz* case, the pickets could not picket around the trucks themselves while they were being unloaded. Of necessity they were limited to picketing the *Ruppert plant entrances* through which the trucks had passed. The placards carried by the pickets stated that the Union's dispute was with Sterling. Nevertheless, the picketing constituted inducement or encouragement of the employees of Ruppert, the secondary employer, to cease handling products on Sterling trucks. As we have previously held,[2] such picketing comes within the proscription of Section 8 (*b*) (4) (*A*), unless we were to agree with the Trial Examiner that the picketing was "direct primary labor activity aimed immediately at the employer involved in the principal dispute" and only incidentally affecting the secondary employer.[3] On the basis of the facts in this case we cannot so agree.

The record in this case discloses that pickets of the Respondent paraded in front of the secondary employer's premises when Sterling's trucks were not physically present at Ruppert's plant and failed to establish that direct and immediate relationship between the picketing and the object picketed necessary to a finding of purely primary picketing. Thus a driver for Sterling testified, without contradiction, that when his truck approached the Ruppert brewery, Respondent's picket was already patrolling the entrance to the plant. On another occasion, when a Sterling truck had entered the Ruppert driveway, a picket appeared and continued to patrol in front of Ruppert's premises for at least 15 and possibly more minutes after all of Sterling's trucks had left the secondary employer's plant. In our opinion, such picketing, unlike that in the *Schultz* case which was directed solely at Schultz' trucks, was not confined to the primary Employer's *trucks,* but extended directly to the secondary em-

[2] *Wadsworth Building Company, Inc.,* and *Klassen & Hodgson, Inc.,* 81 NLRB 802; *Sealright Pacific, Ltd.,* 82 NLRB 271.

[3] *The Pure Oil Company,* 84 NLRB No. 38; *Ryan Construction Corporation,* 85 NLRB No. 76; *Schultz Refrigerated Service, Inc., supra.*

ployer's own premises.[4] The line must be drawn somewhere, and this is where we draw it.

We therefore find, contrary to the Trial Examiner, that the Respondent Union has violated Section 8 (b) (4) (A) of the amended Act by picketing the premises of Jacob Ruppert.

JOHN M. HOUSTON, MEMBER, DISSENTING

In my judgment, the determination of my colleagues that the Respondent violated Section 8 (b) (4) (A) by picketing cannot be supported on the facts of this case. Their decision today appears to be inconsistent with the sound principles enunciated only a few months ago by a majority of the Board in the *Schultz* case.[5]

After most careful and thorough consideration, we specifically stated in the *Schultz* case that, in determining whether picketing is protected as primary action, an "important test is the identification of such picketing with the actual functioning of the primary employer's business at the *situs* of the labor dispute" (emphasis contained in original decision). We found in that case that the test was met by substantial evidence that the labor dispute related to the drivers of Schultz' truck, and that the picketing at the operations of other employers was *identified* with Schultz' business because it occurred in the area of the latter's trucks and because the placards used disclosed Schultz as the struck employer.

In the case before us now, the sole dispute between the Respondent and Sterling related to the conduct of Sterling's terminal operations at Ruppert's plant. The picketing by the Respondent was *strictly* confined to the entrances to Ruppert's unloading platforms [6] *at times* when Sterling's trucks and employees were present or immediately expected. And the placards similarly referred to Sterling alone as the struck Employer.[7] Yet, despite this positive identification of the picketing with Sterling's business at the very situs of the

[4] This distinction, in the opinion of Board Member Murdock, is emphasized by the fact that Sterling's trucks, which the Respondent was allegedly picketing, were at all times beyond the ambulatory range of the patrolling picket. In the *Schultz* case the proximity of the picketing to Schultz' trucks made incidental its effect on the secondary employer's business. Here, the physical situation was such that the Respondent could not relate its picketing at Ruppert's plant directly and immediately to its alleged objective. Conceding that the Respondent may have found itself in a difficult position, Member Murdock does not believe that the doctrine of the *Schultz* case should be extended further to make picketing in front of a secondary employer's premises lawful, where the nexus between the picketing and the truck allegedly picketed is as tenuous as it is in this case. The attempt in the dissenting opinion to harmonize the facts of the two cases serves only to accentuate their distinction.

[5] *Schultz Refrigerated Service, Inc.*, 87 NLRB No. 82.

[6] These platforms were 50 feet or less from the plant entrances and were in open view.

[7] The alleged secondary employer in the present case is not before the Board complaining of any interference with its business, a factor also expressly mentioned as "significant" in the *Schultz* case.

labor dispute, the majority in this case reaches a directly opposite conclusion and finds that the picketing was not primary but secondary action and therefore illegal.

. . . Chairman Herzog and Member Murdock, in an apparent attempt to distinguish the two cases, attach overriding significance to the fact that, on two occasions, picketing was conducted when Sterling's trucks were not on Ruppert's premises. Member Murdock relies, in addition, on the circumstance that the picketing here occurred on the public thoroughfare at the entrance to Ruppert's unloading platforms, rather than around the trucks themselves. Upon analysis, however, I find these distinctions are not substantial or persuasive.[8]

With respect to the picketing at times when Sterling's trucks were not present, my two colleagues refer only to the testimony of driver St. Laurent, to the effect, that when he arrived at the entrance to the unloading platform on March 28, he "saw" a picket there, and to the testimony of Sterling's treasurer, Faria, that on March 29, picketing continued for 15 minutes after one of Sterling's trucks had left the unloading platform. The triviality of these instances, in the face of the overwhelming evidence that the Respondent's picketing was directed solely at Sterling's operations, I should have thought would be readily conceded. However, in any event, as to the March 28 incident, the record shows that Sterling's trucks were then operating on a well-established unloading schedule, concerning which the Respondent was undoubtedly fully apprised; and that late the next morning, when Sterling was proceeding on an off-schedule basis, no picketing whatsoever was commenced until *after* Sterling's truck had entered Ruppert's premises. Therefore, the only realistic conclusion justified by the record is that the arrival of the trucks on March 28 and the appearance of the picket were virtually coincidental. As to the March 29 incident, it is significant that during the 15 minutes found to be so critical by my colleagues, Sterling's treasurer, Faria, was still on the premises, and the picket was apparently unaware that Sterling's other three trucks, which were parked on the public street at some distance from the entrance, had been directed to leave the area. Any picketing during this interval of 15 minutes resulted solely from the misapprehension of the picket, induced by the continued presence of Faria, that other Sterling trucks would immediately enter the premises.

As to the location of the pickets on the public thoroughfare, the necessary implication of Member Murdock's finding would seem to be that, in order to exercise its right to conduct lawful primary picketing in this very common situation, a union must first *unlawfully* trespass upon an employer's property. There is no warrant for such a holding either in the *Schultz* case or in any provision in the Act. The test, as I have already noted, is the identification of the picketing with the operations of the primary employer at the scene of the

[8] It may be observed that at the hearing in this proceeding, which occurred after the issuance of the Intermediate Report in the *Schultz* case, the General Counsel admitted that: "If there ever was a twin case, that [the *Schultz* case] is a twin case to this one."

dispute. Here, the sole dispute related to the backing up or terminal operations conducted by Sterling on Ruppert's premises.[9] And identification of the picketing with Sterling's operations at this actual situs of the dispute was enhanced, rather than impaired, when the Respondent confined its picketing to those very platform entrances where Sterling's trucks unloaded.

Accordingly, as the Respondent's picketing was conducted at the situs of its labor dispute with Sterling and was unmistakably identified with the functioning of Sterling's business by virtue of: (a) the location of the pickets at the entrances where Sterling's trucks were about to be unloaded; (b) the strict limiting of the picketing to those times when Sterling's trucks and employees were present or immediately expected; and (c) the display of placards unequivocally identifying Sterling alone as the struck employer, I would find, under the authority of the *Schultz* case, that such picketing was protected primary activity. Consequently this complaint should be dismissed.

Testimony of Arthur J. Goldberg, General Counsel, Congress of Industrial Organizations, in Taft-Hartley Act Revisions, hearings before the Senate Committee on Labor and Public Welfare, 83d Cong., 1st Sess., 1953, part 1, pp. 581–584

I would like to make this general observation about this [secondary boycott] provision: This provision involves the very difficult question of to what extent boycotts and strikes and other activities in connection with boycotts are to be permitted and to what extent they are to be prohibited by provisions of law.

This section as written practically makes illegal all of the traditional types of boycott operations that unions engaged in and have felt it was necessary for them to engage in in order for them to protect their legitimate interests. I note with considerable satisfaction, Senator Taft, your amendment now proposing to liberalize this section in part, which is contained on page 24 of the committee print, and which reads:

That nothing in (A) of this section shall be construed to make it an unfair labor practice for a labor organization to induce or encourage employees to engage in a concerted refusal to perform work which because of a current labor dispute between another employer and his employees is, for the duration of such dispute, no longer being performed by the employees of such other employer.

Your amendment then would—

SENATOR TAFT: We have met a lot of criticism from that, I must say—at least I have—from the other side, from the employers.

MR. GOLDBERG: I would assume that there would be criticism from that source, and yet it seems to me—

SENATOR TAFT: And there is some proper criticism. Certainly it has to be more clearly defined.

[9] Member Murdock, by requiring the Respondent to invade Ruppert's premises to picket around the trucks, is shrivelling the situs of the dispute from the terminal operations to the trucks themselves.

MR. GOLDBERG: The difficulty in this field in general is always the question of how to define what you are attempting to make legal, and to render illegal. But I say the basic principle of that amendment which protects the right of employees not to work on struck goods is certainly a sound provision. This is something that labor people regard to be immoral, something that they regard to be an unjustified prohibition on their legitimate activity.

SENATOR TAFT: However, the provision was intended to cover the case where a plant is operating and when the strike comes they transfer their work to some other plant. It was certainly not intended to authorize the case of refusal, for example, if you were building a house, to accept millwork from a firm manufacturing millwork, which is an entirely different line of operation. I do not know that it does. I only raise that question. I certainly did not intend to authorize the general theory that just because goods were coming from a plant where there was no union, or even where there was a strike, that the union could refuse to handle those goods in subsequent manufacture into something else. I certainly did not intend that. It has been criticized as perhaps being able to be construed to that effect.

MR. GOLDBERG: Of course, I had hoped that the Senator covered that.

SENATOR TAFT: I think I explained the purpose of it when I introduced it in 1949. I do not think it is fair for a firm which is having a strike to transfer the job to some other place and then make the men work on it there.

MR. GOLDBERG: I agree with that entirely.

SENATOR TAFT: I think that is the main feature. Just how far beyond that it ought to go, that is what we are trying to determine.

MR. GOLDBERG: My own view, the position we have taken before and which we reassert now, is that if you are going to have labor activity that is meaningful in a competitive society, you have got to give the labor organizations the opportunity not only to conduct the boycott that you have defined in the limited way that you have now defined it, but you have got to extend that to a broader area if we really are going to believe in competition between labor and industry in the protection of standards.

SENATOR TAFT: I do not agree to that at all. Fundamentally, the secondary boycott provision is this: It is not a dispute between the employer and his employees. The whole idea is to protect some third party who is not involved in that dispute, who is conducting his business as he sees fit to do it, from being injured by a secondary boycott by the employees, the labor union. . . . This is solely the question of third parties not being injured because of a dispute in which they are in no way involved.

MR. GOLDBERG: Are they not necessarily involved in the dispute when they are handling the goods of a party that is involved in the dispute?

SENATOR TAFT: I do not think they ought to be in any way involved. The answer is "No."

MR. GOLDBERG: Let me put to you, then, again, the case I think I put to you in 1949, which I think still is the classical case, and that is the *Duplex* v. *Deering* case that we discussed in 1949. I looked at it again last night just to refresh my recollection of it.

How can it be said from the facts of that case that this party is a neutral party? Let me recall again what the facts were.

The machinists' union had organized three firms that made presses. They had contracts with those 3 firms to grant the 8-hour day, to establish a minimum wage scale, and to comply with other wage standards. The Duplex Co. refused to do this. It was the fourth firm that made presses. They were the four firms in the United States that made presses. The Duplex Co. operated on a 10-hour day. It refused to establish the minimum wage scale. It disregarded other standards that at least now, by the experience of the times, we would regard to be minimum wage standards.

The machinists' union was then approached by the 3 employers in the industry that they had organized, and the 3 employers in the industry said to the machinists' union, "If you are unable to maintain the standards of this industry, we are going to have to go back on the 8-hour day that we gave you, we are going to have to establish a 10-hour day; we are going to have to establish a contract that contains no minimum wage standard, and we are going to have to abrogate the provisions of our contract with you that provide for fairly tolerable working conditions in the plants."

Faced with that situation, the machinists' union, back in the 1920's then went out and declared a boycott of Duplex products.

SENATOR TAFT: Absolutely unjustifiable; absolutely unjustifiable. Your argument leads to the conclusion that the Government must fix wages in all the plants; that they must see that there is no variation in this scale set up by the unions in agreement. Oh, yes; absolutely. You say that although the Government cannot do that, we will let all the people, by indirect pressure on all their customers, force them to do what these other three people have agreed to do.

No; I think this is an absolute denial of the entire theory of free collective bargaining and free business in the United States.

Incidentally, in this committee, there was not any legitimate objection to outlawing secondary boycotts when we had these hearings in 1947. The committee agreed, I think 13 to 2, that really there was practically no defense against it.

I remember Senator Morse and Senator Ives trying to devise special methods to stop this, which is recognized as an outrage in the labor field. That is the field of secondary boycotts.

I just cannot see any argument for supporting secondary boycotts.

MR. GOLDBERG: I would like to make the argument, I would say that under the facts as I gave them to you, it is not a question of Government fixing wage standards at all. It is a question of allowing people to use economic power against economic power, and by that competition to try to arrive at an adjustment of conflicting interests.

SENATOR TAFT: There was some argument for secondary boycotts when you had no Wagner Act at all, but today if you want to organize a plant you have a method of going in and persuading the employees that there ought to be a union. If you cannot persuade them, then there ought not to be a union and there ought not to be any indirect pressure on their products and their work to make them unionized. . . .

On your same theory, this one case, you could put on a boycott of every nonunion plant in the United States that is not organized, even though they are paying wages higher than your wages, even though there are no sweatshop conditions.

We have a minimum wage law to prevent sweatshop conditions.

MR. GOLDBERG: I think you and I would agree that the minimum wage law we have does not adequately protect against sweatshop conditions, and that it ought to be improved.

SENATOR TAFT: I think it perhaps is not wide enough, but as far as the rate is concerned for the minimum wage, it is all right. Of course, it is not what you would call a standard wage.

MR. GOLDBERG: I hope that this committee will take under consideration the question of improving the minimum wage, but the point I am making is that I think the jungle prevails, not in the way that you indicated, but the jungle prevails when an employer can upset the established labor standards of an industry in the way that Duplex attempted to upset it and was successful in part—

SENATOR TAFT: By persuading men to work for them and refusing to be unionized. The men were satisfied thereby, presumably, because the majority of them did not want to organize a union.

MR. GOLDBERG: But this was a perfectly peaceful appeal. It did not involve violence. This was an appeal by a union to its membership handling this product not to handle a product which they deemed to be unfair to things which the union was striving for.

SENATOR TAFT: What union?

MR. GOLDBERG: The machinists. This was their own membership. That is the point I am making. This would apply under Taft-Hartley.

SENATOR TAFT: They were not making them, because their own members were not in that plant.

MR. GOLDBERG: This was a case of installing the presses. The machinists also represented the installers of the presses, and what they were appealing to were members of their own organization.

SENATOR TAFT: So you can organize the thing on a vertical basis, as the teamsters try to organize the warehouse employees. You can work a secondary boycott to organize industries that are not even organized at all.

MR. GOLDBERG: That assumes, you know, that it is a light thing for a union to declare a secondary boycott situation. It is never a light thing for a union to appeal to its own people to refrain from working, because there is a very great economic inhibition against that. Union people cannot just appeal to people to carry on a boycott. When we say a boycott, we mean that people are asked to strike. That is not the easiest thing for union people to get other people to do.

7: Union Security

For almost as long as unions have existed in this country the issue of the closed shop (or some variation of it, such as the union shop) has been a live one. Whether employees may be obligated to join a union as a condition of employment, and if so under what conditions, has been an issue before legislatures and courts for 150 years. In the earliest recorded conspiracy cases, dating back to the early nineteenth century, judicial opinion tended toward the view that unions could not force membership on unwilling workers. The Massachusetts case of Commonwealth v. Hunt *in 1842 suggested there were certain circumstances, however, under which workers might decide that they would not work alongside anyone who was not a member of their organization.*

At the turn of the century, unionism was faced with a counteroffensive from the employers in the form of the "American plan" or "open shop," which technically admitted union and nonunion employees alike to employment, but which in actuality was usually operated to exclude any but nonunion men. This approach was formalized in the "yellow dog" contract, the obverse of union security, under which employees agreed not to join a union, as a condition of employment.

The yellow-dog contract was made unenforceable by the Norris-LaGuardia Act of 1932. In the period of rapid unionization of the 1930s and early 1940s, unions once again strove to achieve union security provisions. Although the Taft-Hartley Act put an end to union efforts to secure the closed shop (in interstate commerce), it permitted the union shop with certain restrictions. That the controversy is still unresolved is indicated by the continued agitation of employers to eliminate even the restricted union shop and to secure state action outlawing all forms of union security, as permitted by the Taft-Hartley law, and by the opposition of the unions to this employer offensive coupled with efforts to make legal once again the closed shop, at least in certain industries.

THE NORRIS–LAGUARDIA ACT ON "YELLOW–DOG" CONTRACTS

Act of March 23, 1932, 47 U.S. Stat. 70, c. 90

Sec. 2. In the interpretation of this Act and in determining the jurisdiction and authority of the courts of the United States, as such jurisdiction and authority are herein defined and limited, the public policy of the United States is hereby declared as follows:

Whereas under prevailing economic conditions, developed with the aid of governmental authority for owners of property to organize in the corporate and other forms of ownership association, the individual unorganized worker is commonly helpless to exercise actual liberty of contract and to protect his freedom of labor, and thereby to obtain acceptable terms and conditions of employment, wherefore, though he should be free to decline to associate with his fellows, it is necessary that he have full freedom of association, self-organization, and designation of representatives of his own choosing, to negotiate the terms and conditions of his employment, and that he shall be free from the interference, restraint, or coercion of employers of labor, or their agents, in the designation of such representatives or in self-organization or in other concerted activities for the purpose of collective bargaining or other mutual aid or protection; therefore, the following definitions of, and limitations upon, the jurisdiction, and authority of the courts of the United States are hereby enacted.

Sec. 3. Any undertaking or promise, such as is described in this section, or any other undertaking or promise in conflict with the public policy declared in section 2 of this Act, is hereby declared to be contrary to the public policy of the United States, shall not be enforceable in any court of the United States and shall not afford any basis for the granting of legal or equitable relief by any such court, including specifically the following:

Every undertaking or promise hereafter made, whether written or oral, expressed or implied, constituting or contained in any contract or agreement or hiring or employment between any individual, firm, company, association, or corporation, and any employee or prospective employee of the same, whereby

(*a*) Either party to such contract or agreement undertakes or promises not to join, become, or remain a member of any labor organization or of any employer organization; or

(*b*) Either party to such contract or agreement undertakes or promises that he will withdraw from an employment relation in the event that he joins, becomes, or remains a member of any labor organization or of any employer organization.

UNION SECURITY AND GENERAL MOTORS

Charles E. Wilson, President, General Motors Corporation, in Labor Relations Program, hearings before the Senate Committee on Labor and Public Welfare, 80th Cong., 1st Sess., 1947, part 1, p. 464

Do not misunderstand me. I am not in favor of the "yellow dog" contract. I never had one. I never would have had one because I do not believe in those kinds of things.

Likewise, I would not have a closed shop, either. I am never going to sign one. When it gets around to that, it will make a farmer out of me.

From Business Week, October 8, 1955

In less than four months, nearly 600,000 additional UAW members have come under union shop contracts. Of the union's 1,389,091 dues-paying members (Aug. 31 estimate), some 1,215,455, or 87.5%, are covered by straight union shop agreements. New agreements already negotiated but not yet recorded will increase the percentage. Out of 1,583 contracts on file in union headquarters, 989 now provide the union shop.

Tracing this sudden change in the UAW's union security efforts is simple. You have only to go back to June 12, 1955, the date of the new three-year contract between General Motors Corp. and the UAW. That contract provided for the first time at giant GM, the full union shop.

Signing of that agreement broke the log jam that had been piling up for years. In rapid succession, UAW negotiated the union shop at Chrysler, International Harvester, Deere & Co., and in Detroit automotive tool and die shops, among others.

Facts of Life. Why did GM give in this year after resisting the union shop since its initial UAW agreement in 1939? Basically, GM believed that the "principle" had become a pretty shopworn item over the years.

In 1950, it had given UAW a "modified" union shop, under which new employees were required to join UAW but could drop out if they chose at the end of one year of employment. During the five-year contract—from 1950 to 1955—GM hired 600,000 new employees. Of these, only 600 elected to withdraw from UAW after a year's time.

And GM knew this year that UAW was determined to end the modified shop and win full coverage. In the light of practical facts of life, GM believed it would be a pretty small issue over which to take a strike.

Few Objectors. When the end came, GM had some 16,000 employees who were not UAW members. A polite letter went out to all of those, informing them that the new contract required them to join UAW by Aug. 26 or face discharge.

The only resistance popped up in Indianapolis where a non-member unsuccessfully took the case to court. After the deadline passed, there were about 100 employees who objected to unionization on religious principles; the union is investigating each individual case. Less than a dozen—those who simply refused to join the union—were discharged.

INDIVIDUALISM vs. UNIONISM

Testimony of Walter P. Reuther, President, United Automobile Workers, in Tart-Hartley Act Revisions, hearings before the Senate Committee on Labor and Public Welfare, 83d Cong., 1st Sess., 1953, part 1, pp. 409–418

MR. REUTHER: We think, you see, that the union is an attempt to extend the democratic processes in the industrial community; that organized society is based upon the principle that within the framework of a given society the people who make up that society have to work out rules and regulations to govern the relationship of one to the other.

Collective bargaining through the union is an attempt to extend that principle into the industrial community. People have rights and privileges and obligations in the community as a whole, but within industry they had no rights in the past. Collective bargaining is an attempt to establish their rights as economic citizens within the industrial community.

Obviously, in order to do that, they have to work out rules and regulations. They have to have the machinery of self-government. The union represents that kind of machinery.

The union performs some very important and essential functions. We handle grievances. We handle the grievances of all the workers. We have umpire machinery. The unions pay for the umpire machinery. When he hands down a decision, all the workers get the benefits. We have legal services. All the workers get the benefit of the cases we may process in unemployment compensation. All the workers get the benefit because we establish precedents; we work out basic policies. We have a medical department. We work on health problems. We work on occupational diseases. All the workers get the benefit of these.

Since all the workers in the industrial community get the benefits of these services performed by the union, made possible by the union, we believe that since all the workers share in the services all the workers ought to share in the cost of providing those services.

THE CHAIRMAN: Might I say this: I have had some independent union representatives wait upon me recently, and they think the solution is proportional representation. They do not see why they should be compelled to accept a union that may have 51 percent of the votes. They think if they have 49 percent or if it is divided into 3 or 4 different groups, there should be proportional representation in the bargaining agreement.

Would that appeal to you, or do you think that is unsound?

MR. REUTHER: That is the French system, and that is the shortest road to chaos you can travel, because then you get a competition of irresponsibility, seeing who can outbid the other fellow to try to capture a few more percent.

THE CHAIRMAN: It seems to me what you are arguing for is definitely a government within the government. If you are going to set up a government within the government, we are going to be compelled to police certain internal affairs of the unions.

MR. REUTHER: It is government by majority rule, and what is wrong with that? We fought the Revolutionary War around a very fundamental principle, and we were right: Around the idea of taxation without representation.

This is the other side of that coin. This is the matter of representation without taxation. One principle is as sound as the other, because if it is wrong to be taxed without representation, it is wrong to have representation without taxation.

Since all the workers in the industrial community have a right to vote democratically in determining whether our union is going to be the bargaining agency, we cannot get sole bargaining rights unless a majority of the workers support us at the National Labor Relations Board. So having gotten majority support, we then represent the machinery by which the workers in the industrial community govern themselves and have their work done. They all get the benefits of that machinery; they ought all to pay the taxes which make that machinery possible.

That is all we are asking. It seems to me that is a very sound thing.

The only test ought to be, No. 1, Is the government within the industrial community, represented by the union, established by democratic majority decision? No. 2, is its membership open to all the people who have a right to participate in that industrial government?

SENATOR DOUGLAS: You mean is the union open?

MR. REUTHER: That is right. No. 1, is it democratic decision by majority rule? No. 2, is it open membership? Those are the limitations.

SENATOR DOUGLAS: On that very point, I would like to ask some questions. I think your argument is overwhelming and convincing on the question of the union shop. But when you move from the union shop, where the employer has the initiative in hiring and the men after being hired join the union, to the closed shop, where the men must join the union before they can be hired, then you get into an initial difficulty. It is just this: suppose the union is a closed union, whether by absolute prohibition of entrance or by excessive initiation fees or by unduly prolonged apprenticeship periods, or what not. Then you may be giving privileges to those inside the union, but certainly those who are outside and who, if they could come in, would be good union men, suffer.

What would you say on that question if you have a closed shop? Is there a legal obligation upon us to see that the union should be an open union? . . .

MR. REUTHER: . . . I personally think that it is wrong for a union to have a closed membership in which they attempt to build a labor monopoly in order to exploit the advantages of a monopoly. I think that is morally wrong, I think it is economically wrong.

SENATOR DOUGLAS: Do you think that problem should be attacked through governmental legislation?

MR. REUTHER: I think you ought to try to correct the abuses where there are specific abuses.

SENATOR DOUGLAS: By legislation?

MR. REUTHER: I think the labor unions ought to do it themselves.

SENATOR DOUGLAS: But if they do not?

MR. REUTHER: If they do not, then I think if you are going to permit the closed shop to be applied, then I think there ought to be safeguards. . . .

SENATOR PURTELL: Mr. Reuther, I am intrigued by your answer to Senator Douglas. In other words, where these abuses exist, you say what we ought to do is threaten, "and if you aren't a good boy we will pass legislation."

I would assume, therefore, that until such time as we do say that, we can expect a continuation of these abuses? If they are bad and they should be corrected and are not being corrected, is not the answer legislation?

MR. REUTHER: The point is that I think you ought to put the first responsibility on the unions themselves to correct the abuses where they exist, but you ought to do it under circumstances that will not deny the application of principles by those unions who are not abusing them. Taft-Hartley just blankets the thing and just says nobody can do this. You try to rationalize the justification for that by getting into this whole discussion about the right to work.

I think that that idea also has been greatly misunderstood, because I think we all recognize that what we are trying to preserve in the world is human freedom. We are trying to broaden it and strengthen it and give more people the rights to enjoy it.

But human freedom is not an absolute value; it is a relative value. You can exercise what we call human freedom in a given society only in your relationship to other people, both in the local community, in the State community, in the national community, and ultimately in the world community. You have no human freedom excepting in your relationship to other people. All of these things we call our basic human freedoms are relative values. They are not absolute values.

Take freedom of speech. That is not an absolute thing. It is a relative thing. You have a right to exercise freedom of speech, but it is curtailed in certain situations. You cannot stand up in a crowded theater and yell "Fire," because that takes you beyond the framework in which you can exercise the right of freedom of speech. You can drive your car, but we have traffic laws. You have to do it a certain way. As a matter of fact, the laws do not make it harder to drive. Without traffic laws you could not drive a car at all.

That is the way with the right to work. It also can be a qualified basic right. The qualification ought to be that within the framework of this democratic industrial community, through the union, with open membership and the democratic right to say what is right and what is wrong, it seems to me at the point where you have a democratic union and every worker has access to membership, every worker has an equal voice in determining what the policies and program of that union are, who its leadership will be, at that point any curtailment of the right to work within the framework of that kind of democratic structure, is no more or greater curtailment of your basic rights than the way freedom of speech is curtailed.

It seems to me that we get our ideas all mixed up in this field. This right to work seems like a sacred thing that is being violated. It is not being violated. It is being worked out within the democratic framework of the union machinery. . . .

SENATOR GOLDWATER: Mr. Chairman.

I am very much interested in Mr. Reuther's development of the closed shop and the union shop. There is only one question in this whole field in my mind. What about the man who just does not want to belong to a union?

MR. REUTHER: Well, if a fellow works in a General Motors plant and does not want to belong to a union, he does not have to work there.

SENATOR GOLDWATER: But suppose he wants to work there?

MR. REUTHER: If you want to live in a certain community and you want the benefits of the work of that community, you have to pay taxes in that community. If you do not, you do not have to live in that community. That is the freedom of choice. The only check is that it has to be a democratic choice, decision; it has to be a majority democratic decision.

Inside of the industrial community, General Motors has 400,000 employees. How can a complex industrial society like ours work out machinery within this industrial community to meet these problems unless it can be done by a democratic decision of the people involved?

SENATOR GOLDWATER: I get down to the individual who does not want to belong to a union. Let us extend your thinking a little bit further. Take the matter of churches. Certainly churches benefit everybody. Yet we all do not support churches. Should we include laws to tax everybody to support churches in the community? Whether all of us agree or not, organizations like the Chamber of Commerce, for instance, do a lot of good for the people who live in the community, but I do not have to belong to the Chamber of Commerce and neither do you. Yet, because I am a member and pay my dues, I feel pretty much like you, as a union man, feels about the man who will not join your union, but I recognize the right of that competitor of mine or any other friend to say "yes" or "no" to membership in an organization that he will admit benefits him.

It gets down to that, and that is, in my mind, the only question: What about the individual?

MR. REUTHER: The UAW-CIO, for example, to use a specific case, are certified as the sole collective bargaining agent. We represent every General Motors worker in our units. No church represents all the people in the community. You are dealing with an entirely different kind of thing. The church is a fraternal religious organization that you can choose to belong to or choose not to belong to; but our unions are the sole bargaining agent under the law. We represent every General Motors worker. When we process a grievance, every General Motors worker gets the benefit of that. If we have a case that goes to the court on some workmen's compensation case, that sets a principle, and every GM worker gets the benefit of that protection that we want. If we have our doctors go in and check on the dust in a foundry or the fumes in a factory plant and we take corrective steps to protect the health of the workers, every worker in that plant gets the benefit of that.

The church does not perform that kind of function in the community. The church deals with the spiritual values. You can either choose to get them or you can choose not to get them.

But we are by law the agency by which all workers in a given factory take care of their industrial problems. In other words, we really are like a government within that factory, within that industrial community. If you are going to have a government within the industrial community, you have a right to insist that it is a democratic government; you have a right to insist that the workers who make up the industrial citizens in that industrial community have a right to elect their officers democratically, have a right to make democratic majority decisions. But having made the democratic majority decisions, the people in the minority are obligated to go along with the majority just as they are when you vote taxes for schools in your community. What is the difference? It is the same principle.

SENATOR GOLDWATER: I do not agree with you there. I see what you are getting at, and I think we could probably spend a whole year arguing about that point.

I keep getting back to the one question: Suppose a man does not want to belong to a union? You are not a government. The dues to the union cannot be compared to taxes. They do not bring all the benefits that taxes bring. I merely inject that.

MR. REUTHER: They do in the industrial community.

SENATOR GOLDWATER: I wanted to get your thinking on what about the individual, because it all gets down, as you say, to the freedom of the individual, his desire to belong to a union or not, his desire to—let us forget churches—his desire to belong to the Chamber of Commerce or not, or to any other organization that might be helpful, to support the Red Cross or not, the Community Chest or not.

MR. REUTHER: You go out to the Ford plant. I worked for 6 years in the Ford plant under the old system before we had a union. You talk to the workers out there. When they voted 88,000 to 1,000, that was an expression that they had found a new freedom. The union has given them greater freedom than we ever had, freedom from terror, and intimidation, and insecurity.

SENATOR GOLDWATER: I do not disagree with you. I agree with you. I think the unions have done wonderfully. But there are still a thousand men who do not want to belong to the union. You see what I am getting at. To my mind, you are tampering with the basic freedom that this Government is set up to give the people.

SENATOR GRISWOLD: It seems to me, Mr. Reuther, in the field of civil rights, you do not believe that because 51 percent of the people make a decision one way, that they should force their opinion upon the other 49 percent. We are talking about the rights of minorities, and a great deal of our Constitution and a great deal of the Bill of Rights is to protect the minority against the excessive demands on the part of, say, 51 percent of the people to force their will upon the minority. I do not altogether believe that 51 percent of the people in any community or in any economic group have a right to force their rights upon the other 49 percent. There might be a situation in a State where they force everyone to belong to the Democratic Party or the Republican Party just because a majority voted that they wanted the Democratic Party or the Republican Party to represent them in the field of government, but certainly you would say that was contrary to the rights of human beings.

MR. REUTHER: I am opposed to the majority taking away the rights of the minority. We are not talking about that. We are talking about the question of whether they ought to belong and pay their taxes in an industrial union. They do not take away their rights. As a matter of fact, it facilitates their rights.

SENATOR GRISWOLD: In some ways it does take away their rights, to some extent, to work there without belonging to the union. That is a minority right.

MR. REUTHER: I am never able to understand this, Mr. Chairman: The American Medical Association has taken the closed shop principle and applied it with a vengeance. In the average city, if you do not belong to their setup, worked out by their quota system and everything, you cannot get a hospital bed. It is quite all right for the American Medical Association to apply the principle of the closed shop to their profession, but when a group of workers try to protect their interests by applying that same principle, it suddenly becomes un-American and a violation of all the basic values.

SENATOR GRISWOLD: You should apply the rule you referred to in answer to Senator Douglas. You had better work out the wrongs in the situation and not use that as an argument to prove that you are right in your situation.

MR. REUTHER: The principle is sound. . . .

SENATOR DOUGLAS: . . . may I offer a suggestion which might clear up some of this very real difficulty. I do not know that it will effectively do it. There is an inevitable conflict in a few cases between effective collective action and individual conscience. There is no doubt about that. I am wondering if the provisions which are made in some unions and mass industries could not generally be followed out: namely, that where a man's religion or his conscience really restrain him from joining the union, if he pays the equivalent of union dues and thus bears his share of the cost of the benefits which he receives without being an active participant, could that not be regarded as satisfactory even if he does not become a formal union member.

MR. REUTHER: Senator Douglas, we do that every day of the week. There are certain religious groups who, for reasons of conscience, feel that they cannot participate. We have worked those out. We have worked it out with the Seventh Day Adventists, the Brethrens, and other groups. We have had no difficulty, because that is a matter of being sensible and reasonable. But that is something quite different from a worker who just does not want to belong to a union because he says it violates his principles.

SENATOR DOUGLAS: I understand. I mean, could not some such arrangement as that meet, say, 99 percent of the real conflict, not the artificially engendered conflict?

MR. REUTHER: I think it could. I do not think you would have any trouble working it out where it is a matter of conscience. You will find the unions are willing and have been willing and are doing it, working out such practical problems.

SENATOR DOUGLAS: Would you be willing to have some such provision as that put in the law?

MR. REUTHER: Certainly. We would not object to formalizing what we are doing in practice.

COMPULSORY UNIONISM

Statement of Herman W. Steinkraus, on behalf of the Chamber of Commerce of the United States, regarding proposed National Labor Law Revision, in Labor Relations, hearings before the Senate Committee on Labor and Public Welfare, 81st Cong., 1st Sess., 1949, part 5, pp. 2462–2464

It would be appropriate at this point to mention the closed shop. The Wagner Act made it an unfair labor practice for an employer to discriminate against employees by reason of union membership or lack of it, but permitted unions to make a closed-shop contract with an employer whereby he could avoid that prohibition, in part, by discriminating for union members. In other words, it was wrong for an employer to discriminate but all right for a union to do so or force the employer to do so. The result is illogical. If compulsion is wrongful conduct for an employer, it is equally wrongful for a union. If a monopoly is wrongful conduct for an employer, it is equally wrongful for a union. There is no subtle change from wrong to right merely because of the character of the person perpetuating the wrong.

The chamber has long contended that compulsory unionism interferes with the free and uncoerced choice of employees with respect to collective bargaining. Employees should be free to join or not to join a labor organization. Their right to work should never be dependent on union membership.

If unions cannot recruit and hold members on their merits, they should not be allowed to force employees into membership. If I am unable to persuade a customer to buy my product, I am not allowed to sell it to him by compulsion. Why should any different rule apply to unions?

Moreover, this compulsion at times works another way. A qualified employee may want to work and be willing to join the union which holds a closed-shop contract. If the union, however, won't admit him to membership he is denied employment opportunity. This, too, is wrong. It is unjustifiable monopoly of a basic and cherished right: the right to earn a living. The closed shop, coupled with a closed union, has been too common a device for abusing the rights of employees for Congress simply to close its eyes to it.

A compulsory unionism contract restricts the plant management in an unwarranted and disadvantageous manner in the selection and retention of suitable employees. Under such a contract, the employer would be able to hire only persons who are willing to become members of the recognized labor organization if they are not already members. Other persons who have good and sufficient reasons of their own for either preferring membership in a different labor organization, or in none at all, would either refuse to work for the employer, although they might be highly desirable and useful employees from every standpoint, or they would have to pay additional initiation fees and double dues, if they want to retain membership in another union of their choice.

Under a compulsory unionism contract, the employers would be compelled to discharge any employee, no matter how long his period of employment or how satisfactory, if such employee is unwilling for some reason of his own, to be a member of the recognized labor organization or is unwilling to pay dues to it. This might easily cause serious interference with the efficient operation of the plant.

The closed or union shop involves mandatory dues payments. This deprives the union members of their democratic control of their organization. The members lose their right to resign and stop paying dues, which is their most effective means of preventing arbitrary or unscrupulous action, or even racketeering, by their leaders. It permits the union leader to be a dictator and destroys the principle of majority rule. It forces a member of the union to quit his job as the only escape from supporting an organization which may have become wholly unsatisfactory to him.

Compulsory membership in a particular union violates the basic principle that employees should not be required by the employer to take part in any organization or activity or enroll in any benefit plan in order to secure or keep a job. It is a sound principle that all such participation should be strictly voluntary.

The attempt of the unions to eliminate "free riders" through the closed shop is unfair to the minority group. No one ever heard about "free riders" until the unions started to collect "fares" in the form of initiation fees, dues, and assessments. This restriction on freedom of choice of the worker (who, many times, cannot afford to leave his job and community in search of another) is like compelling Republicans in a county or town which has voted Democratic to contribute to the support of the Democratic Party or leave the locality. All must pay their assessed taxes for public services. But taxes cannot be collected to maintain the party treasury.

Compulsory unionism is harmful to the rights of the unorganized worker, the worker who does not want to join a union. Recent Supreme Court decisions have indicated that legislation which protects the rights of the unorganized worker may be enacted by the States where they feel it necessary to correct a situation which is inimical to the public welfare. Denial of the right to work of a worker who happens not to sympathize with the union is denial of a fundamental right. It is said that a worker who cannot get a job because of closed-shop restrictions can go to a nonunionized area to get a job. Far from a defense of compulsory unionism, that statement is a strong argument for outlawing it.

An employee should have the right to continue to live in the place where he may have lived all his life. He should not be arbitrarily forced to spend his savings and disrupt his family life. No, this argument shows most clearly one of the basic failings of the closed shop and why it should not be legalized.

These types of abuses, multiplied many times, were what led Congress to outlaw the closed shop. The arguments against it have not lost their cogency at all. Basic limitations on workers' personal liberty are involved in any closed-shop contract. Restraint, often amounting to absolute, arbitrary monopoly, on an employer's control of his business, of his right to hire employees he considers most suitable for his organization, of his communication lines with his employees, exists under any closed-shop contract. The basic principle of the right to work is flagrantly disregarded. Nor are such practices made less of an evil by calling them union security measures, rather than compulsory unionism.

FREEDOM OF ASSOCIATION AND MAJORITY RIGHTS

Testimony of Robert B. Watts, Vice President and General Counsel, Consolidated Vultee Aircraft Corp., San Diego, Calif., in Taft-Hartley Act Revisions, hearings before the Senate Committee on Labor and Public Welfare, 83d Cong., 1st Sess., 1953, part 2, pp. 716–717

On the subject of compulsory unionism, we go all the way. We say that the proviso of section 8 (a) (3) should be taken out. We think that you come to grips at this point with the basic concept of individual freedom. We think that the only reason and justification for the present Federal toleration of the union shop is the so-called free rider argument. And we say, in response to that, that when the statute enunciates as the policy of the United States, that there should be a freedom of workers to associate, it means what it says; and that there is equally a freedom on the part of those who do not wish to join unions but to remain by themselves and to amass, if they please, their own financial resources, in order to combat the union at a later election. Indeed we think that the suggestion that the unions have now become so much endowed with sovereignty as to refer to themselves as government, as they have before this committee, indicates the unconscious degree to which these labor leaders have been led in their acquisition of power.

We say, gentlemen, that freedom of association is at the root of this act. There is nothing in this act which guarantees the development and creation of labor unions. This act guarantees the freedom of employees to organize and to choose whomever they wish to represent them. They can choose a movie actor if they wish. This act guarantees that, having organized themselves and having selected a representative, their representative is entitled to bargain freely with the employer.

SENATOR TAFT: That sounds like an easy thing, but we really took the step right there to limit freedom. Because we say that if a majority want X as a bargaining agent, the right of the other people to bargain themselves or to choose their own bargaining agent is destroyed.

MR. WATTS: I agree with that, sir.

SENATOR TAFT: So that really the fundamental concept of the whole business of enforcing collective bargaining is far more restrictive of individual liberty than the union shop, in my opinion, because they cannot bargain; those people are deprived of the right to bargain. Now, that we have accepted, and so, when you go on the union shop theory and say that you have to join the union, it does not seem to me to be nearly as important a deprivation as that which takes place at the very basis of the Wagner Act.

MR. WATTS: Except that I suggest, Senator, that it is not as unrealistic to protect the right of those individuals who represent the then minority, and who, perforce, have to be represented in bargaining by the majority.

SENATOR TAFT: You say you have got to let X bargain for you. I do not know why you should not say you have to pay X to bargain for you. I do not see the difference.

MR. WATTS: What I am suggesting is that you ought to have the right, as the minority, to oppose X on the next occasion of an election.

SENATOR TAFT: Oh, yes. You have the right to do that. You can vote the union out.

MR. WATTS: Well, I think I have indicated my point here, which is that we believe that there isn't any halfway business on this compulsory union membership.

SENATOR TAFT: I think I would dispute that entirely. I think the union shop is entirely a different thing from the closed shop, fundamentally different. Do you have many union shops in the industry?

MR. WATTS: No; we don't have many. We have some. And those have been brought about very much against our will and under the circumstances of bargaining which I have described earlier, under the aegis of governmental representatives.

SENATOR TAFT: Well, the essential difference is very clear. One is that under the union shop the employer reserves the right to put anybody to work he wants to put to work. Under the union shop anybody who wants to get a job can get a job without the consent of the union. Those are the essential freedoms that are maintained, which maintains freedom of transfer in the whole labor field and gives them the right to go into the industry which they want to. In other words, the closed shop does eliminate most of the freedom which we want to preserve. The union shop, though, does not seriously infringe upon it.

IS THE CLOSED SHOP DEMOCRATIC?

By Leonard John Turner, in The Painter and Decorator, June, 1953

Would we say that those who come from other lands and work and enjoy the fruits of our country should not be subject to the laws and taxes which our Government imposes for the welfare of all? Should we allow them to impose their own way of life on ours? Should we have to change our laws to suit those who have come from decadent and "foreign" lands, merely because they are not used to prosperity as we know it? It would be a fine kettle of fish if only the dutiful and patriotic citizens of Our Country were made punishable under the law and taxable.

"Oh, I didn't take out citizenship papers, so you can't punish me for breaking the law," would be quite logical under open-shop citizenship. "I don't need to pay this State tax because I only took out papers for another State." It sounds pretty silly, doesn't it, when put this way; but that is the argument the supporters of the open-shop are handing Our People. But that is how some non-Unionists and some anti-Unionists are thinking. Enough to make a Judge sputter and fume to hear such silliness. . . .

Some men object to being "forced" to join a Union and stand on their constitutional rights to contract with their employers on an individual contract basis. Have we the right to deny him that privilege? You will note that I am stating the arguments as the "opposition" expresses them. Let the non-Union man look at the matter in another way, I plead.

Just as when the frontiers of land were closed we were no longer a pioneer country, so have the frontiers of Industry closed. Whereas in the early settlements there was little if any law enforcement and might was right, so in the early days of Industry might was right and the man who was in the strongest position was a law unto himself. But today law enforcement has come to Industry in the form of Labor Unions and Brotherhoods. Standards of conduct are established democratically and are democratically controlled by organizations of majorities of workmen in the various industries. All workmen in America have benefited from the struggle and work of Unions. Better standards of living, improved working conditions and wages have been gained for all in industries through the *leveling upwards* of the unionized workingman.

"But," you may say, "in this third grouping of forces we have to respect the minority right." That is true—in part.

The minority right extends only to the right to express dissent in Local Meetings, in District or State Council Meetings or in the National Conferences of a Union or Brotherhood. The minority also has the privilege of staying away from meetings and withholding its vote. That is the right of every individual in a Democracy.

But the rights of an individual do not extend to the right of non-payment of taxes. All workingmen owe it to themselves and to their country to join a Brotherhood or Union and to pay dues willingly. They also owe it to their fellow workers to become self-governed and to obey the Industrial laws which they themselves have set up.

The Constitution of the United States and the British North America Act have set a precedent for us to show how we may delegate various phases of Our sovereignty to several Governments. Our Federal rights we delegate to Washington—or Ottawa—and our State or Provincial rights to State or Provincial Government. Our civic rights are in the control of City Officials and Our working rights are delegated to Our Union Locals and Federations.

"If you are afraid that you will lose your personality and just be lost in the mob if you join a Union, then you are planning your careers under a delusion," I recently told a group of technical school students. No one in America has ever lost his or her individuality by becoming a citizen and by exercising the citizen's right to act in the voting booth or to speak his mind on a platform. How much are you or I going to lose of our precious little personality by bringing it down to the Local meeting and testing it out on the floor of the meeting? Life is a friction with one's fellow beings. Activity in the life of your Local is living as it is planned in the democratic way.

LEAVING FREE CHOICE TO THE INDIVIDUAL

Testimony of Frederick G. Atkinson, Vice President for Personnel, R. H. Macy & Co., New York, appearing on behalf of the American Retail Federation, in Taft-Hartley Act Revisions, hearings before the Senate Committee on Labor and Public Welfare, 83d Cong., 1st Sess., 1953, part 2, pp. 1095–1098

We believe that unions deserve and are entitled only to the support which they earn but not to support, financial and otherwise, which they obtain by the coercion of union shop or in other forms of compulsory union membership. . . .

THE CHAIRMAN: In a plant which we will say is organized, where union X is voted to be the bargaining agent, where you get a vote of, say, 51 percent or 52 percent or something like that to support union X, you admit that union is the bargaining agent?

MR. ATKINSON: For representation purposes, yes, sir.

THE CHAIRMAN: For representation. And even the 49 percent, which you say should not be compelled to join the union, are represented by that bargaining unit. Now, does your thinking contemplate any way by which the 49 percent that may be benefited by that bargaining would pay their share of the freight, or do you think that is not necessary?

MR. ATKINSON: There is traditionally an imputed benefit to those who are not members of the union. The argument on this, which has been persuasive in my mind, is this: We all benefit to a greater or lesser degree from things to which we do not directly pay. We benefit from the work of the Red Cross, from that of the Boy Scouts of America, from that of hundreds of voluntary associations to which we may or may not subscribe. Because we contribute to the Red Cross one year is, to my mind, no reason why we should be compelled thereafter, under penalty of loss of our employment, to contribute every year in the future. Or because we enjoy some indirect benefit from what the Red Cross does is no reason why we should all be forced to contribute to it.

If you were to carry to its logical conclusion the doctrine that every one must pay for every imputed benefit which he enjoys directly or indirectly, we would have no money left with which to buy our groceries.

I personally see no reason why we should have a legal compulsion to pay for an imputed benefit, which in some cases the individual simply does not believe in, the one who does not want to join the union, or who does not want to subscribe to the Red Cross.

THE CHAIRMAN: I do not think that analogy is quite apt. I think in an industry where we have a recognition of the right of the employees in the industry to choose negotiators as their bargaining agents, and that has been legalized, where we recognize collective bargaining as the heart of the whole management-labor relationship—you would agree with that?

MR. ATKINSON: Quite so.

THE CHAIRMAN: If that is true, if you have provided a way to determine who will be the people to do the sole negotiating for the workers, I think it is a different case from your Red Cross analogy, or a different case from the chamber of commerce, by which we all benefit but to which we do not all contribute.

Now, I have difficulty in saying that those who benefit by that whole process have not some responsibility to it, although I am not arguing about compulsory unionism. I am not saying that is necessary. I want to find some alternative which recognizes the fact that there are some costs involved to the people in doing their bargaining and negotiating.

MR. ATKINSON: My answer to that would be that, one, we should set up as their representative the organization which represents the majority, and, secondly, they should be participants to the extent that they believe their own best interests dictate. They should not be participants by reason of any form of compulsion which says, "You must pay this tax because somebody else says you enjoy a benefit from it." That would be my answer, sir. . . .

The employee who does not wish to be a member of a union, which for bargaining purposes includes him in its representation, it seems to me, is entitled to join the union or stay out. He is not entitled to assert himself as a union official or a committee member if he is not a member of the union. But he should have the free choice to either leave it to this group to represent him, or to get in and undertake to instruct them. And if he wants to get in and undertake to instruct them, as many workers do, of their own free will, why then he obviously should place himself in good standing as a member. But if he chooses not to participate in this, if he thinks it is not to his best interest, and he prefers to disassociate himself from it, I think that also should be his right.

THE CHAIRMAN: Should he be compelled to strike in case the leaders decide there should be a strike and 51 percent are in the union that called the strike and 49 percent are not? Should the 49 percent then be compelled to participate in the strike?

MR. ATKINSON: You are raising a completely different question, sir. Except when there is violence, the decision among employees as to who goes out on strike very often is not consistent with union membership. . . .

THE CHAIRMAN: Let us suppose a secret ballot is taken in favor of a strike.

MR. ATKINSON: Yes?

THE CHAIRMAN: And that secret ballot, say, is 51 percent for and 49 percent against. That makes that strike legal.

MR. ATKINSON: It represents the will of the majority. That is correct.

THE CHAIRMAN: Now, then, you would say that the minority that were against the strike would not have to pay any attention to the vote for a strike?

MR. ATKINSON: Well, this is a more subtle matter. The decision whether to go out on strike is a function of too many different things. It may be a question of personal conviction or principle that one should never cross a picket line regardless of the merits of the dispute. There are others who feel that it is important to get this week's pay and, therefore, who do not want to be deprived of it, and put that ahead of some considerations of union action or principle. So that, in the absence of forceful prevention of the worker from going to work, these democratic votes that you describe as the strike issue do not tend to be controlling. They do not tend to deprive the man who wants to go to work of his right to do so—again I say, in the absence of violence or force that might keep him out of the plant. He may be in trouble with his union. They may say, "You have violated our picket line. You went to work when we said you shouldn't." But that is not a basis for losing his employment, because the act itself protects him as long as he pays his dues.

THE "RIGHT TO WORK" LAWS

The Labor Management Relations Act of 1947, Section 8 (a) (3), outlawed the closed shop in interstate commerce and introduced certain restrictions on the union shop. In addition, Section 14 (b) permitted states to pass more restrictive legislation, outlawing all forms of union security, if they so wished. Under this provision so-called "right to work" laws have been passed in a number of states making unlawful or unenforceable collective agreements which required membership or dues payment as a condition of employment. In other states employer committees have been formed to work for passage of such legislation. The materials which follow relate to these efforts.

Excerpts from a publication of the Industrial Relations Division, National Association of Manufacturers, 1956

TWENTY QUESTIONS ABOUT THE RIGHT-TO-WORK

1

Q. What is the right-to-work controversy all about?

A. Because a number of states have sought to strengthen the basic rights of their citizens to work without having to join a union, organized labor has rolled its big guns into position to fight these laws.

Essentially these laws make it unlawful to deprive a person of a job because he does not belong to a union—or because he does belong. They also make it unlawful for an employer to enter into agreement with a union to make membership in such unions a condition of employment. In short, they insure the right to work *with* or *without* union membership.

The only issue at stake is whether employees are to be forced to join a union in order to hold a job.

2

Q. Why are union officials opposed to right-to-work laws?

A. One would think there could be no argument in a free society against a man's basic right to work without having to join a union. And yet union officers have announced that their #1 target is to eliminate state right-to-work laws.

This is a curious thing—the more so because all their objections do not succeed in hiding their one real fear—namely, that when unionism is placed on a voluntary basis they have to get their new members on the basis of *meriting* the employee's support.

This is the way every other organization in the country operates. You sell a man on the value of membership and then you keep him sold by performing a useful service.

It is therefore easy to see why union leaders are so wrought up. Over the years, closed shop and union shop contracts have made the organizer's job easy. The new employee has to accept union membership along with his new job. If he fails to pay dues, he is discharged. It's that simple!

It would seem that unions are afraid to test their value to employees by giving men and women the American right to refuse to join if they do not wish to. . . .

17

Q. How are employee relations affected where a union controls the work force in a plant through compulsory unionism?

A. Where a union has the power to compel membership—and can coerce the individual—it is tempted to use this power in many ways.

Knowing that they can control the entire work force in a plant, union officers are more prone to make bargaining demands on a take-it-or-leave-it basis and to use strike threats arbitrarily.

The employer may be obliged to discharge employees—even his most able and experienced employees—if they should fail to pay dues.

Members have no effective way to protest union activities of which they disapprove since they cannot resign from the union and remain on the payroll. This can lead to discontentment and frustration on the job.

For good employee relationships, individual employees should have freedom of expression, but under forced unionism, the voice of the individual is effectively drowned out. . . .

19

Q. Why is there a movement in other states for the enactment of right-to-work laws?

A. Because more and more people are becoming aware that without such laws, even in this free country, one's right to work may be conditional on the whims of a union organization and that it may be valid only as long as payments are made to that particular private organization.

The public more and more is recognizing the danger of this worsening situation and is seeking to correct it by enacting protections of a man's freedom to get and hold a job without the compulsion of joining a union or remaining a union member.

20

Q. Why is compulsory unionism—in any form—a menace to America?

A. Because it is one of the most basic issues of our times. After nearly two centuries of freedom in this nation we are now confronted with this fundamental question:

Must an American citizen belong to a private organization—called a labor union—in order to earn his living at his job?

Compulsory unionism denies free men the right to choose their own course of action—and this is the bedrock foundation on which America was built.

No argument for compulsory unionism—however persuasive—can possibly justify invasion of the right of individual choice.

For a society which is dedicated to the freedom and sanctity of the individual, it is tragic to realize that we have permitted compulsion by a single group— a total denial of the individual's freedom to act.

In 1955 the legislature of Kansas passed a "right to work" bill outlawing all forms of union security. On March 28, Governor Fred Hall vetoed that bill, in a message from which the following excerpts have been taken.

VETO MESSAGE OF HOUSE BILL NO. 30, BY GOVERNOR FRED HALL

The enactment of the "right-to-work" bill may be remembered as a dark hour in Kansas legislative history. I doubt that there has ever been a time that the people of Kansas, the members of the legislature and the governor have been subjected to a greater campaign of propaganda. House Bill 30 is a lobbyist bill. The words "right-to-work" have become a magic phrase, and, like magic, few really understand them.

The campaign to enact this law began several years ago and was instigated by a few men who would profit by such a law. They carried their propaganda campaign through every community in the state. They have used every method at their command including many respectable organizations to influence and crystallize public opinion in favor of this bill. We can only speculate how much money has been spent and is still being spent on radio, telegrams, and newspapers to influence the legislature and the governor in their judgment.

The legislative record of this bill is almost incredible. It has been proposed for several sessions beginning, I believe, in 1947. I recall that it was defeated in a committee of the house of representatives two years ago. It was referred to the legislative council and has been studied by the council the past two years. It was not recommended by the council to this legislature. Neither the house committee nor the senate committee of this legislature recommended the passage of the bill. The chairman of the house committee pleaded for consideration of the legislative council recommendations. The chairman of the senate committee declared the "right-to-work" bill does not cure any of the ills of labor or of management. The chairman of this committee also served as the chairman of the legislative council committee. The council committee investigated the claims of "Right-to-Work, Incorporated," the official lobby organization for the "right-to-work" bill. . . .

Under ordinary circumstances no bill could have survived this kind of history.

I have been deeply disturbed by the efforts of the proponents of House Bill No. 30 to turn the farmers of Kansas against labor in Kansas. In the senate debate a senator said, "Farmers are more interested in this bill than any other group. One thing that has disturbed farmers is a statement of Walter Reuther of the CIO that labor is raising a fund of $25 million to get the guaranteed annual wage."

The senator added, "This means if you guarantee wages for the working man you must guarantee profits for the groceryman and it can only lead to a Socialistic Government."

This is not a sound argument. It has nothing to do with either the rights of individuals to work or not join a union. It does betray the real purpose of House Bill No. 30. It is not legislation for the problems of today but for the fears of tomorrow. This argument goes to the very foundations of America. America is essentially a classless country. Those who would pit one group of people against another to make it otherwise are doing their country a great disservice. The rights of all groups in America are entitled to equal consideration and protection.

President Eisenhower expressed the rightful place of labor when he said,

Today in America, unions have a secure place in our industrial life. Only a handful of unreconstructed reactionaries harbor the ugly thought of breaking unions. Only a fool would try to deprive working men and working women of the right to join the union of their choice. I have no use for those, regardless of their political party, who hold some foolish dream of turning the clock back to days when unorganized labor was a huddled almost helpless mass. The right of men to leave their job is a test of freedom. Hitler suppressed strikes. The drafting of strikers into the Army would suppress strikes. But that also suppresses freedom. There are some things worse, much worse, than strikes—one of them is the loss of freedom.

I am aware of the fact that many states in the union have enacted laws similar to House Bill No. 30. In doing so I believe they have acted contrary to the great heritage and freedoms of America. Throughout the country this law has become a symbol to labor of its loss of freedom. We are not obliged to follow their lead. Many wrongs do not make a right and the hucksters tactics cannot make a wrong thing a right thing. It is time to face up to this issue and set an example for others to follow. The people of Kansas believe in the right of labor to organize and in the principle of collective bargaining. I will not approve any law which destroys this right and this principle. House Bill No. 30 will ultimately do both. It is not constructive, but punitive, legislation. It is clearly contrary to the best interests of all the people of Kansas.

It is with great personal regret that I must differ with you on the merits of this bill. I am hopeful that on further reflection you will agree with me. This is not an easy decision to make. I have no alternative. It would be wrong for this bill to become law in Kansas. As the Governor it is my duty to say so and to act accordingly.

From a speech, "Trends in Labor Relations for 1957," by Herbert R. Northrup, Vice President, Penn-Texas Corporation, given at the Ninth Annual New England Congress, National Metal Trades Association, Providence, R.I., April 9, 1957

"LOYAL EMPLOYEES" AND JOINERS

. . . The emotional reaction to shorter work weeks, automation and engineering problems all put together are mild compared to the feelings engendered by the union shop issue. When Indiana became the 18th state to pass the so-called "right-to-work" law, it became inevitable that the fight over this legislation which bans all forms of compulsory unionism would be extended. Indiana is the first really industrialized state to pass such a law. It is most significant that, although the demand for this legislation was pushed by some industry groups, notably the National Association of Manufacturers, it was actively opposed by large business in Indiana. According to TIME Magazine, executives of the Radio Corporation of America, Seagram's, the Allison Division of General Motors, and Cummings Engines were among those who opposed the enactment of this law. Support for the law, in terms of votes, came largely from farmer and small business-minded legislators.

I am no friend of compulsory unionism. It seems to me at best an anomaly that unions expect the employer to maintain employee union membership. One would expect that unions would be able to handle that themselves. Certainly compulsory unionism seems a strange bedfellow to a democratic state. Nevertheless, I think it is a real question whether management ought to be in the forefront of any activities on behalf of such legislation.

We oppose governmental intervention in labor disputes. Yet one effect of a right-to-work law is to deprive management of the right to negotiate about the union shop or other such forms of compulsory unionism. Such negotiations are sometimes valuable in obtaining desirable objectives. I frankly do not like to be deprived of this right to negotiate.

Those of us who hold this view are in the minority among business executives, but it is interesting to note that we do have some friends. For example, J. Irwin Miller, Chairman of the Board of the Cummings Engine Corporation, had this to say, and I quote:

The classic argument against the union shop is the right-to-work argument.

The average American manager feels that there is a character known as the loyal employee, and this is the fellow who is supposed to figure that joining the union is a fate worse than death. Well, this man is in the same category in my opinion as the Easter Bunny and Santa Claus. I have never found him.

Actually, the really valuable man to management is not the fellow who stays out of the union, but rather the one who gets into the union, participates in the union organization and tries to bring to bear a factual point of view instead of an emotional one. In all the labor controversies that I have ever been involved in, the man who stayed out of the union and merely collected benefits was no help to management's cause.

EMPLOYEE REACTION IN AEROSPACE ILLUMINATES WIDESPREAD OPPOSITION TO COMPULSORY UNIONISM

From Compulsory Unionism, General Electric Employee Relations News Letter, April 5, 1963

Over the years, few employees in the relatively new aerospace industry have been required to join a union or to pay union dues in order to get or keep their jobs. Of the approximately 150,000 union-eligible employees in the industry's bargaining units, about 100,000 are members of the two largest unions in the industry—the United Automobile Workers (UAW) and the International Association of Machinists (IAM). About 50,000 employees in the bargaining units represented by these two unions are not union members.

UNIONS BEGIN ALL-OUT DRIVE FOR UNION SHOP

Even before the 1962 aerospace contract negotiations opened, UAW and IAM, in a joint public statement, announced that they were sending union task forces to the gates of "virtually every aerospace manufacturer and missile site" for an all-out drive to get the Union Shop. The plants and missile sites were saturated with Union Shop "educational" material.

In mid-May, both UAW and IAM opened negotiations with Douglas, General Dynamics, Lockheed, North American, and Ryan—five of the major companies in the aerospace industry. In addition to pay and benefits increases, the "Union Shop" was the principal demand. The unions' educational campaign among employees continued.

Throughout the month of June, reports from the bargaining sessions indicated that pay and other economic issues would not be a serious stumbling block to settlement, but that the company negotiating teams were uniformly rejecting the demands for the Union Shop. Early in July, UAW and IAM announced that unless the companies capitulated, all aerospace plants of the five concerns, working on defense materials vital to the security of the nation, would be struck on July 23.

EARLY SETTLEMENT REACHED AT DOUGLAS AIRCRAFT

In mid-July, Douglas Aircraft signed an Agency Shop agreement with UAW and IAM, which would require several thousands of its non-union employees in bargaining units to pay a fee equal to union dues and assessments to the union, on threat of losing their jobs.

Since the legality of the Agency Shop was still unsettled, Douglas agreed that should the Agency Shop be outlawed in the courts, management would accept a Union Shop if two-thirds of Douglas bargaining unit employees voted approval.

On August 7, Douglas employees received a letter from the company, notifying them that "each non-union member in the bargaining unit must pay a service fee to the union as a condition of continued employment." The fee was set at $5.00 a month, and employees were urged to use the payroll deduction plan to assure payment.

Secretary of Labor Goldberg stated that the Douglas settlement was a welcome one, reached through free collective bargaining. Union spokesmen indicated that this settlement had set a pattern which ought to be acceptable to the other aerospace companies. The fact that this did not become the pattern was due in no small measure to the action of the Douglas employees themselves, as later events revealed.

INTERVENTION ORDERED UNDER THREAT OF STRIKE

The other four companies continued to resist the union demands that they force some 45,000 of their employees into union membership against their will, or fire them. On July 22, the day before the strike deadline, President Kennedy announced that he was appointing a three-man "fact-finding" Board to intervene in the aerospace negotiations. The Chairman selected was Professor George W. Taylor of the University of Pennsylvania. This Board was directed to investigate the dispute and recommend terms for settlement. At the President's request the unions postponed the strike deadline.

Negotiations at General Dynamics, Lockheed, North American and Ryan continued under the direction of the Taylor Board. Reports from these negotiations indicated that the companies were being urged to either grant the Union Shop, or to accept the "pattern" settlement established by the Douglas agreement. . . .

NEGOTIATIONS MOVE TO WASHINGTON

Early in September, the Taylor Board called the companies into extraordinary bargaining sessions in Washington, and on September 11 the Board made its recommendations to the President.

The Board urged that votes on the issue should be taken in the plants. Wherever two-thirds or more of those voting approved, all present and future employees in the bargaining unit would be required to join the union as a condition of employment. In support of this recommendation, the Board said: "In the overwhelming majority of collective bargaining relationships, the contemporary accommodation recognizes the union's claim to at least financial support from all of those whom it legally represents. Thus, neither stated public policy nor the increasingly prevalent private practice support the position of the companies in this case that individual freedom of choice in the matter of union membership or support should be regarded as an absolute right." The President accepted the recommendations of the Board.

EMPLOYEES REJECT UNION SHOP AT NORTH AMERICAN, GENERAL DYNAMICS, AND RYAN

In accordance with the recommendations of the Board, employee elections were scheduled at North American for October 19, at General Dynamics for October 23 and at Ryan for November 1.

In the meantime, the fact that pay and other economic issues were not a factor in the controversy was shown by a contract settlement between Lockheed and IAM covering employees at the company's plant in Georgia, where the Union Shop is forbidden by state law.

The results of the employees voting at North American plants in three states, at four plants of General Dynamics, and at Ryan at San Diego were a stunning blow to the unions. In none of these three companies did the Union Shop receive the two-thirds vote necessary for adoption.

All in all, more than 21,000 employees in the plants of these three companies voted against being forced into compulsory union membership. Obviously, numbers of the union members themselves had rejected forced union membership in the voting, despite the unions' massive campaigns directed at employees over the preceding several months. . . .

[At Boeing] the vote was 21,879 for and 7,762 against forced union membership. Since the union officials claimed 80% membership among bargaining unit employees, the fact that 26% of those voting voted against the Union Shop would indicate that many of the union's own members voted against compulsory unionism.

AEROSPACE VOTING ON COMPULSORY UNIONISM

In not one of the votes conducted by the Taylor Board at General Dynamics, North American, and Ryan did the union shop receive the two-thirds majority the Board had set for acceptance. The vote at Boeing, conducted by the Boeing Aerospace Board, was not binding on the parties.

	For Union Shop	Against Union Shop	Percent Against Union Shop
Gen. Dynamics (IAM)	9,268	7,822	45.8%
No. American (IAM)	19,232	12,899	40.2%
Ryan (UAW)	833	544	39.6%
Boeing (IAM)	21,879	7,762	26.2%

8: Labor Monopoly

From their earliest days unions have been branded as monopolies operating at the expense of the community. It is also true that from their earliest days there have been those who have maintained, whether rightly or wrongly, that the degree of monopoly power exercised by unions is necessary if they are to secure favorable terms from employers. As Horace Greeley once expressed it, in the absence of such collective action wages would be forced downward "just as surely as water runs down hill."

The interesting question, then, is not whether unions are monopolies— the Taft-Hartley Act, which requires an employer to deal exclusively with the majority representative of his employees, obviously gives them a certain monopoly advantage (which may, however, be pallid alongside the employer's advantage as the "exclusive" employer of the union's membership). The more significant issues are how much monopoly power should be allowed to the unions and what forms it may take. Most of the materials which follow deal with these questions.

ORGANIZED LABOR

Report of the Attorney General's National Committee to Study the Antitrust Laws, Stanley N. Barnes and S. Chesterfield Oppenheim, cochairmen, March 31, 1955, pp. 293–306 [*]

At the outset, we emphasize that appraisal of the Nation's labor-management relations policy goes beyond this antitrust study. It follows that we assume, as Congress recently "declared," the "policy of the United States" to be elimination "of certain substantial obstructions to the free flow of commerce" by "encouraging . . . collective bargaining and by protecting . . . workers' . . . full freedom of association [and] self-organization . . . for the purpose of negotiating the terms and conditions of their employment or other mutual aid or protection." [1]

Accordingly, our inquiry considers only those union activities, not directed at such established union ends, but instead at direct restraints on commercial competition. This Committee believes that union actions aimed at directly

---

[*] Footnotes have here been renumbered for the convenience of the reader.
[1] 29 U.S.C. § 151 (1952).

fixing the kind or amount of products which may be used, produced or sold, their market price, the geographical area in which they may be used, produced or sold, or the number of firms which may engage in their production or distribution are contrary to antitrust policy. To the best of our knowledge, no national union flatly claims the right to engage in such activities. We believe that where the concession demanded from an employer as prerequisite to ordering the cessation of coercive action against him is participation in such a scheme for market control, this union conduct should be prohibited by some statute.

Within this scope of our inquiry, we consider, first, the extent to which judicial interpretations of the Clayton [2] and Norris-LaGuardia Acts [3] remove these labor practices from the Sherman Act. Second, we analyze whether these union restrictions, not reached by antitrust, were intended by Congress to be outlawed by the Labor-Management Relations Act of 1947.[4]

1. ANTITRUST COVERAGE

Some twenty years after the passage of the Sherman Act, the Supreme Court, in *Danbury Hatters*,[5] considered its application to union activities. There the union inspired a nationwide consumers' boycott of plaintiff's non-union-made hats. The result was a substantial drop in shipments of plaintiff's hats to out-of-state customers. The Supreme Court held this activity by the union a violation of the Sherman Act, apparently because the union sought to and did restrain interstate commerce in plaintiff's hats.

In apparent response, Sections 6 and 20 of the Clayton Act sought to exclude certain activities in the course of a "labor dispute" from the antitrust laws. Section 6 declares that "the labor of a human being is not a commodity or article of commerce." It further provides that "nothing contained in the antitrust laws shall be construed to forbid the existence and operation of labor . . . organizations, instituted for the purposes of mutual help, and not having capital stock or conducted for profits, or to forbid or restrain individual members of such organizations from lawfully carrying out the legitimate objects thereof; nor shall such organizations, or the members thereof, be held or construed to be illegal combinations or conspiracies in restraint of trade under the antitrust laws." Supplementing that provision, Section 20 barred issuance of Federal injunctions prohibiting activities such as strikes, boycotts or picketing "in any case between an employer and employees, or between employers and employees, or between employees, or between persons employed and persons seeking employment, involving, or growing out of, a dispute concerning terms or conditions of employment." Section 20 concludes with the broad language: "[N]or shall any of the acts specified in this paragraph be considered or held to be violations of any law of the United States."

[2] 15 U.S.C. §§ 12 *et seq.* (1952).
[3] 29 U.S.C. §§ 101–110, 113–115 (1952).
[4] 29 U.S.C. §§ 141–188 (1952).
[5] *Loewe* v. *Lawlor*, 208 U.S. 274 (1908).

The Supreme Court narrowed this exemption in the *Duplex* [6] and *Bedford Cut Stone* [7] cases. There the scope of Section 20 was limited to disputes between an employer and his own employees. Both these involved economic pressures created by concerted refusals to work on rather than to consume, as in *Danbury Hatters*, the plaintiff's product.

Thus in *Duplex*, members of the International Association of Machinists and other craft union members in New York refused to install plaintiff's presses manufactured in Michigan with non-union labor and shipped to out-of-state markets. This attempt to reduce the shipment of Duplex presses was held to violate the Sherman Act.

The *Bedford Cut Stone* case differed only in that the plaintiffs, an association of employers producing and shipping around 70 percent of the cut stone used throughout the country, had ceased recognition of the union and were threatening its very survival in the quarries. Members of the union employed by building contractors in various states refused to handle cut stone shipped by any of the plaintiffs; and the resulting cessations of stone shipment were declared to be restraints illegally caused by the union.

The immunity under Section 20 was also marked out in the *Coronado Coal* [8] cases. These involved no boycott but rather a mine shut-down caused in part by a concerted walkout and in part by wanton destruction of the mine's physical facilities. Obviously Section 20 of the Clayton Act did not immunize such acts of violence. Nevertheless, the Supreme Court found that the resulting stoppage had only an "indirect effect" on interstate commerce and, accordingly, held that there was no violation of the antitrust laws. However, when the plaintiff later showed that the union intended to keep the plaintiff's non-union mined coal out of interstate markets, thus eliminating its competition with union mined coal, the Court held that this specific intent made the restraint "direct" and thus violative of the Sherman Act. [9]

A partial reaction to the *Duplex* [10] and *Bedford Cut Stone* [11] restrictions of Clayton Act Section 20, was the Norris-LaGuardia Act of 1932. [12] This aimed "to restore the broad purpose which Congress thought it had formulated in the Clayton Act but which was frustrated, so Congress believed, by unduly restrictive judicial construction." [13] Accomplishing this end, "labor dispute" was there defined to include "any controversy concerning terms or conditions of employ-

[6] *Duplex Printing Press Co.* v. *Deering*, 254 U.S. 443 (1921).

[7] *Bedford Cut Stone Co.* v. *Journeymen Stone Cutter's Association*, 274 U.S. 37 (1927).

[8] *United Mine Workers of America* v. *Coronado Coal Co.*, 259 U.S. 344 (1922); *Coronado Coal Co.* v. *United Mine Workers of America*, 268 U.S. 295 (1925).

[9] This result was later confirmed, where the restraint was effected solely through the exercise of peaceful economic pressures. *Alco-Zander Co.* v. *Amalgamated Clothing Workers*, 35 F. 2d 203 (E.D. Pa. 1929).

[10] *Duplex Printing Press Co.* v. *Deering*, 254 U.S. 443 (1921).

[11] *Bedford Cut Stone Co.* v. *Journeymen Stone Cutter's Association*, 274 U.S. 37 (1927).

[12] 29 U.S.C. §§ 101–110, 113–115 (1952).

[13] *United States* v. *Hutcheson*, 312 U.S. 219, 236 (1941).

ment . . . regardless of whether or not the disputants stand in the proximate
relation of employer and employee." [14] In addition, Section 20 barred Federal
injunction of enumerated union organizational and economic pressure activities.[15]

In *Apex Hosiery Co.* v. *Leader*,[16] the Court found it unnecessary to rely on
Norris-LaGuardia in holding that an organizational strike, though interfering
with interstate hosiery shipments, did not violate the Sherman Act. That Act,
the Court noted, aimed at "restraints," like those this Committee now considers,
"upon commercial competition in the marketing of goods or services." [17] In
Apex, however, it was "plain that the. . . . [union] did not have as its purpose
restraint upon competition in the market for petitioner's product. Its object was
to compel petitioner to accede to the union demands" for organization.[18] From
this decision there emerges a distinction, deemed essential by this Committee,
between union activities aiming, on the one hand, at furthering rightful union
objectives and, on the other, at directly "suppressing [commercial] competition
or fixing prices" of commercial products.[19]

The antitrust impact of Norris-LaGuardia was first construed by the Supreme
Court in *United States* v. *Hutcheson*.[20] There involved was a strike by one union
against an employer who had assigned work to a competing union's members.
Removing such conduct from the Sherman Act, the Court held that Congress,
by the passage of the Norris-LaGuardia Act, had in effect overruled the *Duplex*
construction of Section 20 of the Clayton Act. As a result, the Court concluded
that all union self-help conduct specified in the concluding clause of Section 20,
as well as Section 4 of Norris-LaGuardia, was now immunized from Sherman
Act sanctions.

Hutcheson's rationale, however, was, in its own language, limited to "where
a union acts in its own self-interest and does not combine with nonlabor
groups,[21] . . ." While *Hutcheson* treated union pressure which fell short of
coercing employer participation, *Allen-Bradley Company* v. *Local No. 3*,[22]
decided some five years later, involved a consummated union-employer scheme.
There, Local No. 3, comprised of electrical workers in the New York area,
agreed with "contractors . . . to purchase equipment from none but local
manufacturers who also had closed-shop agreements with Local No. 3," and
with manufacturers "to confine their New York City sales to contractors employing the Local's members." [23] These contracts, the Court found, were "but
one element in a far larger program in which contractors and manufacturers

[14] 29 U.S.C. § 113 (c) (1952).
[15] 29 U.S.C. § 104 (1952).
[16] 310 U.S. 469 (1940).
[17] *Id.* at 495.
[18] *Id.* at 501.
[19] *Ibid.*
[20] 312 U.S. 219 (1941).
[21] *Id.* at 232.
[22] 325 U.S. 797 (1945).
[23] *Id.* at 799.

united . . . to monopolize all the business in New York City." [24] This fact of union-employer combination was held to distinguish *Allen-Bradley* from *Hutcheson* and, in turn, to subject Local No. 3 to the Sherman Act.[25]

It is not yet settled whether *Allen-Bradley* permits antitrust prohibition of an agreement between one union and one employer requiring conduct whose object is some direct market restraint. The majority there assumed, without deciding, that "such an agreement standing alone would not have violated the Sherman Act." [26] However, as the separate opinion emphasized, employer inspired agreements were not solely involved; instead some respondents were "individually coerced by the union's power to agree to its terms. It is, therefore, inaccurate," that opinion went on, "to say that the employers used the union to aid and abet them to restrain interstate commerce." [27] Accordingly, it may be that the employer connivance which *Allen-Bradley* requires might be inferred largely from a labor-management contract agreed to at union insistence.[28]

Even in the absence of such connivance, where the activity involved both aims, in the language of the *Apex* decision, at "suppressing [commercial] competition or fixing prices" [29] and is not sanctioned by the Labor-Management Relations Act, antitrust proceedings may not be foreclosed. In *Hawaiian Tuna Packers* v. *International Longshoremen and Warehousemen's Union*,[30] for example, fish canners sought treble damages from Local 150, made up of some crew members and boat owners who apparently were also crewmen. The complaint alleged that Local 150 demanded that the plaintiff canner contract to buy a season's catch at fixed rates per pound. Upon plaintiff's refusal, the union cut off its fish supply and, as part of its plan to coerce plaintiff to fix prices, agreed with fishermen in competing waters to boycott plaintiff. Upholding the complaint against the defendant's motion to dismiss, the court held that a demand to fix prices made by a combination of crewmen and owner crewmen brought the case within *Allen-Bradley*.[31]

---

[24] *Id.* at 809.

[25] Similarly note *Brotherhood of Carpenters* v. *United States*, 330 U.S. 395, 399–400 (1947); see also *Philadelphia Record Co.* v. *Manufacturing Photo-Engravers Ass'n. of Philadelphia*, 155 F. 2d 799 (3d Cir. 1946); but see *Albrecht* v. *Kinsella*, 119 F. 2d 1003 (7th Cir. 1941).

[26] 325 U.S. 979, 809 (1945); see also *id.* at 818.

[27] *Id.* at 814.

[28] In *Loews Inc.* v. *Basson*, 46 F. Supp. 66 (S.D.N.Y. 1942), a union comprising projectionists, deliverers and cutters sought to compel a movie producer-distributor to license only exhibitors who employed union projectionists. The producer-distributor objected, but the court held nonetheless its entry into the proposed contract would constitute an illegal "combination between a union and a nonlabor group" (*id.* at 72); cf. *Anderson-Friberg Inc.* v. *Justin R. Clary & Son*, 98 F. Supp. 75, 82 (S.D.N.Y. 1951); but see *Meier and Pohlmann Furniture Co.* v. *Gibbons*, 113 F. Supp. 409 (E.D. Mo. 1953).

[29] 310 U.S. 469, 501 (1940).

[30] 72 F. Supp. 562 (D. Hawaii 1947).

[31] *Id.* at 566.

Beyond connivance, however, that court held that the facts alleged failed to state a case involving or growing out of, as the Norris-LaGuardia Act requires, a "labor dispute." That Act, the court reasoned, "was not intended to have application over the disputes over the sale of commodities . . . [or] to include controversies upon which the employer-employee relationship has no bearing." [32]

Supporting the suggestion that a dispute involving the object of direct market control may not constitute a "labor dispute" within Norris-LaGuardia are analogous decisions upholding state action restricting labor activities not sanctioned by Taft-Hartley.[33] *Giboney* v. *Empire Storage Co.*,[34] for example, involved picketing by union peddlers of an ice supply plant to bar ice sales to nonunion peddlers. If Empire had agreed to stop selling ice to nonunion deliverers, the Supreme Court concluded that such conduct would have violated the state antitrust statutes. Accordingly, since no question of conflict with the Federal labor relations scheme was even raised,[35] the Court upheld application of the state policy whose "purpose . . . is to secure competition and preclude combinations which tend to defeat it." [36]

Summing up, our analysis of these "three 'interlacing statutes' " [37] suggests that commercial restraints by unions may be vulnerable to antitrust proceedings:

(1) Where the union engages in fraud or violence and intends or achieves some direct commercial restraint; [38]

(2) Where the union activity is not in the course of a labor dispute as defined in the Norris-LaGuardia Act.[39] Construing this statute, the Supreme Court has recognized "its responsibility to try to reconcile" two "declared Congressional

[32] *Id.* at 566; similarly, note *Columbia River Packers Ass'n.* v. *Hinton,* 315 U.S. 143 (1942); see also *Louisville & N. R. Co.* v. *Local Union No. 432,* 104 F. Supp. 748 (S.D. Ala. 1952); *Pacific Gamble Robinson Co.* v. *Minneapolis and St. Louis Ry. Co.,* 85 F. Supp. 65 (D. Minn. 1949).

[33] See, for example, *Giboney* v. *Empire Storage & Ice Co.* 336 U.S. 490 (1949); *Whitaker* v. *State of North Carolina,* 335 U.S. 525 (1949); *Lincoln Federal Labor Union* v. *Northwestern Iron & Metal Co.,* 335 U.S. 525 (1949); *AFL* v. *American Sash & Door Co.,* 335 U.S. 538 (1949).

[34] 336 U.S. 490 (1949).

[35] It was not necessary for the Court to consider there whether the union activity involved ran afoul of the Taft-Hartley subsection 8 (*b*) (4) (*A*). Its legality under that provision, however, seems open to question. Initially, it seems clear that "an object" of the picketing was, as that section requires, to foreclose Empire from "doing business with any other person." The primary issue would be whether the union activity constituted, within the meaning of that provision, encouraging "the employees of any employer to engage in a . . . concerted refusal in the course of their employment to . . . handle . . . any material . . . or to perform any services." Cf. *National Labor Relations Board* v. *International Rice Milling Co.,* 341 U.S. 665, 670 (1951).

[36] *Giboney* v. *Empire Storage Co.,* 336 U.S. 490, 495 (1949).

[37] *Allen-Bradley Co.* v. *Local No. 3,* 325 U.S. 797, 806 (1945).

[38] Cf. *Apex Hosiery Co.* v. *Leader,* 310 U.S. 469, 501–504 (1940); 29 U.S.C. § 104 (*i*) (1952); *Coronado Coal Co.* v. *United Mine Workers of America,* 268 U.S. 295 (1925).

[39] See 29 U.S.C. § 113 (*c*) (1952).

policies." The "one seeks to preserve a competitive business economy; the other to preserve the rights of labor to organize to better its conditions through an agency of collective bargaining." Accordingly, its task is in each case to determine "how far Congress intended activities under one of these policies to neutralize the results envisioned by the other." [40] Accomplishing this task may require giving content to the Norris-LaGuardia Act's general definition of "labor dispute." We have noted that recent decisions suggest that courts may infer Congressional intent to apply antitrust to those labor activities, not sanctioned by the Taft-Hartley Act, which aim at direct commercial restraint.[41]

(3) Where a union combines with some nonlabor group to effect some direct commercial restraint.[42] . . .

2. RELEVANT PROVISIONS OF THE LABOR-MANAGEMENT RELATIONS ACT OF 1947

Against this background of possible avenues for antitrust suits, Congress in 1947 considered amendments to the National Labor Relations Act. The bill passed by the House, the Conference Committee Report notes, "contained a provision amending the Clayton Act so as to withdraw the exemption of labor organizations under the antitrust laws when such organization engaged in combination or conspiracy in restraint of commerce where one of the purposes or a necessary effect of the combination or conspiracy was to join or combine with any person to fix prices, allocate costs, restrict production, distribution, or competition, or impose restrictions or conditions, upon the purchase, sale, or use of any product, material, machine, or equipment, or to engage in any unlawful concerted activity." [43] Explaining omission of such provisions from the enacted Bill, the Conference Report continued: "Since the matters dealt with in this Section have to a large measure been effectuated through the use of boycotts, and since the conference agreement contains effective provisions directly dealing with boycotts themselves, this provision is omitted from the conference agreement." [44]

The so-called boycott provisions provide in relevant part that "it shall be an unfair labor practice for a labor organization or its agents to engage in, or to induce or encourage the employees of any employer to engage in, a strike or a concerted refusal in the course of their employment to . . . handle or work on any . . . materials . . . or to perform any services, where an object thereof is: (A) forcing or requiring . . . any employer or other person to cease using . . . or otherwise dealing in the products of any other producer . . . or to cease doing business with any other person . . ." or "(D) forcing or requiring any employer to assign particular work to employees in a particular labor

---

[40] *Allen-Bradley Co.* v. *Local No. 3*, 325 U.S. 798, 806 (1945).

[41] See e.g., *Hawaiian Tuna Packers* v. *International Longshoremen & Warehousemen Union*, 72 F. Supp. 562 (D. Hawaii 1947); see also *Columbia River Packers Assoc.* v. *Hinton*, 315 U.S. 143 (1942); cf. *Giboney* v. *Empire Storage Co.*, 336 U.S. 490 (1949).

[42] See e.g., *Allen-Bradley Co.* v. *Local No. 3*, 325 U.S. 797 (1945).

[43] 93 Cong. Rec. 6380 (1947).

[44] *Ibid.*

organization or in a particular trade, craft, or class rather than to employees in another labor organization or in another trade, craft, or class. . . ." [45] Moreover, it further provides that "Whoever shall be injured in his business or property by reason of any violation" of these provisions "may sue therefor . . . and shall recover the damages by him sustained and the cost of the suit." [46]

These provisions have been applied to enjoin certain union activities aimed [47] at restricting the use of competing products in a given area.[48] *United Brotherhood of Carpenters and Joiners of America* v. *Sperry,*[49] for example, involved union picketing and blacklisting of a builder using prefabricated building material. The court, granting an injunction pending hearing, found that such union

[45] 29 U.S.C. § 158 (1952). The language of subsection (*D*), incidentally, would in all probability encompass the union activities held not subject to antitrust coverage in *United States* v. *Hutcheson,* 312 U.S. 219 (1940). Similarly note *United States* v. *Carrozzo,* 37 F. Supp. 191 (N.D. Ill., 1941), *aff'd sub. nom.* 313 U.S. 539 (1941).

[46] 29 U.S.C. § 187 (*b*) (1952); see, e.g., *Longshoremen's and Warehousemen's Union* v. *Juneau Spruce Corp.,* 342 U.S. 237 (1952).

[47] Relevant here is a Supreme Court holding that "under this section it is not necessary to find that the *sole* object of the union activity was an illegal one." (See *National Labor Relations Board* v. *Denver Building and Construction Trades Council,* 341 U.S. 675, 689 [1951].)

[48] For cases ordering cessation of some union efforts to block use of more efficient products see *Joliet Contractors Association* v. *National Labor Relations Board,* 202 F. 2d 606 (7th Cir. 1953); *cert. denied* 346 U.S. 824 (1953); *National Labor Relations Board* v. *United Brotherhood of Carpenters and Joiners of America,* 184 F. 2d 60 (10th Cir. 1950).

Note also *In re Washington and Oregon Shingle Weavers Council,* 101 N.L.R.B. 1159 (1952) (Shingle Weavers Council ordered to "cease and desist from . . . encouraging their members to . . . strike" against a shingle company (*Id.* at 1163) as part of the union effort to eliminate "all unfair Canadian or other 'nonunion' shingles from the United States market." [*Id.* at 1168]), order enforced *National Labor Relations Board* v. *Washington-Oregon Shingle Weavers District Council,* 211 F. 2d 149 (9th Cir. 1954); *In re Bakery Drivers Local 276,* 100 N.L.R.B. 1092 (1952) (Bakery Drivers Union ordered to cease and desist from encouraging employees of various retail outlets to engage in a concerted refusal to handle bakery products of a company which the union was seeking to organize). Similarly, note *Construction and General Laborers Local 320,* 93 N.L.R.B. 751 (1951); *In re International Brotherhood of Teamsters, Chauffeurs, Warehousemen and Helpers of America, Local 87,* 87 N.L.R.B. 720 (1949), order enforced, *National Labor Relations Board* v. *Service Trade, Chauffeurs, Salesmen & Helpers, Local 145,* 191 F. 2d 65 (2d Cir. 1950). For cases where the Board has enjoined a union, as part of a scheme to pressure an employer of a plant already organized, from encouraging workers of a customer concertedly to refuse to handle the product of the employer involved in the dispute, see *In re Metal Polishers Local 171,* 86 N.L.R.B. 1243 (1949); *In re Wine, Liquor and Distillery Workers Union, Rectifying and Wine Workers International Union of America, A.F. of L. Local 1,* 78 N.L.R.B. 504 (1948), order enforced, *National Labor Relations Board* v. *Wine, Liquor and Distillery Workers Union, Rectifying and Wine Workers International Union of America, Local 1,* 178 F. 2d 584 (2d Cir. 1949).

[49] 170 F. 2d 863–869 (10th Cir. 1948).

actions "handicapped" the builder and "delayed [him] in carrying forward . . . [his] program of purchasing and erecting" prefabricated houses.[50] These labor activities were later held by the Board to be an unfair labor practice and its order requiring their cessation was ordered enforced by a circuit court.[51]

Similarly, *Joliet Contractors Association* v. *National Labor Relations Board* [52] involved a union by-law which, one circuit court found left members with no "choice but to refuse to work when discovery was made that preglazed sash was being used." [53] The record there revealed, moreover, that in several instances glaziers on a job, in compliance with this by-law, walked off the job when preglazed sash was purchased. As to these instances of restraint, the circuit court affirmed the Board's order requiring a union to "desist from applying its by-laws . . . to induce and encourage . . . a strike or concerted refusal in the course of . . . employment . . . where an object thereof is to require their employer . . . or other person to cease doing business with any other employer or any person who uses or sells preglazed sash." [54]

As these two instances suggest, certain means for curbing union activities aimed directly at suppressing commercial competition may be proscribed by the boycott provisions of the Labor-Management Relations Act. However, only those activities " 'specifically provided for' in the Act" [55] are restricted. The result, in the language of the Court in the *Joliet Contractors* [56] case may be "numerous apparent incongruities." There, for example, "if two or more glaziers refuse to accept employment because of the use of preglazed sash there is no violation as they have not concertedly refused to work in the course of their employment. However, if they discover the use of preglazed sash after they are on the job and then refuse to work, it is a violation because they have done so in the course of their employment. At the same time, if there is only one glazier on each of several jobs and they each refuse to work, it is not a violation because their refusal is not concerted. These incongruities and others which could be mentioned are unavoidable because of the plain unambiguous language em-

---

[50] *Id.* at 867.

[51] See *United Brotherhood of Carpenters and Joiners of America* (Wadsworth), 81 N.L.R.B. 802 (1949), order enforced, *National Labor Relations Board* v. *United Brotherhood of Carpenters and Joiners of America*, 184 F. 2d 60 (10th Cir. 1950).

[52] 202 F. 2d 606 (7th Cir. 1953), *cert. denied* 346 U.S. 824 (1953).

[53] *Id.* at 612.

[54] *Id.* at 611. There the Board had held as an unfair labor practice the union's inducement of glaziers already on a job to cease installing preglazed sash (99 N.L.R.B. 1391, 1410, 1415 [1952]). However, the Board held not within the Act union inducement of its members, not yet on a job, not to work on preglazed sash (*Id.* at 1412–1413). The result, in the language of the court affirming this order, may be "numerous apparent incongruities," *Joliet Contractors Association* v. *National Labor Relations Board*, 202 F. 2d 606, 611 (7th Cir. 1953), *cert. denied* 346 U.S. 824 (1953), thus permitting certain union pressures against use of new products.

[55] *National Labor Relations Board* v. *International Rice Milling Co., Inc.*, 341 U.S. 665 (1951).

[56] 202 F. 2d 606, 611 (7th Cir. 1953); *cert. denied* 346 U.S. 824 (1953).

ployed by Congress in enumerating the elements required to constitute a violation." [57]

3. CONCLUSIONS AND RECOMMENDATIONS

As the limitations of our inquiry require, no one of our conclusions or recommendations implies any change of labor's freedom under the antitrust laws to act in concert in order to promote union organization or bargain collectively over wages, hours, or other employment conditions. Reported cases indicate, however, that some unions have engaged in some practices aimed directly at commercial market restraints by fixing the kind or amount of products which may be sold in any area [58] or their market price.[59] Such activities run counter to our national antitrust policy.

Some means for carrying them out may be enjoined by the Labor-Management Relations Act,[60] whose enforcement, we note, is presently dependent on receipt of formal complaints. Moreover, such union activities are, to some but as yet unfixed extent, now subject to antitrust coverage. As a practical matter, these union restraints usually gain commercial significance to the extent that there is employer participation—either voluntary or coerced.[61] However, to repeat, we believe that where the concession demanded from an employer as prerequisite to ceasing coercive action against him is participation in or submission to such a scheme for market control or commercial restraints, this union conduct should be prohibited by statute. Accordingly, to the extent that such commercial restraints not effectively curbed by either antitrust or Labor-Management Relations Act exist, then we recommend appropriate legislation to prohibit these union efforts at outright market control.

Regarding such legislation, this Committee recommends:

a. It should cover only specific union activities which have as their direct object direct control of the market, such as fixing the kind or amount of products which may be used, produced or sold, their market price, the geographical area in which they may be sold, or the number of firms which may engage in their production or distribution. By "object" this Committee means only the immediate concession demanded from an employer as a condition precedent to halting coercive action against him. In drafting such legislation, greatest care should be given to protecting labor's "full freedom of association [and] self-

---

[57] *Id.* at 612.

[58] See e.g., *Allen-Bradley Co.* v. *Local No. 3*, 325 U.S. 797 (1945); *Joliet Contractors Association* v. *National Labor Relations Board*, 202 F. 2d 606–611 (7th Cir. 1953), *cert. denied* 346 U.S. 824 (1953); *United Brotherhood of Carpenters and Joiners of America* v. *Sperry*, 170 F. 2d 863 (10th Cir. 1948); cf. *United States* v. *American Federation of Musicians*, 47 F. Supp. 304 (N.D. Ill. 1942), *aff'd* 318 U.S. 741 (1943); *United States* v. *Carrozzo*, 37 F. Supp. 191 (N.D. Ill. 1941); *aff'd sub. nom.* 313 U.S. 539 (1941).

[59] See e.g., *Columbia River Packers Association* v. *Hinton*, 315 U.S. 143 (1942); *Hawaiian Tuna Packers* v. *International Longshoremen and Warehousemen Union*, 72 F. Supp. 562 (D. Hawaii, 1947).

[60] See cases n. 48, *supra*.

[61] Cf. *Allen-Bradley Co.* v. *Local No. 3*, 325 U.S. 797, 809 (1945).

organization . . . for the purpose of negotiating the terms and conditions of their employment or other mutual aid or protection" as now provided in 29 U.S.C. § 151 (1952).

  b. Unlike the present Labor-Management Relations Act,[62] the Government should have power to proceed, on its own initiative, without formal complaints from others. A coerced employer, for example, might find it advantageous to acquiesce rather than complain. Thus, were the Government dependent upon formal complaints of others to initiate actions, some wrong to the public interest might go uncorrected.

  c. Unlike the Sherman Act, such legislation should not contain provisions for private injunction. In the labor-management area, private injunctive remedies under the Sherman Act have in the past been subject to abuse. In any legislation, therefore, primary reliance should be on Government-initiated enforcement.

Walter Adams dissents from this majority report. In his words:

Should Congress find that union commercial restraints not curbed by antitrust or Taft-Hartley are widespread, the majority suggests a possible approach for halting them. This suggestion, however, is so general that its enactment would confuse rather than clarify existing law. Moreover, because of its vagueness, it might be construed—erroneously perhaps—as prohibiting some union activities generally regarded as normal and necessary.

Thus the majority suggestion aims at "specific union activities which have as their direct object control of the market." To the extent that the limits of challenged union conduct are defined in terms of "object" (i.e., intent), the proposal is subject to potential abuse. Unlike the Taft-Hartley Act, it does not pinpoint specific malpractices in terms of a clearly delineated course of conduct. Instead, it makes broad recommendations of an undefined and unknown impact.

In dissenting, I am not unmindful of the concern over allegedly widespread labor abuses. I believe, however, that corrective legislation—if, when and by whomsoever proposed—should be based on a careful and comprehensive investigation of all the facts within the context of market reality. Such legislation, if and when enacted, should become part of our labor-management code, and not part of the antitrust laws. Raymond Dickey joins in this dissent, but adds his view "that present Labor-Management Relations Act and antitrust provisions can effectively curb those commercial restraints by unions which concern the majority."

NATIONAL UNIONS ARE MONOPOLISTIC COMBINATIONS

Statement on behalf of the National Association of Manufacturers, filed with the Attorney General's National Committee to Study the Antitrust Laws, with

---

[62] 29 U.S.C. § 160 (b) (1952) provides that the Board may issue complaints and hold hearings apparently only "[w]henever it is charged that any person has engaged in or is engaging in any such unfair labor practice."

specific reference to immunities accorded organized labor, in Current Antitrust Problems, hearings before Antitrust Subcommittee (Subcommittee No. 5) of the House Committee on the Judiciary, 84th Cong., 1st Sess., 1955, part 2, serial no. 3, pp. 1810–1812

. . . Organized labor is one of the strongest economic forces existing in the United States today. If citation be needed, mere reference to the many recent nationwide rail, coal, and steel strikes will demonstrate not only that monopoly power is possessed by some international labor organizations but also that such power is exercised for the purpose and with the effect of restraining, impeding, and preventing commerce.

This monopoly power is exercised, it should be stressed, by the international organization—a combination of unions—not by the local unions which are primarily concerned with negotiating mutually satisfactory terms and conditions of employment with an employer. It is achieved partly by constitutional provisions similar to article XVII of the United Steelworkers of America (CIO), which provides:

"Section 1. The international union shall be the contracting party in all collective-bargaining agreements and all such agreements shall be signed by the international officers. . . ."

As an indication of the effectiveness of such constitutional provisions, take the case of a small plant, Marvel Industries, which bargained with a local union and reached agreement calling for substantial wage increases. The contract was signed by the company, the bargaining committee, and the international representatives assigned to the case, then ratified by the employees. About a month after it was put into effect, the international union returned the contract, stating it must be redrafted to comply with requirements of international union policy and ordered a strike to enforce the increased demands. After 4 weeks the company, to save its business, capitulated to the international union (House labor hearings, 1953, pt. 6, p. 1886).

As indicated, it is the combination of labor organizations acting as a national or international union which poses antitrust analogies and which requires antitrust remedies and limitation. It is elementary that business concerns, acting alone, may lawfully do many things which if done in combination or concert would bring down the wrath of antitrust. No one would deny, for example, the clear right of an individual steel producer, acting independently, to curtail production or raise or lower prices for economic reasons. By the same token, no one would deny the right of the employees of an individual employer to strike, as a union, for more favorable working conditions. To repeat, it is when unions combine or agree or conspire together to take joint action, as in the recent nationwide strikes, that the antitrust philosophy against the exercise of monopoly power should apply. Certainly there can be no doubt today that the exercise of such monopoly power as has been witnessed in recent years is at least as damaging, if not more so, than the same tactics if undertaken by business organizations through combinations or conspiracy. Yet the one is prohibited while the other is freed of restraint and in fact encouraged.

An antitrust approach to the problem of labor monopoly need not necessarily attempt to itemize particular activities and conduct which should be considered violations of antitrust laws. Rather the problem should be attacked at its roots —the power and dominance of the national or international union over its local constituents.

Normally it is not the activities of an isolated local union dealing with one or more employers in a community which raises antitrust analogies; it is the combination, conspiracy, or agreement between several or all locals of an international union which result in actions adversely and unreasonably affecting the economy.

It should constantly be borne in mind that the antitrust laws are the laws of free commerce and trade; and that the labor laws are simply that, i.e. laws which are designed to establish the ground rules for the conduct of negotiations between employers and their employees for the single broad purpose of reaching an agreement on terms and conditions of employment. Thus it is entirely proper and appropriate for specific practices by labor organizations to be dealt with in the law of labor-management relations as a means to bring about a better atmosphere in which to conduct the negotiations looking toward mutually satisfactory agreement. Such specification of unwarranted labor conduct would be to the law of labor relations what the Clayton, Robinson-Patman, and Federal Trade Commission Acts are to the basic antitrust law. In other words the specific would complement the general in the public interest.

The broad philosophy of the Sherman Act, however, should and must deal with monopoly power, whether it be manifested in combinations of employers or in combinations of unions, since in either instance it is the free economy of the Nation, not merely relations between employers and employees which is threatened or adversely affected. Accordingly an approach to the problem of union monopoly power should be based on the philosophy of the Sherman Act.

This need not necessarily be accomplished, however, by attempting to apply its present provisions through appropriate amendments to the Clayton and Norris-LaGuardia Acts. Rather a new section or sections should be added to the Sherman Act. These should be so designed as to deal directly with the monopoly power of national or international unions. To use traditional antitrust language, for example, the proposed new provisions could embrace contracts, combinations, or conspiracies between local unions, whether or not affiliated where the purpose or necessary effect thereof is unreasonably to impair, diminish, impede, obstruct, or prevent the production or movement of goods for or in interstate commerce.

It may be contended that a Sherman Act approach to the problem, along the lines suggested above, would break up international and national unions. The short answer to that argument is that strong national unions existed prior to adoption of the nationwide stoppage techniques.

International unions are not unlike the modern business or trade association in structure. Moreover many of their present practices, and the "congressionally permitted" restraints imposed by them . . . are not unlike methods which some trade associations adopted in the early days of their growth. When trade

associations engaged in monopolistic activities, the Sherman Act was not used
to compel disbandment but to eliminate monopoly practices. This policy is
consistent with our national traditions; it should guide us in dealing with the
monopoly power of organized labor.

THE MONOPOLY POWERS OF UNIONS SHOULD BE CONFINED TO CERTAIN OBJECTIVES

*Testimony of Thurman Arnold, Washington, D.C., in Economic Power of Labor
Organizations, hearings before the Senate Committee on Banking and Currency, 81st Cong., 1st Sess., 1949, part 1, pp. 71–74*

. . . The unions are, in my judgment, and should be in a peculiarly advantageous position. They are attempting, and in many industries are succeeding,
in monopolizing the supply of labor, and I think that they are probably entitled
to do.

I think that they probably need the strength, if they can get it without illegal
means, of Nation-wide unions which control the production. At least that is the
principle of even the Taft-Hartley Act, which is supposed to be a slave-labor
bill, and I think that it would be idle to dispute that at this time. The water has
run under that dam, so we have a situation where labor is exempt from the
antitrust laws, is not treated the same way with business in one respect, and
that is that labor by voluntary methods can monopolize the labor supply, or at
least attempt to monopolize the labor supply, and every union in the United
States, of course, is now attempting to do it, some with greater success, and
some with less success. That is the set-up of the unions.

The unions having had that power, however, it is a very dangerous thing to
subject them to no curbs whatever. . . .

If we are going to give them monopoly power, we must confine their use of
that power to certain objectives.

Now, what are these objectives? I think that wages and hours is a legitimate
union activity, anything that concerns wages and hours. . . .

When, however, this wages-and-hour becomes used as a pretext to restrict
production, and achieve control over management and production, it then
falls or should fall, it seems to me, upon the prohibitions of the Sherman Act
as an illegitimate activity of labor.

Now, I recognize the fact that if there can be no very sharp line . . . they
will always come before the court under the guise of a wage-and-hour controversy, but we must allow the court, I think, the power to determine whether
in fact it is.

There is no possible way of tying down the antitrust laws to any definite
formula. The court must have that fact-finding power. I think, in the case that
we have got before us, it is perfectly clear that the purpose of the strike has
nothing to do with health or recreation or real wages and hours.

I think, if you pass a law which made that purpose an illegitimate purpose,
you would find close questions between what was a legitimate wage-and-hour
demand and whether an employer's attempt to increase production came within

what we call the speed-up system. You would have questions of fact which the court must decide, and yet I know of nowhere we can put that power except in our courts, and I think that the refusal of any group to allow such questions of fact to be decided among the courts is a dangerous thing. I don't say that the unions are any different from industry. I have been debating with Senator Capehart in a friendly way about the basing-point system. Certainly the matter of whether a basing-point system is used in restraint of trade or whether it isn't is a question of fact which can't be defined very precisely, yet I think that those matters should be left to the courts, and neither labor unions nor industry should have an escape of saying, "We might lose an unjust case, and this throws our activities into confusion; and, therefore, we want an exception from the antitrust law."

So, it seems to me your bill should do what the Taft-Hartley Act does not do at all, doesn't consider, and that is to define the legitimate purposes of labor unions.

Now, I would say that the legitimate purposes of labor unions could be roughly described as those having to do with wages and hours, health, safety, their legitimate activities in promoting the strength of the union, and perhaps you could spell out a number of others.

It would take some thought to draft such a bill; and, having done that, I think the bill should define a few of the outstanding practices and brand them as illegitimate, and those practices which I would brand as illegitimate objectives would be, and I will name them again: . . . A strike to erect a tariff wall around a locality; the exclusion of efficient methods from industry; the refusal of unions to allow independent firms to remain in existence; the activities of unions in imposing and maintaining artificial prices or restricted production of any form; and the make-work system.

IS LABOR TO BE TREATED AS A COMMODITY?

Statement of Arthur J. Goldberg, General Counsel, Congress of Industrial Organizations, in Current Antitrust Problems, hearings before the Antitrust Subcommittee (Subcommittee No. 5) of the House Committee on the Judiciary, 84th Cong., 1st Sess., 1955, part 3, pp. 2146–2148

The chamber, the NAM, and the Farm Bureau all ask that Congress outlaw industrywide, or areawide, or pattern collective bargaining. Such bargaining is, in their view, the epitome of labor monopoly.

This charge that national or regional or pattern bargaining is "monopolistic" and "a restraint of trade" reverts, of course, to the basic fallacy that human labor is to be treated as a commodity, and that organizations of those who have nothing to sell but the use of their minds and bodies constitute "restraints of trade."

This approach . . . is a false one. The issue is not one of monopoly versus competition, and the use of antitrust phraseology in this context serves only to mislead. The purpose of the antitrust laws is to preserve competition; but surely no one is suggesting that unions should compete with each other to see who can supply human labor at the lowest price. And surely no one is suggesting that individual workers should compete with each other to work at the lowest wage.

There is some suggestion in the chamber's statement that industrywide bargaining, and regional and pattern bargaining, are destructive of competition among the employers of labor. I do not believe, however, that such a charge can be generally supported. Such industries as men's and women's clothing, glassware, hosiery, pottery, and the silk and rayon dyeing and finishing industry, in all of which there is a long history of national or regional bargaining, are highly competitive. Professors Lester and Robie of Princeton, after studying 7 industries in which national or regional bargaining had existed for more than 10 years, came to the conclusion that such bargaining has no tendency whatever toward increasing monopolistic, noncompetitive, price policies. See Lester and Robie, Wages Under National and Regional Collective Bargaining, Princeton University Press (1946).

It is, of course, true that industry or area or pattern bargaining tends to prevent employers from competing with each other by paying lower wages than their competitors. But it is neither socially nor economically desirable for employers to compete with each other by paying lower wages. Further, uniform wage scales among employers do not eliminate price competition in the sale of the employers' products. As Lester and Robie state, "Indeed, elimination of wage cutting has tended to stress efficiency of management as the most important factor in competition."

The chamber statement asserts that "the excessive costs of pattern bargaining can force smaller firms out of business." And the statement adds . . . :

"Furthermore, giant unions have not hesitated to impose even tougher demands on small and middle-sized companies unable to resist the tremendous economic power of the giant industry unions. The effect of such union tactics obviously has been to reduce competition, violating at least the spirit of our national antitrust policy."

At this point the chamber's viewing with alarm becomes self-contradictory. The charge that unions "impose even tougher demands" on small and middle-sized companies means, if it means anything, that the unions are deviating from pattern bargaining, and that the chamber is complaining about the deviation. The assertion is in any event quite unrelated to fact.

The real question is not preserving competition against monopoly but a question of power as between workers and employers. The chamber objects to industry or areawide bargaining, and the NAM to bargaining by national unions, not because it reduces competition among the employers in the sale of their products, or because there should be competition among employees to supply labor cheaply, but because it gives greater bargaining power to labor. That is the issue, and unrelated antitrust questions are brought in simply to confuse it.

Does nationwide, or regional, or pattern bargaining give too much power to labor? I think the answer to that question, as a general question, is unqualifiedly "No." There is no evidence that in any major industry the financial strength or the bargaining power of a union is larger than the financial strength or bargaining power of the employers. Can you compare the United Steelworkers of America, with assets of approximately $20 million, with a single corporation like the United States Steel Corp., with assets of $3 billion, and say that the union has the overwhelming power? Of course not. Does this committee really think that it is necessary to break up the Steelworkers Union into fragments so that the Steel Corp. will not be overpowered by the union during the current negotiations? Of course not.

In its prepared statement, the chamber of commerce asserts that . . . :
". . . industrywide bargaining . . . is a clear-cut illustration of the inequity or double standard in our antitrust laws which prohibits monopolistic combinations on the employer side, but permits comparable power combinations on the union side."

This assertion is sheer nonsense. If there is industrywide bargaining, the industry is by definition acting as a unit, and there is no double standard.

The fact that we have defended industrywide or areawide or pattern bargaining may leave the impression that unions are solely responsible for the establishment of these types of bargaining. However, that is not the case, and we do not want to take credit that is not wholly due us.

Indeed, industrywide or areawide bargaining can never be the sole creation of the union. Under the doctrines of the National Labor Relations Board employers may in appropriate situations bargain jointly if they and the union both so elect. However, an individual employer always has the option to refuse to agree to joint bargaining in the first place; and the further option to withdraw from joint bargaining at appropriate times.

The situation is essentially the same as respects "pattern bargaining," where a leader in the industry negotiates an agreement with the union and the pattern thus established is followed by the other companies in the industry. Unions may have some influence in preserving or extending pattern bargaining, but its creation is essentially due to decisions of management, which, in turn, reflect the economic organization of the particular industry. Let me illustrate.

One industry which is always singled out as an example of pattern bargaining is the steel industry. That is an industry I happen to know something about, since I have the honor to be general counsel of the United Steelworkers of America as well as of the CIO.

The fact is that it was the steel industry, not the union, which initiated the practice of following a pattern in wage movements. The industry follows a pattern not only on wage movements, but on prices, and it has been doing so for many years. Indeed, a disinterested study on wage movements in the steel industry from 1913 to 1932 shows that these wage movements followed a pattern even during those years, long before the union appeared on the scene. This study was made by Mr. George Seltzer, at the University of Chicago, and was financed by a grant from the Rockefeller Foundation. In his study, entitled "Pattern Bargaining and the United Steelworkers," Mr. Seltzer reaches the following conclusions on wage movements during the period 1913–1932:

"They show general agreement in the timing and amount of wage changes throughout the industry. . . . The United States Steel Corp. took the lead in 11 of the 14 general wage changes during this period; no other basic-steel firm assumed the leadership role more than once."

Mr. Seltzer concluded:

"It seems clear that the USA-CIO did not initiate uniformity of wage behavior in the basic-steel industry. This uniformity is rooted in the product and labor market structure of the industry.

"The synchronization of the wage behavior of basic-steel firms is in part a reflection of the larger business strategy prevailing in the industry."

Mr. Seltzer, I should make it clear, was talking about the uniformity of wage movements, rather than about the uniformity of individual wages. While the movement of wages followed a pattern in the steel industry before the establishment of the union, it is also true that the union has substantially contributed to the establishment of wage uniformity—that is, to equal pay for equal work. In the days before the union, wage rates for the same job varied widely not only from plant to plant but within a single plant, and there was little attempt at scientific job evaluation. Now, job evaluation plans jointly operated by the companies and the union seek to insure wage uniformity throughout the basic-steel industry.

Again, before the creation of the union there was a very substantial differential between northern and southern wage rates, and there were other intermediate regional differentials. In successive collective-bargaining contracts negotiated over the years, the union gradually succeeded in eliminating all of these regional wage differentials.

Thus while the union was not responsible for establishing the pattern of wage movements in the industry, it has contributed to establishing a more uniform pattern of wage rates. Frankly, we are quite proud that we have done so. We believe in equal pay for equal work. We believe that steelworkers in the South should receive the same pay as steelworkers in the North. They do the same work, their living costs are the same, and the steel they make sells for the same prices. We do not see why they should not receive the same pay. Or, to go back to an antitrust formulation, we do not believe that the Nation's economic well-being would be promoted by requiring that these steelworkers compete with each other as to who will work more cheaply.

I have no doubt that the same general picture is true of other industries where pattern bargaining prevails. This type of bargaining exists primarily in industries like steel, automobile, meat-packing, rubber, and oil, where one or more large corporations dominate the industry. Long before there were unions in these industries, the dominant corporations in the industry set the pattern both for the prices of the industry's products and for the wages of its employees. This following of a pattern came about as a matter of deliberate choice by the corporations, or because of the structure of the industry, or some mixture of the two. In any event it was not foisted by unions on an unwilling industry.

Today strong national unions exist in nearly all of these industries. It is fortunate that they do. For without them the giant corporations would have a free hand in fixing wages as they saw fit. It is only the existence of powerful unions that has enabled the workers in these industries to get higher wages, secure decent living standards for themselves, and make their contribution to maintaining national purchasing power.

I do not wish, however, to leave any impression that we believe that industrywide or area or pattern bargaining is the only proper type of bargaining, or necessarily the best type in all situations. That is not the case. We are not in favor of any of these types of bargaining, as a general proposition, any more than we are in favor of companywide or of local plant bargaining, or of craft bargaining, or of any of numerous other types or combinations. All of these diverse types of bargaining have emerged as responses to the needs and realities of particular situations. Presumably both industry and management have found them desirable and workable, and certainly there is no indication that any of these various types of collective bargaining has harmed the public interest.

UNIONS ARE ALREADY RESTRICTED

Statement of Andrew J. Biemiller, Member, National Legislative Committee, American Federation of Labor, in Current Antitrust Problems, hearings before Antitrust Subcommittee (Subcommittee No. 5) of the House Committee on the Judiciary, 84th Cong., 1st Sess., 1955, part 3, pp. 2028–2033

The effort to extend antitrust laws to unions is spear-headed by continued references by industry to so-called monopolistic power of unions and to giant unions. This is simply part of a semantic campaign designed to delude some of the public into believing that it might make sense to apply the antitrust laws to union trusts.

It is true that union membership has increased during the past two decades and that the financial position of unions generally has improved. But an examination of union strength and growth must be kept in proper perspective.

The total financial resources of all unions combined has been liberally estimated as perhaps as high as $1 billion. This is a rough estimate made by Prof. Nathan Belfer in his examination of union finances in Trade Union Investment Policy, Industrial and Labor Relations Review, Cornell University, April 1953. But this figure, standing alone, is highly misleading. These financial resources are not under the direction or control of any one organization.

THE CHAIRMAN: Would the fact of the merger of the CIO and the AFL make any difference in your characterization?

MR. BIEMILLER: Not as we see the situation. I am coming right to that.

Organized labor in this country is not centrally controlled. Even when the merger of the American Federation of Labor and the Congress of Industrial Organizations will be completed, the new federation will be made up of more than 145 separate national and international unions which determine their own policies. They in turn are made up of more than 60,000 local unions which are largely autonomous.

The various unions never act as a single unit. Each controls its own finances. The American Federation of Labor, for example, no more controls the treasuries of its affiliated organizations than the United States Chamber of Commerce controls the combined assets of its member corporations.

The federation itself, incidentally, had a financial balance of but $1.5 million at the end of its last fiscal year's operations. Its total receipts for a year to cover all its expenses came to but $5.5 million. This is less than, for example, the Government's expenditures for the management of its Fish and Wildlife Service and it amounts to less than a fifth of the budget for the Weather Bureau. . . .

. . . The strength of unions lies, not in relatively meager treasuries, but rather in their membership.

While a union needs certain income to function, its ability to improve worker living standards is rooted essentially in its members' willingness to act together and, if necessary, to withhold their labor. If legislation is enacted to eliminate or restrict the right of workers concertedly to withhold their labor and peacefully to persuade the public to withdraw its patronage from a particular employer, the union's strength is effectively dissipated even if it has a substantial treasury. . . .

Actually, it is in the absence of a union that there is a monopoly in the employment relationship. Without a union, the workers can hardly increase wages or improve conditions through individual efforts. The employer alone decides. He truly has monopoly power over unorganized workers. It is only with the establishment of a union that workers can take some effective part in determining their conditions of work. . . .

The abuses of which antiunion employers complain, either are already the subject of congressional regulation or are not actually significant abuses.

Those who argue that unions should be brought under the antitrust laws find it easy to utilize such time-worn phrases as "labor monopoly," "racketeering," and "featherbedding." These individuals find it far more difficult to state exactly what union activities constitute such a threat to the free enterprise system that they need to be the subject of specific action by Congress.

We have examined most diligently the recent arguments of those who favor placing unions under the antitrust laws. Frankly, we have found very few specific complaints regarding union conduct and nothing that is at all new.

Among the alleged types of union activity which antilabor spokesmen have mentioned as monopolistic in character are the following:

1. Various types of secondary boycotts.
2. Pressure for the hiring of unnecessary labor.
3. Jurisdictional disputes.
4. Price fixing and control of the market.
5. Opposition to technological improvement.
6. Industrywide bargaining.

What is the status of these issues today? First of all, it should be noted that Congress has seen fit over the opposition of organized labor to write into the Taft-Hartley law a number of provisions dealing with some of these points. The statute, for example, includes specific provisions against activities noted by points 1, 2, and 3.

Not only does the law include these provisions which declare certain union activities to be unfair labor practices subject to Government prosecution through the National Labor Relations Board, but in another section of the law the Congress provided that an injured party could sue for damages from any injuries received as a result of these activities.

Under each of these provisions, in the Taft-Hartley law, action has been taken against unions and union officials. Yet, we find the United States Chamber of Commerce appearing before this committee complaining that the NLRB has not interpreted this law correctly and that Congress should therefore pass a different type of statute. If this were done, it would open the way for certain types of union activity to be punished in three different ways, prosecutions by the NLRB, civil suit for damages, and prosecution by the Department of Justice.

Let me merely point out that organized labor, too, is very dissatisfied with these provisions of the Taft-Hartley law and with the manner in which the NLRB has interpreted them. We, too, believe that Congress should act regarding this problem.

We believe that as the law is now written and interpreted it unfairly penalizes certain union activities. However, we believe that the proper forum in which to argue this is the debate over the merits of the Taft-Hartley law. Merely because the Taft-Hartley law has not operated to the satisfaction of the chamber of commerce is no reason why Congress should pass a completely new law assigning authority to act in these matters to another Government agency whose jurisdiction would overlap and conflict with the functions of the NLRB.

Point four in the campaign against unions concerns so-called price fixing and control of the market through joint action with employers. Organized labor does not advocate collusion of this sort between unions and employers. Instances of such activity are extremely rare. On this issue the Supreme Court has made it quite clear that a union which joins with an employer in collusive action completely loses its immunity to antitrust action. Thus, no further legislation of any sort is needed to bring this type of activity by any union under the antitrust laws.

MR. KEATING: Do you have a reference to a decision which covers that?

MR. BIEMILLER: It is the Allen-Bradley case . . .

The fifth point involves alleged union opposition to technological improvement. It would be difficult today to find a dispute which has arisen as a result of union opposition to technological change as such. The disputes which have arisen over technological improvement rather reflect the union concern over the lack of adequate consideration for workers who may be directly and adversely affected by technological innovations.

The A.F. of L.'s attitude is best expressed by a paragraph in a recent article by President Meany for *Fortune* magazine:

Certainly the trade-union movement does not oppose technological change. There can be no turning back to a negative or shortsighted policy of limiting progress. . . . The answer to technological change lies in smoothing its transitions and cushioning the shocks that attend it. This means, in the immediate sense, the establishment of severance pay, retraining of skills, reorganization of work schedules. These are social costs that industry will have to bear in order to avoid the wasting of human resources—and to avoid our calling on Government to bear these costs if industry fails to do so.

It would be an exceedingly dangerous precedent to give employers by law an absolute right to introduce technological changes regardless of the effect on their workers, with the workers forbidden to take action to protect their own job rights and livelihood.

We believe that careful consideration of the implications of such legislation will convince the Congress against any action to make illegal union efforts to gain severance pay, transfer rights, gradual change, or other measures to ease any adverse social impact on workers of technological innovations.

The sixth item in the list of alleged union abuses, industrywide bargaining, has received thorough discussion in recent years. This discussion has helped to clarify the fact that there are in the United States today very few instances of complete industrywide bargaining. Many cases of so-called industrywide bargaining turn out, upon examination, to involve bargaining for a single large company or for a group of firms in a particular locality or region.

It is often forgotten that both labor and management have to agree on the scope of the bargaining unit. Where bargaining is conducted on an industry basis, this development has been the result of mutual agreement after both parties have weighed its possible effect on all aspects of the bargaining relationship.

It is important to remember that Congress itself has given thorough consideration to the issues involved in industrywide bargaining. In 1947 during the discussion on the Taft-Hartley law by the 80th Congress, a specific proposal to ban industrywide bargaining was rejected.

The American Federation of Labor does not endorse any particular bargaining system. We believe that the national interest is best served if unions and employers are free to choose for themselves the type of bargaining unit that best fits their particular situation. Prohibiting industrywide bargaining by statute would inject the Federal Government further into the framework of collective bargaining and could only lead to disrupting peaceful labor-management relations.

Let me conclude with several summary observations.

Proposals to restrict certain union activities through application of the antitrust laws are not rooted in any demonstration of genuine need for such drastic legislative action. They are rather the reflection of a continuing effort of certain employer groups to use any means possible to carve out areas of union activity from the scope of legitimate activity. . . .

We do not believe the particular minor or occasional activities of unions which certain employers have complained of warrant legislative consideration. But even if they did, a remedy as broad as the application of the antitrust laws is much too far-reaching.

Extension of the antitrust laws to unions would place under a legal cloud many traditional and necessary union activities. In many instances it would undoubtedly cut off the only effective means unions have to protect and aid workers.

The national interest is best served, not by increasing the avenues of legal entanglement for unions, but by minimizing restrictions on unions, for union activity to protect and improve worker status is in the interest of society as a whole. Any possible gain to society from curbing union activities by applying the antitrust laws would be far outweighed by the loss incurred from the stifling of union efforts in behalf of workers.

FREEDOM OF ASSOCIATION OR MONOPOLY?

Testimony of Walter P. Reuther, President, United Automobile Workers, in Labor-Management Relations, hearings before the House Committee on Education and Labor, 83d Cong., 1st Sess., 1953, part 3, pp. 1026–1029

MR. GWINN: I have never been able to see how you arrive at what a fair wage is in a monopolistic situation where you control completely the worker and the number of them.

MR. REUTHER: We do not control the workers at all, and I do not control a single worker in America. What do you mean about that?

MR. GWINN: What percentage of the General Motors workers are in your union? . . .

MR. REUTHER: I would say that in the plants under contract, probably 95 percent.

MR. GWINN: For all practical purposes, then, you are a monopoly, an absolute monopoly.

MR. REUTHER: Would a Congressman be a monopoly if 95 percent of the people in his district voted for him? Would that make you a monopoly?

MR. GWINN: I would like to have that experience, and I would not know what to say about it.

MR. REUTHER: We have had that experience, and we have had 95 percent of the General Motors workers vote for us, and that does not make us a monopoly.

MR. GWINN: What is a monopoly except control of the asset or the commodity or the service?

MR. REUTHER: But no one has control over anybody, I don't control a single General Motors worker. They have much more control over me than I have over them. I am obligated to do what they tell me to do, but they are not obligated to do what I tell them to do. . . .

MR. GWINN: It would not make any difference whether you personally were controlling them or whether the union was controlling them. It is obvious, is it not, Mr. Reuther, that when 95 percent of the workers in the automobile industry are united as one, that for all practical purposes, it is a monopoly of the service or the working forces in that industry?

MR. REUTHER: Well, the purpose of collective bargaining is to facilitate workers acting together. Obviously, if you have them all acting together, that is collective bargaining and that is not a monopoly. How else would you do it?

MR. GWINN: Well, it seems to me when you get to the point where you have 95 percent of all the workers operating as a unit to get what they want, that you have no free market left and, therefore, you have no free choice.

You talked a good deal about freedom this morning, and I was very much interested in your devotion to freedom. If you take 95 percent of the workers together, is the employer free to do anything except what those 95 percent operating together demand of him?

MR. REUTHER: He surely is free, and he is free to say, 'No," and they often say "No."

MR. GWINN: Well, he certainly is not free to go into the market and find other workers, is he?

MR. REUTHER: Well, you see, labor is not a commodity which you go and shop for in the free market place. Labor is something different than a commodity, and if you want to give American labor the status of another commodity you can go out and shop for on the free market place, you have missed the whole point. We are trying to develop collective bargaining, to advance.

MR. GWINN: No; it seems to me it is quite offensive to have a monopoly of human flesh, and I think that they are different. When you have 95 percent of all the workers united together so that neither the employer can find any free market at all for other workers and the employer has no choice at all, nor the man who is not a member of the union has any choice but to wait on what the 95 percent do, then you have a tight, fierce, absolutely decisive monopoly in the situation. This free collective bargaining that you talk about under those circumstances cannot exist, can it?

MR. REUTHER: Well, the workers have a right through the democratic decisions which they make to withhold their labor power, and the management has a right to withhold their job opportunities.

They can say, "O.K., we won't operate the plant under your conditions, and you won't work under our conditions," and so you have got the free play of two economic forces. Now, the only substitute for that, and the only substitute for the free play of economic forces in those circumstances is to have the Government make the decision; and when we start traveling that road, we are on the way to the destruction of everything that we are trying to defend in the struggle against communism.

I say you cannot substitute a Government decision for a decision which of necessity ought to be a voluntary one made between two parties.

Now, the General Motors Corp. does not even have to talk to anybody. They have got a small board of directors, and they make a decision, and that is their decision. They are not divided, and it is not 95 percent. It is 100 percent. They make a decision to commit their economic force in the implementation of a certain policy decision, and the union challenges that through the decision of the workers. We are no more of a monopoly in the exercise of our power than they are, and they are not a monopoly in that sense.

The whole concept of monopoly is where you get into the field where you are carrying out practices which are unethical and which are deliberately directed toward the restraint of free trade and free competition. We are not doing that.

MR. GWENN: That is all that we are talking about now, and where is the free competition in this whole business?

MR. REUTHER: The competition is between the General Motors Corp. and its workers at the collective-bargaining table. That is where the competition is. And if you do not think that there is intense competition, you ought to sit down and try to get more out of these big corporations. I have had that experience, and it is not easy.

If you think they have abdicated their power, and if you think they have surrendered, if you think that they are easily pushed around in the face of this powerful force you are talking about, I wish we could get some of the magic you think we have got, because we could use it at times.

MR. GWINN: It seems to me by the very definition of the terms, you have eliminated all choice and all freedom when you unify all of your forces, and you certainly effect a monopoly situation on all the competitors of General Motors when you monopolize, in collective bargaining, the bargaining table, and also have in your force the total labor force under command. I do not see how you can see it differently.

MR. REUTHER: You just treat labor as a commodity, and labor is not a commodity. Labor is people.

MR. GWINN: I know; that is an old story, and I do not treat it as a commodity. I want to make it free, and I am talking about freemen and not a commodity. That is what we are trying to get at here, so that we will have some basis for arriving at what is a fair wage or what is a fair price. The public is interested in this.

MR. REUTHER: Sure. But before we had strong unions, Congressman, the employer by arbitrary decisions decided the level of wages, and he just said, "This is it," and the worker either took it or went hungry. It was only when we developed unions and we began to make collective bargaining work that the individual worker, in conjunction with his fellow worker, began to be able to counteract the arbitrary economic decisions made by the employer. And at the point where the worker develops an economic strength comparable or at least sufficiently strong to begin to get a measure of justice, you come up and say, "It is a monopoly."

UNION COULD CONTROL PRODUCTION, MANUFACTURER SAYS

From the Hosiery Worker, published by the American Federation of Hosiery Workers, April, 1952

Reading, Pa.—The [American Federation of Hosiery Workers] can work effectively against the evil of overproduction if it is able to organize from 80 to 100 per cent of the industry, Samuel F. Rubin, President of the Full Fashioned Hosiery Manufacturers of America, Inc., said in his address to the Convention here this month.

Rubin pointed out that there is no legal way for manufacturers to control inventories and production. Any attempt by manufacturers to join together to accomplish this end is as illegal as collaboration to fix prices. But the Union in its contractual agreements with the manufacturers could control production if it were dominant in the industry and thus function to restore stability to this badly overproduced industry.

He hailed the relations between the American Federation of Hosiery Workers and the Full Fashioned Hosiery Manufacturers of America, Inc., as a triumph of peaceful collective bargaining. . . .

THE WAGE PROBLEM IN TEXTILES

From Textiles: Crisis for America—A Special Report, Textile Labor, vol. 17, September, 1956, pp. 21–22

. . . By what law of man or nature must a worker who sweeps lint be worth little more than half the pay of a worker who sweeps iron-fillings?

The solution of the wage problem is so simple that we hesitate to put it down. Let's insist, first, that it has nothing to do with the nature of the textile industry or the profit-margins of the employers; nor does it concern the ferocious competition in the textile markets.

The wage problem can be solved by the simplest of all methods—union organization. And this, in turn, would help no end to cure the ills. . . . Here's why:

If textile workers were 100% unionized, or close to it, they'd submit the same basic proposals to all employers in each division. No employer could complain that he was being penalized unfairly.

Would this constitute a labor-management "conspiracy" against the consumer, as some intellectuals argue? Not at all. [Just 55¢ added to the price of a $50 man's suit would bring average pay of woolen and worsted workers up to $1.97 an hour, the national standard in manufacturing. What's inflationary about that? Only 25¢ added to the price of a $20 dress would raise the average hourly pay of cotton-rayon workers to the same $1.97 level. Is this too great a burden to place on the consumer?]

Would this eliminate competition? Not at all. Though basic wages would be uniform, there would be an endless variety of differences based upon manhour output, the use of new and better machinery and processes.

Would this hurt the employers? Not at all. It would help them. To put it as bluntly as possible, a mill margin of 2% on a unit cost of $1 is 2¢; a mill margin of 2% on a unit cost of $2 is 4¢. If textile wages are doubled, the employers would be better off and the consumer would hardly notice the difference.

But no one employer—even now—can himself establish a new and higher wage pattern. It can be done only if all employers separately agree to union proposals.

9: The Grievance Procedure

The grievance procedure is to most unionists the heart of collective bargaining. The day-to-day applications of the terms of the agreement determine whether a person receives the wage rate to which he is entitled, is given first refusal of a job opening to which his seniority gives him claim, is not laid off out of turn, can call his foreman to account for discriminatory treatment or unwarranted discipline. Any "gripe" over his treatment can have its outlet in a recognized process in which his union representative takes the matter up with his supervisor. If the issue is unresolved at this stage and if the union believes his complaint is well founded, management people at several higher levels can be required to reexamine the matter in conferences with union officials. If these bilateral discussions fail to produce agreement on whether the employee has been fairly treated, the union may demand arbitration. For John Jones, the man at the bench, the grievance process is the subject's right to dispute the king; it is the means by which management's exercise of power can be made reasonable and responsible. The cases that follow illustrate how this process operates.

THE GRIEVANCE PROCESS

Excerpts from Making Grievance Procedure Work Successfully, handbook of District 50, United Mine Workers, 1945

We have watched three different types of grievance committees. One is the blustering, threatening type that goes in with an obvious chip on its shoulder and immediately antagonizes the management. Very often its attitude forces the management into a fight, even though the case is reasonable.

Another is the timid, fearful type which presents its case as though it were begging some favor from the supervisor. Its meetings with management are reminiscent of the days of the employee representation plans and the other company unions. Fearful of incurring the displeasure of the management, it accepts the company's answer without question or argument.

The third type is polite but firm. It presents its case courteously and calmly. It neither cowers before the superintendent nor does it threaten to throw him out the window. It doesn't beg favors but asks for justice. It has an air about

it of knowing that it is right and it lets the superintendent know that it intends
to fight the case until justice is done.

Which type of Committee do you think is most likely to be successful?
Which type do you think wins the respect of management? Which type is
practicing real collective bargaining? Which type represents your Local Union?

YOUR AGREEMENT

Before you can interpret your agreement or know whether a proper grievance exists, you must know your contract. Become thoroughly familiar with it;
know what your rights and what your limitations are. Print or mimeograph
enough copies for a full distribution to the membership. Every officer, shop
steward, and member of the grievance committee, at least, should have a copy.

There is no such thing as a standard contract for all our diversified industries.
Each agreement has been negotiated with a view toward obtaining as much as
possible for the workers in their own field. One feature in our contracts is,
however, standard: the section on adjusting disputes and grievances. Since this
is the section which concerns us, we are printing it here:

ADJUSTMENT OF GRIEVANCES

Should any difference arise between the Company and the Union, or its
members, as to the meaning and application of this agreement, or should
any local trouble of any kind arise in any plant, there shall be no suspension of work on account of such differences but an earnest effort shall be
made to settle such differences immediately in the following manner:

First, between the aggrieved employee and the foreman of the depart-
men involved. The department steward may accompany the aggrieved
employee;

Second, between a member or members of the Grievance Committee,
designated by the Union, and the foreman or superintendent of the department;

Third, between a member or members of the Grievance Committee,
designated by the Union, and the general superintendent or manager of
the work or his designated assistant;

Fourth, between the representatives of the National organization of the
Union and the representatives of the executives of the Company; and

Fifth, in the event the dispute shall not have been satisfactorily settled,
the matter shall then be appealed to an impartial umpire to be appointed
by mutual agreement of the parties hereto. The decision of the umpire
shall be final. The expenses and salary incident to the services of the
umpire shall be paid jointly by the Company and the Union.

The need for following each step set forth in your agreement must be
stressed. Skipping a single step may prove costly. Although technical interpretations of the letter of the agreement are troublesome and undesirable because
they lead only to frequent friction between the company and the union,
nevertheless there are certain parts of the contract which must be carefully
followed.

The steps for adjustment of grievances is such a part of the contract because all remedies must be exhausted under the provisions of the agreement before further action can be taken.

GRIEVANCE MACHINERY

We suggest that your grievance machinery consist of shop stewards and the general grievance committee.

Shop Steward. The shop steward is elected by the workers in the department, division, or job. In addition to assisting with grievances, he should be responsible for the collection of dues in the particular department which he serves as steward. It is his duty to try to settle disputes which arise on the job when a worker is unable to reach a satisfactory agreement with his foreman. All grievances presented to him for adjustment must be written out in full on the grievance report. If he is unable to secure a settlement of the grievance, he should report it to the general grievance committee for further action.

General Grievance Committee. The general grievance committee usually consists of four members with the president of the local union serving ex-officio. The general grievance committee and the company's representatives should hold regular meetings. The local union should present its facts by means of the record on the grievance report and its witnesses. Both sides should be permitted to ask questions. If an agreement can be reached, it should be reduced to writing and signed by both parties.

If no agreement can be reached, the general grievance committee and the union membership should carefully consider the question of whether or not to appeal to an impartial umpire. This step should only be taken if the committee and membership feel confident that the grievance is right and just and the union's case is sufficiently strong to outweigh the arguments advanced by the company. In such case, consult your regional director of District 50 and ask that a field representative be assigned to the case.

Impartial Umpire. If it is decided to appeal the case to an impartial umpire, great care must be taken to secure the fairest possible arbitrator. Care should be taken to secure a person who will judge the case according to logic and justice and not according to technicalities. Judges and lawyers, even though noted for liberal opinions, too often will base their opinions on legal interpretations of the agreement and not necessarily according to what is fair to the aggrieved employee. Make sure, that the person selected has no connections with the company.

A mediator from the United States Department of Labor can usually be depended upon for an honest decision.

THE CASE OF A WILDCAT STRIKE

Ford Motor Company and UAW-CIO, Opinion A-151, 1944

HARRY SHULMAN, UMPIRE

The Chairman of the Flat Rock Plant Committee was given a disciplinary layoff of two weeks. As soon as this became known, a stoppage of work shut the plant down on September 20, 1944. Efforts to persuade the men to return to work proved unavailing. As a final means of effecting a resumption of work, the parties agreed to waive the several steps of the grievance procedure and to bring directly to the Umpire the case of the Plant Chairman and the other employee who was involved in the incident. A hearing at the Umpire's office was scheduled for October 3rd. But on September 30th, the plant went down again for a reason related to the Chairman's disciplinary penalty. The plant was still down on October 3rd when the parties appeared for the hearing, and is still down now.

The Company objected to the holding of the hearing while the employees were on strike. It objected, further, to the consideration of the case at all in the expedited manner. It urged that the special agreement to waive the prior steps of the grievance procedure was made for the purpose of restoring production in the plant; that in stopping work on September 30th and continuing the stoppage thereafter, the men destroyed the consideration for the agreement and abandoned the scheduled procedure.

These positions must be sustained. The current stoppage, like its predecessor, is, of course, completely unauthorized, in defiance of the Union's regularly constituted leadership, in violation of the Constitution and By-laws of both the International and the Local, and in disregard of the no-strike pledge. These features should surely condemn the stoppage in the mind of any thinking worker. But the feature bearing more closely upon the Umpire's function is the fact that the stoppage is an outright breach of the parties' Agreement.

When a Union enters a plant, one of its very first concerns is the establishment of a grievance procedure. For the grievance procedure is fundamental in civilized collective bargaining. A Union and its members can choose, if they like, to settle each day to day dispute by strike action. They could stop work every time a supervisor or other representative of management did something that they deemed improper. But union men long ago recognized that this method of protest would destroy the Union and their own economy. For this method would necessitate a stoppage nearly every day. Now workers live by production. Strikes are costly to workers as they are to management. In normal times an occasional, deliberate test of strength by strikes on matters of major importance may be necessary and desirable. The anticipated victory is then deemed to be worthy of the cost. But wanton and needless use of the strike weapon weakens the weapon itself, casts undue burden on the workers, and threatens to destroy their organization.

The workers who shed their blood and whose families suffered the pain of hunger and privation in order to establish the right of collective bargaining, those workers saw these dangers and rejected this anarchistic method. They asked for a just and civilized reign of order, the collective agreement which states the rights and obligations of the parties for its duration and establishes a regular procedure for their enforcement. They cherished the strike weapon for effective use in crises, when, for example, negotiations for a new contract failed. Even then they sought to preserve the strength of that weapon by permitting its use only after deliberate consideration and decision made by the Union in prescribed ways. Provisions of union constitutions and by-laws state in careful detail how and when authorized strike action is to be taken.

The Ford contract is true to this tradition. It established a grievance procedure which insures final determination in an impartial manner. And it provides that, during its term, the grievance procedure, not strikes or interruptions of production, shall be employed for the adjustment of grievances. This is the rule of order for which generations of working men have struggled. They understood and appreciated it. It should be clearly understood and appreciated now.

It is, of course, entirely obvious that when parties sign a collective agreement, they fully expect that disputes will arise as to its interpretation and application from day to day. That is precisely why the grievance procedure was established. It is the orderly, economic procedure prescribed for those situations in which a violation of agreement is alleged. The obligation to employ this procedure rather than the work stoppage is a solemn contractual obligation which law and honor require to be observed. To employ the stoppage when the grievance procedure is available is to abandon the contract. In no case is the grievance procedure more effective and adequate than in the case of an allegedly improper disciplinary penalty. The aggrieved employee can be fully compensated; and no other employee need suffer any loss. There is no reason for imposing an economic loss on hundreds of employees for the purpose of securing illegally to one of them that which he can get in an orderly, legal manner without loss to any employee.

ROLE OF THE UNION COMMITTEEMAN

Ford Motor Company and UAW-CIO, Opinion A-116, 1944

HARRY SHULMAN, UMPIRE

No committeeman or other union officer is entitled to instruct employees to disobey Supervision's orders, no matter how strongly he may believe that the orders are in violation of agreement. If he believes that an improper order has been issued, his course is to take the matter up with Supervision and seek to effect an adjustment. Failing to effect an adjustment, he may file a grievance. But he may not tell the employee to disregard the order.

The employee himself must also normally obey the order, even though he thinks it improper. His remedy is prescribed in the grievance procedure. He may not take it on himself to disobey. To be sure, one can conceive of improper orders which need not be obeyed. An employee is not expected to obey an order to do that which would be criminal or otherwise unlawful. He may refuse to obey an improper order which involves an unusual health hazard or other serious sacrifice. But in the absence of such justifying factors, he may not refuse to obey merely because the order violates some right of his under the Contract. The remedy under the Contract for violation of right lies in the grievance procedure and only in the grievance procedure. To refuse obedience because of a claimed contract violation would be to substitute individual action for collective bargaining and to replace the grievance procedure with extra-contractual methods. And such must be the advice of the committeeman, if he gives advice to employees. His advice must be that the safe and proper method is to obey Supervision's instructions and to seek correction and redress through the grievance procedure.

Some men apparently think that when a violation of contract seems clear, the employee may refuse to obey and thus resort to self-help rather than the grievance procedure. That is an erroneous point of view. In the first place, what appears to one party to be a clear violation may not seem so at all to the other party. Neither party can be the final judge as to whether the Contract has been violated. The determination of that issue rests in collective negotiation through the grievance procedure. But in the second place, and more important, the grievance procedure is prescribed in the Contract precisely because the parties anticipated that there would be claims of violations which would require adjustment. That procedure is prescribed for all grievances, not merely for doubtful ones. Nothing in the Contract even suggests the idea that only doubtful violations need be processed through the grievance procedure and that clear violations can be resisted through individual self-help. The only difference between a "clear" violation and a "doubtful" one is that the former makes a clear grievance and the latter a doubtful one. But both must be handled in the regular prescribed manner.

Some men apparently think also that the problems here involved are evils incident to private profit enterprise. That, too, is a totally mistaken view, as a moment's reflection will show. The problems of adjustment with which we are concerned under the Contract are problems which arise and require adjustment in the management of an enterprise under any form of economic or social organization. Any enterprise—whether it be a privately owned plant, a governmentally operated unit, a consumer's cooperative, a social club, or a trade union—any enterprise in a capitalist or a socialist economy, requires persons with authority and responsibility to keep the enterprise running. In any such enterprise there is need for equality of treatment, regularity of procedure, and adjustment of conflicting claims of individuals. In any industrial plant, whatever may be the form of the political or economic organization in which it exists, problems are bound to arise as to the method of making promotions, the assignment of tasks to individuals, the choice of shifts, the maintenance of discipline, the rates of production and remuneration, and the various other matters which are handled through the grievance procedure.

These are not incidents peculiar to private enterprise. They are incidents of human organization in any form of society. On a lesser scale, similar problems exist in every family: who shall do the dishes, who shall mow the lawn, where to go on a Sunday, what movie to see, what is a reasonable spending allowance for husband or daughter, how much to pay for a new hat, and so on. The operation of the Union itself presents problems requiring adjustment quite similar to those involved in the operation of the Company—problems not only in the relations of the Union to its own employees but also in the relations between the members of the Union. Anyone familiar with seniority problems knows that the conflict of desires within the Union are quite comparable to those between the Union and the Company. And any active manner of Local 600 knows that the frictions and conflicts within a large Union may be as numerous and difficult as those between the Union and the Company. Such "disputes" are not necessarily evils. They are the normal characteristics of human society which both arise from, and create the occasion for, the exercise of human intelligence. And the grievance procedure is the orderly, effective and democratic way of adjusting such disputes within the framework of the collective labor agreement. It is the substitute of civilized collective bargaining for jungle warfare.

But an industrial plant is not a debating society. Its object is production. When a controversy arises, production cannot wait for exhaustion of the grievance procedure. While that procedure is being pursued, production must go on. And some one must have the authority to direct the manner in which it is to go on until the controversy is settled. That authority is vested in Supervision. It must be vested there because the responsibility for production is also vested there; and responsibility must be accompanied by authority. It is fairly vested there because the grievance procedure is capable of adequately recompensing employees for abuse of authority by Supervision.

It should be definitely understood, then, that a committeeman has no authority to direct or advise an employee to disobey Supervision's instructions; that his authority is expressed in the duty to take the matter up with Supervision and seek an adjustment through negotiations and the grievance procedure; that an employee must obey Supervision's instructions pending the negotiations or the processing of his grievance, except only in the rare case where obedience would involve an unusual health hazard or similar sacrifice; and that disobedience by the employee, or counsel of disobedience by a committeeman, is proper cause for disciplinary penalty. . . .

DISCHARGE OF A UNION STEWARD

Green River Steel Corporation and United Steelworkers, Local 4959, 25 LA 774, 1955

JOHN F. SEMBROWER, ARBITRATOR

SUBMISSION

The discharge on Sept. 9, 1955, of Joseph C. Holland, at that time a second helper on furnace No. 4 working the 12 midnight to 8 A.M. shift, under an accusation of violating Article XIII, the no-strike clause of the Agreement entered into by the parties on Oct. 1, 1954, and still in full force and effect, came before the undersigned as sole arbitrator pursuant to Step 5 of the Grievance Procedure, Article VIII, Sec. 3.

The arbitrator conducted a hearing on Dec. 9, 1955, at Owensboro, Ky., with Keith C. Reese, Esq., representing the Union, and Frank A. Logan, Esq.; Fred B. Redwine, Esq. and Jack A. Keenan, secretary and personnel director, representing the Company.

Although there is no sharp disagreement between the parties as to the physical occurrences surrounding the discharge of Joseph C. Holland, about the only fact on which there is no dispute whatever is that he was discharged on Sept. 9, 1955, terminating an employment which had begun on July 6, 1953, and was without reprimands or other blemishes on his employment record. It is necessary for the arbitrator to make a number of findings of fact as to the collateral matters, based upon listening to and observing the demeanor of the witnesses as they gave testimony which was recorded in shorthand and transcribed.

There was tension in the plant on the night of Sept. 8–9, 1955. Several unauthorized strikes had occurred in the recent past (Tr. 39) *, and the foreman, known in this plant as a melter, one Len Norcia, was so apprehensive that at 1 A.M. he had telephoned the general superintendent, Robert Spence, that trouble was brewing (Tr. 29). An employee, Paul Lott, a motor inspector, early in the shift had exchanged sharp words with Norcia when the latter told him to leave the chemical laboratory, to which it appeared that employees frequently repaired during breaks in their work (Tr. 3). Lott had filed a grievance against Norcia (Tr. 36). Soon after the grievant, Holland, reported to work, a fellow employee, Farmer, told him of the incident involving Lott (Tr. 3), and asked him what he was going to do about it. Holland told Farmer that he was going to "stay out of it," since he had "enough trouble of his own" and Lott was not in his department.

Holland testified (Tr. 5) that Farmer told him at 1 or 1:15 A.M. that "the guys were fed up with how things had been going and that a strike would be in order" (Tr. 4). Holland related that he stuck to his job (Tr. 4) which was interrupted when his glove caught fire, and he went for another. Upon his return he was confronted by Norcia, who asked him where he had been and, by implication at least, criticized him.

At 6:20 A.M., according to Holland's testimony, the "heat" in his furnace had been completed, and as he went for a drink of water, four employees gathered at No. 3 Furnace—Bratcher, Umbreit, Royal and Keller—called him over (Tr. 5) and asked him if he had heard the "rumors" of an impending strike. They asked Holland what he thought of it (Tr. 4), and Holland testified: "I told them all I knew was what Farmer had told me—that I had been busy all night." Holland testified on direct and cross examination that Royal spoke so loudly and animatedly that he could not get in any other remarks (Tr. 5, 10). He was aware that if the men walked out they would be violating the terms of the contract (Tr. 10), and he testified that he did not agree with them (Tr. 10), but on the other hand he didn't feel that the had the opportunity to raise his voice against it (Tr. 10).

Holland felt that Norcia was "watching him like a hawk" (Tr. 10), and he testified that Norcia passed by the group at No. 3 Furnace and said something

* Editor's note: References are to the verbatim transcript of the hearings.

he did not hear (Tr. 5). Then Norcia returned at 6:30 A.M. and said to Holland: "I am sending you home, and he didn't say why" (Tr. 5). Holland's first impulse was to follow Norcia into the office for a talk (Tr. 5), but instead he went to his furnace, picked up his lunch bucket, and headed for the clocks. He heard Norcia call after him (Tr. 5), "Where are you going?" To the answer, "Home; you sent me home," Norcia replied: "Can't a guy get hot once in a while? How about coming back to work?" Holland replied, "No, you sent me home so I am going home" (Tr. 5).

Holland clocked out and walked to his automobile (Tr. 6), and looked back as he drove away, seeing the four other employees walking out after him. He paused at a parking lot near the mill, and the others caught up. Holland testified on direct examination that, "I didn't say much because due to my trouble, my mind was a bit hazy as to the best action for them to take." At about 7:15 A.M., the little group saw the automobile of Robert Washburn, Union representative, and Local President Savu, coming over the hill as they hurried to the scene after receiving a telephone call from the plant superintendent. "Mr. Washburn told me to direct the guys in to work," Holland testified (Tr. 7), and he did so, urging the employees arriving for the 8 A.M. shift to go on in.

A striking aspect of Norcia's version of the incident was his testimony that during the rumors of a strike, and at one time when the whole crew was at No. 3 Furnace and he (Norcia) "told Holland and Farmer that Lott had a grievance filed against me (Norcia) and to let it go to see how it came out, Holland kept quiet." (Tr. 36) On cross examination he elaborated: "I said I didn't hear him (Holland) say a word. He wouldn't talk to me."

Norcia was suspicious of Holland: "Since I knew a strike was coming on, I figured he might be in it." (Tr. 39) Asked why he thought so when he had not heard Holland say a word, Norcia testified, "Holland had a better record on my turn, and I figure he felt if he could get rid of me and get together the melters, the slate would be clean." By way of explanation as to why he pursued Holland and asked him to return to the job, Norcia testified: "Well as Washburn said before that I was an awful mean fellow up there. He has had everybody trying to believe it and I was trying to eliminate that idea." (Tr. 38) Norcia also testified that Holland "hollered to the fellows, 'let's go,' and motioned his arm." (Tr. 37)

This incident also was described by two of the men in the cluster at No. 3 Furnace. Roland Umbreit, first helper and a candid witness who testified that he did not believe in walkout strikes and had told Farmer that he could not leave his furnace charged with steel, related that Farmer, not Holland, was the instigator and that he and the others were trying "to get Farmer not to walk out" (Tr. 20). He testified that Holland's contribution to the discussion was to "relate the story of the glove" (Tr. 20, 22), and "that was all." Clyde Ford, who was discharged after the walkout and no longer works for the Company, said Farmer was the instigator. Neither Ford nor Umbreit saw Holland make any signs or say anything beckoning the others to follow him. (Tr. 23, 24)

As to the reason for the discharge of Holland, Norcia testified (Tr. 39) that he sent him home because: "I figured . . . he wasn't working and because he was instigating the strike. I could kill two birds with one stone." But Jack A. Keenan, the personnel director, answered categorically (Tr. 44) that Holland was discharged because he had violated Article 13. He testified (Tr. 45) that Norcia "didn't state the reason for sending Mr. Holland home was for agitating a strike," but "for not performing his duties." However, Mr. Keenan left no doubt whatever that the reason for Holland's discharge was the alleged violation of Article 13. (Tr. 45)

There was considerable confusion over whether Holland was, in fact, the steward on the shift. Under direct questioning (Tr. 17), Holland testified that, although he appeared on the list of Stewards for D turn, he was not the steward on that particular shift. On cross examination, he acknowledged that there was no other steward on duty and that the one who would have so functioned, one Garner, had not been on duty for upwards of four months. Holland indicated clearly that he thought of himself as a steward: "I did my duty as a member of the union and an employee of Green River Steel to try to settle things before real trouble started." (Tr. 18) He agreed (Tr. 9) that certain employees in his department or area were to tell him about any difficulty.

On direct examination, Holland described a steward's duties: "A shop steward's duty is to take the grief and headache off supervision; to try to work out little troubles before they amount to something big; to more or less help the company run a smooth operation." (Tr. 9) On cross examination he was asked: "You know as a shop steward they recognized you knew that" (i.e. a walkout would be violating the terms of the contract)? (Tr. 10) He did not deny then that he was a steward, but answered: "I suppose so. I was busy working a heat and you have to stay there and work it and you can't be running off unless it is important."

Farmer, in relating Lott's trouble with Norcia to Holland, appeared to regard Holland as steward, and Holland corrected him only to say that Lott was under the jurisdiction of a steward in another department. Umbreit testified (Tr. 23): "Well, I thought Holland was a steward," although he did say that matters often were taken up with Richardson, the Union vice-president, and that "We weren't putting too much faith in a steward at that time." (Tr. 23) Norcia thought Holland was a steward; "I thought he was and everybody else thought he was." (Tr. 41) Tony Brown, the assistant personnel director, acknowledged that Holland was listed on a memorandum of Aug. 29, 1955, from the Union to the Company (Joint Exhibit #2) as steward on D turn, whereas Garner was steward on C turn of which Norcia was the foreman. But he testified (Tr. 48) that the Company regarded the men listed as stewards and union officials.

The following is the only citation from the Agreement made by either party:

ARTICLE XIII—STRIKES PROHIBITED

The employees, the Union, its officers, agents and members agree that so long as this Agreement is in effect, there shall be no strikes, sitdowns, slow-downs, stoppages of work or other interruption or impeding of production, and they will not otherwise permit, engage in, countenance, authorize, instigate, aid or condone such acts. The Company reserves the right to provisional discharge of any employee or employees who violate the provisions of this Article, and agrees that upon such discharge of such employee or employees, it will provide to a Union representative a list of names, check numbers and addresses of employees whom the Company has so discharged.

DISCUSSION

In view of the foregoing summary of the testimony, the following facts emerge:

Holland was discharged, not for failure to do his work, as some of the foreman's testimony seems to indicate, but clearly because of an alleged violation of Article XIII. This was the ground assigned by the Company and carried through Step 4 of the Grievance Procedure, although the personnel manager admits (Tr. 45) that the foreman himself never assigned this ground, and Norcia himself testified that in sending Holland home he was killing "two birds with one stone." (Tr. 39)

Holland's errors, if errors they were, were of omission rather than commission. An employee with a clean record theretofore, he seemed to have determined to try to stay clear of the difficulty swirling around him. His fellow employees were tugging at him on the one hand, and his foreman on the other. The foreman was overwrought, perhaps entirely justifiably, by a gnawing anxiety that there was a covert gathering of forces against him. This undoubtedly was heightened by his consciousness of past criticism of his leadership (Tr. 38). Norcia probably did "watch Holland like a hawk," as Holland testified, and alternately he tried to be stern, as when he made issues of Holland's absence from his furnace, and solicitous, as when he almost pleaded with Holland to intervene on his behalf with the men and to let the Lott grievance take its course, and then urged Holland to disregard his go-home order and to return to the job. Indeed, it was Holland's very silence and refusal to intervene that seemed to disturb his foreman most. This does not make out a case for discharge unless something is added by way of a duty upon Holland to act affirmatively rather than passively. Only Norcia's uncorroborated testimony says that Holland tried to lead the men out with him.

It may not be seriously argued that since the foreman asked Holland to return to the job, Holland never actually was sent home. An order from one's supervisor is not to be taken lightly, and had Holland refused to go home in the first place, he would have been insubordinate and in violation of the Contract. Holland had the right to take the order to go home at face value. But the crucial question remains whether Holland was, in fact, the steward on this shift, and if so, whether this imposed affirmative duties upon him. As to the first issue, it seems clear that ostensibly he was the steward. Technically Holland may not have been the steward on this particular shift, but he had color of being so by virtue of his presence on the list of stewards, the lack of clear-cut understanding as to whether stewards were qualified as such or just for shifts, plus the fact that no other steward was on the job at the time. Holland's own testimony is illuminating on this point. He talked like the steward; in his job he did nothing to inform others that he was not the steward or to point out who was the Union's representative in the plant that night if he was not. To all intents and purposes, it appears that he was the steward and we must so regard him.

Having crossed that bridge, we now may inquire whether, as steward, Holland had a status which made mere inaction culpable in itself. In the development of labor relations the post of steward has become one of recognized importance, dignity and responsibility. "Moreover, the occurrence of a work stoppage, whether sanctioned, or directed or not, imposes an affirmative obligation on the part of the Union (through its officers) to see that the employees involved go back to work," said the arbitrator in 18 L.A. 919, Canadian Gen. Electric Co. Such views are frequently expressed by arbitrators, and increasingly so.

Here the Union fully recognized this responsibility, as amply indicated by Messrs. Washburn and Savu literally jumping from their beds in the dawn and rushing to the scene, their only complaint being that the plant superintendent had not apprised them of the situation sooner. ("I felt they had let it go on all night without calling us then instead of waiting until morning." Mr. Washburn (Tr. 29).) Mr. Washburn testified (Tr. 34) that after he arrived, "We definitely told Holland and Lott in no uncertain terms they were jeopardizing the jobs of the other men and themselves and we directed the boys to see that they reported for work."

To Holland's credit, perhaps, he did so without demurrer, when Washburn showed him the course to follow. But in contrast with the decisive action of his union officials, Holland's shortcomings are all too apparent. Apparently at first he tried to ignore the situation entirely. According to Umbreit, in his testimony on behalf of Holland, he and the other employees at No. 3 Furnace were trying to dissuade Farmer from walking out when they called Holland over. What did he contribute but to tell of his own recent unpleasant experience with the foreman over his flaming glove, which hardly was oil to spread on the troubled water? Holland complained that he did not "have the opportunity" to counter the arguments of Royal, who was urging a walkout, so while he opposed it he did so silently. Finally, after he had been sent home and was across the road with the men who had walked off the job, Holland testified that "I didn't say much because due to my trouble my mind was a bit hazy as to the best action for them to take." It took Mr. Washburn to show him the way; that it was to urge the men to the job and back to work, which to be sure, he then followed. Holland gave an acceptable definition of the steward's role (Tr. 9), but he failed to back it up with action.

In mitigation of Holland's conduct, it may be said that he may have been distracted by harassment which preoccupied him with "his own troubles." The foreman had a vague idea of what he might expect from a steward in helping to hold the situation in line, but he never really presented it squarely and forthrightly to Holland. Finally, the foreman hopelessly confused the issue by ordering Holland home for an offense of not doing his work, which was discarded as the basis for the discharge in favor of a charge of violation of Article XIII. In all kindness, it may be pointed out that neither the foreman nor the steward precipitated into this tense situation that was fraught with so many serious consequences was a man of long experience in his paricular role.

Discharge is the capital penalty of employer-employee relations, and it is fundamental to all legal systems that such charges must be specific and precise. The case for discharge is not made out here, but on the other hand, Holland is not blameless. He has lost wages which may be considered a penalty and a hard-earned lesson. As an employee with a theretofore unblemished record and a union officer who knew the definition of his role if not their application, he deserves the chance of a restoration of his job with full seniority, but without back pay.

AWARD

Accordingly, the Award is that Joseph C. Holland is to be restored immediately to his job as a second helper with full seniority rights including the period of his discharge, and he is not to receive back pay.

THE CASE OF THE LADY IN RED SLACKS

Ford Motor Company and UAW-CIO, Opinion A-117, 1944

HARRY SHULMAN, UMPIRE

A, a Highland Park employee, was reprimanded and docked one half hour because she wore slacks described as bright red in color. The objection was to the color, not to the slacks; the girls are required to wear slacks. And the objection is based on the safety and production hazards that would be created by the tendency of the bright color to distract the attention of employees, particularly that of the male sex.

Protection of employees against safety hazards by the publication and an enforcement of safety rules is an accepted duty of Management which Management must discharge however distasteful the task may be to it or to the employees. If Management determined upon investigation that certain forms of attire tended to distract the attention of employees in a "co-ed" plant with resulting safety hazards and interference with production, and if it published rules prohibiting such forms of attire, it probably could not then be said that such rules were unreasonable or beyond the proper scope of Management's duties.

But such is not the case here. Neither the Company nor the Plant Management promulgated or published any rules as to the color of employees' clothing. The claimed general understanding that bright colors were "taboo" is no more definite than that. What color was proper and what color was "taboo" was apparently a matter depending entirely on the spot reactions of individual Counsellors of Labor Relations officers to particular slacks as they appeared on the scene. And the claimed understanding was the product, not of the publication of a rule, but of alleged repetition by word of mouth and by diverse unspecified persons. Apparently bright green slacks were tolerated. And there was no effort at specification of other articles of clothing, or the fit thereof, which might be equally seductive of employees' attention. Yet it is common knowledge that wolves, unlike bulls, may be attracted by colors other than red and by various other enticements in the art and fit of female attire.

It is clear that there was here no effort to survey the field and to prescribe knowable and enforceable rules. The matter was left largely to idiosyncrasy of circumstance and of persons in authority. That is not the way to prescribe or enforce rules of conduct.

A's reprimand is to be expunged from the record and she is to be reimbursed for the half hour lost in the Labor Relations office.

A QUESTION OF DEMOTION FOR INCOMPETENCE

Standard Oil Company (Indiana) and Central States Petroleum Union, Local 117, Independent, 25 LA 32, 1955

EDWARD C. BURRIS, ARBITRATOR

This is a proceeding instituted by Local No. 117 of the Central States Petroleum Union under the final step of the grievance procedure of the Union's collective bargaining agreement with the Company. In accordance with the provisions of Article II, Section 7, the parties requested the Federal Mediation and Conciliation Service to submit a panel of arbitrators, and from this panel, Edward C. Burris was selected to serve in this case.

On April 16, 1955, a hearing was held in the Company offices of the Neodesha, Kansas, Refinery, with opportunity for presentation by both parties of their positions and with opportunity to present witnesses and to cross-examine the witnesses of the other. At the conclusion of the hearing, the parties requested the opportunity to present briefs in support of their positions, such briefs to be postmarked not later than May 26, 1955. Rebuttal briefs were, by agreement, to be postmarked not later than June 3, 1955. A transcript of the proceedings of the hearing was taken by a court reporter and made available to both parties and to the arbitrator.

ISSUE

The issue for determination is submitted by stipulation of the Union and the Company as follows: Whether or not the Company's action of demoting C. E. Hawthorne from the classification of Machinist Second Year to the classification of Laborer was justified.

CASE HISTORY

The Neodesha Refinery of the Standard Oil Company (Indiana) is engaged in the refining of crude oil into gasoline and related petroleum products. The Company consists of two principal divisions—the Process Division and the Mechanical Division. This case is concerned with the Mechanical Division.

Mr. C. E. Hawthorne is 43 years of age. Prior to his employment as a Laborer by the Standard Oil Company (Indiana) on January 2, 1951, he had had previous experience as a bus driver and as a salesman. In March, 1951, he became a Watchman; on August 5, 1951, a Storehouse Helper; and on February 2, 1953, he became a Machinist First Year under the Company's Progressive Plan. On February 2, 1954, he became a Machinist Second Year.

In a letter dated November 16, 1954, the Union was informed that Mr. Hawthorne was to be demoted to the classification of Laborer, effective November 22, 1954. The letter stated:

This action is being taken because of Mr. Hawthorne's lack of ability to acquire a satisfactory degree of skill as a Machinist.

Mr. Hawthorne entered a grievance, and this grievance was processed through the steps of the grievance procedure and ultimately to arbitration. . . .

POSITION OF THE UNION

The Union contends that the demotion of Mr. Hawthorne is unjustified for the following reasons:

1. The demotion is but the culmination of a series of acts of discrimination against him because of his assertion of his contractual and union rights.

2. Even if the acts complained of were true and constituted an adequate ground for demotion, the Company is precluded from now asserting them because:

A. They occurred prior to Hawthorne's last promotion and were known at that time.

B. Hawthorne was given no warning that his work was not entirely satisfactory.

C. The list of complaints was not presented during the grievance procedure.

3. The complaints against Hawthorne are not valid and do not constitute a sufficient ground for permanent demotion.

4. Hawthorne's demotion is violative of past practice, no other employee in the Progressive Plan having been permanently demoted.

POSITION OF THE COMPANY

The Company contends that:

1. No written rules have been violated.

2. The arbitrator may not substitute his judgment for that of the Company in determining employee ability.

3. Mr. Hawthorne does not have the ability satisfactorily to perform Machinist work.

4. Mr. Hawthorne was offered ample time, and sufficient opportunity to acquire the knowledge and skill necessary satisfactorily to perform assigned work.

5. The Company did not act contrary to any practice or policy established by its own actions or by acquiescing in a course of conduct carried on over a long period of time.

6. In demoting Mr. Hawthorne, the Company acted in good faith and not arbitrarily nor with ulterior purpose.

DISCUSSION OF THE ISSUE

What evidence was disclosed at the hearing concerning the ability or lack of ability of Mr. Hawthorne to do Machinist work?

Mr. W. A. Mason, a Machinist who has been with the Standard Oil Company since 1932 and was with the predecessor company for seven years before that, testified that Mr. Hawthorne was his Helper for approximately three months. Mr. Mason testified that Mr. Hawthorne was polite and courteous, that he was never insubordinate; and when asked to compare him with other people who had been serving him as a Helper, he replied that Mr. Hawthorne "was just as good as any of them." (Record, page 74)

Mr. Charles Eaton, a No. 1 Pumper who has been with the Standard Oil Company and its predecessor refinery since 1917, stated that Mr. Hawthorne had done a good job of maintaining the pumps and that he frequently was able to diagnose pump difficulties and solve them on his own initiative and that he frequently made suggestions as to potential difficulties with other pumps which enabled Mr. Eaton to write out a work order for repairs on these pumps. Mr. Eaton was asked this question: "Then, on the basis of your experience with other mechanics and procedure and effectiveness of other people who came in to work on these particular pumps, could you judge Mr. Hawthorne's ability?" Mr. Eaton's answer was: "I would say it was as good as the average as the other machinists." (Record, page 106)

Mr. Bill Holper, who has been with Standard Oil Company of Indiana for nine years, the last five of which have been at the Neodesha Refinery, stated that Hawthorne's repairs of pumps are "as good as any other Machinist's."

On the other hand, Mr. Robert H. Colwell, Superintendent of the Mechanical Division, did not agree with the opinions of the above witnesses.

Likewise, Mr. John A. Brewer, Assistant Superintendent of the Mechanical Division, stated that Hawthorne visited too much with fellow workers, on occasions was found sitting in windows rather than working, and on other occasions was simply doing nothing.

It should be pointed out, however, that in the very nature of things Mr. Colwell and Mr. Brewer had limited opportunities for personal observation of Mr. Hawthorne's work, and that from their own testimony many of their criticisms of Hawthorne and his work were criticisms which had been passed on to them by Mr. Harold Brown, Machine Shop Foreman. Furthermore, there was considerable uncertainty in the testimony of Mr. Colwell and Mr. Brewer concerning specific times and places, and an admission on occasions that (for example, in the plating up of soaker drums) trouble with leaks on soaker drums was not an uncommon thing and that the Company had been plagued by this type of problem both before Mr. Hawthorne became a Machinist and since his demotion to Laborer.

There were two or three deficiencies in Mr. Hawthorne's work which apparently have some substance. It appears from the testimony that Mr. Hawthorne did have some dislike for climbing ladders or working from high scaffolds; but he testified (Record, page 239) that this fear was no longer present, and neither Mr. Colwell nor Mr. Brewer could cite comparatively recent instances where this had been a problem.

The Company charged Mr. Hawthorne with "lack of success in maintaining tools and equipment while working in the tool room." In cross-examination, Mr. Brewer agreed that this pertained largely to a group of shovels with broken handles. The Company did not contradict Mr. Hawthorne's testimony that while he was working in the tool room it was not his duty to repair shovels, but rather to saw off the handle so they could not be used as salvage. In fact, this entire criticism would be a criticism of his work before he entered his duties as a Machinist.

Mr. Brewer testified that one of Mr. Hawthorne's shortcomings was "an excessive amount of time required to accomplish given jobs." But Mr. Brewer acknowledged that his comments were based upon very casual observations. Indeed, no incidents of this were testified to positively as having occurred since February 3, 1954, the beginning date of Mr. Hawthorne's service as a Machinist Second Year.

Another charge leveled against Mr. Hawthorne was that of "damaged bolts due to the use of nuts having different thread than that on bolts." Apparently this referred to one instance in which one bolt of a group of 24 bolts on a particular plate was so damaged.

The Company charged Mr. Hawthorne with "frequent requests for help when working alone." Yet Mr. Brewer testified that the Machinist who worked on the pump usually had a Helper "the majority of the time" (Record, page 205). Mr. Brewer was not particularly helpful in clarifying this complaint against Mr. Hawthorne.

The Company charged Mr. Hawthorne with "wearing gloves while attempting to do Machinist work." Mr. Hawthorne testified that he had worn gloves on some occasions during the earlier part of his service as a Machinist due to an allergy which had been cured for some time.

Mr. Hawthorne was likewise charged with a lack of initiative. Yet testimony of both Company and Union witnesses was that Mr. Harold Brown did not like for his employees to do things differently from the way that he told them or to attempt to make repairs according to their own diagnosis. Mr. Hawthorne's testimony indicated that on at least one occasion he made a suggestion that steel rings be replaced by hydraulic packing rings and that this had been done with presumably some saving to the Company since the latter type of rings seem to last a longer period of time.

The Union criticized the Company for the lack of an adequate training program for Machinists. Yet it is true that presumably Mr. Hawthorne had the same opportunities for training as did other Machinists. Testimony by two or three Union witnesses indicated that responsible Company representatives stated that it was the Company's responsibility to train the individual and that if the results were not satisfactory, it is the fault of the Company, not the individual. Most of the Company training is in the nature of on-the-job training without specific collateral training.

The over-all picture of Mr. Hawthorne's ability or lack of ability as gleaned from the hearing is that his work, while not outstanding, was reasonably satisfactory. If such were not the case, testimony by Mr. Howard Brown, Mr. Hawthorne's immediate supervisor, would have been very helpful. Judging from the hearsay evidence concerning Mr. Brown's opinion of Mr. Hawthorne's ability, Mr. Brown was somewhat unfavorably impressed. If such opinion is Mr. Brown's evaluation of Mr. Hawthorne's ability, it is quite possible that his attitude may have been influenced by an incident just prior to Mr. Hawthorne's beginning as a Machinist First Year on February 2, 1953. On the occasion in question, Mr. Hawthorne apparently indicated to his Foreman that he wanted to discuss with a higher official, Mr. R. H. Colwell, Superintendent, Mechanical Division, the reason for his not being placed on the Progressive Plan. While assenting to Mr. Hawthorne's doing this, Mr. Hawthorne felt that Mr. Brown was displeased at this action. Following this incident, Mr. Hawthorne was assigned to a somewhat disagreeable task of cleaning all of the ten machines in the machine shop with oil and sandpapering them down. Testimony of several witnesses indicated that this was an unusual procedure and that it was in the nature of a retaliation or punishment for Mr. Hawthorne. Indeed, on his own initiative, Mr. Pfeifer, the Union Steward in the machine shop, requested a hearing with Mr. U. M. Clerkin, Personnel Supervisor, to discuss the matter.

The treatment of Mr. Hawthorne following the accident of August, 1954, in which it was necessary for the first joint of the index finger to be amputated surgically, is another incident which tends to raise a question in the mind of any unprejudiced person concerning the attitude of Mr. Brown toward Mr. Hawthorne.

FINDINGS OF FACT AND CONCLUSIONS

Considering the testimony of all the witnesses for both Company and Union, the arbitrator must find that while there were some deficiencies in Mr. Hawthorne's work, his work was reasonably satisfactory. The arbitrator finds that the recommendation that Mr. Hawthorne be demoted from Machinist Second Year to Laborer was based to a great degree upon the recommendation of Mr. Brown, his Foreman, whose opinions could easily have been colored by his personal feeling toward Mr. Hawthorne.

The arbitrator finds that the judgments of Mr. Colwell and Mr. Brewer concerning Mr. Hawthorne's ability or lack of it were reflections very largely of the opinion of Mr. Brown and that, in the nature of things, this would be expected, and that, therefore, the action in "going along with" Mr. Brown's recommendation should not be construed as criticism of them.

Although the record indicates that on occasions the quality of Mr. Hawthorne's work was discussed with him by his Foreman, Mr. Hawthorne was apparently never given a warning notice for the alleged poor quality of his work during the twenty months he worked in a Machinist classification.

In North American Aviation, Inc., 17 LA 784, a demotion was held to be improper because an employee had received no warning notice during his four years of work.

In Hiram Walker and Sons, Inc., 19 LA 447, a demotion for incompetence was set aside because, among other reasons, the employee had never been given a specific individual warning.

The case for the demotion of Mr. Hawthorne would have been much clearer, had there been convincing evidence that on one or more occasions his Foreman had warned him that failure to improve the quality of his work would lead to demotion.

The Company has no precise standards regarding the quantity or quality of work expected of a Machinist Second Year. Thus, its judgment is based entirely upon the subjective evaluation of the supervisors who worked with Hawthorne. Neither Mr. Colwell nor Mr. Brewer, by their own testimony, were in a position to evaluate the day-to-day work performance of Hawthorne. For reasons unknown to the arbitrator, the Company chose not to place in evidence at the hearing the evaluation of Hawthorne's work by using his Foreman, Mr. Harold Brown, as a witness. Thus, the arbitrator was deprived of the testimony of Mr. Brown who should have been in a superior position to evaluate Mr. Hawthorne's work.

STATEMENT OF AWARD

The arbitrator finds that the Company's action in demoting Mr. C. E. Hawthorne from the classification of Machinist Second Year to the classification of Laborer was not justified and that this error should be corrected by the placement of Mr. Hawthorne again into the Machinist Second Year classification with retroactive compensation at regular straight time hourly rates for the period since his demotion to the time when he shall have been returned to Machinist Second Year classification, less, of course, earnings which he has received at regular straight time rates in his employment with the Company in the interim.

People—including employers!—have become accustomed to the phenomenon of unions bargaining concerning wages and hours and even

job assignments. But at times we encounter situations where manage-
ment's discretion on matters considerably removed from wages and hours
appears to be limited by the union-negotiated collective agreement. In
the arbitration decision which follows, issues are raised by the union
which most managements would instinctively presume should fall within
their sole purview.

A QUESTION OF LAYOFFS

Weber Aircraft Corporation and International Association of Machinists, Lodge
727, 24 LA 821, 1955

EDGAR A. JONES, ARBITRATOR

The following questions were determined by the parties at the hearing to be
a mutually acceptable formulation of the issues to be decided by the arbitrator.
1. Are the layoffs of Freda M. Quinn, Ira A. Stadalman, Ben Westman,
and William A. Wright proper subject matters for grievance within the
provisions of the current collective bargaining agreement between the
Company and the Union dated October 20, 1954?
2. If the answer to (1) is "yes," were the individuals named laid off
for just cause by the Company on April 4, 1955?
3. If the answer to (2) is "no," what award does the arbitrator make?

STATEMENT OF FACTS

In 1951, Weber Aircraft Corporation, a subsidiary of Weber Showcase and
Fixture Co., acquired from Airquipment Company, a subsidiary of Lockheed
Aircraft Corporation, the assets of the business presently operated by the Com-
pany. When Airquipment Company was formed in 1946 out of a division of
Lockheed, IAM Lodge 727 was certified as collective bargaining representative
of the new corporation's employees.

Shortly before the Weber acquisition, the Airquipment management decided
to contract out part of the plant maintenance work. The decision was carried
through by the incoming Weber management. Accordingly, in June, 1951, an
independent contractor whom we shall refer to as the XYZ Co., was engaged
to do the outside window washing on an office building. Eventually, some time
prior to the present grievance, the XYZ contract had been broadened to cover
the washing of inside and outside windows on the Company's two office buildings and its production office.

Weber employees wear a distinctive yellow badge at all times inside the
plant. It is required to be readily visible. The XYZ window washers have always
worn a differently colored badge denoting nonemployees, either white or green,
but never yellow. Weber janitors, members of the bargaining unit, some of
whom are grievants here, worked in and around the same areas as did XYZ
janitors when the latter were washing inside windows.

In November, 1954, in the midst of a decline in its business, the Company undertook a study of the feasibility of contracting out all of its janitorial work. On March 22, 1955, and again on March 28, the vice-president in charge of manufacturing, Mr. Johnson, telephoned the business representative of the Union, Mr. Foote, and informed him that the Company had decided, first, to "sub-contract" all of its janitorial work to an outside firm, which we shall refer to as the ABC Co., on or about April 1, 1955, and, second, to lay off its seven janitors on that date. The Union objected, indicated that it was unaware of the XYZ janitorial contract, and, upon consummation of the Company's decision, processed the grievances of the four employees involved here.

Neither the ABC Co. nor the XYZ Co. are related to Weber Aircraft other than as independent contractors.

RELEVANT CONTRACTUAL PROVISIONS

The Company relies on Article I, Section 6, "Right to Manage Plant":

Except as abridged, delegated, granted or modified by this Agreement, or any supplementary agreements that may hereafter be made, all of the rights, powers and authority the Company had prior to the signing of this Agreement are retained by the Company, and remain exclusively and without limitation within the rights of management.

The Union relies on Article I, Section 2, "Exclusive Representation"; Section 3, "Period of Agreement"; Section 5, "Scope of Agreement"; Section 8, "Union Security"; Article II, Section 1, "Strikes and Lockouts"; Article III, Sectiion 4 (3), "Arbitration"; Article IV, Section 1, "Basis of Seniority"; Article VI, "Employee Privileges"; Exhibit A, "Factory Occupations," listing the "Classification" and "Rate" of "Janitor" at "1.63." Article I, Section 2A, "Exclusive Representation," is as follows:

For the period of this Agreement the Company recognizes and accepts the Union as the exclusive representative of all the employees of the Company, except those listed in Subsection (B), for the purpose of collective bargaining in respect to rates of pay, wages, hours of employment, or other conditions of employment.

Subsection (B) of Article I, Section 2 does not except the classification of "Janitor" from the bargaining unit. Article I, Section 8, "Union Security," establishes a union shop.

UNION POSITION

The substance of the Union's position is that the Agreement, read as a whole, precludes outside contracting despite absence of explicit prohibition. It notes first that the Company refers to its outside contracting for janitorial service as a "sub-contract." This, the Union says, is inaccurate. The arrangement is not in fact a sub-contract in the accepted sense of the word, the sense in which the Union sought in 1954 to negotiate a new provision in this Agreement limiting the Company's right to subcontract. The distinction, the Union feels, is important and not merely a matter of semantics. It turns on whether the Company in good faith sends work out of the plant to be performed elsewhere or, instead, displaces its Union employees with another employer's personnel who then perform the same work on Company premises as did the displaced Company employees. The former may be allowable under the Agreement, but the latter, this case, is not.

The Union cites the Recognition provision [Article I, Section 2] wherein Lodge 727 is recognized as the exclusive representative of all Weber employees including the janitors. It asserts that "the only legal time for excluding of employees from the bargaining unit to be brought up is during negotiations. Where a job is in the bargaining unit and in existence, the Company cannot unilaterally exclude it from the unit. . . . [I]n past negotiations, classifications have been by mutual agreement excluded from the bargaining unit. . . . [as] was that of the Industrial Nurse." (Union Rebuttal Brief, p. 4) The reference is to the 1952 handling by the Company and the Union of the removal from the bargaining unit of the Industrial Nurse job classification. That was negotiated; this was not; that was good labor-management relations; this was not.

In addition, the provision establishing the term of the Agreement [Article I, Section 3] is cited by the Union, together with the denomination and rate of pay of the "Janitor" classification [Agreement, Exhibit A, p. 48], as establishing "the right of job security to work so long as work remains available to him within the plant. The work of these Janitors is still available to them in the plant." [Union Rebuttal Brief, p. 5] Furthermore, the parties contemplated that the Union would represent employees whose work "transpires on the Company's premises at their present plant." [Union Rebuttal Brief, p. 5]

Again, the Union Security provision [Article I, Section 8] insures the Union against layoffs of this nature because, "if the practice perpetrated by the Company in this case was expanded to the other job classifications existing under the Union Agreement, we would see the spectacle of a plant full of people working and the Union not having a single, solitary member among them due to the fact that said employees would be working for agencies which we do not represent." [Union Rebuttal Brief, p. 5]

The Seniority Article [Article IV], the Union urges, is also set to naught by the Company's layoff which renders "the entire concept and provisions of this article completely meaningless." How shall this appear to other Weber hourly-paid employees if it be upheld? "If it is legal for the Company to do what they have done in these cases, then it would evidently be legal for them to delete the entire bargaining unit the same way, by doing the same thing to every employee on the payroll." This is "very unwholesome" since it could lead to the ousting of employees "regardless of how many years they had spent building up the Company by their years of service and seniority." [Union Rebuttal Brief, p. 7] It is an economy, true but, "We venture to say that if the Company did delete the entire bargaining unit en masse by this procedure with one stroke of their unilateral pen, the arbitrator would unquestionably rule against them. The Union's position is therefore relatively simple: If it is illegal to kill 500 people by massacre, then it is also illegal to kill off four people the same way. The magnitude of the killing should not make it any more legal one way or the other." [Union Rebuttal Brief, p. 7] "The Company attempted to show . . . by various documents how much money per hour they would be saving by doing what they did. These savings referred to, of course, are achieved at the expense of our Union Janitors who are covered by our Union Agreement. . . . Whether this was accomplished with good faith or with bad faith is immaterial. The net result was the same: Our Union Janitors suffered loss of their jobs." [Union Rebuttal Brief, pp. 9–10]

Finally, with reference to arbitration decisions on this point,[1] the Union observes that, "there have been decisions both ways on cases of this kind. . . . [T]he arbitrator will have to reach his own conclusions, securing such ideas as he might be able to come up with through study of these . . . cases," noting nevertheless that "many of the cases listed by the Company refer to the sending out of work to other manufacturing concerns for the other . . . concerns to do in their own plant." (Union Rebuttal Brief, p. 12) The Union concludes: "In view of the generous statement and suggestion to the arbitrator contained in the Company's . . . brief [see Company Position, infra], the Union, too, wishes to make a generous statement and suggestion to the arbitrator: Inasmuch as the Union is merely trying to get simple justice for the Janitors, and not trying to unmercifully crucify the Company, we suggest to the arbitrator that we think a fair ruling from him would be to restore the jobs of the Janitors to them with full back pay *minus* any earnings or any unemployment compensation obtained by the Janitors while they were in a state of layoff from Weber Aircraft Corporation." (Union Rebuttal Brief, pp. 12–13)

COMPANY POSITION

The Company's layoff action was premised on its interpretation of the management prerogative clause [Article I, Section 6, supra] of the Agreement. This section reserves to the Company "exclusively and without limitation" all rights not "abridged . . . by this Agreement." The Company points to the lack of any express prohibition of outside contracting and concludes that the Agreement leaves its subcontracting power undiminished, at least in this instance. This interpretation is bolstered, it argues, by the fact that the Union in negotiations preliminary to this Agreement proposed but did not press (at least, did not secure) an express bar on the subcontracting "of any work that could normally be performed by our people so long as there are any people on the recall list for said work." (Company Exhibit # 3)

The Company notes that "good faith is an important element in these outside contractor cases." It then denies emphatically any intent or desire to sap the strength of the Union as the representative of its employees. It cites its policy of bringing back into the plant types of work previously subcontracted by Airquipment, thereby augmenting the Union's strength. It interprets the

[1] The Union cites the following cases: Magnolia Petroleum Co., 21 L.A. 267 (Larson); Stockholders Pub. Co., 16 L.A. 644 (Aaron); Bethlehem Steel Co., 16 L.A. 111 (Killingsworth); Parke Davis & Co., 15 L.A. 111 (Scheiber); Celanese Corp of America, 14 L.A. 31 (Wolff).

Union's concern to be that this action of the Company, if upheld here, "may be used as a precedent to undermine the bargaining unit through contracting out substantial portions of the work normally performed by employees in the unit." It therefore advances the following statement: "Should the arbitrator wish to reassure the Union, in the event this arbitration is decided in favor of the Company, that the decision cannot be used as a precedent for any further outside contracting but that each case must stand on its own facts in light of the overall principle that the Company must use good faith in respect to the bargaining unit, the Company certainly has no objection to such a statement." (Company Brief, p. 12) The good faith of the Company, it argues, is demonstrated, first, by the fact that this outside janitorial contract is just a projection of a long standing practice not hitherto challenged by the Union, and, second, by the economies dictating the action. These latter may be digested from the memorandum (Company Exhibit #1) prepared and on February 7, 1955, submitted by the Plant Maintenance supervisor to the vice-president in charge of manufacturing.

Weber Janitorial Costs [1]

	1953	1954	1955 (est.)
Labor [2]	$22,738.10	$35,363.96	$29,520.00
Supplies	8,027.87	9,165.38	7,200.00
Total	30,765.97	44,529.34	36,720.00
Contract bid [3]	27,564.00	27,564.00	27,564.00
Realizable savings	3,201.97	16,965.34	9,156.00

[1] The memorandum estimated that improved janitorial service to be received from ABC Co. would require, to duplicate it, a capital investment by Weber of $1600.00 for equipment.

[2] Including fringe benefits at $4,320.00 in 1953 ($.20 per hour), $5,400.00 in 1954 ($.25 per hour) and $4,320.00 in 1955 ($.30 per hour). ". . . 1954 janitorial labor costs for Company employees embraced some 21,600 hours as indicated by the statistics on fringe benefits. Under [ABC] maintenance two employees working 40 hours a week for 52 weeks produced 4,160 hours of work. For the afternoon crew, assuming that 12 employees worked 3 hours each, 5 days a week, 52 weeks a year, these hours total 9,360 or total overall hours of 13,520 or almost 8,000 hours less than for Company employees in the janitorial field." (Company Brief, p. 7)

[3] $2,297 per month was the lowest of five (5) bids, including all but a few supplies.

Further, the Company emphasizes that the ABC Co. is in fact an independent contractor, that Weber has no direct supervisory control over ABC employees but, on the contrary, under the terms of the ABC contract must present any complaints it may have to the ABC foreman to whose directions alone the ABC janitors must respond.

Finally, the Company distinguishes the cases relied upon by the Union, advances its own authorities,[2] notes that the trend of decisions supports the Company's position, and concludes thus:

[I]n *all* recent cases the issue of outside contracting has been decided in favor of the Company. In each instance the arbitrators have stressed the factors present in this case, namely, good faith on the part of the Company and the absence of a contract prohibition against the outside contract work. Here . . . good faith . . . is bolstered not only by past practice in outside contracting but by unusually strong contract provisions as construed by the Union itself in contract negotiations. (Company Brief, p. 11)

DISCUSSION

This kind of case is difficult to decide. Strong policies are at loggerheads. The concern of the parties quite understandably reflects the grave import to their respective operations of, on the one hand, the Company's power to subcontract and, on the other, the Union's protection both of the seniority benefits of its members and its own bargaining-unit strength. A clash of conflicting interests in such a vital area can generate a good deal of friction harmful to the continued maturing of the bargaining relationship. These parties are therefore to be commended for the restraint and good will which each has evidenced in the presentation of this case.

It is not unusual, of course, that diverse viewpoints should be reflected among arbitration awards. Here however, there is apparent a tendency even among experienced arbitrators to be dogmatic in quite general terms. Thus, for instance, one arbitrator concludes that arbitrators are "virtually unanimous in holding that a Company may not unilaterally remove a job from the bargaining unit, even where there is no express limitation to that effect in the agreement or when there is a management rights clause."[3] Yet another, in contrary vein, declares that, "The arbitration decisions are unanimously to the effect that the Company has the right to subcontract work unless the contract specifically restricts that right."[4] More accurately, a third finds the cases cut down the middle and concludes, "In summary, previous decisions form no sure guide.

[2] Re Berger, 78 N.Y.S. 2d 528; 9 L.A. 1045 (1948); B. F. Curry, Inc. v. Reddeck, 86 N.Y.S. 2d 674 (1954); Carbide & Carbon Chemical Co., 24 L.A. 158 (Kelliher); Vickers, Inc., 24 L.A. 121 (Haughton); Dalmo Victor Co., 24 L.A. 33 (Kagel); Washington Post Co., 23 L.A. 728 (Healy); Allegheny Ludlum Steel Corp., 23 L.A. 171 (Blair); Tungsten Mining Corp., 19 L.A. 503 (Maggs); Appalachian Electric Cooperative, 19 L.A. 815 (Holly); National Tube Co., 17 L.A. 790 (Garrett); Youngstown Sheet & Tube Co., 14 L.A. 645 (Blair); International Harvester Co., 12 L.A. 707 (McCoy); Amoskeag Mills Inc., 8 L.A. 990 (Copelof); Cords Ltd., Inc., 7 L.A. 474 (Stein); Electro-Physical Labs, 7 L.A. 474 (Kaplan).

[3] Bethlehem Steel Co., 16 L.A. at 113 (Killingsworth).

[4] International Harvester Co., 12 L.A. 707 at 709 (McCoy). Accord: Carbide & Carbon Chemicals Co., 24 L.A. 158 (Kelliher); Elkouri, How Arbitration Works 237 (1952).

There is no long line of decisions supporting the reasoning of either side . . . no sure and guiding light." [5]

A reading of a substantial cross-section of the reported decisions indicates that the only unanimity reflected in the cases is that of diversity. Each is a law unto itself. Collectively, they point up the delusiveness of generalizing about the content of arbitration awards. Cases supporting Company action stress the retention of management of the right to subcontract work where there is no express prohibition in the agreement.[6] Cases upholding Union grievances give paramount emphasis to the effect, collectively or individually, of the Recognition, Seniority, Wage, and Fringe Benefits clauses of the agreement[7] and the stability of the bargaining unit.[8] Past practice in which either party has acquiesced has been given decisive weight in some cases.[9] In others, the location of the work subcontracted, whether on the premises of the Company or those of the independent contractor, has been accorded significance.[10] Whether or not union employees are displaced has been deemed important.[11] Finally, the existence of good faith has been required of the Company[12] which is to say, an effort by the Company to subvert the express terms of the Agreement or to undermine the strength of the Union will not be upheld.[13]

A survey of judicial decisions may indicate how a court in a given jurisdiction may be expected to resolve a similar fact complex if the court conforms to the doctrine of *stare decisis*. A survey of arbitrations may also establish a pattern

[5] A. D. Juilliard Co., Inc., 21 L.A. 713 at 723 (Hogan).

[6] See, for example, Appalachian Electric Corp., 19 L.A. 815 (Holly); Allegheny Ludlum Steel Corp., 23 L.A. 171 (Blair); Amoskeag Mills, Inc., 8 L.A. 990 (Copelof); Ashland Oil & Refining Co., 8 L.A. 465 (Wardlaw); Cords Ltd., Inc., 7 L.A. 748 (Stein); Dalmo Victor Co., 24 L.A. 33 (Kagel); International Harvester Co., 12 L.A. 707 (McCoy); National Sugar Refining Co., 13 L.A. 991 (Feinberg). Of course this can involve interpretation of differently worded clauses. See Washington Post Co., 23 L.A. 728 (Healy).

[7] See, for example, Bridgeport Brass Co., 15 L.A. 559 (Donnelly); Celanese Corp. of America, 14 L.A. 31 (Wolff); A. D. Juilliard Co., Inc., 21 L.A. 713 (Hogan); New Britain Machine Co., 8 L.A. 720 (Wallen); Parke Davis & Co., 15 L.A. 111 (Scheiber). But see Dalmo Victor Co., 24 L.A. 33 (Kagel).

[8] See, for example, Stockholders Publishing Co., 16 L.A. 644 (Aaron).

[9] See, for example, Allegheny Ludlum Steel Corp., 23 L.A. 171 (Blair); Tungsten Mining Corp., 19 L.A. 503 (Maggs); Vickers, Inc., 24 L.A. 121 (Haughton); Youngstown Sheet & Tube Co., 14 L.A. 645 (Blair).

[10] See, for example, Magnolia Petroleum Co., 21 L.A. 267 (Larson); Celanese Corp. of America, 14 L.A. 31 (Wolff). But cf. Stockholders Publishing Co., 16 L.A. 644 at 649 (Aaron).

[11] See, for example, Carbide & Carbon Chemicals Co., 24 L.A. 158 (Kelliher); Electro-Physical Laboratories, Inc., 7 L.A. 474 (Kaplan); Tungsten Mining Corp., 19 L.A. 503 (Maggs).

[12] See, for example, Carbide & Carbon Chemicals Co., 24 L.A. 158 (Kelliher); Cords, Ltd., Inc., 7 L.A. 748 (Stein); Swift & Co., 10 L.A. 842 (Healy); Vickers, Inc., 24 L.A. 121 (Haughton).

[13] See, for example, Bethlehem Steel Co., 16 L.A. 111 (Killingsworth); Dalmo Victor Co., 24 L.A. 33 (Kagel); Magnolia Petroleum Co., 21 L.A. 267 (Larson).

of past judgment. But its effect on future decisions depends on the relative sense of reasonableness it may evoke in a particular arbitrator. It is still a misnomer to use the rather pretentious phrase, "industrial jurisprudence", with reference to arbitration. It is possible, of course, to cumulate groups of "Company" and "Union" decisions on either side of a given point.[14] But, aside from a rough consensus of commonsense, as yet there is no interior logic flowing from interrelated principles characteristic of jurisprudence. Nor is there apt to be so long as courts refrain from imposing (and parties refrain from seeking) judicial review of arbitration awards in much the same ratio as prevails today.[15]

In the instant case, there are two significant factors with opposite pulls on the judgment of the arbitrator.

First is the fact underscored by the Union that the economy sought by the Company at the expense of the janitors involved no more than bringing non-union janitors into the plant to do the work hitherto done by union janitors. To argue that economies are thereby affected does not conclude the case. It is as accurate (and obvious) to observe that a completely nonunion Weber plant would be a good deal less costly than the one in which union wage scale and fringe benefits now prevail. A cursory reading of this or any collective bargaining agreement will readily demonstrate that the collective bargaining process inevitably entails the sacrifice by the Company of many potential dollar economies in the interest of the welfare of its employees.

The Union sought a bar to subcontracting in the 1954 negotiations. But it assertedly dropped its proposal when the Company made evident to it the indispensability of subcontracting in the airframe industry and, more particularly, to Weber Aircraft. It is clear from the Union proposal (see Company Position, supra) that it contemplated the situation where work was sent outside the plant and remained outside while union members were on layoff for lack of work inside the plant. Thus the unaccepted proposal then advanced cannot now be said to have foreclosed the Union's present position concerning the bringing in of an outside firm to do work on plant premises with the consequent layoff and, presumably, eventual discharge of the grievant janitors.

This brings us to the second and converse point. Since 1951 the Company has been doing on a limited scale exactly what the Union complains of in this case. It brought in an independent contractor to wash office windows, work on the premises which the Union janitors certainly could have done. Indeed, for a while the XYZ janitors washed the outside panes and the Weber janitors the inside panes. Eventually, the XYZ janitors did both. This is the past practice exception that has been thought sufficient in some cases to render subcontracting proper which otherwise might be improper under a collective agree-

[14] See, for example, Elkouri, How Collective Bargaining Works (1952).

[15] I do not mean to discount the effect of the unfortunate tendency to judicial preemption of arbitration which perhaps is observable currently. See, for example, Black v. Cutter Laboratories, — Cal. 2d —, 278 P. 2d 905, 23 L.A. 715 (1955); Summers, Judicial Review of Labor Arbitration, 2 Buffalo L. Rev. 1 (1952).

ment.[16] If there were no more to this case than that, the decision would be less difficult.

But the Union denies categorically that it collectively, or its shop stewards individually, had any actual knowledge of the window washing arrangement. The only means of distinguishing between the Weber and the XYZ janitors was the differently colored identification badges worn by employees and non-employees of Weber. No uniform was worn by the outside janitors. Their truck was even unmarked. Further, the testimony of Company witnesses indicated that the company had not notified the Union of the 1951 XYZ contract until March, 1955, and then in connection with this dispute. The Union business representative testified that the first he knew of the XYZ window washers was on March 28, 1955, when the Company vice-president in charge of manufacturing informed him of it by telephone in the course of announcing the impending company action which gave rise to these grievances.

All this seems to boil down to the necessity of a decision by the Arbitrator whether or not the ostensible ignorance on the part of the Union of the status of the XYZ janitors is so incredible as to be beyond belief or, if not, is nonetheless so negligent as to mean that the Union cannot fairly rely now upon its actual lack of knowledge.

The Arbitrator accepts the Union's disclaimer of knowledge. Perhaps it is a source of embarrassment to the Union that its people did not recognize that XYZ rather than Weber janitors were polishing up the windows on the big front door. The Company, after all, is not alleged to have made any effort to camouflage the XYZ janitors or their tall ladders on the outside walls of the office buildings. Yet it remains true that the Company at no time previous to this controversy made known to the Union the existence of its contractual arrangement with the XYZ Co.

The Arbitrator can see no reasonable basis for imposing upon the Union the affirmative duty of ascertaining the unit status of each Weber employee. Indeed, he doubts very much if it would advance the relationship of the parties were his decision to force Union stewards to become snoopers that they might ferret out employment relationships which might otherwise remain unknown to the Union at the peril of an adverse ruling on this issue of past practice in some future arbitration. That would certainly be the effect of upholding the Company's position on the past practice issue here. The Arbitrator therefore concludes as follows: so long as the Company does not inform the Union of the presence on the premises of nonunion employees doing work allotted by the Agreement to union employees, and so long as the Union officials in the plant are in fact unaware of their presence, awareness of the nonunion employees ought not to be imputed to the Union irrespective of actual knowledge.

This conclusion, it should be emphasized, is limited to the issue of past practice raised in this case. It should also be added as a caution that it does not mean that shop stewards can ignore completely the union or nonunion status of employees with whom they come into contact. Circumstances are readily

[16] See note 12 supra.

conceivable where this or another Arbitrator might feel required to find actual knowledge to be the fact despite disavowal by the Union, and this simply because it would be too incredible to believe otherwise. This case has seemed to the Arbitrator, on balance, to fall just short of that incredibility.

The unresolved area of dispute is then reduced to the question of whether the Company retained the power under this Agreement to lay off its janitors in order to bring onto the premises an independent contractor to take over the balance of the Company's janitorial work. It is useless to attempt to decide that question by framing general propositions which make up in forcefulness what they lack in precision. The power to subcontract exists, it is important, but it is not unqualified. This is acknowledged explicitly in the arguments of both parties.

The Company is legitimately concerned lest resolution of this dispute in favor of the Union unduly constrict its use of the subcontracting device in an industry where it is indispensable to business success. The Company's suggestion that the Arbitrator explicitly confine the precedent scope of this Award recognizes the equally legitimate concern of the Union that a decision for the Company could render the Union vulnerable to a process of whittling away of its strength in the unit by subcontracting arrangements.

Mindful of these factors, the Arbitrator adopts the case-by-case approach suggested by the Company and applies it to the resolution of this dispute as follows: it was an unreasonable exercise of its subcontracting power for the Company, while subject to this Agreement, to effectuate an unnegotiated reduction of the bargaining unit by laying off its union janitors and replacing them with nonunion janitors of another employer in order to gain economies in the conduct of janitorial work on its premises.

AWARD

The answers to the questions submitted for decision are accordingly as follows: (1) Yes; (2) No; (3) the Janitors laid off shall be restored without loss of benefits to the "active payroll" status they possessed before their layoff. They shall receive back pay, less earnings or unemployment compensation received by them during their layoff, but only for the periods of their layoff when they were ready and able to perform the duties of their classification.

10: Seniority

Seniority is the device by which the allocation of scarce opportunities is made among workers—who gets the remaining jobs when some have to be laid off, who receives the promotion when numbers of individuals would like to have it, who is called back to work when operations resume after a shutdown, who has first chance to work overtime when there are more people than can be used who would like this opportunity to earn extra income, and so on. Seniority is based on length of service in the defined seniority unit.

In general, workers prefer that scarce opportunities be rationed on this basis, whereas many managers would prefer that scarce opportunities be allocated on the basis of superior ability. But even among workers there are often conflicting views as to how seniority should operate.

A UNION VIEW OF SENIORITY

From Making Grievance Procedure Work Successfully, handbook of District 50, United Mine Workers, 1945

Job security is one of the prime objectives of workers in mass production industries which restrict chances for advancement. The most successful way to prevent favoritism, discrimination, or unfair treatment so far as hiring, advancement, layoff and rehiring after layoff are concerned has been the seniority system.

Seniority means that the worker with longest record of continuous service as the senior employee is entitled to preference. It is written into the contract for the purpose of giving to the employees an equitable measure of security based on the simple and just standard of length of continuous service.

Wherever possible plant-wide seniority is preferable and should be the basis of a seniority system. THIS MEANS THAT THE MEMBERS HAVING LONGEST SENIORITY IN THE ENTIRE PLANT HAVE PREFERENCE IN ANY DEPARTMENT ON THE WORK THAT THEY ARE CAPABLE OF PERFORMING. Older men are entitled to such preference:—

First—Because they have demonstrated their skill for the longest period of time.

Second—Because the management has a responsibility toward men who have given their energy, intelligence, and best years in making profits for the company.

Third—It sets up a single standard capable of being understood by all and easily applied.

Fourth—It prevents the introduction of more and more divisions by the company with the increased possibility of competition within the units of the plants and against the best interests of the union.

Fifth—It is a check against the speed-up by eliminating arbitrary discharge and rehiring since success of the speed-up depends on the worker's constant fear of losing his job at first sign of slackening speed.

Sixth—It is a safeguard against the speed-up system in so far as the standard of production is not set by the youngest workers.

Seventh—It is a defense against discriminatory firing whether based on personal prejudice or antiunionism.

Eighth—Where the system is automatic and simple to understand, it is an important factor in reducing the number of grievances based upon the difficult problems of layoffs, rehiring after layoffs, and promotions.

The commonly stated argument of the company that straight seniority does away with initiative and efficiency is purely without foundation. The seniority systems of the United Mine Workers of America and District 50 are of sufficiently long standing to prove otherwise.

Furthermore, the company's right to discharge inefficient workers has never been taken away. Where the company claims that certain employees with less seniority are exceptionally qualified for specific jobs, the union takes the position that such employees may be retained where advisable, provided a fixed percentage of such employees is agreed upon.

Wherever possible, shop committeemen should be placed at the head of the seniority list during their period of office in order to insure the continuity of responsibility which such an office requires.

Where there are many different departments, each requiring special skill and knowledge, it is often impossible to establish plant-wide seniority or fix arbitrary rules which will apply to all equally. The question of which seniority system shall prevail in your plant is a serious and important one. It should be the subject of careful consideration before a final decision is reached.

Make the seniority rule simple and workable so that it will be clearly understood by the entire plant. Although skill, knowledge, ability, and other intangible factors may be part of your seniority clause, remember that these should and must be only incidental to what seniority really means, namely, continuous length of service.

Your contract may read, "ability and efficiency being equal, seniority shall govern." Since absolute equality is never found, interpret the rule to mean that only striking differences in competency or ability or efficiency warrant a departure from the true meaning of seniority.

Under the union principle of the greatest good for the greatest number, younger men should be protected by providing rules for spreading work during slack periods. This should not be considered as violating the rule of seniority.

THE EMPLOYER'S VIEW OF SENIORITY

Excerpts from Information Bulletin No. 20, Employee Relations Division, National Association of Manufacturers, 1955

Length of service is sometimes used as the sole determinant for granting preference under the seniority principle—it is then known as "straight" or "strict" seniority. In the interest of managerial efficiency, as well as for the best long-range good of employees, many companies modify seniority by making other occupational factors (such as ability, job performance, etc.) of paramount importance, giving weight to length of service only when all other factors are relatively equal.

The question of whether or not seniority is to be the controlling factor in layoffs and other personnel actions looms large in current labor-management negotiations. Labor leaders are becoming more and more insistent that seniority should be the sole determinant in such actions.

This trend is not confined to demands during contract negotiations. Many companies report that although their contracts permit them to maintain well-balanced work forces by utilizing "qualified" seniority, they are under pressure to revert to the use of length of service alone when layoffs become necessary during the life of the contract. In this situation most employers have maintained that management freedom to operate efficiently is best for the employees in the long run. Further, they hold that the principle of the sanctity of the contract is jeopardized by yielding to such demands. . . .

Seniority as the sole criterion in such actions serves neither the best interests of the employer nor the employee. Used this way, it reduces all employees to a common level where no recognition or reward for difference in abilities or performance is possible. Thus, it blocks the advancement of able individuals and destroys their incentive to grow and improve. Straight seniority also penalizes young or new employees because the only way in which they can attain job security, or the opportunity for advancement, is through long service on the job.

The factor of ability is the most generally used and the most important limitation on the length-of-service criterion. Of course, other qualifications such as skill, performance, merit, job knowledge, training, etc., may be taken into consideration.

It is vital to the development and maintenance of good human relationships that the factors used to qualify length of service be measured in as objective and equitable manner as possible. To do so, management should develop adequate techniques, including the best use of:

employee records
job descriptions
merit rating plans
supervisory appraisal ability.

Management not only has the responsibility for developing an accurate, reliable and fair method for evaluating employee skill and ability—one which supervisors understand, accept and cooperate in—but day-to-day actions must support it. For example, if—despite the existence of a policy which gives weight to ability—supervisors follow the path of least resistance and, in the hope of avoiding grievances and union problems, promote strictly in accordance with seniority, the real objective will have been thwarted.

Further, the principle of basing seniority on skill and ability can be made to work only if action is taken with respect to unsatisfactory work performance at the time it is first recognized. It is too late to wait until a layoff is imminent and then suddenly "discover" that a person is not doing a qualified job. This is particularly true if a supervisor has tolerated the alleged unqualified work for a period of time.

The time to tell the employee that he is not doing a qualified job is when the supervisor first discovers it—not when a curtailment looms. To do otherwise is to invite a breakdown of the seniority system, and to disrupt morale. . . .

A major problem in extensive layoffs is "bumping" which may result in job transfers for the greater part of the retained work force. Such situations may be alleviated . . . by restrictions on the number of "bumps" that may result from any one layoff, and by specifying certain occupational groups which cannot be bumped.

Such companies consider that a certain amount of "bumping" is desirable because it protects a company's older employees. It gives employees who have been with the company a long time the opportunity of dropping back to a lower classified job, rather than go "out the door."

The problem of "bumping" in temporary layoffs of relatively short duration can be completely avoided by establishing a separate procedure for such situations, under which layoffs are made without regard to seniority. However, if the layoff is extended beyond a specified number of days at any time, or in a year, then the usual seniority procedure takes effect. . . .

Many managements insist on the exemption of certain employees from the seniority system so as to (1) protect and retain exceptional employees and supervisors, and (2) to insure that during employment cut-backs an adequate work force with the proper proportion of needed skills will be maintained.

In general, these exceptions are handled in labor agreements by:

1. Listing jobs or occupational groups to be exempt or
2. By provisions permitting management to retain—without regard to their seniority—a certain percentage of the work force whose special skills or training, or whose work, is vital to the efficient operation of the plant. . . .

The ability of management to freely select or reject candidates for promotion is a matter of extreme importance.

Only management has the knowledge requisite for matching the candidate's abilities to the requirements of the job. The success of the company reflects the ability of its people—it is vital that each job be filled by the best man available.

Promotion on an objective and equitable basis is basic in sound human relations. Competent management, of course, adheres to this principle but is well aware of the possibility that some of its employees may feel that only the "fair-haired boys" are promoted to the more desirable and better-paying jobs. To eliminate any possibility of this morale-destroying impression among employees, employers give weight to length of service in making selections for promotions.

Union negotiators press for promotions solely on the basis of seniority, provided that the employee wants the job. Experience has shown this to be an undesirable procedure. There is constant agitation to promote the senior employee and give him a trial period to ascertain whether he has the necessary ability. If it develops that he has even the bare minimum qualifications, he usually stays on the job even though employees of greater ability and potentialities, but with less seniority, are available.

The most satisfactory procedure, from the viewpoint of both employee and employer, is to give weight to length of service only when in the opinion of management the qualifications of the candidates are relatively equal.

MANAGEMENT, ON THE IMPORTANCE OF ABILITY IN PROMOTIONS

Comments by personnel and industrial relations directors, collected by Norman J. Pentecost in the preparation of a paper for submission to a research seminar at the Graduate School of Business, Columbia University, 1957

Ability is always an important factor in considering promotions but is more important in some jobs than in others. Where there is a seniority clause, contract language has definite influence on decisions concerning promotions. Arbitration decisions in recent years have made it necessary to balance ability with seniority, meaning that it has not always been possible to promote the best qualified individual. This tends to drive the alert, aggressive short service employee to seek employment elsewhere or to satisfy his ambition in other directions, such as holding Union office.

Seniority clauses greatly influence decisions concerning promotion. By and large, ability becomes an issue only on the higher rated and skilled jobs, and here only where there is a clearly demonstrable difference in *relative* ability as between the applicants.

In our lower grades, seniority governs promotions. The man need only demonstrate during a trial period that he can do the job to the satisfaction of management, subject, of course, to grievance. Regardless of labor grade, the same rule applies to promotions to jobs in higher labor grades within the department. Outside the department in the higher labor grades, we select the man we judge to be the best suited to the job, and ability is the principal factor governing selection.

While it is true that seniority had some bearing on promotions when we had no labor contract, we were not restricted and, as a result, some promotions had the appearance of discrimination which to some extent could be true. Labor contract or no labor contract, no supervisor or manager can help but feel the impact of intangible or subjective influences such as attitude toward the job and company, the ability to get along with people, etc. When not restricted by the terms of a contract, a supervisor will in many cases make selections for promotion with these respective factors in mind, and I believe that our supervisors would not be exceptions.

We always consider ability as an important factor in decisions concerning promotion. Our contract provides that for promotion to any classification above that of helper a man must possess the necessary ability to progress within a reasonable time to the next higher classification in the particular line of work and to ultimately progress to the classification of journeyman. Considering this provision in the contract we do not differentiate between certain types of jobs concerning the importance of ability. Seniority clauses very definitely have had an influence on our decisions concerning promotions. Our contract provides that competency being sufficient, seniority shall prevail. In cases where the margin is very narrow in determining whether a man possesses sufficient competency, I am sure that seniority many times influences our decisions.

Normally, we stress ability more on the skilled jobs. However, if there is a great difference in the abilities of the men concerned, even in the semi-skilled jobs, we introduce aggressiveness, attitude on the job and ability in order to get the best man on the job.

Ability is of less importance in unskilled and semi-skilled occupations as compared to skilled occupations. Seniority clauses have caused us to be more objective in measuring ability and more careful in our decisions. We are occasionally forced to promote employees less desirable because of attitude, cooperativeness, willingness and moral character because of lack of an objective measure and proof of the difference. We include those characteristics in ability, the Union usually does not.

Ability is always a factor in the decisions concerning promotions, the importance of this factor increasing as the skill requirements of the job increase. Where ability and other qualifications are relatively equal seniority governs the selection.

In all promotions, ability to do the job to which promoted is a very important factor. In promotions to higher hourly paid jobs relative ability becomes important, since it is from these higher jobs that future salaried foremen must be selected. Obviously, where supervisory qualifications are required, mere ability to perform a job is not enough. Consequently, it will be noted in the seniority section of our Labor Agreement that when promotions are to be made to the highest hourly paid jobs relative ability becomes a consideration along with seniority. Our feeling is that even in the absence of a labor agreement we would still give some weight to seniority in making promotions. Our Company has a long history of promoting from within, and naturally tries to favor its older employees consistent with getting the required job properly done.

Certainly ability is an important factor in decisions concerning promotion. I think that potential ability or "capability" is also of considerable importance. In instances where we can make value judgments without the pressure from the union to compromise an issue on a "political" basis we could make better decisions. This is based on the realistic assumption that management is better off getting the best man for the job into the job irrespective of seniority.

The individual as well as the union regard seniority as the controlling factor; we insist on ability as governing. There is a distinction between seniority entitling a man to a preferred job and seniority entitling him to consideration for a preferred job. Seniority without regard to the other factors (ability and physical fitness) gears everything to the level of the less efficient, penalizes the good worker for initiative, and eventually brings to a lower level the overall efficiency of the entire group.

Greater consideration is given ability in more skilled jobs. More consideration is given to seniority than was given before our contractual agreements. However, seniority has always been given a great deal of consideration in this Company, in cases where more than one man was qualified for the job.

As the company grew from 5,000 to 30,000 people, it became impossible for supervisors to adequately judge people's ability. There were many claims that via favoritism, relatives and friends were being promoted. We gave in to the pressure and instituted a straight seniority system. I don't think ability matters much in the first five labor grades. The skill needs get stiffer above that though and it's at these higher levels that we sometimes by-pass a senior man. For example, if a job requires some imagination and ingenuity the supervisor is in the best position to judge whether or not the senior man has it. If he picks a junior man and the senior man "hollers," then we must give it to the senior man on a trial basis. Most of the time the supervisor is right. How do we judge imaginativeness? In a lower ranking job, did the man innovate new tools or procedures? It is safe to say that ability is more important in the higher skilled jobs.

My philosophy is that ability and merit should be the sole basis for promotions. It's completely unfair to be unable to reward a young fellow with ability, initiative and ambition because he faces an overwhelming seniority roster. I'm not even convinced that the majority of union members really want it. It's been my experience that it's the unskilled employees who shout the most for a seniority system and not the higher levels of semi-skilled and skilled. This is because they possess no skill or ability qualities to protect them in promotions. I think the skilled and semi-skilled workers prefer to get along without it and get ahead on their ability.

I'll admit that I believe there is a high correlation between seniority and ability on the unskilled and lower semi-skilled levels. The average fellow has the ability and desire to learn the next higher job. We are so advanced technologically today that much of the skill involved has been taken over by the machine. Even though this is true, there still are a few "deadheads" who can't or won't learn the next higher job properly, so the company needs some protection against being forced to promote on seniority even on the lower job levels.

PROMOTION AND THE DETERMINATION OF ABILITY

Kuhlman Electric Co. and United Automobile Workers, Local 778, 26 LA 885, 1956

ROBERT G. HOWLETT, ARBITRATOR

GRIEVANCE NO. 6002

In January, 1956, the Company posted a notice of openings in the second class electrical maintenance classification. Among the employees who applied were Aloysius Piesik, whose seniority dates from May 23, 1944, and Jack Dean, with seniority from September 30, 1947. Both employees were working as second class electrical testers, a classification having a lower wage rate than the job of second class electrical maintenance.

The Company chose Jack Dean, the employee with the lesser seniority, in preference to Aloysius Piesik.[1] Mr. Piesik thereupon filed a grievance reading as follows:

I, the undersigned, with equal ability and more seniority protest the appointment of Jack Dean to the Electrical Maintenance opening. I request the appointment with full rights of seniority credits.

The Company replied as follows:

Selection of the man chosen for the Electrical Maintenance opening was based on ability as determined through interview, interview with department supervisor, evaluation of educational background, problem solving ability, electrical knowledge, continuation of education, and potential for growth in the department. In our judgment the man selected rated the highest on the combination of these factors.

The parties have stipulated that the question for the arbitrator is:

Has the Company complied with the provisions of the Agreement between the parties in the selection of Jack Dean over Aloysius Piesik for a posted opening on Second Class Electrical Maintenance?

The rules pertaining to the promotion of employees are found in Section 9 of Article IV of the agreement:

Where new jobs or vacancies occur, they will be posted on the bulletin boards by Management. Employees having ability for same may make application to the Personnel Manager for these jobs.

[1] There was a dispute concerning other employees, but it was resolved by the parties prior to the submission of Grievance No. 6002 to the arbitrator.

In cases of promotion to higher job classifications within the bargaining unit, the factors to be considered shall be ability and seniority. Where the ability of the employees under consideration for the promotion is substantially equal, then seniority shall govern. The Company shall give the Union the reason for the selection of an applicant under this section if the Union so desires. . . .

Prior to selecting the particular employees for the vacancies, the Company gave each applicant two examinations. One consisted of the Wonderlic Personnel Test, a twelve minute examination prepared for use in industry as a selection instrument in employment and placement, and as an indicator of future possibilities. The test shows general ability rather than aptitude for a specific job. The second test, written by the Company, was designed to show the applicants' knowledge of work in the Electrical Maintenance Department.

The Company had never previously used written examinations of this scope, although short tests containing three questions had been, on some occasions, used in the past. The Personnel Manager testified that the weight given to each test was "about fifty-fifty."

Out of a possible twenty-one, Dean scored fifteen on the electrical knowledge test, whereas Piesik scored seventeen.

On the Wonderlic test, Dean scored twenty-six which, according to the author of the test, places him one point above the level of foreman, production control man, job analysis and time study man, and eight points above the minimum for skilled mechanic, which, the Company says, is the type of work involved in the second class electrical maintenance classification. Grievant scored fourteen, which, according to the author of the test, is one point below the minimum for general factory help and four points below the minimum for skilled mechanics.

In addition to the tests, the Company also considered (1) the educational background of the two applicants, (2) the continuation of their education, (3) age and physical condition, and (4) attitude.

Dean had completed the eleventh grade and passed the United States Armed Forces Institute General Education Development Test at the high school level. Piesik had completed the eighth grade.

Dean was engaged in formal home study courses in radio and television for the past year and a half. The Company reported that the courses consisted of one hundred eighteen regular lessons, eighteen mathematics, algebra and trigonometry lessons and fifteen experiment kits. Dean had completed one hundred one lessons.

Piesik had done outside reading in trade journals and publications concerning electronic controls, time controls, heating ovens and other electrical fields. He had performed service work on television sets and radios.

Dean is twenty-six; Piesik is forty-three.

While both employees are "in apparent good health" a question was raised as to a foot injury suffered by grievant in a foundry prior to his employment by the Company and also as to an impairment of vision.

Dean is described by management as "Quiet type of person, appears eager to learn, tries hard to please and is co-operative." He is said to have "a sincere desire to get ahead and work his way into a more responsible position" and he "has a record of being dependable." Grievant is said to have "a tendency to be somewhat loud and outspoken and not as co-operative as is desirable in helping achieve departmental goals."

POSITION OF THE PARTIES

The Union vigorously objects to the use of the two written tests as one basis for selecting an employee for a vacancy. The Union has no objection to the use of written tests, as such, but urges that they may not be instituted by unilateral action of the Company, as the Union Committee is entitled to know the type of questions and the weight to be given the tests before written examinations may be used as a basis for promotion. The Company, says the Union, had not used written examinations in the past, and the institution of this method of testing is an alteration of the intent and purpose of Section 9 of Article IV. Past practice, it is urged, must be continued until changed by agreement of the parties. The Union also contends:

1. Grievant has had practical experience on the job for which he applied on Saturdays, when other employees have been absent, and during inventory periods.

2. The Company is seeking to promote the "best qualified man" which is not the test established by the contract. The Union says that some of the questions asked on the Electrical Maintenance Department examination were of first class potential, whereas, the job to be filled was in the second class category.

3. Grievant passed the portion of the examination covering electrical knowledge and experience with a higher rate than Dean.

4. Grievant has worked in the Electrical Maintenance Department without supervision.

5. With respect to grievant's impairment of vision, his present job has a higher visual point evaluation than the second class electrical maintenance job.[2]

The Company contends that its sole motivation in selecting an employee for a job "is to pick the best qualified employee with the understanding that if two or more applicants have substantially equal qualifications, then seniority shall be used as the tie-breaker." "The selection," says management, "was based on employee interviews, interviews with the supervisors, evaluation of their educational background, problem solving ability and general elementary electrical

---

[2] The Company has an evaluation plan for all jobs. "Frequent mental/visual attention" has an evaluation of 20 points for second class electric maintenance and an evaluation of 30 points for second class electrical tester, grievant's present job. No distinction is made as to the "mental" and "visual" portion of this particular attribute. Second class electrical maintenance has 628 evaluation points, whereas second class electrical tester has 590. Jobs in the plant range from 328 to 710.

knowledge as measured by brief tests, continuation of education and potential for growth in the department." The Company contends that it is continually searching for a better method of exercising its managerial responsibility of promotion and that it may adopt written examinations unless there is a contract prohibition against their use.

Management further contends that the parties have agreed on a job definition wherein there is required "the use of complicated drawings and specifications, advanced shop mathematics and book formulas, wide variety of precision measuring instruments, broad shop knowledge." [3] Because of this, the Company contends, a high school education is a definite advantage over an eighth grade education. The Company further contends that the written tests were only part of the selection procedure, and that the selection was also made because (1) Dean had a better education than Piesik, (2) his age (the maintenance foreman stated he was looking for employees with a potential for future upgrading), (3) his greater interest in further education, (4) his attitude toward his fellow employees, and (5) the performance of the two employees.

DISCUSSION

Seniority clauses generally (and perhaps of necessity) are founded (or founder) on abstractions, as draftsmen seek to limit length of service as the criterion for promotion and other aspects of job security and job movement. The concepts of "ability," "aptitude," "fitness," "skill," "capability," "merit," and "qualifications," not to mention the appending of adjectives ("required ability," "satisfactory experience," "necessary qualifications") renders difficult the task of the arbitrator. The plaintive cry of one arbitrator speaks for the profession:

> If the parties to collective bargaining agreements do not set up a more specific standard of reference than that contained in the abstract word "ability," then it seems to me that the most they can expect from themselves and their arbitrators are sincere but inexact personal judgments as to the comparative standing of various employees.[4]

Prior to the advent of collective bargaining agreements, management had the power, and the legal right, to promote (and to demote, lay-off and recall) at will. Employees were generally moved from job to job, or in and out of the factory, as productive efficiency required. The unions, often charging favoritism, sought job security for senior employees. Thus there developed limitations on management's freedom to move employees. To say that the contest between seniority and ability results in a head-on collision between job security and

---

[3] This statement is made in the Company brief, and while the statement was not denied by the Union, the job description for the job submitted in evidence, does not express such a high educational requirement.

[4] Gabriel N. Alexander in "Factor of Ability in Labor Relations," published in *Arbitration Today*, Bureau of National Affairs, 1955, pages 60, 61. See also, Douglas Aircraft Co., Inc., 25 LA 600, 603 (1955); Public Service Electric & Gas Co., 12 LA 317, 321 (1949); and Elkouri, *How Arbitration Works*, Bureau of National Affairs, 1952, pages 241–251.

productive efficiency is an over-simplification, but these conflicting viewpoints are always in evidence in both collective bargaining and arbitration where seniority is involved.[5]

Promotion clauses (other than the infrequent ones based solely on seniority *or* competence) are generally divided into four categories: [6]

1. Seniority the Primary Factor. The senior employee is promoted provided he is able to perform a specified requirement of the job, such as "minimum," "normal," "average" or "sufficient." [7]

2. Seniority and Other Qualification Equal. Seniority and another requirement are both factors, but there is no reference as to the weight to be given to each, i.e. "due regard to length of service and ability," and "promotion shall be based upon seniority and capability." [8]

3. Seniority the Secondary Factor. Ability or other qualification is the primary factor unless equal, in which event, seniority will prevail.[9]

4. Ability Limited by an Additional Factor. Ability or other qualification is stated to be the primary factor, but is limited by a qualifying word—usually "relatively" or "substantially." An additional factor is added to type (3), thus creating a penumbra area in which ability may be superseded by seniority.[10]

The Kuhlman Electric Company promotion clause falls within type (4). The senior employee receives the promotion if his ability is *"substantially"* equal to that of the junior employee. Thus, a senior employee may be preferred, even

---

[5] Of course, if length of service, as the sole basis for advancement, should result in a wholesale promotion of inefficient employees, workers would lose their job security, for the enterprise would fail. Perhaps the issue of seniority vs. ability is not as great as the arguments of management and union make it appear. It has been suggested that seniority *may* be as good a guide to future performance as ability. See James J. Healey and Jean T. McKelvey in "The Factor of Ability in Labor Relations," published in *Arbitration Today,* Bureau of National Affairs, 1955, page 45, et seq.

[6] Some arbitrators have suggested there are two types of seniority clauses. See Pittsburgh Steel Co., 21 LA 565, 567 (1953).

[7] International Harvester Company, 11 LA 1190 (1948); North American Cement Corporation, 11 LA 1109 (1949); Aviation Maintenance Corporation, 13 LA 677 (1949); United States Rubber Company, 18 LA 834 (1952); West Virginia Pulp and Paper Co., 20 LA 385 (1953). A trial period is frequently required for the employee promoted under this type of clause.

[8] Standard Oil Company, 11 LA 810 (1948); Pennsylvania Salt Manufacturing Company, 14 LA 12 (1949); International Harvester Company, 21 LA 183 (1953); Callite Tungsten Company, 11 LA 743 (1948); Shell Oil Company, Inc., 4 LA 13 (1946). Trial periods are sometimes required in clauses of this type.

[9] Dewey & Almy Chemical Company, 25 LA 316 (1955); Ford Motor Company, 2 LA 374 (1945); Chrysler Corporation, 14 LA 143 (1950).

[10] Examples of "substantially equal" are Douglas Aircraft Company, Inc., 25 LA 601 (1955); Connecticut Power Company, 13 LA 459 (1949); Southern Bell Telephone & Telegraph Company, 16 LA 1 (1951); Marlin-Rockwell Corporation, 17 LA 254 (1951). Examples of "relatively equal" are Acme Steel Co., 9 LA 432 (1944) ("relatively equal" seems to mean the same as "equal"); Hercules Powder Company, 10 LA 624 (1948); Seagrave Corporation, 16 LA 410 (1951); Bethlehem Steel Company, 24 LA 820 (1955).

though his ability is less than that of some junior employee, but the exact line between employees is difficult to draw. The problem is well stated by Arbitrator Whitley P. McCoy, former Director of the Federal Mediation & Conciliation Service:

> The term "substantially equal" has a meaning obviously different from the unmodified word "equal." "Equal" might conceivably be construed as meaning "substantially equal," but "substantially equal" could not possibly be construed as meaning "exactly equal." The parties, in writing this section, quite apparently contemplated a situation where one applicant would be slightly better qualified than another, but not substantially so, in which case seniority should be the controlling factor. So they provided that where the qualifications are *substantially* equal seniority should govern. This provision means that the superiority of one over the other must be by a substantial margin, not so slight as to cause doubt or to leave room for reasonable question. This seems so clear as not to require elaboration.[11]

The word seems to be used in the subject contract as meaning "about" or "approximately." [12]

Of importance in this arbitration is the fact that Section 9 does not refer to general ability or native ability, but ability "for the promotion"—ability to perform the particular job sought. This is emphasized by the first portion of Section 9, which states that when new jobs or vacancies are posted on the bulletin boards "employees having ability for same (the new job or vacancy) may make application therefor." It is therefore necessary to relate each employee's qualifications to the job to be filled in making the decision to promote or not to promote.[13]

Management in its testimony and argument stressed the importance of securing the "best qualified" or "highest qualified" employee, the employee with the "greatest ability" or "most ability," or with "potential for upgrading." The Union, on the other hand, tried to create a type (1) seniority clause out of Section 9. It contended that under past practice seniority prevailed if the employee could "do the job," but no evidence was presented to substantiate this theory. Neither theory is correct under the type (4) clause (Section 9) which is the subject matter of this discussion.

The Company's interest in securing the best qualified employee for promotion is understandable. Management is interested in the success of its enterprise and one aspect of successful operation is competent employees. Possibly the Union should have as great an interest in general competence and ability, for

[11] Southern Bell Telephone & Telegraph Company, 16 LA 1, 10 (1951). Should "substantially" or "relatively" ever be used as modifying "equal"? Are not two persons or things either equal or *not* equal? We may take comfort in the use by the framers of our Constitution of "more perfect union."

[12] It has been held that "relatively" cannot mean "about" or "approximately," but means that applicants must be compared, thus making the phrase "relatively equal" mean "equal." Acme Steel Company, 9 LA 432, 435 (1947).

[13] Douglas Aircraft Company, 25 LA 600, 603 (1955).

the success of the business will redound to the benefit of all employees. However, the contract language must control unless and until changed.

A job description of second class electric maintenance was adopted as of September 23, 1953:

> Under general supervision, perform routine electrical maintenance operations, such as replacement of burned out bulbs and tubes, cleaning electrical fixtures, regular routine lubrication and inspection of motors, replacement of fuses: replacement or repair of switches, portable tools, extension cords, run conduit or wire according to sketch or diagram or detailed instructions; assist in trouble shooting; repair an installation of electrical and connected mechanical equipment.

Dean and Piesik must be compared with respect to the factors used by the Company in promoting Dean, in order to determine whether the two are *substantially* equal—or, in the alternative, whether Dean is *substantially* superior to Piesik. The arbitrator is convinced that Dean is *superior* and that under a type (1) clause Dean would be entitled to the promotion. But is he sufficiently superior (i.e. "substantially superior") to justify a disregard of Piesik's seniority? [14]

Educational Background. While formal education is not a guarantee of success in any job, it is a factor to be considered. Dean is superior to Piesik, in this regard.

Continuation of Education. The Company stresses the fact that Dean has taken formal home study courses, while Piesik's study has been confined to informal reading. The Union seeks to minimize Dean's efforts on the ground that Dean's study of radios and television is not of assistance in the job sought because the Company does not manufacture these products, and algebra and trigonometry are not used in the second class electrical maintenance job. It seems evident that any study in the field of electricity and electronics will benefit an employee at the Kuhlman plant and that such study should be encouraged. While the testimony with respect to Dean's work was hearsay and Piesik's testimony was general, it appears that both these employees have displayed interest in study which will be helpful to them as employees of the Kuhlman Electric Company.

Health. Both employees appear to enjoy good health, except for Piesik's eyes. He testified that he does not need to wear glasses, and that he can see moving objects from the side, although he does not see them clearly. In further support of his physical ability, he pointed out that he had been performing his present job in a satisfactory manner, and that since 1951 he has done part time work as a second class electrical maintenance employee. The arbitrator must take note of the fact that the mental and visual demand for the second class electrical maintenance classification is less thn that for second class electrical tester, the present classification of both Piesik and Dean. No evidence was submitted by the Company with respect to Piesik's alleged foot ailment; and he

[14] Some arbitrators give weight to the difference in the seniority of applicants for a job, but such a comparison is not pertinent under the clause here involved. International Harvester Company, 21 LA 183 (1953).

testified that it did not bother him, and he could climb if the job required it. The fact that Dean, at twenty-seven, is several years younger than Piesik, who is forty-three, is not an advantage insofar as this job is concerned. It would appear that Dean may be slightly superior to Piesik with respect to health.

Attitude. "Attitude" is difficult to determine, although the particular attribute is important—the degree thereof depends on the job to be performed. No persuasive testimony was presented by either Company or Union with respect to the attitudes of the two employees. The Electrical Testing Department foreman, who might be expected to know more about the attitude of both Dean and Piesik than any other supervisor, was not called to testify. The Company laid stress on an "interview" between Piesik and Guzdzial, the Maintenance Department foreman. The Union contends this was not a "formal" interview. A conversation did take place, although it is patent that there was no exhaustive treatment of Piesik's ability to fill the vacancy. The foreman testified that he asked Piesik whether he had done anything since his last interview which should be added. Piesik replied in the negative, but no testimony was offered with respect to the prior interview. The Company stated that "all applicants were interviewed" but there is no testimony with respect to the results of the interview with Dean.

While the strict rules of evidence do not apply in arbitrations, the arbitrator must hold that there has been no evidence on the issue to support the Company's allegation with respect to Dean's superiority in "attitude" as compared with Piesik.

The Examinations. In some respects this arbitration was presented as though the issue were the right of the Company to require written examinations rather than Dean vs. Piesik.[15]

The Union urges that before the Company may require written tests, it must be consulted in order that the Union committee may know the types of questions which will be asked and the weight which will be given to them.

The Company urges that it is attempting continuously to develop the best method of finding the best qualified men for promotion, that promotion of employees is a management responsibility and that unless the contract prohibits the use of written examinations, the Company may require applicants to submit to them.

The Company is correct up to a point. It is not bound by established practice in its method of determining "ability." [16] The Company may not, however,

---

[15] The exhibits disclose that a grievance raising this general issue had been filed by the Union, and that arbitration was contemplated; but subsequently a determination was made not to submit this issue to arbitration.

[16] Mr. Guzdzial testified that prior to the filling of the present vacancy (1) applicants were tried out, (2) selections were ordinarily made from the Electrical Testing Department, (3) it was hoped that people interested in the Electrical Maintenance Department would take formal training, but there were no written tests, (4) it was felt that the method in use was not adequate, (5) the past practice had been satisfactory in line with those who had applied for the jobs, and (6) the Company was looking for people with potential.

unilaterally change the qualifications of a job. Thus, in Pennsylvania Salt Manufacturing Company, 14 LA 12 (1949), a Board of Arbitration held that a Company did not have the right to require a high school education and high school chemistry or equivalent where these requirements had not existed before. An examination might be of such difficulty that it would, in fact, result in a change in the qualifications.[17]

The electrical knowledge test is specifically related to the job sought by Dean and Piesik. The Wonderlic Test is related only generally to promotion to second class electrical maintenance. The Company's testimony and argument were directed primarily toward showing the importance of the Wonderlic test as a measurement of general ability and potential of the employees examined. As the Personnel Manager said, the Company is seeking employees to promote "not just for the moment but for promotion in the department." Meritorious as this idea may be it is not within the contemplation of Section 9, which limits "ability" to "*the* promotion" which the employees under consideration are seeking to secure. While the Wonderlic test is not an examination which, if required as a condition to being considered for a job, changes the qualifications of the job (and hence is contrary to the existing requirements), the Company has given it greater weight than the contract language justifies. Dean may be a man who, after service as a second class electrical employee, will be well qualified for promotion to first class, while Piesik may reach his ultimate peak as a second class. This, however, is not the contract basis for promoting the junior employee over the senior employee, if their abilities to fill the second class electrical maintenance job ("ability . . . for the promotion") are *substantially* (or about) equal.

Experience. In neither brief nor testimony did the Company make much of the respective experience of the two employees within the plant. The Union sought to give the impression that the work performed by Piesik in the Maintenance Department was almost constant; and it was not until the arbitrator asked just how long Piesik had worked on various second class electrical maintenance operations that it appeared that this work was confined to three or four days in each of the years 1953, 1954 and 1955, although considerably more extensive in 1951 and 1952. Piesik testified that he worked, at times, without supervision.

Mr. Guzdzial testified that when Piesik worked in the Maintenance Department, he was usually used to clean motors, overhead cranes and ventilator fans and for pulling wires. He also said that Piesik was called in primarily because he was acquainted with stock and that he was called in to "help, not to take the place of a second class man." He had told Piesik, during the interview, that he believed he would have no trouble in passing the electrical test.

Dean had never performed any work in the Maintenance Department.

[17] See also Standard Oil Company, 11 LA 810 (1948); International Harvester Company, 21 LA 183 (1953). See American Can Company, 10 LA 613 (1948) for an excellent discussion of the use of aptitude tests. There was no limiting contract language which prevented the employer from giving considerably more weight to the tests than is possible here.

Satisfactory performance of an employee in operations of the vacant job is a factor in determining "ability." Other things being equal, the man who has had some experience on a job can become a competent employee in the classification faster than a man who has had no such experience. The testimony disclosed that in previous promotions, experience has been considered.

The job descriptions disclosed that the second class electrical maintenance job is a more difficult job than second class electrical tester, but the tester job is good preparation for the maintenance job.

A reference to "job rate data sheet" for second class electrical maintenance discloses that the attribute of "education" (112 points) requires "knowledge of electricity and electronics, use of measuring instruments, such as meters and gauges." From the testimony, including the electrical knowledge test, it appears that both Dean and Piesik are reasonably qualified for this second class maintenance job. The job (under the attribute of "experience," with 132 points), according to the data sheet, requires approximately one year to learn. Dean may have the ability to learn more rapidly, but Piesik already knows some of the operations. From the Wonderlic test, it appears that Dean is probably superior in the ability under "Initiative and Ingenuity" to "plan and perform sequence operations," and to "make general decisions as to quality and tolerances"; this attribute being evaluated at 84 points out of a total of 628.

In summary, Dean and Piesik rated approximately as follows:

Educational Background. Dean is superior.

Continuation of Education. Dean may have a slight advantage over Piesik.

Physical Condition. Dean may have a slight advantage over Piesik. Age is not a factor for the vacant job.

Attitude. The testimony was inconclusive with respect to either of the men.

Electrical Knowledge. Piesik has a slight advantage over Dean.

Problem-Solving Ability. (Wonderlic Test) Dean is substantially superior to Piesik, but this test is primarily directed toward general ability and not qualifications for the specific job here involved.

Experience on the Job. Piesik is superior to Dean. There was no testimony as to which employee is superior as a second class electrical tester.

The two employees are within the area of substantial equality for the job of second class electrical maintenance, hence Piesik, the senior employee, rather than Dean, should have been selected for the promotion.

The grievance made no request for retroactive pay in the event it were held that Piesik was entitled to the promotion; and the Union spokesman stated that the Union was "not interested" in back pay. Consequently, none is awarded.

11: Strikes

The one aspect of collective bargaining of which the public is more conscious than any other is probably strikes. In many minds the word "strike" would be freely associated with the word "union."

Since the public is generally not concerned with the several thousand small strikes which occur in any year, but may become irritated and inconvenienced by a few major strikes, it is the latter which governments—both state and Federal—have sought to control in some manner. The wave of strikes which broke over the nation following the ending of wage controls after World War II aroused public resentment from consumers who had for four war years been waiting to buy automobiles and refrigerators and houses which—at the moment when fulfillment seemed imminent—these work stoppages were now denying them. One consequence of this widespread exasperation was the writing into the Taft-Hartley Act of Title II, giving the government certain specific powers in strike situations which threatened public health and safety. And in nine states legislation was passed giving state governments powers of intervention in certain types of walkouts.

As the materials reproduced here will indicate, however, there has been continuing disagreement over the effectiveness and desirability of strike-control procedures. On the one hand, there are some—principally in the business community—who are satisfied to leave the present provisions untouched. There are numerous others, however, who regard the emergency-strike procedures as relatively ineffective and undesirable—some because they do not go far enough and others because they go too far.

HOW MUCH DOES A STRIKE COST YOU?

Flyer issued by the National Association of Manufacturers

If you are an employee in a manufacturing firm who takes home (after all deductions) $60 a week, and . . .

IF THE STRIKE LASTS		
	2¢	it will take you 1 Year and 23 Weeks
	4¢	it will take you 38 Weeks
	6¢	it will take you 25 Weeks
1 week	8¢	it will take you 19 Weeks
and your hourly gain is...	10¢	it will take you 15 Weeks
	16¢	it will take you 9 Weeks
	20¢	it will take you 7 Weeks

to make up for pay lost.

IF THE STRIKE LASTS		
	2¢	it will take you 5 Years and 40 Weeks
	4¢	it will take you 2 Years and 46 Weeks
	6¢	it will take you 1 Year and 48 Weeks
4 weeks	8¢	it will take you 1 Year and 23 Weeks
and your hourly gain is...	10¢	it will take you 1 Year and 8 Weeks
	16¢	it will take you 38 Weeks
	20¢	it will take you 30 Weeks

to make up for pay lost.

IF THE STRIKE LASTS		
	2¢	it will take you 14 Years and 22 Weeks
	4¢	it will take you 7 Years and 11 Weeks
	6¢	it will take you 4 Years and 42 Weeks
10 weeks	8¢	it will take you 3 Years and 31 Weeks
and your hourly gain is...	10¢	it will take you 2 Years and 46 Weeks
	16¢	it will take you 1 Year and 42 Weeks
	20¢	it will take you 1 Year and 23 Weeks

to make up for pay lost.

IF THE STRIKE LASTS		
	2¢	it will take you 21 Years and 34 Weeks
	4¢	it will take you 10 Years and 43 Weeks
	6¢	it will take you 7 Years and 11 Weeks
15 weeks	8¢	it will take you 5 Years and 21 Weeks
and your hourly gain is...	10¢	it will take you 4 Years and 17 Weeks
	16¢	it will take you 2 Years and 37 Weeks
	20¢	it will take you 2 Years and 9 Weeks

to make up for pay lost.

Source: "Your Personal Strike Cost Computer" Harmon E. Snoke, Bridgeport, Conn.

IF THE STRIKE LASTS	2¢ it will take you 28 Years and 44 Weeks
	4¢ it will take you 14 Years and 22 Weeks
	6¢ it will take you 9 Years and 32 Weeks
20 weeks	8¢ it will take you 7 Years and 11 Weeks
and your hourly gain is...	10¢ it will take you 5 Years and 40 Weeks
	16¢ it will take you 3 Years and 32 Weeks
	20¢ it will take you 2 Years and 46 Weeks
	to make up for pay lost.

THE TAFT-HARTLEY ACT ON NATIONAL EMERGENCY STRIKES

TITLE II—CONCILIATION OF LABOR DISPUTES IN INDUSTRIES AFFECTING COMMERCE; NATIONAL EMERGENCIES

Sec. 201. That it is the policy of the United States that—

(a) sound and stable industrial peace and the advancement of the general welfare, health, and safety of the Nation and of the best interests of employers and employees can most satisfactorily be secured by the settlement of issues between employers and employees through the processes of conference and collective bargaining between employers and the representatives of their employees;

(b) the settlement of issues between employers and employees through collective bargaining may be advanced by making available full and adequate governmental facilities for conciliation, mediation, and voluntary arbitration to aid and encourage employers and the representatives of their employees to reach and maintain agreements concerning rates of pay, hours, and working conditions, and to make all reasonable efforts to settle their differences by mutual agreement reached through conferences and collective bargaining or by such methods as may be provided for in any applicable agreement for the settlement of disputes; and

(c) certain controversies which arise between parties to collective-bargaining agreements may be avoided or minimized by making available full and adequate governmental facilities for furnishing assistance to employers and the representatives of their employees in formulating for inclusion within such agreements provision for adequate notice of any proposed changes in the terms of such agreements, for the final adjustment of grievances or questions regarding the application or interpretation of such agreements, and other provisions designed to prevent the subsequent arising of such controversies.

Sec. 202. (a) There is hereby created an independent agency to be known as the Federal Mediation and Conciliation Service (herein referred to as the "Service," except that for sixty days after the date of the enactment of this Act such term shall refer to the Conciliation Service of the Department of Labor). The Service shall be under the direction of a Federal Mediation and Conciliation Director (hereinafter referred to as the "Director"), who shall be appointed by the President by and with the advice and consent of the Senate.

The Director shall receive compensation at the rate of $12,000 per annum. The Director shall not engage in any other business, vocation, or employment. . . .

(c) The principal office of the Service shall be in the District of Columbia, but the Director may establish regional offices convenient to localities in which labor controversies are likely to arise. The Director may by order, subject to revocation at any time, delegate any authority and discretion conferred upon him by this Act to any regional director, or other officer or employee of the Service. The Director may establish suitable procedures for cooperation with State and local mediation agencies. The Director shall make an annual report in writing to Congress at the end of the fiscal year. . . .

FUNCTIONS OF THE SERVICE

Sec. 203. (a) It shall be the duty of the Service, in order to prevent or minimize interruptions of the free flow of commerce growing out of labor disputes, to assist parties to labor disputes in industries affecting commerce to settle such disputes through conciliation and mediation.

(b) The Service may proffer its services in any labor dispute in any industry affecting commerce, either upon its own motion or upon the request of one or more of the parties to the dispute, whenever in its judgment such dispute threatens to cause a substantial interruption of commerce. The Director and the Service are directed to avoid attempting to mediate disputes which would have only a minor effect on interstate commerce if State or other conciliation services are available to the parties. Whenever the Service does proffer its services in any dispute, it shall be the duty of the Service promptly to put itself in communication with the parties and to use its best efforts, by mediation and conciliation, to bring them to agreement.

(c) If the Director is not able to bring the parties to agreement by conciliation within a reasonable time, he shall seek to induce the parties voluntarily to seek other means of settling the dispute without resort to strike, lock-out, or other coercion, including submission to the employees in the bargaining unit of the employer's last offer of settlement for approval or rejection in a secret ballot. The failure or refusal of either party to agree to any procedure suggested by the Director shall not be deemed a violation of any duty or obligation imposed by this Act.

(d) Final adjustment by a method agreed upon by the parties is hereby declared to be the desirable method for settlement of grievance disputes arising over the application or interpretation of an existing collective-bargaining agreement. The Service is directed to make its conciliation and mediation services available in the settlement of such grievance disputes only as a last resort and in exceptional cases.

Sec. 204. (a) In order to prevent or minimize interruptions of the free flow of commerce growing out of labor disputes, employers and employees and their representatives, in any industry affecting commerce, shall—

(1) exert every reasonable effort to make and maintain agreements concerning rates of pay, hours, and working conditions, including provision for adequate notice of any proposed change in the terms of such agreements;

(2) whenever a dispute arises over the terms or application of a collective-bargaining agreement and a conference is requested by a party or prospective party thereto, arrange promptly for such a conference to be held and endeavor in such conference to settle such dispute expeditiously; and

(3) in case such dispute is not settled by conference, participate fully and promptly in such meetings as may be undertaken by the Service under this Act for the purpose of aiding in a settlement of the dispute.

Sec. 205. (a) There is hereby created a National Labor-Management Panel which shall be composed of twelve members appointed by the President, six of whom shall be selected from among persons outstanding in the field of management and six of whom shall be selected from among persons outstanding in the field of labor. Each member shall hold office for a term of three years, except that any member appointed to fill a vacancy occurring prior to the expiration of the term for which his predecessor was appointed shall be appointed for the remainder of such term, and the terms of office of the members first taking office shall expire, as designated by the President at the time of appointment, four at the end of the first year, four at the end of the second year, and four at the end of the third year after the date of appointment. Members of the panel, when serving on business of the panel, shall be paid compensation at the rate of $25 per day, and shall also be entitled to receive an allowance for actual and necessary travel and subsistence expenses while so serving away from their places of residence.

(b) It shall be the duty of the panel, at the request of the Director, to advise in the avoidance of industrial controversies and the manner in which mediation and voluntary adjustment shall be administered, particularly with reference to controversies affecting the general welfare of the country.

NATIONAL EMERGENCIES

Sec. 206. Whenever in the opinion of the President of the United States, a threatened or actual strike or lock-out affecting an entire industry or a substantial part thereof engaged in trade, commerce, transportation, transmission, or communication among the several States or with foreign nations, or engaged in the production of goods for commerce, will, if permitted to occur or to continue, imperil the national health or safety, he may appoint a board of inquiry to inquire into the issues involved in the dispute and to make a written report to him within such time as he shall prescribe. Such report shall include a statement of the facts with respect to the dispute, including each party's statement of its position but shall not contain any recommendations. The President shall file a copy of such report with the Service and shall make its contents available to the public.

Sec. 207. (a) A board of inquiry shall be composed of a chairman and such other members as the President shall determine, and shall have power to sit and act in any place within the United States and to conduct such hearings either in public or in private, as it may deem necessary or proper, to ascertain the facts with respect to the causes and circumstances of the dispute.

(b) Members of a board of inquiry shall receive compensation at the rate of

$50 for each day actually spent by them in the work of the board, together with necessary travel and subsistence expenses.

(c) For the purpose of any hearing or inquiry conducted by any board appointed under this title, the provisions of sections 9 and 10 (relating to the attendance of witnesses and the production of books, papers, and documents) of the Federal Trade Commission Act of September 16, 1914, as amended (U.S.C. 19, title 15, secs. 49 and 50, as amended), are hereby made applicable to the powers and duties of such board.

Sec. 208. (a) Upon receiving a report from a board of inquiry the President may direct the Attorney General to petition any district court of the United States having jurisdiction of the parties to enjoin such strike or lock-out or the continuing thereof, and if the court finds that such threatened or actual strike or lock-out—

(i) affects an entire industry or a substantial part thereof engaged in trade, commerce, transportation, transmission, or communication among the several States or with foreign nations, or engaged in the production of goods for commerce; and

(ii) if permitted to occur or to continue, will imperil the national health or safety, it shall have jurisdiction to enjoin any such strike or lock-out, or the continuing thereof, and to make such other orders as may be appropriate.

(b) In any case, the provisions of the Act of March 23, 1932, entitled "An Act to amend the Judicial Code and to define and limit the jurisdiction of courts sitting in equity, and for other purposes," shall not be applicable.

(c) The order or orders of the court shall be subject to review by the appropriate circuit court of appeals and by the Supreme Court upon writ of certiorari or certification as provided in sections 239 and 240 of the Judicial Code, as amended (U.S.C., title 29, secs. 346 and 347).

Sec. 209. (a) Whenever a district court has issued an order under section 208 enjoining acts or practices which imperil or threaten to imperil the national health or safety, it shall be the duty of the parties to the labor dispute giving rise to such order to make every effort to adjust and settle their differences, with the assistance of the Service created by this Act. Neither party shall be under any duty to accept, in whole or in part, any proposal of settlement made by the Service.

(b) Upon the issuance of such order, the President shall reconvene the board of inquiry which has previously reported with respect to the dispute. At the end of a sixty-day period (unless the dispute has been settled by that time), the board of inquiry shall report to the President the current position of the parties and the efforts which have been made for settlement, and shall include a statement by each party of its position and a statement of the employer's last offer of settlement. The President shall make such report available to the public. The National Labor Relations Board, within the succeeding fifteen days, shall take a secret ballot of the employees of each employer involved in the dispute on the question of whether they wish to accept the final offer of settlement made by their employer as stated by him and shall certify the results thereof to the Attorney General within five days thereafter.

Sec. 210. Upon the certification of the results of such ballot or upon a settlement being reached, whichever happens sooner, the Attorney General shall move the court to discharge the injunction, which motion shall then be granted and the injunction discharged. When such motion is granted, the President shall submit to the Congress a full and comprehensive report of the proceedings, including the findings of the board of inquiry and the ballot taken by the National Labor Relations Board, together with such recommendations as he may see fit to make the consideration and appropriate action.

NATIONAL EMERGENCY DISPUTES [*]

From the First Annual Report of the Federal Mediation and Conciliation Service, 1948, pp. 55–58

Boards of Inquiry. The current provisions of the act (sec. 208 (*a*)) make the submission of a report by a statutory board of inquiry a condition precedent to the President requesting the Attorney General to apply for an injunction. If the dispute threatens a national stoppage of critical proportions, it becomes necessary for the President to appoint the board a sufficient period of time in advance of the deadline date in order to afford it an opportunity to convene, to investigate, to hold hearings, to prepare and submit its report, and to give the Attorney General a reasonable opportunity to apply to the courts for an injunction in anticipation of a stoppage. Experience under the current provisions demonstrates that approximately 10 days to 2 weeks is required, as a minimum, to enable boards of inquiry satisfactorily to perform their statutory duties in most national emergency situations.

The Service has found that appointment of a board of inquiry in advance of a stoppage deadline and the scheduling of hearings before such a board, has the effect of interfering with the collective bargaining of the parties, particularly in relationships in which it is traditional not to reach a settlement until the eleventh hour. Mediation cannot be performed effectively when either the representatives of the Service or of the parties are before a board of inquiry, or when the parties await the report of the investigations of such a board. Further, the record will disclose that the relatively short period of time afforded to such boards to investigate the facts relevant to a dispute has exposed them to criticism and has afforded them insufficient time to operate at maximum efficiency and effectiveness.

Experience has also demonstrated that despite the great national importance of several disputes, relatively little publicity was given to, or public notice taken of, the reports of boards of inquiry. This may have been due to the fact that these boards were forbidden to make recommendations which might reasonably be expected to be given wide publicity, and restricted themselves to an exposition of the issues in controversy and the positions of the parties thereon. Although the facts relevant to a dispute may not have been known in the detail

[*] This account does not undertake a critical evaluation of the basic structure and merits of the national emergency dispute provisions in the act. It does attempt to set forth the special experience of the Service with particular provisions thereof.

in which they were set forth in the reports of the boards of inquiry, it is believed that they were generally matters of public knowledge. Apparently the Congress required board of inquiry reports to be submitted and made public because of the desirability of mobilizing public opinion behind a settlement of the controversy. This desire has not been fulfilled to a satisfactory degree.

It should also be observed that under current provisions of law, if the Federal Mediation and Conciliation Service does not make a public recommendation of settlement (a procedure it will normally refrain from adopting because nonacceptance of its recommendation might destroy its future usefulness to the parties) a dispute might well run the 60-day period prior to the deadline date and the 80-day period of the injunction—a period of 20 weeks—without any public recommendation of settlement calculated to bring public opinion to bear on the parties.

Use of the Injunction. It is the experience of the Service that in some of the national emergency disputes occurring in the last year the issuance of an injunctive order did much to forestall a national crisis and to assist in achieving a peaceful settlement. Similar claims for the utility of injunctions, such as are provided in current law, as a means of protecting the national welfare, cannot be made in respect of other national emergency disputes. Indeed, the final report of the board of inquiry in the maritime dispute involving the Pacific coast longshoremen's union observed that the employers and unions in that dispute regarded the injunction period as a "warming up" rather than a "cooling off" period (p. 27). National emergency disputes vary widely in their facts and circumstances, and it is unlikely that any machinery can be devised that will guarantee satisfactory handling in all situations.

One of the conclusions which the Service is undoubtedly justified in drawing from its experience of the last year is that provision for an 80-day period of continued operations, under injunctive order of a court, tends to delay rather than facilitate settlement of a dispute. Parties unable to resolve the issues facing them before a deadline date, when subject to an injunction order, tend to lose a sense of urgency and to relax their efforts to reach a settlement. They wait for the next deadline date (the date of discharge of the injunction) to spur them to renewed efforts. In most instances efforts of the Service to encourage the parties to bargain during the injunction period, with a view to early settlement, falls on deaf ears. Further, the public appears to be lulled into a sense of false security by a relatively long period of industrial peace by injunction and does not give evidence of being aware of a threat to the common welfare which would produce a climate of public opinion favorable to settlement. Whether this experience dictates the desirability of a shorter injunction period or an injunction period of indefinite duration the Service expresses no opinion at this time.

Last Offer Ballots (sec. 209 (b)). In every national emergency dispute to date the results of a ballot conducted by the National Labor Relations Board pursuant to section 209 (b) of the act have been overwhelmingly for rejection of the employer's last offer. For reasons which need not be elaborated here it is fair to assume that the likelihood of any ballot in the future having a contrary result, is small and remote. These ballots are expensive to conduct, and the experience of a year demonstrates that they do nothing to promote settlement of a dispute. To the contrary, they are a disrupting influence in collective bargaining and mediation. The last or final offer of an employer which the National Labor Relations Board is under an obligation to submit to ballot, is not likely to be the ultimate offer in fact, on the basis of which a settlement will be reached. Most decidedly this was the case in the disputes involving the Oak Ridge National Laboratories, the West coast maritime and longshoremen's unions and the Atlantic coast longshoremen's union. Unions and their membership appear to regard such last offers as counteroffers in bargaining which, if accepted, mean a repudiation of union leadership. Experience with the strike ballots required by the War Labor Disputes Act as well as the Labor Management Relations Act, 1947, discloses that workers are not likely to repudiate their representatives in the course of contract negotiations.

A vote turning down an employer's last offer places additional obstacles and difficulties in the way of a settlement. Union representatives must necessarily accept the vote as a mandate from the rank and file of workers that they may regard as practicable and possible bases of settlement only those offers of employers substantially more favorable than the one rejected. With foreknowledge of this consequence, employers tend to keep in reserve, and not to represent as a last offer which may be submitted to ballot, concessions which might result in a settlement. Union leadership and employees, aware that employers assess the situation in this manner, act accordingly. Thus, the mandatory last offer ballot sets into action a cycle of tactical operations by both parties which cancel each other out and delay serious efforts to arrive at a prompt resolution of their differences.

The national emergency dispute provisions discussed above (sec. 209 (b)) require the National Labor Relations Board to conduct a ballot of employees on the last offer of their employers. Section 203 (b) directs the Service in the generality of cases within its jurisdiction to suggest to the parties that they agree to submit the last offer of the employer to a secret ballot of the employees. The experience of the Service with this provision has not been such as to justify the conclusion that it has contributed materially to the settlement of disputes.

AN ALTERNATIVE STRIKE PROCEDURE

Testimony of Walter P. Reuther, President, United Automobile Workers, in Taft-Hartley Act Revisions, hearings before the Senate Committee on Labor and Public Welfare, 83d Cong., 1st Sess., 1953, part 1, pp. 393–406

PLACE THE RESPONSIBILITY ON CONGRESS

MR. REUTHER: . . . Going on now to the national emergency provisions, we recognize the fact that, if and when the welfare, the safety, and the security of our Nation are in jeopardy, as the result of a labor dispute, that the Government, as the agency of all the people has an obligation to act in order to protect the public good. Nobody can argue against that point of view. Certainly, the public interest transcends the narrower interest of the parties in any labor dispute. We recognize that obviously, if you cannot defend the whole of our free society, then we as free labor or free management can't enjoy rights within that free society. So that we do not argue as to the right of the Government to interefere. But we believe that Government interventions ought to be only in those situations where you actually have an emergency.

SENATOR IVES: Who is going to determine that?

MR. REUTHER: I think in the first case it ought to be determined by the President, and that the remedies ought to be worked out by the Congress. That is what I suggest. We believe that under Taft-Hartley with all the steps predetermined by law, a great deal of the pressures which make collective bargaining work are removed from the collective-bargaining table. And because of that, issues that might normally be resolved by the give and take of collective bargaining are not resolved and, therefore, you get a dispute. We believe that if you could wipe out the predetermined steps in Taft-Hartley that deal with national emergencies, and say to the parties, "It is your baby; it is your responsibility. You step up to it," and let the Government intervene only in the event of an emergency that does actually jeopardize the public safety and the public welfare in each specific situation on a tailor-made basis by specific acts of Congress, then the parties would not know what was going to happen, and that would give them a sense of urgency to sit down and bargain.

SENATOR IVES: That is exactly what I have tried to do in a couple of bills I introduced.

MR. REUTHER: That is right. And we think that the bills you have introduced embody this same basic approach and we think it is sound. I have sat in a lot of bargaining situations. I have sat down with corporations having as many as 400,000 employees covered by a contract. I know from practical experience that you do more collective bargaining an hour or two before the deadline than you do in 2 months before that time, because that is the nature of the animal. Everybody figures "We will see what the other fellow is going to do."

You wait, and you maneuver, and you try to get yourself in the position where you can get the best bargain out of it. So you wait until the last minute before you begin to yield and make concessions and begin to put everything on the table.

THE CHAIRMAN: Would you approve, Mr. Reuther, if we attempted to get the mediation service into the picture earlier than we do today? Would that help?

MR. REUTHER: Sometimes mediation helps. If the parties don't understand each other, mediation helps them to get some of the misunderstandings out of the way and get a better clarification of the areas of dispute. But if the parties are merely holding back for the purpose of maintaining the strongest bargaining position, then conciliation won't change that, because the problem there is not misunderstanding. They understand each other too well. And that is why they are not moving. But the point is—and this is a practical matter, this is not theory; you know, you get from theory to practice in collective bargaining very abruptly; this is the practice of collective bargaining. You are sitting there on two sides of the table, and the fellows say, "We have 2 weeks yet. There is no hurry." Then they have 1 week and then they have a couple of hours and then they get down to brass tacks. If Taft-Hartley says there is an 80-day injunction hanging out here, and industry feels "Well, this is going to be big enough, this will create a big enough emergency so that we can get a Taft-Hartley injunction," when they have 1 hour, they really haven't 1 hour; they have 1 hour plus 80 days. The result is that there is no pressure, there is no urgency. The weight of responsibility on the parties is not there. And without the pressure of responsibilities on the parties at the collective-bargaining table, collective bargaining won't work. . . .

There are a number of real advantages not to bargain if you think the Government will come in and bail you out for 80 days. First of all, you will not put your offer on the table, because if, out of Taft-Hartley intervention the Government sets up a fact-finding board, and supposing the company was really willing to give 10 cents and they lay 10 cents on the table, they figure well the fact-finding board will start with 10 cents and will compromise the thing with the 10 cents toward the union position. But if you don't put any figure on the table, then the fact-finding board will start with zero and maybe they will compromise at 10 cents instead of 10 cents plus. So there is every incentive not to bargain, there is every incentive not to lay anything on the table. Then, also, when you are dealing with large corporations and large industries—for example we used to say back in General Motors that 1 penny was worth $6 million. Well, if you can withhold a few pennies for a few months, that runs into many, many millions of dollars. Therefore, the 80-day injunction thing may delay a settlement for a period, retroactive wage increases may not be granted, and the company can save many millions of dollars by the simple process of delay. We believe, and I say this very sincerely, based upon the practical experience that we have had in collective bargaining, that any Government machinery that tends to lessen the sense of urgency, that tends to minimize the full weight of the responsibilities on the parties at the bargaining table, will discourage and weaken collective bargaining and will increase the possibilities of greater areas of disputes, and therefore, create the need for greater Government intervention in the long pull.

SENATOR DOUGLAS: Mr. Chairman, may I ask another question at this point?

THE CHAIRMAN: Senator Douglas.

SENATOR DOUGLAS: Does not the requirement that toward the end of the 80-day period the workers must vote on the last offer of the employer, tend to restrain the employers, at least in the early stages of negotiation, from really offering as much as they might later give under free collective bargaining?

MR. REUTHER: Our whole experience, Senator Douglas, has been that the minute we get involved in the 80-day period, there is less collective bargaining than at any other time. If you will get the statement of Mr. David Cole, who was the head of the Federal Mediation and Conciliation Service, and get Mr. Ching's statement when he headed that agency, they will tell you that their experience has been in practical situations where they went in and tried to mediate and conciliate, that there was no give and take whatever during the

80-day period; the situation was just rigidly frozen there, everybody waiting for the thing to get out of the way so they could get back to collective bargaining, the corporation obviously taking care of the 80-day because every day they didn't have to make a wage adjustment they were saving money.

SENATOR HILL: I was just going to say this, in line with the statement you are making, I suppose you are going to comment on the effect that the injunction has on labor's position. The injunction is only against labor, not against management and labor. What does that do to weaken labor's position or what does that do to encourage management not to bargain collectively? Are you going to comment on that?

MR. REUTHER: Workers having exhausted the efforts to arrive at a reasonable and satisfactory settlement of the issues in dispute through collective bargaining have as their final recourse the withholding of their labor power. That is the only thing they have to sell in the free market so they decide to withhold it and not sell it. Workers threaten the use of that economic weapon only as an effort to change the status quo. The status quo is not satisfactory. The injunction is using the power of the Government and the courts to maintain the status quo. Obviously the use of the injunction is always on the side of management. There is no such thing as the impartial intervention of Government. If Government intervenes through the process of the issuance of an injunction, it is intervening on management's side of the argument, because it is maintaining the status quo which the workers want to change. There is no such thing as an impartial intervention. The Government intervenes to maintain the status quo and that is exactly what the company wants to maintain, the status quo. The status quo is unsatisfactory and that is why the workers want to change it. That is obviously why we object to the use of the injunction because the injunction is a weapon used to maintain the status quo and bolster the position of the employer in opposition to the position of the workers.

THE CHAIRMAN: That wouldn't be true, would it, if you had your ultimate settlement retroactive to the beginning of the dispute. You would simply maintain the status quo until you get the final decision. If you make it retroactive, I think that will meet the argument you are making now, that the workers are necessarily damaged by the injunction.

MR. REUTHER: Many times, you see, collective bargaining is a very complex process. The ability of a group of workers to make a good bargain as of one calendar date may not be the same at a later calendar date. You may not be able to overcome that by any retroactive adjustment. You must also remember that when you work out a retroactive adjustment, that has an impact on the total economic package in other respects. So you can never recapture or re-create the elements in a given collective bargaining situation at a later date, because you are dealing here with a living, dynamic kind of process that changes.

Now, if you say you go back to the period before the 80 days began, you can't re-create the thing. There may be situations in the industry where the seasonal aspect of the production cycle may have a great bearing upon the ability of workers to get what they consider to be a satisfactory arrangement.

Eighty days later, maybe, the pressure in the industry has tapered off a great deal and the employer can coast for a while. So the minute the Government intervenes to interfere with the give and take of free collective bargaining and the free play of economic forces, the Government automatically, by the nature of the problem, intervenes on the employers' side.

SENATOR IVES: Mr. Chairman?

THE CHAIRMAN: Senator Ives.

SENATOR IVES: I think there is one thing that all of us have kind of ignored in our conversation on this subject. Of course we want justice, equity, fairness and all of those things, where labor is concerned and where management is concerned. But in this particular instance we are dealing with a national emergency, and you yourself stated that the President is the one who should determine what constitutes a national emergency and when it occurs. The national emergency of the type we are talking about requires production. How are we going to get production during all of this period of time when the controversy exists and which, of itself, seems to be causing a work stoppage? That is the big question. It is the public interest that is involved which overshadows some of these other things while this period exists. What is your answer there?

MR. REUTHER: Well, to begin with the number of situations in which we did really have the kind of national emergency which threatens safety and the welfare of the whole Nation, the community, the number of those kind of situations are very few.

SENATOR IVES: Well, it occurred in the steel dispute, for example, last year.

MR. REUTHER: They are very few. That is one of the bad features of Taft-Hartley. Every time some management has a bellyache, they get a Taft-Hartley injunction. Every time there is some slight inconvenience, they get a national emergency Taft-Hartley injunction. . . .

When you have an emergency, then the Government has an obligation to move. But we believe that you should let the parties in collective bargaining carry on their work under the full pressures of the responsibilities and the urgencies of given collective-bargaining situations. If industry makes a fair offer to labor, the labor people have to think that over, they have to say to themselves, "Is this a reasonable proposition? Do we take it back to the men and try to nail the thing down and settle it?" If it is a reasonable provision, you will find that the labor leaders will take it back to the men involved and they will nail it down, the thing will be settled. On the other hand, if the labor people offer management a reasonable proposition, they have to think, are they going to risk a strike? the loss of production? the loss of their profits? and if that is reasonable, I think that they will, under circumstances where the weight of the responsibilities is on the parties, they will find an area of agreement. But if both of them figure, "Why should we try to work it out? The Government is going to take over for 80 days," then you transfer the responsibility. Under Taft-Hartley industry knows precisely what will happen. Under the proposal that we suggest, having the thing wide open, with the Government, through the President in the first instance, certifying a national emergency, and then having Congress make a tailormade answer to that problem, we believe that both parties then would feel, "Well, we better work it out ourselves because we don't know what those people in Washington are going to do to us."

SENATOR IVES: I follow you until you talk about Congress making a tailormade answer to the problem. How is Congress going to make that tailormade answer? That is the thing that has been bothering me no end. If you can tell me how they are going to do it, I wish you would. I think somewhere, in the area I have tried to cover in my two bills, an area you are talking about, is the answer to what we are seeking. But that is the question. How is Congress going to make a tailormade answer to the problem?

MR. REUTHER: I think the tailormade answer must reflect the elements of a given situation. If you are dealing with one type of situation, you may come up with one type of answer. In another situation, you would vary your answer.

SENATOR IVES: I tried to approach it this way, by steps, so that Congress could be apprised of the situation in time. And the tailormade answer that you are talking about might possibly be evolved under those conditions. I don't think there is any sureness that it would be, but I gathered from your prepared testimony here that you do not like the steps that I suggest. You want to slash right in, "The President declares a national emergency. Congress acts." You know what happened in 1946 when Congress contemplated drafting strikers, at least an effort was made to draft everybody that wouldn't go to work under certain conditions. I would not dare leave the thing like that without preliminary effort in the hands of the Congress.

MR. REUTHER: First of all, I can envision the possibility of a national emergency arising only in a very limited area of this total problem. And certainly, it wouldn't be something that came out of the clear blue sky. The administration would know, the Congress would know, that this was coming up. If at the last minute labor and management were able to resolve it, everybody could say, "Thank God, that is behind us." On the other hand, having been apprised of the situation in the course of its development, then you could meet it. In other words, if the situation is so urgent as to take away from men the right to act as freemen, it is also of such urgency as to require the Congress to sit down and do something about it in terms of that specific problem.

SENATOR IVES: You want to make sure that when the Congress sits down to act on it that it does the right thing and nothing else. How best can you arrive at what would be the best thing?

MR. REUTHER: I would run a chance of having Congress do the right thing in specific national emergencies rather than have a law that does the wrong thing in all situations.

SENATOR IVES: I am not talking about the law. What criticism have you regarding the bills, either one or both, that I have introduced, in which I tried to make that approach, intelligently and by comprehensive steps?

MR. REUTHER: Let me try to answer that. We are in agreement on the basic approach. We agree that it is an attempt to minimize the area of intervention and to maximize the responsibility on the parties at the bargaining table. We are together.

SENATOR IVES: That is correct.

MR. REUTHER: Now, the difference between our approach and yours is that you provide some intermediate machinery to go into effect—a sort of a fact-finding board and so forth for the 30- and 60-day period, as I understand.

SENATOR IVES: No 30-day period. Just a 60-day in one, no limit in the other, no period at all.

MR. REUTHER: Our difference there is that we believe that even that amount of machinery will tend—although not to the extent that Taft-Hartley does—your bill is a much more realistic approach than Taft-Hartley. But we believe that the number of national-emergency situations will be so infrequent that if the President could certify them, he could have the Conciliation Department working on them, and all the information would be gathered without this intermediate machinery. That would tend to maximize the pressure and the responsibility at the bargaining table. Your bill is better than the present Taft-Hartley machinery; there is no question about that in our mind. But we believe that having no machinery at all but having the machinery and the solution tailor-made in each situation is the most effective way to deal with this problem.

SENATOR IVES: We at last arrive together again. I say tailormade. That is what I am trying to have, something that will be tailormade when the Congress does act. But I don't follow you in reaching to that tailormade proposal.

MR. REUTHER: We don't want anything to detract from the pressures of the bargaining table until they really are in trouble. Then you can move fast. As I say, this is not something that is going to come out of the blue sky. You are going to know about it. The President can certify it. In certifying it, he could make recommendations. He could say "I think under this situation you ought to do thus and so" to meet the problem quickly. Then Congress can sit down.

SENATOR IVES: I think I get your point. You think it is up to the President to advise the Congress as to the action which should be taken, that Congress should act upon his proposal?

MR. REUTHER: I think he ought to certify to you the character of the emergency requiring your action, and he could say to you, I think, that this and this ought to be the approach. And you could either accept his recommendations or you could not.

SENATOR IVES: Suppose the Congress should not accept them?

MR. REUTHER: Then you make your own.

SENATOR IVES: Under conditions at a time when the Congress might not be fully acquainted with all the facts. How about that?

MR. REUTHER: That is why you have machinery in Congress to get the facts. You take the auto industry. I just do not see how we can create a national emergency, unless all the production of the auto industry were on defense work.

SENATOR IVES: I do not think you could. But you certainly could do it in steel, as was shown last year, and it could be done in coal as was demonstrated a couple of years prior to that time.

MR. REUTHER: In any situation where a national emergency could be created, you would know about that. There are only a handful of those possibilities, you would know about them. I say it gets back to this fundamental question, that when you take away from freemen the right to withhold their labor power, that is a very basic step, and it is one that you should not do as a blanket proposition, it is one that you ought to do only when there are situations of a compelling enough nature to justify that kind of a drastic step. I would put that full responsibility on the Congress, because when Congress does that, I don't think it will do it lightly. I think that you will have to have a real emergency before Congress will do that.

SENATOR IVES: You will have to have a real emergency, but you want to make sure that the Congress is sufficiently acquainted with conditions and is able to act intelligently when they do occur.

MR. REUTHER: You see, if you had a situation, if an industry that was dragging its feet in a given collective-bargaining situation felt it could get an 80-day injunction, it will say "Why should we settle? We can get an 80-day injunction." Under Taft-Hartley they drag their feet. But if that same industry feels "Maybe they will seize the property, and maybe they will establish right away that any wage adjustments would be retroactive. They may do a lot of things that industry does not like," maybe that will exert greater pressure upon industry to do something about it. On the other hand, labor would not know what would happen to them. They wouldn't know whether they would be put through the wringer on it. Maybe we better sit down. At the point where there is a great deal of uncertainty as to what the Government will do when it intervenes, you will get a greater sense of urgency at the bargaining table to settle than you will when the parties know in advance what is going to happen, because it is already predetermined. We think that any steps that are predetermined by law tend to minimize the pressure at the bargaining table, and anything that minimizes the pressure makes for inability to get together. . . .

SENATOR LEHMAN: May I ask a question? It is not quite clear to me at what point you advocate that Congress may intervene in a strike or threatened strike. Would you recommend that the intervention of Congress can be had only on the issuance of a proclamation by the President certifying to an emergency, or would you give Congress the discretion to intervene on its own responsibility in advance of the issuance of a proclamation?

I ask that because I was wondering whether you had in mind that Congress should be given the right to bring pressure to bear on the two disputants in the hope of compelling a reasonable and fair settlement. I am not quite clear what you have in mind.

MR. REUTHER: I think as a normal procedure it would be the responsibility of the executive branch of the Government to be in close contact with the developing situation and make recommendations. That would not preclude, however, under our understanding, the right of Congress to intervene without having the matter referred by the executive branch of the Government. Congress certainly has the right, and if in its judgment it felt it was justified in intervening without having the matter referred by the executive branch of the Government, you could intervene directly.

SENATOR LEHMAN: The reason I ask that, as I interpret your testimony it is to the effect that if both sides to a dispute are uncertain in respect to what action Congress might take or recommend, pressure could be brought to bear to cause a settlement to be made, is that correct?

MR. REUTHER: That is right.

SENATOR GRISWOLD: Mr. Chairman.

It seems to me there has been no discussion about how you are going to put into effect or enforce this tailormade decision that Congress might make. Really what you are talking about doing is making Congress the top-level wage board, and then what are they going to do? What if Congress comes out with a tailormade decision saying, "We will retain the status quo indefinitely," and then what if the men refuse to work? What happens?

MR. REUTHER: The point is, I think you have to work on the assumption that both labor and management have some sense of responsibility in that kind of emergency situation. If people are going to defy the decision of the appropriate Government agencies, you have a state of insurrection.

I ask you, what would happen if, having the Taft-Hartley 80-day emergency provision, every labor union in a situation that was a potential national emergency said, "Let's just set our time schedule 80 days ahead. We will drift through the 80-day injunction period and then we will strike at the end of it." What would you do then? You would have to meet and act upon that kind of emergency. You would have to meet that emergency. So what we say is, meet that same responsibility that you have at the end of the 80 days without the use of the 80 days, and get the full benefit of the pressures at the collective bargaining table.

SENATOR GRISWOLD: I do not quite understand how that 80-day provision is of particular damage to either side as long as the decision that comes out at the end of the 80 days is retroactive. Most strikes are for economic benefits, and if they are retroactive, just as Senator Smith pointed out, I do not see where you have been damaged any, and in the meantime the public interest has been protected. At least, that is the theory.

The point I make is, what if Congress comes out with a tailormade decision and says, "We will retain the status quo for 90 days or 120 days or 6 months, and then the decision at the end of that time will be retroactive." What if an organization, either of managers or of labor, say, "We refuse to operate on that basis"? Are you not going to have to go into the courts and have injunctions, bring a mandamus and a lot of other legal actions, and throw the whole force of Government into really the maintenance of the decision that Congress may have made?

MR. REUTHER: Obviously, if Congress made a tailormade decision to meet a certain emergency situation and either party to the dispute defied Congress and the emergency continued, then in order to protect the welfare you would have to use the full power of the Government, in court action, et cetera. You would have to do that because the public good must be protected.

SENATOR GRISWOLD: That is the theory back of the Taft-Hartley law, is it not? . . .

MR. REUTHER: Senator, the point we are making is that the uncertainty in the situation creates greater pressure on the parties and a greater sense of urgency to settle. But under Taft-Hartley, where you have the treaty type of thing, they know exactly what is going to happen, so the pressure is not there.

SENATOR GRISWOLD: If we adopted that plan and had a tailormade decision, do you approve of putting strong clauses in there to provide for the enforcement of the decision that Congress may make, using all the processes of Government to put it into effect? You would not disapprove of the most stringent provisions in the act if it was a tailormade decision for that particular case? Do I understand you correctly?

MR. REUTHER: Our proposal obviously contains within it the idea that if the Government is going to tailormake a decision, then the Government obviously has to exercise its authority in the implementation of that decision. Otherwise, it is an academic exercise.

SENATOR GRISWOLD: If Congress in its decision decided instead of them making the tailormade decision, to set up a board that would make a tailormade decision, what is the difference? What if Congress decided, instead of our trying to judge all of these economic and social matters that are involved in a labor dispute, we will set up a board of experts which will in each case make a tailormade decision? Then could not Congress put strong provisions in that act to make that decision effective? That is the normal way that the Government operates. This whole executive department that you speak of is really a product of the executive branch of Government, is it not? The Constitution provides for a President, but it does not say what duties the Department of Labor will have or anything, so it is just a matter of congressional act as to what the National Labor Relations Board shall do, and the General Counsel can do. All these things that are discussed here are really congressional decisions.

MR. REUTHER: This gets back to the fundamental problems in the world between our free society and the totalitarian part of the world. If we cannot find the social mechanisms by which we can resolve the areas of economic conflict between labor, management, and other economic groups, and if we have to rely upon Government by creating machinery, then we are in trouble.

We want to put the maximum reliance upon the voluntary processes by having the parties not be able to look to Government for the use of predetermined machinery. We want to minimize that in order to maximize the voluntary process.

However, in those isolated and remote cases where the voluntary process creates a national emergency of the size and proportions that jeopardize the public safety and welfare, then the Government, as the agency of all the people, has an overriding obligation to intervene. But the intervention is not predetermined, nor is the particular type of intervention predetermined. It is that uncertainty that puts the greatest amount of pressure on the voluntary process and encourages it to operate.

In our kind of world there is no substitute for the voluntary process. That is the whole concept of a free society, to try to find a way to maximize the voluntary process, that people will participate in the voluntary process out of a sense of moral and social responsibility. The minute you predetermine Government intervention, you make it more difficult for the voluntary process to operate. That is the whole basic idea we are trying to advance.

SENATOR GRISWOLD: I can understand the viewpoint that you would like to make the decision voluntarily on both sides, but if Congress acts in the heat of emotion or perhaps because boys are being killed some place or men are being shot during a period of labor strife in Chicago, I do not believe the decision by Congress will be as fair to the public as it might be if the Congress in its wisdom set up a fair-minded board which would be ahead of the problem, which would see it coming a year ahead or 6 months or 3 months ahead and make their decision on the basis of long study of the details of the question. Certainly Government does not operate that way. That is why you set up departments of Government, the Federal Trade Commission, the Federal Power Commission, the Federal Communications Commission, so they, being theoretically experts in that particular field, can make a long study of the problem and arrive at a sound decision in the interest of the public. I do not believe that every time there is a dispute on the Fair Trade Act or pertaining to whether TV should go into an area or whether or not we should broadcast baseball games, Congress should suddenly be asked to make a tailormade decision to answer that particular question. I do not believe it will work.

MR. REUTHER: We have been working at this thing and we do think it will work. That is why we propose it. We think this is the way to get collective bargaining to work and to settle these things at the bargaining table, and that the number of areas in which the Government will have to intervene will be very limited.

If you intervene on this basis, we think that you will minimize the need for intervention. Where you have to intervene, it seems to me that Congress can act in a rational and intelligent manner and create machinery to try to bring about an adjustment that will reflect equities.

In the situation where the railroad workers were threatened with being put in the Army, Congress was not stampeded. Congress acted very sensibly and did the right thing in that situation. We have that much faith in Congress. We think the choice here—

SENATOR IVES: They came very near being stampeded, as I recall. If it had not been for Senator Taft, they might have been.

MR. REUTHER: Being very nearly stampeded is not as serious as being stampeded, you see.

SENATOR PURTELL: Does it not appear, Mr. Reuther, since we are talking about national emergency, since the Government will only intervene in a particular sense in the public interest, it would be timesaving if there were predetermined methods so we could handle this thing? Having exhausted or having given great thought and care to the method to be employed, we could apply it immediately and save the necessary time in the public interest to solve what is then a national emergency.

MR. REUTHER: You are choosing between two sets of values. You are choosing between: Do you want to have the machinery handy so you can bring it into play very quickly; and how much pressure does that detract from the bargaining table? Which is the more desirable? Do you want the maximum pressure at the bargaining table, or do you want convenient machinery handy?

We say that the advantages that make for maximum pressure at the bargaining table, that will encourage the voluntary process and strengthen that, that that is a more important value than the handy machinery. That is the difference here.

FREE AND RESPONSIBLE COLLECTIVE BARGAINING AND INDUSTRIAL PEACE

From the Report to the President by the Advisory Committee on Labor-Management Policy, May 1, 1962

III. COLLECTIVE BARGAINING CAN AND SHOULD BE STRENGTHENED BY MAKING IT MORE RESPONSIVE TO THE PUBLIC, OR COMMON, INTEREST

Preserving the free and voluntary nature of decision making which collective bargaining represents requires a full realization by representatives of labor and management that the privilege they enjoy to agree or disagree on terms and conditions of employment can be preserved only if it is exercised responsibly.

We believe that the parties have for the most part learned to respect each other's responsibilities, with management recognizing the union's representative functions to advance the welfare of its constituency and labor acknowledging the responsibilities which a system of private ownership and free competitive enterprise places on management to operate efficiently and profitably.

The growing complexities of our own industrial society and the instabilities of the international setting now require that the parties recognize not only their own individual responsibilities but their joint responsibility to the society of which they constitute an important and integral part. This calls for improved private and public procedures and techniques and above all for an increased measure of maturity.

A. THE MOST PROMISING OPPORTUNITIES FOR MAKING COLLECTIVE BARGAINING MORE RESPONSIVE TO THE PUBLIC INTEREST LIE WITH THE PARTIES THEMSELVES

Collective bargaining implies necessarily the right of the parties to disagree. We also believe that in a mature labor-management relationship economic force should be resorted to only as an ultimate weapon and reserved for disputes which do not respond to other and more reasonable means of resolution. Its frequent and repeated use is a sign not only of unimaginativeness but also of a considerable degree of irresponsible inflexibility in one or both parties.

The role of the United States in its relations with the other nations of the world, its programs for assuring adequate economic growth and full employment, the effects of major technological developments on the economy at large, and the functions of wages, prices, and profits in the economic system are all matters of vital interest. Yet unless their contextual relationship to collective bargaining is understood they can only too easily be ignored.

If unions and managements are to give consideration to these broader national interests, they can do so only within a framework of reliable information concerning the state of the economy, reasonable expectations as to the future, and a frank interchange of opinion between union, management, and Government representatives as to the significance of these data for industrial relations.

We have proposed, and the President has approved, the convening of periodic conferences of labor, management, and public officials under Government auspices which will be addressed to national and international influences affecting economic problems.

Conferences of this type should help clarify the context for responsible collective bargaining and develop a more informed viewpoint for future negotiations. They will obviously not provide formulas for the disposition of matters at issue between parties engaged in negotiations. Nor do we believe that such formulas would be desirable or in the interest of preserving free collective bargaining. But conferences of this kind can apprise the parties of relevant governmental objectives and policies and also provide an opportunity for industry and labor spokesmen to offer constructive recommendations to the Government.

B. FACTFINDING PROCEDURES SHOULD BE IMPROVED

There are areas in which the assistance of third parties in the collective-bargaining process can be useful.

One such area is in developing the facts pertinent to agreement. Fuller cooperation by labor, management, and Government in developing and making available pertinent data can facilitate sound and equitable collective bargaining decisions based on reason with a minimum disruption of operation.

There is obviously no magic formula for placing questions about the need for and pertinency of particular facts beyond dispute; such questions frequently are an integral part of the bargaining itself. Other aspects of the particular relationship between the parties may also have a legitimate bearing on questions of factual disclosure or development. Factfinding approaches, including questions as to whether and under what circumstances a joint endeavor might be most helpful, must of course be left to the parties themselves in the natural development of their bargaining relationship.

Yet, factual data, always valuable, can be of greater value than heretofore recognized at the early stages of negotiations. In preparation for negotiations the parties might jointly determine what information is relevant to issues which have been or are likely to be raised. If the facts sought are in the public domain, or obtainable through public agencies such as the Bureau of Labor Statistics, Department of Labor, or the Bureau of the Census, Department of Commerce, a joint request should be addressed to such agencies as far in advance as possible, specifying the data desired.

At other times it is likely that the facts sought relate to company or industry operations and must be developed by the parties themselves. We recommend greater experimentation by the parties with techniques of factfinding by jointly appointed outside experts or by personnel drawn from their own staffs.

C. OTHER FORMS OF THIRD-PARTY ASSISTANCE CAN BE USED TO GOOD ADVANTAGE

Third-party expert assistance goes beyond its use solely in factfinding. While the objective is for the parties themselves to reach agreement, on any issue concerning which this proves difficult or impossible we believe they may make effective use of various available private techniques in order to achieve agreement. Calling on third parties for private mediation, recommendations on all or some crucial issues, comparative analysis of a particular problem, or voluntary arbitration—these are well-known and worthwhile techniques. They may be used singly or in combination as well-intentioned parties may agree would suit their purposes under the given circumstances.

The form of third-party assistance is secondary to the parties' willingness to enlist such assistance. Whether they obtain it from Government or from some private agency, or whether it takes the form of mediation, factfinding, recommendations, or voluntary arbitration is less important than the good faith of the parties and their willingness to let it function in their mutual interest.

We do not in any sense imply that the use of third-party procedures is a preferable objective, or that the use of third parties will lead to more desirable long-range relationships or sounder settlements. These are only supplementary procedures. The central emphasis must be on the development of bilateral relationships based on sufficient maturity, sophistication, and judgment to enable the parties to work out solutions appropriate to their particular circumstances. Responsibility flourishes best in an atmosphere of self-reliance.

D. STRENGTHENING OF THE PUBLIC MEDIATION PROCESS WILL CONTRIBUTE TO BOTH THE EFFECTIVENESS AND THE RESPONSIBILITY OF PRIVATE COLLECTIVE BARGAINING

In all but relatively few exceptional cases the Federal, State, and local mediation services provide the only appropriate form of governmental service. At the national level the National Mediation Board renders these services in the railroad and air transportation industries, and the Federal Mediation and Conciliation Service in other industries. Local service and intrastate industries are in many instances serviced by State or city agencies.

Mediation can be of great help in encouraging more forthright use of reasoning and pursuasion, and in disabusing an overly suspicious party of the impression that the other has come to the bargaining table with ulterior purposes. This service is not easily performed, and, as many experienced mediators agree, it would be wise to develop means of imparting greater vigor and influence to the function of mediation as a greater help in collective bargaining.

We understand that in order to function more effectively, the Federal Mediation and Conciliation Service currently has plans to raise the professional status of its mediation staff, to participate actively at an earlier stage in the more difficult and important cases, to make more use of panels of mediators, and to establish the national labor-management panel provided for in the Taft-Hartley Act, while continuing to remain an entirely voluntary process. We also suggest that regional counterparts of this panel could be of help.

IV. PRESENT PROCEDURES FOR THE HANDLING OF CRITICAL AND NATIONAL EMERGENCY DISPUTES SHOULD BE IMPROVED, IN THE LIGHT OF EXPERIENCE, TO PROMOTE BOTH FREE COLLECTIVE BARGAINING AND THE NATIONAL INTEREST

In the case of major disputes, involving whole or important segments of critical industries, extraordinary measures may be found necessary. Normal mediation may prove unequal to the task of removing a strike threat or ending an actual strike.

It is our view that the emergency dispute provisions in the present law can and should be improved to cover more adequately the necessities of these situations.

Extraordinary measures should be applied with great restraint, and only when no other means are available to protect the national health and safety. Whenever it becomes necessary to place restraints or inhibitions on the freedom of the parties to pursue what they consider to be legitimate objectives, it is imperative that methods be provided for equitable solution of the disputed issues.

The Committee accordingly recommends, in place of the present emergency dispute provisions of the Taft-Hartley Act, the following procedures:

(1) The Director of the Federal Mediation and Conciliation Service would have the authority to recommend to the President the appointment of an Emergency Dispute Board in any collective-bargaining situation in a major or critical industry which may develop into a dispute threatening the national health or safety. This board would be authorized to mediate between the parties and to recommend procedures or techniques to them which appeared conducive to settlement. The board should work closely with the Federal Mediation and Conciliation Service. When deemed necessary the board could seek authorization from the President to make, and would be empowered with his approval to make, recommendations to the parties as to terms of settlement of the issues in dispute.

The members of this board would represent the public, it being recognized that in certain cases it would be advantageous to include members with labor or industry background. The board could be appointed at any stage in the negotiations, and the decision whether to set up any such board would rest with the President.

(2) The President would be authorized to direct the Emergency Dispute Board to hold a hearing on the question of whether a strike or lockout or threatened strike or lockout in a major or critical industry threatens the national health or safety. Upon receipt of the board's report, the President would be authorized to determine whether such threat exists, and to declare, if he so finds, the existence of a national emergency. On the declaration of such emergency, the President would be authorized to direct the parties to continue or resume operations in whole or, to the extent practicable, in part, until agreement regarding the dispute was reached, but in no event longer than 80 days. The President's declaration of emergency should be subject to judicial review at the instance of any affected party.

(3) Upon such declaration of emergency, the board would be authorized to continue mediation as between the parties, to make findings of facts regarding the issues in dispute and related matters, and to make recommendations to the parties and the public at the President's discretion regarding settlement of these issues, including any recommendation which might appear appropriate regarding the effective date of any adjustment in pre-

vious terms and conditions. The board would also be authorized to make recommendations at any time to the parties regarding any changes in terms or conditions of employment which in its judgment should be put into effect during the 80-day period on a concurrent or retroactive basis.[1]

(4) We recommend eliminating, in view of its demonstrated ineffectiveness in the past, the last-offer ballot procedure contained in the present law.

(5) If, despite the efforts of the Emergency Dispute Board, it appeared likely that there would be a strike or lockout at the expiration of the 80-day period, the President would be authorized to refer the matter to Congress, with his recommendations for appropriate action.

Even though the additional governmental powers recommended are mild compared with other suggestions which have been made for dealing with critical and national emergency disputes, we regret that a further intervention by Government into free collective bargaining is necessary. Nevertheless, inasmuch as the welfare of vast numbers of our citizens who are not directly concerned in these disputes is involved, and the economy of the country is often adversely affected, we conclude that there is a clear need for more effective governmental action under existing circumstances.[2]

[1] MR. MEANY, MR. DUBINSKY, MR. HARRISON, MR. KEENAN, MR. MCDONALD, AND MR. REUTHER: The proposal that the board would be authorized to make recommendations to the parties regarding any change which in its judgment should be put into effect during the 80-day period on a concurrent or retroactive basis seems ineffective and illogical. If the President has authority to order the employees to continue or resume work for 80 days, he should have authority to order whatever terms and conditions of employment he finds to be equitable.

[2] MR. FORD: The present national emergency provisions have had remarkable success in fulfilling their intended purpose. I would confine changes to eliminating the requirement for a vote on the employer's "last offer."

In my opinion, the remaining changes indicated here would weaken the whole concept of free collective bargaining, and would not help to alleviate national emergency strikes.

To extend the scope of sanctioned intervention to any "major or critical industry" would set up a standard that is undesirably vague, and that seems to me clearly to be broader than the concept of disputes imperiling the national health or safety now embodied in the law.

Orders to continue or resume operations should be issued through judicial process, as at present, rather than at the discretion of the President.

Factfinding boards with power to recommend terms of settlement would be both unjustified and unwise. I do not agree with the statement that this provision is necessary because the act, as it now stands, limits the freedom of the parties to reach settlement in their own way. The act only postpones strikes and lockouts; it does not prohibit them. The past performance of the factfinding-with-recommendations approach is not impressive. The record indicates that its use severely weakens collective bargaining and is likely to lead ultimately to compulsory arbitration.

12: Wage Determination and Inflation

The question of the degree of union influence on wages has been a diffi-cult one to solve through statistical studies. Many hold that unions are not only responsible for high wages, but also for higher prices that result from these higher wages. Labor has mixed views about the impact of unionism on wages. On the one hand, to claim that unions do not raise wages places unions in a secondary economic role; on the other hand, to claim that unions raise wages makes unionism a ready scapegoat for assigning the cause of inflation.

The wage "guideposts" of the Council of Economic Advisers are in-cluded in this chapter as well as criticism leveled at the use of national productivity changes as a criterion for noninflationary wage increases.

UNION RESPONSIBILITY FOR WAGE CHANGES

From Economic Intelligence, published by the United States Chamber of Commerce, December, 1953

Recent studies indicate that both the layman and some economists tend to exaggerate the extent to which labor unions can and in fact do raise wages. Such an error may undermine a balanced and sensible judgment about appro-priate labor legislation and proper public labor policies.

UNION BATTLES NEWSWORTHY

Union wage battles are newsworthy. Under collective bargaining, wage rates tend to be fixed and rigid for a year or two. Then either with or without public fanfare wage rates go up 5% or 10%. The fact that the wage change is expressed as an accomplishment of the union, and the change is identified with a few definite personalities, makes for "personal" news. Forces that work themselves out slowly and unnoticeably in nonunionized companies suddenly come to a head in unionized plants. They must then be handled at a definite time and the consequences may appear dramatic and obvious.

Wage changes in union shops and in nonunionized plants are illustrated in the accompanying diagram. Wage changes in nonunionized companies operate without fanfare, impersonally and more or less steadily. So they tend to go unnoticed.

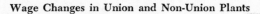

Wage Changes in Union and Non-Union Plants

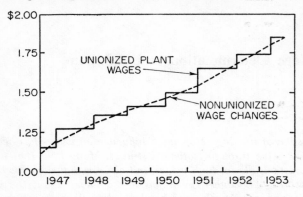

Many studies have been made to determine the effect of unions on wages. The evidence is conflicting, confusing and contradictory. But a growing number of economists are coming to the conclusion that by-and-large the same forces that permit and generate wage changes in nonunionized plants operate in roughly the same way in unionized plants.

100 YEARS HISTORY

Let us look at the period covering the last hundred years. In the 25-year period 1853 to 1878 hourly earnings rose 71% while the cost of living rose 25%—or, about one-third as fast as wages. Very few establishments were unionized then.

In the 50-year period 1853 to 1903, hourly earnings rose by 127%, while the cost of living rose only 38%. Only a very small fraction of our economy was unionized.

In the 75-year period 1853 to 1928, hourly earnings rose 569% while the cost of living rose 171%—or less than one-third as fast. Both money wages and real wages rose greatly. This three-quarters of a century was a period of few unions, except for the World War I period. Employers' rivalry in the labor market for scarce labor, and the competition in the goods market to sell goods, forced a free, unregulated, relatively nonunionized economy to spread the benefits of rising investment per worker and improved tools of production broadly among all.

In the last 20 years—a period of fabulous union growth—the share of the national income going to labor, while shifting a bit from year to year, has not changed perceptibly. In 1936, for example, compensation of employees, according to Department of Commerce figures, was 66% of our national income. In 1952 the figure was almost the same—66.3%. Yet during this period we have had the Wagner Act, minimum wage laws, political promotion of unions, and a terrific amount of labor turmoil, strikes and threats of strikes and enmity. Even if it were conceded that unions through one all-out effort could raise their members' share of the national income by 2% or 3%, this would be no more than the normal rise in productivity which occurs year by year.

In the World War II boom (say, 1939 to 1948) unorganized workers in some sectors of the economy had substantially greater wage increases than the unionized. For example, average annual fulltime earnings of domestic servants in 1948 were 272% of such earnings in 1939. The figure for nearly 100%-unionized auto workers was only 192%, while farm labor wage rates rose by 250%. In World War I wage rates in the nonunionized coal mines increased more than in the unionized in spite of feverish activity in the unionized sector.

AUTOMATIC WAGE INCREASES

Before General Motors adopted the cost-of-living escalator plus the 2½% annual improvement factor, a careful study was made of the hourly earnings in manufacturing generally, as well as in General Motors plants.

Had the General Motors formula been adopted by the American economy generally in 1940, the average hourly earnings in June 1951 (a year after Korean inflation began) would have been within 1 cent of the actual hourly earnings. The President of General Motors pointed out that if this had been done in 1940 we "would certainly have saved a lot of friction and strikes. . . ."

Indeed, if this formula had been generally adopted in 1910, more than 40 years ago, and adhered to throughout two world wars and a great depression, average hourly earnings would today be within a few cents of what they are in fact. Furthermore, the same would be true for the trend of actual hourly earnings based on this formula on a year-by-year basis. We are not arguing here for the General Motors formula, but merely trying to throw light on what governs wages.

In fact, there is good evidence that some unions have held wages down. This is partly attributable to the fact that contracts are ordinarily opened only once a year. It is also due to the fact that union leaders insist on getting credit for wage increases. Thus to cite the case of one farm implement company, in July 1952 when the contract expired the union made very extreme demands. Management offered a wage increase varying from 5¢ to 9¢ per hour. The offer was turned down and up to November 1953 employees have gotten no increase whatsoever.

A study of wage movements from 1909 to the present shows no systematic correlation with the percentage of workers unionized. Perhaps many workers are becoming aware of this. At any rate, since the mid-1940's the percentage of the labor force unionized has declined fairly steadily. Yet since 1945 average hourly earnings in manufacturing increased 74%, with roughly similar increases in other sectors of the economy, some of which are less unionized and some more unionized.

This brings us back to Taft-Hartley changes. Market forces account for basic wage changes—union and nonunion. A competitive free market economy *automatically* passes into the hands of workers the gains of rising productivity.

In fact, under competition there is no way for investors, savers, stockholders or businessmen to keep the gains of technological progress to themselves.

This all has an important bearing on whether there is need for any relaxa-
tion of Taft-Hartley in terms of the economic progress and welfare of the
American worker.

From the AFL News-Reporter, December 18, 1953

WAGE HIKES "FREE GIFT OF BOSSES," SAYS THE CHAMBER OF COMMERCE

Yes, dear wage earners of America, there is a Santa Claus. And you'd never
recognize him behind those whiskers if it hadn't been for the sharp detective
work of Dr. Emerson P. Schmidt, research director for the United States
Chamber of Commerce.

Dum, ta, dum, tum. The good doctor went hunting through statistics in
search of the facts, ma'am, with a veritable dragnet, and he came up with a
great discovery. Briefly stated it is this: The great gains scored by you American
workers in the past 16 years were not due to unionization, not won by struggle,
but—get this!—the free gift of your bosses!

If it is a little difficult for you to picture your employer climbing down your
chimney and stuffing your Christmas stockings with free and unsolicited wage
increases, just listen to what Dr. Schmidt has to say in the latest issue of "Washington Report, "published by the Chamber of Commerce:

"A competitive free market economy automatically passes into the hands of
workers the gains of rising productivity."

AUTOMATICALLY, mind you.

What about the strikes, the picketing, the weary hours of negotiation to
wrest higher wage rates and better working conditions from the employers?

All that is just sound and fury, signifying nothing, says Dr. Schmidt. His
statistics SHOW that the percentage of national income going to wage earners in
1952 was no higher than in 1936.

What about these statistics? If you have always suspected that statistics are
stranger than fiction, listen to what Boris Shishkin, AFL economist, has to say
about Dr. Schmidt's.

In 1936, says Shishkin, average wages in manufacturing industries were only
$21.78 a week. Now, with most of those factories unionized, the average has
been raised to $71.91 a week. That's not all. The unions have improved working
conditions, obtained vacations with pay, paid holidays, retirement pensions,
health benefits and many other forms of security for the workers.

Before declaring a war of statistics between the clashing conclusions of the
two economists, it should be pointed out that Dr. Schmidt failed to mention
that 1952 was a year of unparalleled prosperity for business and rising profits
took a greater share of the national income than in 1936. Farm income was
also far higher. Therefore the percentage represented by personal income out
of the whole kitty of national income is not, of itself, particularly significant. It
is not representative.

But it is fruitless to try to answer statistics with other statistics. And those of
you who have served on the firing line in the struggle of labor to improve its
status should not allow your blood pressure to shoot up because of Dr. Schmidt's

effort to disguise your employer as Santa Claus. After all, everyone knows it just ain't so.

Did you ever hear of a real Santa Claus who would fight against paying his helpers the legal minimum wage of 75 cents an hour, or $30 a week in these times of high living costs? Do you think Santa Claus would try to wipe out your Social Security funds, as the Chamber of Commerce is doing?

Dear wage earners of America, when you strip the false whiskers off Dr. Schmidt's Santa Claus it become obvious that he is an old phony.

PROSPECTS OF INFLATION

By Charles O. Hardy, Vice President, Federal Reserve Bank of Kansas City, in Prices, Wages, and Employment, Postwar Economic Studies No. 4, Board of Governors of the Federal Reserve System, Washington, 1946, pp. 23–24

. . . Even if wage increases are allowed only when no price increase is necessary, the net effect of collective bargaining under present standards is still inflationary. For stability of prices does not mean stability of all prices; it means that some prices rise and others fall. If the excessive profit margins that would otherwise lead to competitive price reductions are regularly absorbed in wage increases, the cases where prices rise for other than wage reasons are not offset in the general average by cases where they decline. In addition, higher prices in one industry often mean higher cost of materials in another, and higher wages in one industry create added pressures in others. Hence, unless the upward pressures are counteracted with anti-inflationary credit and fiscal policies, which reduce other prices to offset the cases where cost increases force higher prices, the price level steadily rises. . . .

The fact is that collective bargaining with strong unions, price stability, and full employment are incompatible. We can have any two of these, but not all three. So long as union power is not dampened down by unemployment there is no apparent power in the state strong enough to check a parallel upward sweep of wages and prices.

The basic difficulty is that although the unions have a degree of monopoly power that is sufficient to make them irresistible in their respective fields, the bases are not broad enough to bring their specific interests into balance with the over-all consequences of their policies. The decision whether to demand wages so high as to force higher prices is made by each industrial union separately; the price consequences are spread over the whole community. No union's successful demands will raise its own members' living costs by nearly as much as it will increase their incomes. Even if each unionist believed that the effect of a series of wage increases in different industries would be nullified by the resulting inflation, it would still be good policy for each union to try to get its increases first and make them bigger than the average.

A NEW FORCE FOR INFLATION

National Association of Manufacturers, 1956

When an industrywide union, exercising monopoly control over the labor supply of an industry, demands wage increases which discount productivity gains far in advance, possible price reductions of mass-produced products are prevented and buying power is shifted unfairly from the public as a whole to the favored few who happen to work in the industry in question.

Furthermore, competition cannot act to restore the proper balance. Any new concern, attracted to the industry by growing demand, would have to submit to dictation by the same union and would not be permitted to establish labor costs which would reflect the true value of the services rendered in the economic situation then prevailing.

Thus, union monopoly power distorts economic rewards in favor of those who are under the umbrella of the monopoly, to the detriment of all other economic interests. In the situation which prevails today, where monopoly power over the labor supply is a reality in most of the nation's basic raw materials, manufacturing, transportation and communications industries, persistent inflation is a constant threat. . . .

The obvious remedy in the situation is to curtail the power of industrywide unions to engage in monopolistic practices and restore bargaining to the local level.

INFLATION OR STABILIZATION?

From Steel and the National Economy, 1956, United Steelworkers of America, Pittsburgh, Pa.

Contentions by management and by anti-labor spokesmen that all wage increases must result in price increases—that higher wages must lead to inflation —are without basis in theory, in practice and in fact. Rising wages and inflation are not part and parcel of a single phenomenon. Industry need not, and most employers do not, raise prices every time wages are increased. So much has been said and written proving that wages must rise relative to prices, that only economic isolationists in their remote-from-reality hideouts continue to prattle about higher wages causing inflation.

Contentions that wage rates can be increased without limit and still have no impact on prices are equally irresponsible. But, a healthy economy requires that wages and salaries must rise relative to prices and the only meaningful question is the degree to which wages can and must increase relative to prices.

Unions have never contended that higher wages could be paid without higher prices regardless of the size of the wage increase. Rather, labor has contended that the level of profits and changes in productivity should be taken into account in determining how much wages can be increased without increasing the general price level. On the other hand, those who steadfastly fight against wage increases attempt to propagate the view that every wage increase must result in a price increase.

It is unequivocally clear that unless wages and salaries increase somewhat more than prices, our economic growth will be halted. As our productive capacity and output of goods and services expand, there must be an increase in the real buying power of consumers. Except for inventory and investment booms which cause busts, our economy can grow no faster than the market for its products. The mainstay of that market is the purchasing power of our workers. . . . More than four-fifths of America's total output of goods and services, excluding what is bought by the Government, is purchased for personal consumption. It is the income of the wage and salary earners that accounts for the bulk of personal consumption. Rising real wages are an absolute prerequisite to economic prosperity and economic growth.

The history of our industrial development is a history of rising output per man-hour of work. The rate of change in productivity has varied from time to time, but the increase in efficiency—in production per man-hour—has been persistent and substantial. Workers can share in the benefits of rising productivity only through rising real wages. But even more important from the economic point of view is the continuing need for higher real wages as a basis for sustained high levels of production and income and employment.

Economists have long argued whether the benefits of rising productivity should be shared through constant prices and higher wages or through constant wages and lower prices, or a combination of the two. Most economists are at least dubious, if not firmly opposed, to a goal of declining prices. Falling prices tend to discourage investment and to retard economic expansion. Even if general price declines were desirable, it is doubtful that prices would actually be reduced by those industries which can best afford it—those whose firm grip on the market has permitted them to reap the profits by setting their prices high.

As the economy has grown, business enterprises have developed in size and scale and in organization, bringing much less price flexibility than was true in the past. Many objective analyses have been made demonstrating the growing stickiness of prices, especially for industrial products. Even when economic activity and productivity have risen relative to wages, there is little evidence of a readiness by the large industrial corporations to cut prices. Rather, our increasingly monopolistic industries tend to change their prices only in one direction, namely upward. If labor were to forego demands for higher wages and wait for employers to pass on the benefits of higher productivity through lower prices, we would surely experience short and intensive booms with tremendous profits and inadequate buying power, followed by severe depressions and mass unemployment. This is not a promising path to economic progress.

Labor often seeks wage increases that are proportionately higher than the rise in productivity, because wages have lagged in the past and profits have become exorbitant. Once labor's share is reasonable, increases should primarily take into consideration changes in productivity. In industries where productivity is rising at a lesser rate than for the total economy, wages should be increased in proportion to the over-all rate, even though some price increase might be necessary. In industries where productivity is increasing very rapidly, wages should rise more than in proportion to the national increase in productivity. This might well leave room for price declines.

The above policies would permit all workers to share in the improving productivity of the economy with extra benefits to workers in those industries where technological advancements are most rapid. It would result in only a slight upward trend in prices.

It should be noted that a percentage increase in wage rates proportionate with changes in productivity results in a sharing of the benefits of productivity between management, labor and investors. Not all the benefits of increased efficiency and mechanization are expected nor sought by labor.

History has demonstrated not only that wages can rise relative to prices, thus providing the increased purchasing power without which our economy would stagnate, but also that there can be substantial increases in wages with virtually no change in prices or living costs. . . .

In many areas where prices are not truly free, such as the steel industry, but are subject to some degree of control—control by monopolistic firms—wage increases have been passed on in the form of higher prices, with consequent booming profits. . . .

Some corporations try to justify their price gouging on the grounds that they need more profits to finance expansion. . . . Other companies frankly say that they seek to make all the profits they possibly can so that when depressions come they will be better able to weather the storm. This is truly a cynical and dangerous view because such behavior, if widespread, will induce depressions. We need wage and price policies based on confidence in America's future and on a sense of responsibility for the welfare of the entire nation. There are still too many employers who deviate from such policies.

INSTITUTIONALIZED INFLATION

From the 1955 annual report of United States Steel Corporation

Of great importance to industry and hence to U.S. Steel is the development of what appears to be a permanent and alarming peacetime trend of cost and price inflation. . . .

Two basic roots of the inflationary tendency are discernible. The first one is the institution of industry-wide labor unions, headed by leaders who, with power to bring about industry-wide strikes, seek always to outdo each other in elevating employment costs in their respective industries. The legislative and social framework within which they function compels them to compete in elevating this basic cost.

The other root is the Government's "full employment" policy under which the money supply must be inflated fast enough to accommodate the inflating employment cost, lest that mounting cost bring about its natural result of pricing some people out of their jobs, even though only temporarily. It takes ever more dollars to cover ever rising costs and prices if industry's full output is to be purchased. The money supply—people's bank deposits subject to check plus their pocket currency—was in 1955, on a per capita basis, 2.7 times what it was in 1940. This is equivalent to 6.8 per cent per annum compounded.

The abuse of labor monopoly privilege and the monetary policy that transfers to the public in higher prices the penalty of that abuse appear to be the main elements of institutionalized inflation. It would be most helpful in this regard if those responsible for determining wage costs and fiscal policies were constantly aware of the inflationary potentials of their decisions.

EFFECT OF RECENT WAGE AND PRICE INCREASES IN STEEL

From Bulletin—Steel 1951–1955, A Comparison of Values, a memorandum issued by a stock brokerage firm, member of the New York Stock Exchange, July 7, 1955, p. 8

Last week steel wages were raised by 15¢ per hour on average and this was followed by price increases estimated to average $7.35 per ton. President C. F. Hood of U.S. Steel stated that the price increase was designed not only to compensate for the higher wage costs but also for "the steadily mounting costs of purchased goods and services, of state and local taxes, and of new construction." The excess of the price over the wage increase appears indeed to be substantial.

In 1954, average hourly earnings at U.S. Steel were $2.488 so that the wage increase was 6%. On the other hand the price rise amounted to 5.8%. In 1954 wages and salaries were 37.5% of U.S. Steel's sales volume but the wage rise will spread to other industries upon which the steel companies depend for raw materials and services. In the past, the cost of such products and services bought by U.S. Steel about equalled the company's wage costs, and it may be assumed that these costs will go up by about 50% of the wage rise.

On this basis it appears that the price increase exceeds the direct and indirect costs of the wage boost by about $2.00 to $2.50 per ton of steel shipped. If translated into earnings after taxes it can be estimated that the new prices will add about 40¢ per share to U.S. Steel's earnings this year, about $1.20 to the earnings of Bethlehem and corresponding amounts to the earnings of the other companies.

From a pamphlet issued August–September, 1956, by the same firm

STEELS AFTER THE STRIKE

The steel strike and the ensuing wage settlement and price increases have improved rather than impaired the investment position of the industry. Burdensome inventories have been absorbed and high capacity operations are likely to prevail during the rest of the year. Although the price increases have not quite come up to expectations they should more than offset the higher wage costs. In spite of recent moderate advances steel stocks continue to appraise existing capacity at only a fraction of reproduction costs, and the steel group remains the last major undervalued group in the market.

The main features of the new wage settlement in the steel industry are as follows:

1. Wage increases variously estimated to average between 20.3¢ and 25¢ per hour for the first year and between 45.6¢ and 55¢ for the next three years, depending on whether higher social security taxes, vacation payments, etc. are included.

2. A three-year non-reopenable contract as against two-year agreements in the past which could be reopened every year as to their wage clauses.

3. A 52-week supplementary unemployment benefit plan and a cost-of-living clause permitting wage increases twice a year tied to the cost-of-living index and practically applicable only on the upside.

To compensate for the higher costs the industry has posted price increases which range in the case of U.S. Steel from $7 to $21 and more per ton and reportedly average around $8.50 per ton or 6¼% of the prices existing before the strike.

In order to gauge the impact of wage settlement and price increases on the earnings of the steel industry the following factors have to be considered:

1. Assuming that about 20 man-hours are needed to produce one ton of finished steel, a 20¢ increase per hour in employment costs is equivalent to $4 per ton. It may be assumed further that the indirect effect of the wage rise on raw materials will over a period of time amount to another $2 per ton. Against this the increase in base prices is $8.50 per ton, so that the profit of the industry per ton of finished steel would be improved by about $2.50 per ton. While this subject is highly controversial, our estimate of the increment to profits is probably conservative as it may take less than 20 man-hours to produce a ton of steel, and besides this there has been a continuous increase of perhaps 3% per annum in productivity over the years and thus there is some compensation against wage increases. . . .

GUIDELINES FOR NONINFLATIONARY WAGE AND PRICE DECISIONS

From The 1962 Report of the Council of Economic Advisers, pp. 188–189

Individual wage and price decisions assume national importance when they involve large numbers of workers and large amounts of output directly, or when they are regarded by large segments of the economy as setting a pattern. Because such decisions affect the progress of the whole economy, there is legitimate reason for public interest in their content and consequences. An informed public, aware of the significance of major wage bargains and price decisions, and equipped to judge for itself their compatibility with the national interest, can help to create an atmosphere in which the parties to such decisions will exercise their powers responsibly.

How is the public to judge whether a particular wage-price decision is in the national interest? No simple test exists, and it is not possible to set out systematically all of the many considerations which bear on such a judgment. It is possible, however, to describe in broad outline a set of guides which, if followed, would preserve overall price stability while still allowing sufficient flexibility to accommodate objectives of efficiency and equity. These are not arbitrary guides. They describe—briefly and no doubt incompletely—how prices and wage rates would behave in a smoothly functioning competitive economy operating near full employment. Nor do they constitute a mechanical formula for determining whether a particular price or wage decision is inflationary. They will serve their purpose if they suggest to the interested public a useful way of approaching the appraisal of such a decision.

If, as a point of departure, we assume no change in the relative shares of labor and nonlabor incomes in a particular industry, then a general guide may be advanced for noninflationary wage behavior, and another for noninflationary price behavior. Both guides, as will be seen, are only first approximations.

The general guide for noninflationary wage behavior is that the rate of increase in wage rates (including fringe benefits) in each industry be equal to the trend rate of overall productivity increase. General acceptance of this guide would maintain stability of labor cost per unit of output for the economy as a whole—though not of course for individual industries.

The general guide for noninflationary price behavior calls for price reduction if the industry's rate of productivity increase exceeds the overall rate—for this would mean declining unit labor costs; it calls for an appropriate increase in price if the opposite relationship prevails; and it calls for stable prices if the two rates of productivity increase are equal.

These are advanced as general guideposts. To reconcile them with objectives of equity and efficiency, specific modifications must be made to adapt them to the circumstances of particular industries. If all of these modifications are made, each in the specific circumstances to which it applies, they are consistent with stability of the general price level. Public judgments about the effects on the price level of particular wage or price decisions should take into account the modifications as well as the general guides. The most important modifications are the following:

1. Wage-rate increases would exceed the general guide rate in an industry which would otherwise be unable to attract sufficient labor; or in which wage rates are exceptionally low compared with the range of wages earned elsewhere by similar labor, because the bargaining position of workers has been weak in particular local labor markets.

2. Wage-rate increases would fall short of the general guide rate in an industry which could not provide jobs for its entire labor force even in times of generally full employment; or in which wage rates are exceptionally high compared with the range of wages earned elsewhere by similar labor, because the bargaining position of workers has been especially strong.

3. Prices would rise more rapidly, or fall more slowly, than indicated by the general guide rate in an industry in which the level of profits was insufficient to attract the capital required to finance a needed expansion in capacity; or in which costs other than labor costs had risen.

4. Prices would rise more slowly, or fall more rapidly, than indicated by the

general guide in an industry in which the relation of productive capacity to full employment demand shows the desirability of an outflow of capital from the industry; or in which costs other than labor costs have fallen; or in which excessive market power has resulted in rates of profit substantially higher than those earned elsewhere on investments of comparable risk.

It is a measure of the difficulty of the problem that even these complex guideposts leave out of account several important considerations. Although output per man-hour rises mainly in response to improvements in the quantity and quality of capital goods with which employees are equipped, employees are often able to improve their performance by means within their own control. It is obviously in the public interest that incentives be preserved which would reward employees for such efforts.

Also, in connection with the use of measures of overall productivity gain as benchmarks for wage increases, it must be borne in mind that average hourly labor costs often change through the process of up or down grading, shifts between wage and salaried employment, and other forces. Such changes may either add to or subtract from the increment which is available for wage increases under the overall productivity guide.

Finally, it must be reiterated that collective bargaining within an industry over the division of the proceeds between labor and nonlabor income is not necessarily disruptive of overall price stability. The relative shares can change within the bounds of noninflationary price behavior. But when a disagreement between management and labor is resolved by passing the bill to the rest of the economy, the bill is paid in depreciated currency to the ultimate advantage of no one.

PRODUCTIVITY AND COLLECTIVE BARGAINING

From Productivity and Wage Settlements, United States Chamber of Commerce, 1961

Using past national productivity improvements as a wage settlement guide involves another possible serious defect. To a considerable extent productivity improvements are due to the shifting of human and other resources from economic activities with low productivity to activities with higher productivity; the search for better rewards—both worker and investor rewards—encourages such shifts. But insofar as the data for previous productivity improvements reflect such shifts, the rise in productivity is not available for *future* upward wage and salary adjustments; remunerations and price adjustments have already occurred as the shifts took place, with some lags at times.

For example, suppose an industry has had a 5.0% average improvement in over-all productivity during the last decade. But this industry is *currently* experiencing only 2.0% rise in productivity, or none at all. These past gains in productivity will have already been absorbed in the economy—in the form of increased wages, rents, profits and through more stable or even falling final product prices. Since the only productivity figures that can be made available reflect productivity improvement of past periods, should labor demand a share of an increase in productivity for which it has already benefited, as have other groups who have a claim on the industry's gains?

It is not possible to reach backward, in a new wage settlement, to adjust wage rates for the future—an adjustment which has already been absorbed into the economy.

Productivity improvements of earlier years may not be repeated. Wage settlements are, inevitably, forward looking; productivity indices are backward looking. Productivity changes even of the recent past, not to speak of the more remote past, furnish little or no clues to the future.

In measuring past productivity changes, the results depend upon the time period used or the time intervals. In the 50 year period from 1909 to 1959, according to one measure, the average annual increase in output per man-hour was 2.2%. But for shorter periods, such as three, five or nine year periods, the changes ranged from −1.8% (1912 to 1917) to 4.8% (1933 to 1941), as can be seen in the chart on page [274].

NATIONAL PRODUCTIVITY: A GUIDE TO ALLOWABLE WAGE INCREASES?

Since we never know the future, of what value would these data be, even if all the foregoing pitfalls were resolved, in settling a wage demand as of a given date in any particular firm?

Perhaps leaning over backwards to find *some* possible use for the productivity measures, Professor John W. Kendrick (who has analyzed the data most carefully) made this statement:

In the short run, it is apparent that the economy-wide average increase in hourly labor compensation consistent with price stability can serve only as a *rough general guide to the increases appropriate in particular firms, or in particular industries where bargaining is on an industry-wide basis.* The actual increases will have to be more or less than the indicated average depending on particular market situations, if structural flexibility in the economy is to be maintained.[1] [Italics supplied]

Possibly even this is an undue concession to those who would argue that wage settlements for the future should be geared to recent productivity changes. For example, suppose a university or a business enterprise is in dire need of some specific type of talent and know-how which is in short supply. Will some national average of productivity or some industry average be *any guide whatsoever* to the employer in determining his offering price for the talent? Obviously not. If he wants the personnel he must pay the going rate. If an industry or company is stagnating or declining, on the other hand, should it still follow some national or industry average productivity change?

It has frequently been suggested that some government authority should pronounce annually in advance how much average wages might rise in the year ahead without impairing the national interest and the *general* welfare; the implication being that this would serve as a guide to employers confronted

[1] John W. Kendrick, "The Wage-Productivity-Price Issue," *California Management Review*, Vol. II, No. 3, Spring, 1960.

ANNUAL RATE OF CHANGE
IN REAL PRIVATE PRODUCT PER MAN HOUR
(for the man and his technological aids supplied by investors)
PERCENT CHANGE IN OUTPUT PER MAN HOUR

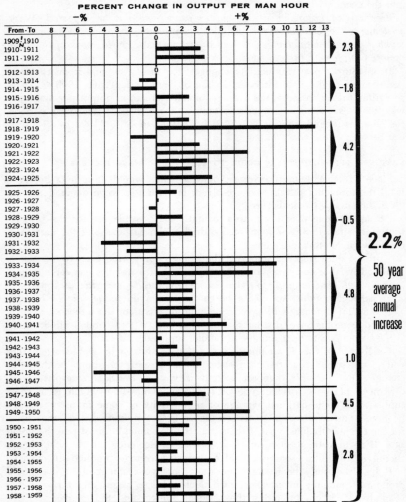

Sources: U.S. Congress, Joint Economic Committee, *Productivity Prices and Incomes,*
U.S. Govt. Print. Off. (1957), Table 5, p. 91; U.S. Dept. of Labor, BLS Bulletin
#1249, Table 1, p. 5 and supplementary press release June 28, 1960.

with a wage demand or, to a union official about to determine the size of his demands. The *ECONOMIC REPORT OF THE PRESIDENT* of January 1960, for example, implied or suggested this approach:

. . . Settlements should not be such as to cause the national average of wage rate increases to exceed sustainable rates of improvement in national productivity. A national wage pattern that fails to meet this criterion would put an upward pressure on the price level. Hourly rates of pay and related labor benefits can, of course, be increased without jeopardizing price stability. Indeed, such increases are the major means in our free economy by which labor shares in the fruits of industrial progress.

How useful then is the following statement as a guide for a specific wage settlement?

But improvements in compensation rates must, on the average, remain within the limits of general productivity gains if reasonable stability of prices is to be achieved and maintained. Furthermore, price reductions warranted by especially rapid productivity gains must be a normal and frequent feature of our economy. Without such reductions we shall not be able to keep the price level as a whole from advancing. (Page 8.)

Here again, it is the competitive market process which should provide the mechanism for such desirable price declines. . . .

ANOTHER LOOK AT THE "WAGE GUIDEPOSTS"

From General Electric Relations News Letter, August 13, 1963

THE "LOST" PRODUCTIVITY OF THE FARM SECTOR

An important element in the theory of the noninflationary guideposts is that industries with above-average productivity growth should show price decreases as an offset to price (cost) increases in industries with below-average productivity growth. This has been termed "compensatory pricing.". . .

However, in the case of the agricultural sector of the economy, the farm price support program prevents the consumer from gaining, through lower agricultural prices, the full benefits of the cost savings resulting from the 6% annual gain in the output per manhour of the farm sector.

The substantial annual increase in the productivity of the farm sector accounts for a six-tenths percentage point increase in the output per manhour of the private sector during the postwar period. Thus, while output per manhour of the private sector of the economy increased by 3.0% from 1947 to 1960, the omission of the farm sector reduces that increase from 3.0% to 2.4%.

In President Kennedy's 1962 message to Congress on agriculture he cited four independent studies which agree that if there were no subsidy programs wheat prices would be sliced almost in half, barley 28%, soybeans 38%, oats 25%, grain sorghums 22%, dairy products 17%, and non-price supported commodities would also drop.

It would seem, therefore, that for purposes of a general noninflationary guidepost, an allowance should be made for the fact that some part of the cost savings in farm productivity is not available as an offset to higher prices in industries with below-average productivity.

This is the "lost" productivity of the farm sector which inflates the "noninflationary" guidepost.

THE EXCLUSION OF THE GOVERNMENT SECTOR

Another inflationary bias in the general guidepost results from the exclusion of the government sector in the calculation of the rate of increased productivity.[1]

Some observers in the field of productivity have indicated that the efficiency of government rises less than that of other sectors of the economy,[2] so that the annual rate of increase in output per manhour for the private sector is higher than the rate of gain for the entire economy, including government. In his estimates of the long-term rate of productivity advance of the entire economy, including government, Professor Fabricant [3] indicates a downward adjustment of .2% from the annual rate of gain of the private sector.[4]

Regardless of the rate of change in productivity in the government sector of the economy, however, government must hold and recruit its labor supply in competition with the private sector; and government employees as a matter of equity expect compensation increases as other employees receive them. Just recently the Senate and the House of Representatives passed a $1.2 billion military pay raise bill. It grants an average 12.6% increase, the first in five years.

The use of the *higher* rate of productivity increase in the *private sector* as the basis for compensation increases *throughout the economy* means that such increases will exceed the productivity of the *whole economy, including gov-*

---

[1] On the other side of the coin, there is some downward bias in all measures of productivity because of the difficulty in measuring quality changes. This is the opposite effect to that in the Consumers Price Index, which some sources state has an upward bias since the Price Index reflects increased prices due to quality improvements.

[2] Studies of Henry D. Lytton of a sample of seven civilian components of Government indicate productivity in these components for the years 1947–1957 to have increased about five-eighths as much as the private sector of the economy. This is on the basis of output per unweighted manhours. This group of components experienced declines in 1958 and 1960 and had but a .2% increase in 1959. The failure of productivity to rise in recent years, Lytton said in 1961, "appears at least superficially due to a rather sustained tendency in the last three years of the Eisenhower administration, as well as in the Truman-Eisenhower change-over year (fiscal 1953) to increase employment even though the work to be done was not increasing as much—or at all." Henry D. Lytton, "Public Sector Productivity in the Truman-Eisenhower Years," *Review of Economics and Statistics*, May 1961, p. 182.

[3] "Productivity: Its Meaning and Trend," *Challenge*, October 1962. See also "Basic Facts on Productivity Change," National Bureau of Economic Research, p. 5, and John W. Kendrick "Productivity Trends in the U.S."

[4] This is based on the Commerce Department convention of assuming no productivity increase for government workers, which undoubtedly imparts a downward bias to the total economy estimates, as indicated by the studies of Henry D. Lytton.

ernment, because the productivity of the government sector is below that of the private sector. Thus, a guidepost based on the productivity of the private sector alone has an inflationary bias.

This is an increasingly important factor. Governments have over eleven million employees on Federal (including military), State and local payrolls. This is more than double the 4.8 millions in 1940. Government employment has been growing three times as fast as private employment, and it is projected to grow faster in the years ahead, particularly in State and local government agencies where employment is expected to rise by more than 50% between 1960 and 1975.[5]

[5] "Manpower Report of the President," U.S. Department of Labor, March 1963, p. 96.

13: Automation

The next three chapters deal with probably the greatest economic problem today—the number and rate of the chronically unemployed. This paradox of hard-core unemployment in the midst of economic prosperity results from a number of causes. One—but only one—is the rapid change in technological processes, symbolized by the word "automation," which makes less employable those whose skills and training are no longer needed, and even less employable those without skills or training. This is the subject of the present chapter. Chapter 14 examines some of the devices by which workers have sought job security, and Chapter 15 is concerned with governmental programs seeking solutions to the related problems of unemployment and poverty.

AUTOMATION: PROMISE AND PROBLEMS

By Walter P. Reuther, from the American Flint, April, 1956

In the spread of automation and the prospective large-scale industrial use of atomic energy—and the possible practical utilization of solar energy, as well —we are faced with mighty forces whose impact on our economy can be vastly beneficial or vastly harmful, depending on whether we succeed or fail in achieving economic and social progress that will keep pace with changing technology.

We have been told so often that automation is going to bring on "the Second Industrial Revolution" that there is, perhaps, a danger we may dismiss the warning as a catch-phrase, and lose sight of the fact that, not only the technique, but the philosophy of automation is revolutionary, in the truest sense of the word.

Automation does not only produce changes in the methods of manufacturing, distribution, many clerical operations, and in the structure of business organization, but the impact of those changes on our economy and our whole society bids fair to prove quite as revolutionary as were those of the First Industrial Revolution.

The revolutionary change produced by automation is its tendency to displace the worker entirely from the direct operation of the machine, through the use of automatic control devices.

In other words, automation is a technique by which whole batteries of machines, in some cases, almost whole factories and offices, can be operated according to predetermined automatic controls. The raw material is automatically fed in, the machine automatically processes it, the product is automatically taken away, often to be fed automatically into still another machine that carries it automatically through a further process. In some cases, the machine is self-regulating—that is, it is set to turn out a product within certain tolerances as to size or other factors, and if those tolerances are exceeded, the machine itself detects the variation and automatically adjusts itself to correct it.

POTENTIAL BENEFITS

What is the attitude of the trade union movement to this new technology of automation?

First of all, we fully realize that the potential benefits of automation are great, if properly handled. If only a fraction of what technologists promise for the future is true, within a very few years automation can and should make possible a four-day work-week, longer vacation periods, opportunities for earlier retirement, as well as a vast increase in our material standards of living.

At the same time, automation can bring freedom from the monotonous drudgery of many jobs in which the worker today is no more than a servant of the machine. It can free workers from routine, repetitive tasks which the new machines can be taught to do, and can give to the workers who toil at those tasks the opportunity of developing higher skills.

But in looking ahead to the many benefits which automation can produce, we must not overlook or minimize the many problems which will inevitably arise in making the adjustment to the new technology—problems for individual workers and individual companies, problems for entire communities and regions, problems for the economy as a whole.

What should be done to help the worker who will be displaced from his job or the worker who will find that his highly specialized skill has been taken over by a machine? What about the businessman who lacks sufficient capital to automate his plant, yet has to face the competition of firms whose resources enable them to build whole new communities in some areas, while others are turned into ghost towns? How can we increase the market for goods and services sufficiently and quickly enough, to match greatly accelerated increases in productivity?

Obviously, there will be problems for the workers who are displaced from their jobs by automation. This is not merely a problem of finding a new job. By its very nature, automation will tend to eliminate unskilled and semiskilled jobs, while the new jobs it creates will be at a much higher level of skill.

Another aspect of the same problem is that of the worker with a specialized skill who finds that his skill has been made valueless because a machine has taken over his job—such as the skilled machine operator displaced by a self-operating lathe or the bookkeeper whose job is taken over by an electronic "brain."

If automation is going to displace any substantial number of workers in either of these two ways, we will need a carefully organized retraining program to give them the opportunity of acquiring the skills they will need. Such a program must take into account the needs of the workers, the fact that most of them will be mature men and women to whom the learning of new skills may not come easily, and that they have to live and support their families while they are acquiring these skills. The program will require not merely training facilities and expert vocational guidance; it will have to include provision for training allowances to replace lost wages during the training period.

An alternative solution will have to be found in the case of older workers, not old enough for normal retirement, but too old to learn new skills or to adjust to the demands of the new technology. In some of our collective bargaining agreements, we have already laid the foundations for a system of early retirement which could help to meet such situations.

But in the very nature of most private pension plans, the problem cannot be solved through collective bargaining alone. Industrial pension plans are based on the assumption that the worker, when he retires, will also be eligible for social security benefits. Much as we have improved the level of private pensions in recent years, a worker who is forced to retire before the age of 65 would find it impossible to maintain a decent standard of living on his industrial pension alone. There is thus the need for earlier social security payments to workers who are forced into retirement before the age of 65 because technological changes have taken their jobs from them and their age makes it impossible for them to find other work.

The growth of automated factories can create problems of dislocation not only for individual workers but for the whole communities. It is often cheaper to build a new plant from the ground up, so that the whole design of the buildings can be related to the industrial process, than to attempt to remodel an existing plant.

In addition, corporations frequently seem to prefer to employ on automated processes workers who have had no experience with older methods. Thus, an employer whose only concern is his own profit, may decide that it is to his advantage to build a new plant in a new location, perhaps hundreds of miles away, without any consideration for the old community.

Even today, there are scores of distressed communities in our nation, where hundreds of thousands of workers have been left stranded by shutdown plants, industry migration, closed coal mines and curtailed operations of railroad repair shops. The impact of automation will possibly create additional pockets of substantial unemployment, even if high employment levels are maintained nationally.

Government assistance is required to aid in solving the pressing problems of such communities at present; government assistance has not yet been forthcoming, despite campaign promises made in the fall of 1952. Additional government aid will be needed in the future, as the new technology becomes widespread.

If the result of automation is that a large number of workers in a plant have to learn new skills, it is just as reasonable to expect the employer to pay the cost of retraining, including the payment of wages during the retraining period, as it is that he should pay the cost of building the new plant or installing the new equipment. When a plant is moved to a new locality, the employer has a responsibility not merely to retrain those workers who wish to move with the plant, but also to bear at least part of their cost of moving and new housing.

With the spread of automation, there will be a growing need for specialized semi-professional technicians, as well as for professional engineers and skilled workers. The education system of the nation should be preparing now to meet these requirements.

ADJUSTMENT PERIOD

From the viewpoint of the national economy, the greatest problem posed by automation is the threat of violent fluctuations in employment and production during the period of adjustment to the new technology. With the wide-spread introduction of automation speeding up the potential output of goods and services, there is the possibility that markets may not grow fast enough to sustain high employment levels. . . .

One of the fruits of automation which we should welcome is the opportunity it gives us to meet the present and growing social deficits in health, housing, schools, highways, natural resources, and other public services. Through increased productivity, our economy can meet the cost of these long-delayed measures without strain—and their achievement will help, by creating new jobs, to ease any necessary adjustments in employment.

It is within our power to see to it that these economic and social changes take place in an orderly and evolutionary manner—towards improved standards of living and social welfare, and extension of leisure and new horizons of individual opportunities for educational and cultural achievements. Such evolutionary changes in the coming decade will require forethought, planning and guidance. . . .

If we accept the challenge of the new technology, if we use foresight and act wisely and vigorously, we can help to usher in an age of abundance and freedom, the like of which the world has never known.

ATTITUDES TOWARD AUTOMATION

Excerpts from an address by Malcolm P. Ferguson, President, Bendix Aviation Corporation, at the 3d International Conference of Manufacturers, New York City, November 29, 1956

"Wholehearted acceptance" of automation is most common among representatives of management. Many go so far as to say it is absolutely *essential* to attainment of national goals.

Ralph J. Cordiner, president of General Electric, testified at hearings held by the American Congress to explore automation and technological changes that the United States will require an estimated 40 per cent more goods and services by 1965 though it will have only 14 per cent more people in the labor force. Industry must be encouraged, he said, to invest in more productive machinery and methods. Faster progress in the newer field of automation seems to us to be the only available solution to this problem, Mr. Cordiner said, particularly in situations where we have exhausted the known economic possibilities in the more familiar field of simple mechanization.

George Meany, president of the AFL-CIO, recently expressed an attitude very close to "whole hearted acceptance" of automation. He was quoted as saying, in part, that "automation, coupled with atomic power, will change the lives of all of us" and "labor sees no reason to fear the time when factories will run virtually on an automatic basis, with machines operating machines." But he went on to say that there will still be plenty of work to be done by people and, "if it becomes possible to put into effect a shorter work week to *maintain full employment*, let us promptly accept this opportunity to lighten the burdens of the American people."

The attitude of "acceptance with reservations" is more common among labor leaders. They agree that automation is a good development, but some of them insist that planned intervention—either through government or through collective bargaining—is necessary to protect people against the alleged "bad side effects" of automation.

There is real danger that these fears about objectionable corollary effects may seriously slow down automation by imposing an additional cost upon production. If such burdens offset the savings from increased efficiency, the incentive for technological improvements may be impaired or destroyed. . . .

It is elementary that long-run improvements in national economic welfare can have no other basis than increases in productivity. During the two centuries since the beginning of the industrial revolution, the level of living in the Western World has been raised tremendously. The chief impact of automation will be to permit the continuation of this historical improvement of human welfare.

In discussing the impact of automation on employment, a distinction must be made between labor displacement through technological change and technological unemployment. To say that automation will cause labor displacement is by no means equivalent to saying that it will bring about unemployment.

If you were to go along with the statements of some labor spokesmen that automation holds out the fear of dislocation, distress, unemployment and misery, you would have to say that technological progress, in and of itself, destroys jobs and does not create new ones. This leaves one wondering how the United States could have advanced so far technologically without a continuous increase in unemployment and without the welfare measures certain American labor leaders advocate for the future.

Automation, actually, will create new jobs as well as new and higher skills. The industry itself must produce automation devices, controls and equipment of all kinds of which computers themselves will be a substantial product. There will be engineering, development, sales, servicing and maintenance of product and all of the other requirements of this new industry involving machines, mechanical and electrical devices, hydraulics and electronics.

In discussing attitudes toward automation—or what you might describe as the "politics" of the matter—here are some interesting points:

The record of economic growth in the United States makes it seem almost absurd to fear unemployment as a result of improved technology. Let's have a look at it: Since 1870 productivity in the American economy has quadrupled. In other words we are, on the average, able to do any given task with one-fourth as much labor as it took in 1870. Yet the number of persons employed by private business has increased from about 12 million in 1870 to about 60 million at present. Productivity has more than doubled since 1900, yet the rate of unemployment has actually declined slightly since then—it was 5.1 per cent of the civilian labor force in 1900, 4 per cent in 1955, and still lower in 1956. Our economy provides 67 million jobs, many of which would not exist if it were not for our advanced economy.

Thus the real problem involved in the relationship of automation to unemployment is the problem of labor displacement and the need for people to adapt themselves to new jobs and opportunities rather than the problem of mass unemployment.

People will shift from lines of work in which their services are no longer needed to other, often better jobs. There is no virtue in keeping more people at work making automobiles than are actually needed. To do so would be to cheat society of the services these people would be performing and to cheat the people themselves of new opportunities.

The great increases in agricultural productivity through mechanization would not have enriched our lives and the lives of our farmers if we had insisted on keeping *three-quarters of our population* on farms, as was the case in our grandfathers' time. It is by freeing labor for other tasks that agricultural progress has made one of its chief contributions to the rising standard of living for all of us.

Cases can be cited of whole industries that increased their total employment after the introduction of automation. The use of dial equipment by the telephone industry, beginning about 1920, is one such instance. Since 1920 the operating telephone companies have more than doubled their employment. The use of continuous-flow methods in the oil refining industry also began about 1920 and this industry's employment has about doubled, too. The reason for this outcome is the development of more and cheaper methods of producing telephone service and motor fuels, resulting in a greater expansion of their use.

Realistic estimates of the rate of labor displacement that may be anticipated from automation indicate that it will be very minor indeed compared to the rate of labor displacement that is going on all the time, from other causes. The U.S. labor force is in a continuous state of flux right now with about 6 million people entering it or leaving it each month.

It seems reasonable to hope that automation will result in jobs becoming more interesting, less tiring, and, in general, more personal. Muscular labor already has been largely eliminated by machine production, but some monotonous, repetitive jobs have been created. Automation will tend to alter this type of job.

Automation will probably offer opportunities for eliminating jobs which create special risks to health and safety. In some fields, it can reduce the likelihood of individuals coming into contact with dangerous or toxic substances. It may contribute to the productive power of older workers and open many opportunities where age handicaps are no longer important. Fatigue can be reduced because automation will tend to eliminate jobs where the operator is paced by the machine.

Management will, of course, play a big role in determining progress toward automation. But it will not only initiate automation. It will be in the midst of all the changes which the new technology will bring and *will have to adapt itself* to them. *We will need more management* . . . tighter control and coordination of every detail of the production process . . . and probably more individuals at every level making more decisions of a management type than they had previously.

AUTOMATION—FRIEND OR FOE?

Excerpts from the General Electric Employee Relations News Letter of April 8, 1955

WHY DOES—AND MUST—BUSINESS AUTOMATE AS FAST AS POSSIBLE?

The urge for survival, growth, strength, profit and usefulness—in the face of temperate and intemperate competition—is what spurs business to automate as fast as feasible. Technological advance gives the customer lower costs, higher quality, greater quantity and broader variety of products and services. The business which fails to keep in the front row of pioneers of such advances soon finds it has lost its customers and jobs to the one that does stay up front.

A recent article in the Lynn IUE-CIO newspaper scolded us for losing a big order. The union paper claimed we had not put in as much automatic labor-saving equipment as the midwestern competitor who got the business. If the editor's claim had been correct, his position would have been extremely well taken.

For the question is not whether a given *industry* or all industry will automate as far and as fast as feasible. The only question for its employees—as well as for all others concerned—is whether a given *company* will be among the leaders of the parade, or will try to follow, or will even earlier fall by the way-side.

WHAT MAY PEOPLE BE PERSUADED TO FEAR?

There has always been resistance to change, fear of the unknown. New machines have always been distrusted—until the favorable facts at last become widely known.

An 1830 propaganda cartoon on our office wall shows all the dire disasters to be expected from the introduction of steam power in factories. It even went so far as to recommend that mothers bear no more children since steam would take away any possibility of jobs for them.

At the turn of the century, the motor car was questioned by most sober people—and seemingly feared or hated by almost as many on both economic and moral grounds. The automobile now gives us the world's largest industry—and hundreds of times the jobs which the harness, coach, and buggy-whip factories supplied. We have even forgotten how we distrusted that great labor and accident saver, the self-starter, when it was introduced.

It would have been permissible for anyone to expect that the dial telephone was going to eliminate operators and cut telephone employment. Just the opposite has happened, of course, because the dial savings made it possible to increase the value and attractiveness of the service and to bring on the great expansion in the installation and use of phones that has occurred—so that in just the last ten years the number of telephone operators in this country has increased by 79 per cent.

THE SHORT-TERM FALSE ALARM

This is not to say that there *might* not occasionally be a relatively few *short-term* displacements here and there from the automation process itself—even though the gloomiest detractors of automation are finding it hard to uncover any really convincing evidence of such displacements.

The immediate result sought from the automation process is a reduction in relative cost and a resulting more attractive competitive offering to customers. The employer is likely to get more business as a result of the more attractive offering on the item automated—and hence retain or increase employment even though there are fewer employees per *new unit of output*.

On the other hand, his customers may not want more of this particular item but will apply their new savings to additional purchases of other kinds of goods from other makers. Then in the absence of sufficient natural attrition of the work force employed on that item, there may be temporary layoffs by this particular employer unless he has a large and varied local operation in which there are other openings as a result of the turnover or expansion in the rest of his lines there.

But, in any event, the employer must automate to stay alive and to keep all or the bulk of his jobs alive—and he can only automate if he gets his costs down appropriately. If he tries to keep on the payroll people he does not need, his costs are too likely to prevent him from meeting competition and from supplying *any* jobs at all. So it is imperative to the rest of his employees, as well as to him and all others concerned—that he remove from his payroll any substantial surplus of employees not needed.

Fortunately, there are two alternatives for any such few that might be temporarily displaced.

The first is that—as history shows—any such displacements can normally expect to be quickly absorbed in the new jobs created as the new savings go into added purchases. Incidentally, job opportunities have grown fastest in industries like ours where technological progress has gone forward the fastest.

Second—if the times are such that some general unemployment interferes temporarily with this reemployment—the employer has provided out of his funds alone an unemployment compensation which is set at the proportion of the employee pay that is judged appropriate by the citizens in each state through their legislatures there. For those employees at the lower end of the earning scale—these being the ones most likely to experience the few displacements that may occur—the benefits tend to go up to around 65 per cent of their normal take-home pay and to last as long as a half year.

The point is that there is no royal road to technological progress and, if we want to continue to see our level of living go up, some risks by *all* are inescapable. Since it is no longer a question of whether industry in general will automate, but only whether a *given company* will be a leader or fall behind, anybody who is temporarily displaced by improvements in that company would lose his job anyhow—along with all the other employees in that company losing their jobs—if it should fall back in the parade.

DESPITE CHAMBER OF COMMERCE COMMERCIALS, LABOR DOES NOT OPPOSE AUTOMATION

From the Oil, Chemical and Atomic Union News, April 4, 1955

Some leaders in American business and industry are now hard at work building up the idea that the American worker is afraid of progress.

Specifically, the charge is that labor is opposed to the introduction of automation in the fear that it will produce mass unemployment.

On the contrary, all the evidence available indicates that organized labor is NOT opposed to automation as such but wants to make sure that its impact on the economy is cushioned and that the worker will get his share of its benefits.

In addition, there are strong signs that the "myth" of labor opposition to automation actually will be used to fight against such labor demands as the guaranteed annual wage and similar benefits.

Within recent weeks, "Washington Report," published by the U.S. Chamber of Commerce, has been devoting itself to what it calls "the attack on automatic machines" with organized labor as its obvious target.

Recently, it published an old 19th Century handbill calling upon the people of Philadelphia to keep the Camden and Amboy railroad out of the city. The appeal of the handbill, addressed to "artizans, mechanics, citizens," was based on the dangers of a railroad running through the city's streets, the ruin of trade and the annihilation of the prosperity and comfort of Philadelphia.

"Washington Report" published the handbill under the head, *"The Fearful Always Attempt To Halt Progress,"* and declares that it is in the tradition of those who are afraid that automatic machines will create mass unemployment and may create a depression.

Later, "Washington Report" returned to the battle with an article headed "Attack on Machine Called 'Vicious Propaganda' by Ben Fairless."

"Washington Report" chimed in with its declaration that "the attack on automatic machines continues unabated."

Significantly, it then remarks, "general belief in such propaganda would hamper the development and the use of machines. For instance, a guaranteed wage to prevent technological unemployment could be a major roadblock to technical progress."

Now, in reality, what has been the attitude of today's labor leadership toward automation?

We have a number of examples showing clearly that American labor leadership is NOT fighting the introduction of automatic machinery, but that it does see grave cause for concern that automation will be introduced without the slightest regard for the workers displaced and without the slightest planning for the social and economic consequences that will follow.

Past experience has taught American labor leaders that the workingman is the chief one left to "pick up the pieces" when there are great technological changes made in the economy.

Thus they have been pounding away on the theme that while business and industry are holding out bright hopes for an increase in jobs as a result of automation, business and industry are saying little and doing less about jobs during the period of transition.

Writing in a current issue of the magazine *Fortune*, AFL Pres. George Meany declared flatly that *"the trade union movement does* NOT *oppose technological change."* He added that *"the answer lies in cushioning the shocks that attend it."*

CIO Pres. Walter P. Reuther appeared before the Joint Congressional Committee on the Economic Report to comment on President Eisenhower's recent Economic Report. Outlining the tremendous potential of the automatic factory, Reuther spoke of productivity increases in the days ahead "which may well be tremendous, making possible the creation of abundance in terms undreamed of before."

"These growth potentials," he said, "will make possible vast improvements in the living conditions of the American people. They can be a major asset in developing both national strength and power and stability of the free world."

But he declared, "from the Administration we have received no analysis of this potential, no guideposts for future economic growth, no discussion of the probable temporary dislocations arising from automation, no preparation of the Congress and of the people to meet the new technology and to use it for the benefit of the nation."

Thus organized labor has clearly stated that it is NOT fighting automation. Instead, it sees just as great a potential in automation for the future well-being of the nation as does industry.

But American labor has expressed determination that the dislocations inevitably caused by automation shall be cushioned and, further, that automation will serve not merely to increase profits, but to give workers a better life.

THE BENEFITS AND PROBLEMS INCIDENT TO AUTOMATION AND OTHER TECHNOLOGICAL ADVANCES

Report from the President's Advisory Committee on Labor-Management Policy, January 11, 1962

Three central propositions have emerged in the Committee's consideration of the significance and impact of automation and other technological advances.

First, automation and technological progress are essential to the general welfare, the economic strength, and the defense of the Nation.

Second, this progress can and must be achieved without the sacrifice of human values and without inequitable cost in terms of individual interests.

Third, the achievement of maximum technological development with adequate safeguards against economic injury to individuals depends upon a combination of private and governmental action, consonant with the principles of the free society.

Automation and technological change have meant much to our country. Today the average worker in the United States works shorter hours, turns out more goods, receives higher wages, and has more energy harnessed and working with him than a worker anywhere else in the world. Increasingly, machines are relieving men of heavy physical labor and of dangerous and repetitive work. Competition in the world markets has been possible against foreign countries whose standards of living are below our own, though this advantage is diminishing. Finally, in a world split by ideological differences, automation and technological change have a tremendous and crucial role to play in maintaining the strength of the free world.

For these reasons, we emphasize at the outset the imperative need for and desirability of automation and technological change. Indeed, increased productivity and fuller utilization of resources are urgently needed to improve our rate of economic growth. They are likewise needed to improve our competitive position in world markets. Failure to advance technologically and to otherwise increase the productivity of our economy would bring on much more serious unemployment and related social problems than any we now face.

It is equally true that the current rate of technological advance has created social problems and that an acceleration of this rate may intensify these problems.

While advancing technology has given rise to new industries and jobs, it has also resulted in employee displacement; and the fact that new work opportunities are eventually created is no comfort or help to the displaced individual who cannot, for one reason or another, secure comparable or any employment. While employment has expanded in some industries, the net effect of rising output per worker, of the growing labor force, and of other factors has been an increase in the volume of unemployment during the past few years—even as total employment has reached new heights.

The impact of technology on agricultural employment has been particularly great. Along with other factors, it has resulted in over 1,600,000 workers—20 percent of the total—leaving the farms since 1950. Yet farm output has increased 28 percent, making available to our people an abundance of food, while there was famine in some of the Communist countries. This increased output enabled this country to be of substantial assistance to needy people elsewhere in the world.

Our purpose, then, is to seek that course of action which will encourage essential progress in the form of automation and technological change, while meeting at the same time the social consequences such change creates.

We recognize that the subject of automation and technological change cannot be dealt with apart from two broader subjects: increased productivity in general, and unemployment.

We are preparing a separate report on economic growth, and only note here the basic importance of such growth to any consideration of the problems— and the opportunities—automation and technological advance present.

Regarding technological advance and unemployment, it is clear that unemployment has resulted from displacement due to automation and technological change. It is impossible, with presently available data, to isolate that portion of present unemployment resulting from these causes. Whether such displacement will be short-run depends to a considerable extent on our ability to anticipate and plan for programs involving technological change and to make better use of various mechanisms for retraining and relocating workers who find themselves unneeded in their former occupations. We have necessarily given general consideration in this report to some aspects of the broader unemployment problem and to the prospects of more effective use of the work force.

A long stride toward solution of the unemployment problem will be made if we first recognize the nature of the problem. We regard the following factors as important in this connection:

1. The recent rate of economic growth in the United States has been insufficient to reduce unemployment to a tolerable level.
2. The exact extent of unemployment attributable to automation and technological change is unknown, since it is greatly complicated by other factors, such as:
   a. The economic recession of 1960–61.
   b. The unusually high entrance rate into the labor market, caused by the great postwar population increase. In the next 10 years it is expected that there will be a net gain in the labor force of 13½ million workers.
   c. Chronic unemployment in distressed areas.
   d. The effects of the rapid advances which have been made by foreign competitors.
   e. Changing consumption patterns.
   f. The changing nature of jobs which often leaves a gap between job requirements and qualifications of applicants. During the 1950's there was a 58 percent increase in the number of skilled technical and professional workers. Unskilled workers, with only a limited education, found it more difficult to get, or hold, a job. In this connection, the

Department of Labor projections indicate that unless steps are taken to reduce the dropout rate among high school students, some 7½ million of those new workers joining the labor force in the 1960's, or more than 30 percent, will not have completed high school, and over 2½ million of them will not even have completed grade school.

   g. Discrimination against workers on the basis of age, sex, race, and creed.

   h. Multiple jobholding by individuals.

   i. The continuing movement of workers away from the farms.

3. Public employment service facilities have been inadequate as well as seriously uneven in their effectiveness with respect to helping workers find new jobs, counseling them as to the kind of jobs which are liable to be available in the future, and advising them as to job prospects in other geographical areas.

4. The mobility of workers is reduced by factors running contrary to the demands of a dynamic society, and an economy in transition.

   a. The nontransferability of pension, seniority, and other accumulated rights may result in an employee's being dependent upon his attachment to a particular job as the sole means of protecting his equities.

   b. Desirable and essential mobility is affected by reluctance to leave home—because of personal ties, or because other members of the family may be working; by the cost of moving and possible losses on local property; and by the insecurity of jobs in a new locality.

5. Educational and informational facilities have been inadequate in that:

   a. The requirements for general education prior to vocational and professional training have not kept pace with the shift in job opportunities.

   b. The required types of vocational and technical training and retraining are often not available, e.g., for workers leaving the farm.

   c. There has been an inadequate liaison among school systems, industry, and government with respect to future job requirements, and in fact there is insufficient information about the nature of such jobs.

   d. There has been inadequate financial support for needy students.

   e. Counseling facilities have been generally inadequate.

6. Proper retraining facilities, and a system of financial support for workers while retraining, have been lacking.

These are some of the relevant circumstances of a society in which automation and technological advance are essential motive forces. The operation of these forces within the social context creates serious displacement problems—not as a necessary price of progress but as the stern consequence of failure to recognize and provide for these problems. We reject the too common assumption that continuing unemployment is an inherent cost of automation.

We believe, rather, that a combination of energetic and responsible private and public action will permit the advancement of automation and technological change without the sacrifice of human values, and that such combined efforts can cope satisfactorily with the total unemployment problem—including whatever part of it may arise from the displacements which result inevitably from the introduction of new devices and processes.

We do not attempt here an exhaustive exploration or enumeration of all the ways and means of achieving maximum technological progress with the minimum of individual disadvantage. Our suggestions can be only representative of a broader set of possibilities. We recognize, furthermore, that the totality of any combination of recommendations must be viewed in the light of such relevant factors as their costs to individual enterprises, their effect on the Federal budget, and their influence on general price levels.

We recommend that serious consideration be given the following measures:

1. Adoption by the government and others of policies which will promote a high rate of economic growth and fuller utilization of resources. A much higher rate of growth is essential and is the best device for reducing unemployment to tolerable levels. We will include in our forthcoming report on economic growth suggestions in this area.

2. Acceptance by government agencies of the responsibility for collecting, collating, and disseminating information with respect to present and future job opportunities and requirements in a rapidly changing society.

3. Cooperation between government and private organizations in the field of education in improving and supporting educational facilities to the end that:

    a. New entrants to the labor force will be better qualified to meet the occupational demands of the future;

    b. The dropout rate at grade and high school levels will be reduced;

    c. Better vocational, technical, and guidance programs will be available;

    d. Rural and depressed areas, where surplus workers reside, will be better served;

    e. Financial support will be available for deserving and needy students; and

    f. There will be a general upgrading in the quality of our education.

4. Acceptance by management of responsibility for taking measures, to the maximum extent practicable, for lessening the impact of technological change, including:

    a. Adequate lead time.

    b. Open reporting to the employees involved.

    c. Cooperation with representatives of the employees to meet the problems involved.

    d. Cooperation with public employment services.

    e. The timing of changes, to the extent possible, so that potential unemployment will be cushioned by expected expansion of operations and normal attrition in the work force (through separations resulting from retirement, quits, and so forth).

5. Support from both public and private organizations for retraining of workers who have been and will be displaced.

    a. Private employers and unions faced with automation or technological changes should make every reasonable effort to enable workers who are being displaced, and who need to be retrained, to qualify for new jobs available with the same employer, and to enjoy a means of support while so engaged.

    b. Where it is not possible for the employer to reabsorb displaced workers, appropriately safeguarded public support in the form of subsistence payments should be available to industrial and agricultural workers who qualify for and engage in retraining.

    c. Unemployment compensation laws should be liberalized to permit and to encourage retraining.

6. Support from both public and private sources, with due consideration to the circumstances of the enterprise involved, for the displaced worker who is seeking new employment.

    a. The duration, coverage, and amount of unemployment compensation, where inadequate, should be increased and made subject to realistic uniform minimum requirements under the Federal-State system.

    b. Employer supplementation of public unemployment compensation should be accomplished through severance pay, supplemental unemployment benefits, and similar measures.

    c. Attention should be given to provision for the special case of the worker who is displaced during the period when he is approaching retirement. This may appropriately include consideration of provision for early retirement, through private arrangements or social security measures; but alternative possibilities of more constructive temporary uses of such services warrant exploration.

7. Support from both private and public sources to the end that a worker's job equities and security may be protected without impairment of his mobility. This will warrant consideration, taking into account relevant cost factors, of such measures as:

    a. Financial aid in the transfer of employees to other plants in a multi-plant system, and protection of existing rights for individuals so transferred.

    b. The use of public funds in order to give financial aid in the transfer of unemployed workers from one area to another where the result will be to provide continuing employment.

    c. The improvement of public and private protection of pension rights.

    d. The recognition by unions, individual employees, and employers of the necessity of adapting seniority and other rules in order to facilitate mobility of workers, while providing protection for the equities of employees.

The Committee notes particularly the need for further study and exploration of this vital area.

8. Vast additional improvement of the public employment service so that it can effectively place, counsel, and relocate workers both locally and

across State lines. We note with approval the start which has been made in this direction.

9. Vigorous and unremitting efforts by all segments of the population—including government, employers, unions, and employees—to eliminate discrimination in employment because of race, creed, age, or sex.

10. There are pressing national needs to be met, and an abundance of manpower available to meet these needs. This matching of manpower and national needs, which is part of the vital context of the automation and technological advance problem, will obviously be affected by various broader governmental policies. Reserving fuller consideration of this area for our economic growth report, we nevertheless note here that:

   a. When technological changes or other factors develop particular pockets of unemployment, this becomes an additional reason for the undertaking, particularly at the State and local levels but with Federal assistance where this is necessary, of public development projects for which there is need independent of the employment need itself.

   b. Every effort should be made to maintain on an up-to-date and ready-to-go basis a schedule of needed public development projects, particularly those which could be started most quickly and which would be of short or controllable duration, so that the initiation of such projects can in the future be advanced, and the flow of projects already under way can be speeded up, if the manpower situation warrants this.

   c. If the operation of the economy, including the effect of automation and technological change, creates or leaves an intolerable manpower surplus, consideration should be given to monetary and fiscal measures—including the possibility of appropriate tax reductions—which would give promise of helping alleviate this situation.

   d. Governmental action along the lines suggested here, stimulated in part by the need to meet unemployment situations, would obviously have to take account of other considerations, including particularly the maintenance of national economic stability and security. We simply assert, however, the coordinate importance of stability and growth.

11. The need for goods and services must not be left unfilled, particularly in a time of international crisis. At the same time, high unemployment is intolerable. In the light of our current responsibilities to meet world conditions, and in view of our unmet needs at home, we consider the development of programs directed at the achievement of full employment as being more signficant at the present time than the consideration of a general reduction in the hours of work. A reduction in the basic work period has, however, historically been one means of sharing the fruits of technological progress, and there may well develop in the future the necessity and the desirability of shortening the work period, either through collective bargaining or by law or by both methods. In connec-

tion with such a development, consideration would necessarily be given to the extent to which purchasing power could be maintained along with a reduced work period.[1, 2]

We affirm our conviction that the infinite promise of automation and technological advance can be realized without loss or cost of human values. America can enjoy the fruits of higher productivity without having to accept, as the inevitable result, serious social consequences growing out of the displacement of workers.

The recommendations made here suggest our view of a broader pattern of possible courses of action which would necessarily have to be adapted to particular circumstances, but which permit the constructive and responsible uses of technology and automation. We see no barriers—except misunderstanding, timidity, and false fear—to the accomplishment of this purpose by a coordination of private and public programs wholly consonant with the essential concepts of the free society.

We assert the necessity of automation and technological development to the maintenance of American standards of living and to the fulfillment of this country's role of leadership in freedom's fight for survival. We assert equally the obligation and the capacity of Americans—as individuals and as a group—to use these new instruments and methods to enrich the lives of *all* of us.

We see no reason for alarm if out of a greater sense of common purpose we can achieve the good will and the determination to act together.

[1] MR. MEANY, MR. DUBINSKY, MR. HARRISON, MR. REUTHER, and MR. KEENAN are of the view that this paragraph should read as follows:

"The need for goods and services must not be left unfilled, particularly in a time of international crisis. At the same time, high unemployment is intolerable. In the light of our current responsibilities to meet world conditions, and in view of our unmet needs at home, we consider the development of programs directed at the achievement of maximum output and full employment as most significant at the present time. However, if unemployment is not reduced substantially in the near future we will have to resort to a general shortening of the work period through collective bargaining and by law. In connection with such a development, consideration would necessarily be given to the extent to which purchasing power could be maintained along with a reduced work period. A reduction in the basic work period has historically been one means of sharing fruits of technological progress."

[2] MR. MCDONALD, MR. REUTHER, and MR. KEENAN comment as follows:

"We agree that, in the light of the considerations stated, the most desirable solution now to the problem of unemployment is the development of programs which will achieve full employment at forty hours per week. Saying that this is the most desirable solution is not, however, the same thing as saying that we have in fact achieved that solution or that we will in fact achieve it in the near future. And only the fact of full employment—not a statement of its desirability—can properly serve as the premise for the statement that the necessity for shortening the work period will only develop 'in the future.' If we fail, as we have so far failed, to achieve the most desirable solution we will have to move more quickly than we are now moving in the direction of shortening the work period."

AUTOMATION IS BECOMING A CURSE

From an address by President George Meany to the 5th Annual Constitutional Convention of the AFL-CIO, November 14, 1963

A remark was made a few minutes ago that automation could be a blessing. Well, I have heard that phrase, "Automation can be a blessing, or it can be a curse, it can relieve human labor, make it easier for people, they won't have to strain themselves."

Well, ladies and gentlemen, I've heard that for a number of years, and I have come to the conclusion—there is no longer any question in my mind, and I say this with deep sincerity—there is no longer any question in my mind as to the direction in which automation is going today.

There is no element of blessing in it. It is rapidly becoming a real curse to this society. When you study what's happening, you realize that this is a real threat. This could bring us to a national catastrophe. Every big corporation in America is in a mad race to produce more and more with less and less labor without any feeling as to what it may mean to the whole national economy.

The fact that they're reducing purchasing power in their own plant, they're eliminating customers in their own plant doesn't seem to bother them because they feel if they produce cheaper they will get customers some other place.

Their plans for expansion are staggering, and every one of them call for more and more pushbutton operation with machines to push the button, if you please, even eliminating the human element there.

Serious-minded scientists and public officials who are knowledgeable on this subject see jobs being eliminated at the rate of tens of thousands a month. Competent technologists in this field think of the day a few years hence when all the production we need will be furnished by less than twenty-five per cent of the manpower we have.

Then we're told by a prominent industrialist who has turned statesman, that the argument about automation is just a bugaboo. The important thing is to balance the budget. This is our greatest secret weapon. We will balance the budget and Moscow will put up the white flag of surrender.

Yes, there has got to be a change in the thinking. They have got to understand that while many of them believe that automation will eventually supply more jobs, I don't know what they have to prove this, but I am quite sure a good many sincerely believe this, then what happens until that takes place? Do we get our purchasing power from the push-buttons?

We have a great system in this country, the greatest system of government ever devised by the minds of men, in my opinion. It has brought more benefits to those who work for wages than has any other system on earth. We can be proud of this system and proud of this great country but we cannot be blind. We cannot take the position that this system is invulnerable, that it cannot collapse.

This system can go down the drain on this very one problem, and it's a problem for all the country, not just labor, unless our business community, our great captains of industry and our politicians wake up to this problem.

14: Job and Income Security

The struggle for job security takes a number of forms. Some—such as spreading work among more workers through a reduction in hours, or seeking to forestall railroad mergers—we do not have space to examine. One of the most widely discussed security programs in recent years has been the supplemental unemployment benefit plan, which was pioneered at the Ford Motor Company and which originally took the form of a union demand for a guaranteed annual wage.

Another method by which workers seek to protect their jobs is through work rules which, in one way or another, oblige an employer to hire more labor for a job than he might do on his own.

GUARANTEED ANNUAL WAGE

From a resolution adopted by the 14th Constitutional Convention of the United Automobile Workers, Atlantic City, N.J., 1953

Workers and their families live by the year, a biological need which they share with stockholders and corporation officials. Corporations also live by the year. Interest rates, depreciation charges, taxes, executive salaries—all these items in the cost of keeping corporations alive are computed as annual costs.

The time has come to consider labor costs as annual costs also, because to the workers they are annual costs. Workers must provide for their needs every day in the year. They cannot meet those needs when they are left without jobs or earnings for weeks or months at a time. But little will be done to insure that they have jobs throughout the year until employers are given a greater financial responsibility in stabilizing employment.

The guaranteed annual wage is not a cure-all for our economic problems, but it can be the beginning, and the focal point, of a general attack on the basic problem of maintaining full employment in peacetime.

We have seen repeatedly how financial responsibility can convert management to social responsibility. A sound guaranteed annual wage plan will arouse management's social conscience and stimulate its social ingenuity by putting pressure on its pocketbook nerve. The guaranteed annual wage will compel management to take steps in its plants to end the instability of employment for which it is directly responsible. It will lead management to cooperate more readily in developing national economic measures designed to maintain full employment and full production by eliminating the causes of instability over which individual plant managements have no control. Industry will have cause to welcome rather than to oppose improved legislation to maintain the incomes and living standards of unemployed workers and their families.

Above all, the guaranteed annual wage will mark an end to irresponsible actions of employers which create needless unemployment, dislocation and hardship. It will end, for example, irresponsible decentralization of production and movement of plants which, though profitable to the employer, are costly to the workers and to the community in disrupted lives and weakened local economies.

No management in its right mind will pay to keep some of its workers in idleness while it hires others to do their work at new locations. The guaranteed annual wage will compel management to plan the extension or movement of its plants into new areas on a socially and economically sound basis by gearing decentralization to the expansion of markets and plant relocation to the orderly and gradual absorption of its existing work forces into other employment.

THE FORD SUPPLEMENTAL UNEMPLOYMENT BENEFIT PLAN (OCTOBER 20, 1961)

ARTICLE II. ESTABLISHMENT OF FUND

The Company shall establish, in accordance with this Supplemental Unemployment Benefit Plan, a Fund with a qualified bank or banks or a qualified trust company or companies selected by the Company as Trustee. The Company's contributions shall be made into the Fund, the assets of which shall be held, invested and applied by the Trustee, all in accordance with the Plan. Benefits and Separation Payments shall be payable only from such Fund. The Company shall provide in the contract with the Trustee that the Fund shall be held in cash or invested only in general obligations of the United States Government.

ARTICLE III. MAXIMUM FUNDING

SECTION 1. MAXIMUM FUNDING

There shall be a Maximum Funding of the Fund for each calendar month after November, 1962. The Maximum Funding of the Fund for each calendar month after November, 1962 shall be determined by multiplying the Average Full Benefit Rate by sixteen (16) and this result by the sum of

(i) the number of Covered Employes on the Active Employment Rolls, and

(ii) the number of persons laid off from work as Covered Employes who are not on the Active Employment Rolls but who have Credit Units; both numbers shall be as determined by the Company as of the latest date for which the figures are available prior to the first Monday in the month for which the Maximum Funding is being determined.

The computation of the Average Full Benefit Rate for the purpose of determining Maximum Funding shall be made monthly and shall be the average during the preceding months, not to exceed twelve (12), subsequent to the month of September, 1962, and immediately prior to the month next preceding the month for which Maximum Funding is being determined. The average shall be determined by dividing the sum of all Full Benefits paid during the period for which the computation is made by the number of such Benefits. A Full Benefit for the purpose of this computation shall mean a Regular Benefit which has been paid for a Week of layoff and which has not been reduced because of Other Compensation as defined in Section 2 (a) of Article VII and a Benefit paid to an applicant ineligible to receive a State System Unemployment Benefit for the reason specified in Section 2 (b) (3) (v) of Article V.

The provisions of this Section 1 shall not be construed to change in any manner whatsoever the provisions of Section 6 of Article X.

SECTION 2. FINALITY OF DETERMINATIONS

No adjustment in the Maximum Funding or the Credit Unit Cancellation Base shall be made on account of any subsequently discovered error in the computations or the figures used in making the computations, except in the case where after discovery of an error adjustment is practicable, and then the adjustment shall only be prospective in effect, unless such adjustment would be substantial in the opinion of the Company. Nothing in the foregoing shall be construed to excuse the Company from making up any shortage in its contributions to the Fund.

ARTICLE IV. CONTRIBUTIONS BY COMPANY

SECTION 1. COMPANY CONTRIBUTIONS

With respect to each Pay Period commencing on or after September 1, 1961, and prior to the first month for which the Maximum Funding is to be determined under Section 1 of Article III and with respect to each Pay Period thereafter for which the current market value of the assets of the Fund is less than the Maximum Funding, the Company shall make a contribution to the Fund in an amount to be determined by multiplying Five Cents ($.05) by the total number of hours for which Covered Employes shall have received pay from the Company (excluding any hours for which Benefits hereunder are payable) for such Pay Period (or such lesser amount as will bring the total market value of the assets in the Fund up to the Maximum Funding for such month).

Notwithstanding any other provisions of this Plan, the Company shall not be obligated to make any contribution to the Fund with respect to any Pay Period for which the current market value of the assets in the Fund is equal to or in excess of the Maximum Funding for such Fund, and no contribution to the Fund for any Pay Period shall be in excess of the amount necessary to bring the total market value of the assets in such Fund up to the Maximum Funding for such Fund.

Contributions with respect to Covered Employes at any additional Plant at which the Collective Bargaining Agreement becomes applicable shall commence with respect to the first Pay Period beginning after (i) the date of certification by the National Labor Relations Board of the Union as the collective bargaining representative of Employes at such Plant or (ii) if recognition is by agreement, the effective date of the agreement by which the Company recognizes the Union as the collective bargaining representative of Employes at such Plant.

SECTION 2. SCHEDULED SHORT WORKWEEK CONTRIBUTIONS

(a) Notwithstanding any other provisions of this Plan, the Company shall not be obligated to make any contribution to the Fund with respect to Short Week and Special Benefits for Scheduled Short Workweeks, for any Pay Period for which such Benefits are paid and for which the Credit Unit Cancellation Base is Three Hundred Dollars ($300) or more; provided, however, with respect to a month for which the Credit Unit Cancellation Base is less than Three Hundred Dollars ($300), the Company shall contribute to the Fund an amount equal to the lesser of (i) the amount of Short Week and Special Benefits for Scheduled Short Workweeks for which the Company was not obligated to make any contribution to the Fund with respect to Pay Periods commencing during the preceding month, or (ii) the amount necessary to bring the Credit Unit Cancellation Base up to Three Hundred Dollars ($300) for the month with respect to which such contribution is made. The amount of any such contribution will be added to the market value of the assets of the Fund for purposes of determining the Credit Unit Cancellation Base to be used for all purposes under the Plan for the month with respect to which any such contribution is made to the Fund.

(b) In addition to the contributions required by Section 1 of this Article and Subsection (a) of this Section 2, for any Pay Period for which the Credit Unit Cancellation Base is less than Three Hundred Dollars ($300) the Company shall contribute to the Fund an amount, determined for each Pay Period, equal to the amount of Short Week and Special Benefits for Scheduled Short Workweeks which have been paid from the Fund for such Pay Period under Section 1 (b) of Article VII and Section 3 of Article XIII.

SECTION 3. WHEN CONTRIBUTIONS ARE PAYABLE

Each contribution by the Company shall be made on or before the close of business on the first regularly scheduled workday in the second calendar week following the pay day for the Pay Period with respect to which the contribution is being made.

ARTICLE V. ELIGIBILITY FOR WEEKLY SUPPLEMENTAL BENEFITS

SECTION 1. APPLICATION FOR WEEKLY SUPPLEMENTAL BENEFITS

No person shall be eligible for a Weekly Supplemental Benefit unless and until he shall have made due application therefor in accordance with the procedure established by the Company hereunder and shall have met the eligibility requirements of Section 2 or Section 3 of this Article.

SECTION 2. ELIGIBILITY FOR A REGULAR BENEFIT

An applicant shall be eligible for a Regular Benefit only if he is on layoff from the Company with respect to the Week for which application is made and the first day of such Week is on or after January 1, 1962, and if

(a) such layoff:

(1) was from the Contract Unit;

(2) occurred in a reduction in force or temporary layoff, including a layoff because of the discontinuance of a Plant or an operation, or occurred or continued because the applicant was unable to do the work offered by the Company although able to perform other work in the Plant to which he would have been entitled if he had had sufficient seniority;

(3) was not for disciplinary reasons, and was not a consequence of (i) any strike, slowdown, work stoppage, picketing (whether or not by Employes), or concerted action, at a Company Plant or Plants, or any dispute of any kind involving Employes, whether at a Company Plant or Plants or elsewhere, or (ii) any fault attributable to the applicant, or (iii) any war or hostile act of a foreign power (but not government regulation or controls connected therewith), or (iv) sabotage, or insurrection, or (v) any act of God; provided, however, that if a layoff for one or more of the reasons in this Section 2 (a) (3) was not for all of the working days of such Week, an applicant shall not be considered ineligible for a Benefit for the remainder of the working days in such Week solely because of this Section 2 (a) (3); and

(b) with respect to such Week, the applicant:

(1) had to his credit a Credit Unit or fraction thereof;

(2) has registered at and has reported to an employment office maintained by the applicable State System if required under such State System;

(3) has received a State System Unemployment Benefit not currently under protest by the Company or was ineligible to receive a State System Unemployment Benefit only for one or more of the following reasons: (i) because such Week is the second "waiting week" of layoff of the applicable State System or (ii) because he did not have prior to his layout a sufficient period of work or earnings in employment covered by the State System or (iii) because of a limit under the State System of the period of time for which the State System Unemployment Benefits are payable to the applicant or (iv) because of the period he worked or because he was employed by the Company or otherwise for wages or remuneration in an amount equal to or in excess of his Estimated State System Earnings Limit or (v) because he is serving a "waiting week" of layoff under the applicable State System during a period while he has sufficient seniority to work in the Plant but is laid off out of line of seniority in accordance with the terms of the Collective Bargaining Agreement; provided, that the provisions of this item (v) shall not be applicable to a layoff under the provisions of Section 16 (d) or Section 21 of Article VIII of the Collective Bargaining Agreement or (vi) because he has refused an offer of work by the Company which he had an option to refuse under an

applicable collective bargaining agreement or which he may refuse without disqualification under Section 2 (*b*) (4) of this Article V or (vii) because he is receiving military terminal pay or (viii) because he is automatically retired from the Company without a retirement benefit under the Company's retirement program or (ix) because he was eligible for or receiving statutory benefits for retirement or disability which he could have received while working full time or (x) because he failed to claim a State System Unemployment Benefit for such Week if by reason of his pay received or receivable from the Company such State System Unemployment Benefit would have amounted to less than Two Dollars ($2) or (xi) because he was participating in a vocational training or retraining program established or approved under an act of Congress providing for such training and for benefits or subsistence allowances to unemployed individuals participating in such training or under similar provisions of a state law or (xii) because he was unable to do work offered by the Company but he is laid off or continued on layoff because he is able to perform other work in the Plant to which he would have been entitled if he had had sufficient seniority.

(4) has not refused to accept work when recalled pursuant to the Collective Bargaining Agreement, and has not refused an offer by the Company of other available work which he had no option to refuse under the provisions of an applicable collective bargaining agreement at the same Plant or at another Plant in the same labor market area (as defined by the State Employment Security Commission of the state in which the Plant from which he was laid off is located; those Plants presently covered by the Detroit Area Availability List Agreement shall be considered to be in the same "labor market area"); provided, however, that refusal by skilled Tool and Die, Maintenance and Construction or Power House Employes or apprentices of work other than work in Tool Room Departments, Maintenance Departments and Power House Departments, respectively, shall not result in ineligibility for a Benefit.

(5) was not eligible for, and was not claiming, any accident or sickness or other disability benefit (other than a disability benefit which would be payable to the applicant, whether or not he was working full time, or a survivor's allowance under Workmen's Compensation laws), whether publicly or privately financed, or a pension or retirement benefit financed in whole or in part by the Company, provided that if an applicant was not eligible for, and was not claiming, such benefits with respect to all of the working days of such week, he shall not be considered ineligible for a benefit for the remainder of such working days solely because of this Section 2 (*b*) (5);

(6) was not in military service;

(7) did not receive any unemployment benefit from, or under any contract, plan or arrangement of, any other employer; and he was not eligible for such a benefit from, or under any contract, plan or arrangement of, any employer with whom he has greater seniority than with the Company; and

(8) did not receive any unemployment benefit from, or under, any other supplemental unemployment benefit plan to which the Company has con-

tributed as an employer and was not eligible for such a benefit from, or under, any such plan in which he has Credit Units which were credited earlier than the oldest Credit Units credited under this plan;

(9) qualifies for a Regular Benefit computed under the Plan of at least Two Dollars ($2);

(10) was not eligible for a Short Week Benefit under Article XIII; and

(c) with respect to such Week the Credit Unit Cancellation Base was Twelve Dollars and Eighty Cents ($12.80) or more.

(d) An applicant who is automatically retired from the Company and who is not eligible for a retirement benefit under the Company's retirement program shall be considered to be on layoff for purposes of this Section 2.

SECTION 3. ELIGIBILITY FOR A SPECIAL BENEFIT

An applicant shall be eligible for a Special Benefit for any Week beginning on or after January 1, 1962

(a) with respect to which all of the eligibility conditions for a Regular Benefit are satisfied except the condition set forth under Section 2 (b) (9) of this Article V;

(b) during which he works for the Company and the total Compensated or Available Hours (as defined in Section 2 of Article XIII) are less than forty (40); and

(c) with respect to which (i) the pay received or receivable from the Company was not equal to or in excess of his Estimated State System Earnings Limit, or (ii) the period worked for the Company was not sufficient to disqualify him for a State System Unemployment Benefit or "waiting week" credit; provided, however, that no Special Benefit shall be payable if he is eligible for a Regular Benefit with respect to such Week in an amount that is the same as or higher than such Special Benefit; and provided, further, that a Special Benefit shall not be payable for any Week for which holiday pay or pay for scheduled vacations is the only pay received or receivable from the Company.

SECTION 4. PROTEST OF APPLICATION FOR STATE SYSTEM UNEMPLOYMENT BENEFIT

With respect to any Week for which an applicant for a Weekly Supplemental Benefit has applied for and been denied a State System Unemployment Benefit, which denial is being protested by the applicant through the procedure provided therefor under the State System, and also with respect to any Week for which the applicant has received a State System Unemployment Benefit, payment of which is being protested by the Company through the procedure provided therefor under the State System (and such protest has not, upon appeal pursuant to the procedure set forth in Article XI, been held by the Board to be frivolous), the Weekly Supplemental Benefit shall not be paid to the applicant, but, if the applicant is eligible to receive a Weekly Supplemental Benefit under the Plan except for such denial, or protest, of the State System Unemployment Benefit, the payment of such Weekly Supplemental Benefit shall be suspended until such dispute shall have been determined. If the dispute shall be finally determined in favor of the applicant, the Weekly Supplemental Benefit shall be paid to him if such Benefit is a Special Benefit for a Scheduled Short Workweek or if he had not exhausted Credit Units subsequent to the Week of the Weekly Supplemental Benefit in dispute; if the dispute shall be finally determined adversely to the applicant, he shall be disqualified for such Weekly Supplemental Benefit, except as otherwise provided in Section 2 (b) (3) of this Article V.

SECTION 5. BENEFITS PAYABLE AFTER APPEAL

In the event that an appeal pursuant to Section 5 of Article XI of the Plan with respect to entitlement to a Benefit is decided in favor of an applicant, said Benefit shall be paid to him if such Benefit is a Special Benefit for a Scheduled Short Workweek or if he had not exhausted Credit Units after the Week of the Benefit in dispute.

ARTICLE VI. CREDIT UNITS

SECTION 1. ACCRUAL OF CREDIT UNITS

(a) Credit Units shall have no fixed value in terms of either time or money, but shall be a means of determining duration of Benefits under the varying circumstances from time to time prevailing. Credit Units shall be credited to an Employe, at the rates specified in Subsections (b), (c), and (d) of this Section for Workweeks occurring while he is an Employe for which he receives pay commencing on or after June 1, 1955; provided, however, that

(1) No Employe may have to his credit at any one time more Credit Units than the greater of the following:

(i) twenty-six (26), or

(ii) after August 31, 1958, and prior to September 4, 1961, such number, not to exceed thirty-nine (39), as shall equal the maximum number of weekly State System Unemployment Benefits payable for weeks of total unemployment within a benefit year with respect to the applicable State System, or

(iii) after September 3, 1961, fifty-two (52); provided, however, that an Employe shall not accrue Credit Units in excess of 39 for any Workweek commencing prior to September 3, 1961; and

(2) No Employe shall be credited with any Credit Unit prior to the first day as of which he (i) has at least one (1) year of Seniority, and (ii) is on the Active Employment Rolls in the Contract Unit (or was on such rolls within thirty (30) days prior to such first day); but as of such day he shall be credited with Credit Units based upon his Workweeks occurring while he is an Employe after June 1, 1955, and subsequent to his Seniority date. An Employe who has Credit Units to his credit as of the last day of the Week shall be deemed to have had such Credit Units during all of such Week.

(b) For Workweeks commencing between June 1, 1955, and May 31, 1957, both inclusive, Credit Units shall be credited to each Employe with less than ten (10) years of Seniority at the rate of one-quarter (.25) of a Credit Unit for each Workweek for which he receives pay from the Company for at least thirty-two (32) hours, and to Employes with ten (10) or more years of Seniority at the rate of one-half (.50) of a Credit Unit for each such Workweek.

(c) For Workweeks commencing between June 1, 1957, and August 31, 1958, both inclusive, Credit Units shall be credited at the rate of one-half (.50) of a Credit Unit for each Workweek for which the Employe receives pay from the Company for at least thirty-two (32) hours.

(d) For Workweeks commencing on or after September 1, 1958, Credit Units shall be credited at the rate of one-half (.50) of a Credit Unit for each Workweek for which the Employe receives any pay from the Company, and, for any Workweek commencing on or after January 1, 1962, for which the Employe does not receive pay from the Company but for which he receives a Benefit pursuant to Section 2 (b) (3) (v) of Article V.

(e) For the purposes of accruing Credit Units under this Section 1—

(1) hours paid for at premium rate shall be counted only as straight-time hours;

(2) all hours represented by pay in lieu of vacation shall be counted as hours in the Workweek covered by the pay day as of which payment in lieu of vacation is made;

(3) back pay shall be considered as pay for any Workweek or Workweeks to which it may be allocable; and

(4) the provisions of Section 5 (a) of Article IX shall not affect the accrual of Credit Units pending possible reinstatement of the Plan in the applicable state.

SECTION 2. FORFEITURE OF CREDIT UNITS

(a) A person shall forfeit permanently all Credit Units with which he shall have been credited if at any time

(i) he shall incur a Break in Seniority, except a person who is automatically retired and who is not eligible for a retirement benefit under the Company's retirement program, provided, however, that if a person has incurred a Break in Seniority by reason of his retirement under the total and permanent disability provisions of the Retirement Plan established by agreement between the Company and the Union and shall subsequently have his Seniority reinstated, his Credit Units previously forfeited shall again be credited to him as of the date his Seniority is reinstated, or

(ii) he shall be on layoff from the Contract Unit for a continuous period of twenty-four (24) months, except that if at the expiration of such twenty-four (24) month period he is receiving Benefits his Credit Units shall not be forfeited until he ceases to receive Benefits, or

(iii) he shall wilfully misrepresent any material fact in connection with an application by him for Benefits under the Plan.

ARTICLE VII. AMOUNT OF WEEKLY SUPPLEMENTAL BENEFIT

SECTION 1. WEEKLY SUPPLEMENTAL BENEFIT

The Weekly Supplemental Benefit payable to any eligible applicant for any Week commencing on or after January 1, 1962, shall be (i) if he performed no work for the Company during such Week a Regular Benefit as computed below, or (ii) if he worked for the Company during such Week but is not eligible for a Short Week Benefit under Article XIII, the greater of a Regular Benefit or a Special Benefit, as computed below:

(a) Regular Benefit

A Regular Benefit shall be the lesser of

(1) an amount which, when added to the applicant's State Benefit and Other Compensation (as defined in Section 2 of this Article) for such Week, will equal 62% of his weekly straight-time Ford wage, computed as provided in Subsection (c) of this Section, plus One Dollar and Fifty Cents ($1.50) for each Dependent up to a maximum of four (4) Dependents, or

(2) Forty Dollars ($40), provided, however, that this Forty Dollar ($40) maximum shall not apply to an applicant ineligible to receive a State System Unemployment Benefit for the reason specified in Section 2 (b) (3) (v) of Article V;

(b) Special Benefit

A Special Benefit shall be an amount which when added to that part of the applicant's State Benefit and Other Compensation (as defined in Section 2 of this Article) for the Week which is in excess of the applicant's pay received or receivable from the Company will equal the product of the number by which forty (40) exceeds the number of Compensated or Available Hours (as defined in Section 2 of Article XIII), with any fractional hour expressed as a decimal to the nearest tenth, during such Week, multiplied by:

(i) in the case of a Scheduled Short Workweek as defined in Article XIII, 65% of his Base Hourly Rate (plus 65% of any applicable cost-of-living allowance then in effect but excluding all other premiums and bonuses of any kind), or

(ii) in the case of an Unscheduled Short Workweek as defined in Article XIII, 50% of his Base Hourly Rate (plus 50% of any applicable cost-of-living allowance then in effect but excluding all other premiums and bonuses of any kind).

The minimum Two Dollar ($2) Benefit requirement as set forth under Article V, Section 2 (b) (9), shall not apply with respect to the payment of any Special Benefit.

An applicant ineligible under Section 2 (a) (3) or 2 (b) (5) of Article V for a Weekly Supplemental Benefit for a part of a Week shall be entitled to a Weekly Supplemental Benefit in a reduced amount equal to one-fifth of the full Weekly Supplemental Benefit computed under (a) or (b) above, whichever is applicable, for each work day of the Week in which he meets all the eligibility requirements of Section 2 of Article V.

(*c*) For purposes of this Plan, an applicant's weekly straight-time Ford wage shall be computed by multiplying his Base Hourly Rate (plus any applicable hourly cost-of-living allowance in effect at the time of computation of the Weekly Supplemental Benefit, but excluding all other premiums and bonuses of any kind) by 40, except, however, that for a Part Time Employe such Base Hourly Rate (plus any applicable hourly cost-of-living allowance in effect at the time of computation of the Weekly Supplemental Benefit, but excluding all other premiums and bonuses of any kind) shall be multiplied by the number of hours such Employe is regularly scheduled to work during a Workweek.

SECTION 2. STATE BENEFIT AND OTHER COMPENSATION

(*a*) "State Benefit and Other Compensation" for a Week means the full amount of the State System Unemployment Benefit, if any, received or receivable by the applicant for such Week (or the estimated amount that would have been received by the applicant for such Week if he had not been ineligible therefor solely as set forth in items (i), (ii), (iii), (vi), (vii), (viii), (ix), (x), (xi) and (xii) of Subsection (*b*) (3) of Section 2 of Artivle V), including any dependency allowances, plus

(1) all pay received or receivable from the Company (including without limitation holiday payments and payments for scheduled vacations but not payments in lieu of vacation), and, except as otehwise provided for in determining the amount of a Special Benefit, the amount of unearned pay computed, as if payable, for hours made available by the Company, but not worked, for such Week; provided, however, that all of the pay received or receivable by an applicant for a shift which extends through midnight shall be allocated, regardless of the method of allocation used by the state, (i) to the day on which the shift started if the applicant is on layoff with respect to the corresponding shift on the following day, (ii) to the day on which the shift ended if the applicant was on layoff with respect to the corresponding shift on the preceding day, and (iii) according to the pay for the hours worked each day, if the applicant was on layoff with respect to the corresponding shifts on both the preceding and the following days; and, in any such event, the Forty Dollar ($40) maximum provided in Subsection 1 (*a*) (1) of this section shall be modified to the extent (if any) necessary so that the applicant's Benefit will be increased to offset any reduction in the Applicant's State System Unemployment Benefit which may have resulted solely from the allocation of the applicant's earnings for such a shift otherwise than as prescribed in this Proviso.

(2) all wages or remuneration, as defined under the law of the applicable State System, in excess of Ten Dollars ($10) received or receivable from other employers for such Week; and

(3) the amount of all other benefits in the nature of compensation or benefits for unemployment, received or receivable under any state or federal system (such as, for example, the so-called readjustment allowances which were payable under federal law to veterans of World War II for such Week.

(*b*) For purposes of Subsection (*a*) above, the estimated amount that would have been received by the applicant shall be an amount equal to whichever of the following amounts is applicable:

(1) If the applicant has had a weekly benefit rate, which is currently applicable, established under the State System, an amount equal to such benefit rate plus any dependents allowances so established;

(2) If the applicant is ineligible for State System Unemployment Benefits under Section 2 (b) (3) (iii) of Article V, an amount equal to the State System weekly benefit rate which applied to the most recent week for which he received a State System Unemployment Benefit plus any dependents allowances thus applicable; or

(3) for any other applicant, an amount equal to the State System weekly benefit rate which would be payable to an individual having the same number of dependents as the applicant and having weekly earnings equal to the applicant's weekly straight-time Ford wage as computed under Section 1 (c) of this Article.

(c) Notwithstanding any other provision of this Article, with respect to an applicant who is eligible for a Regular Benefit but is ineligible to receive a State System Unemployment Benefit because of a limit under the State System of the period of time for which the State System Unemployment Benefits are payable to the applicant (as specified in Subsection 2 (b) (3) (iii) of Article V), State Benefit and Other Compensation shall not include any estimated State System Unemployment Benefit.

(d) In the event the amount of the State System Unemployment Benefit received by an applicant for a state week shall be for less, or more, than a full state week (for reasons other than the applicant's receipt of wages or remuneration for such state week):

(1) because the applicant has been disqualified or otherwise determined ineligible for a portion of his State System Unemployment Benefit or for one or more days of such state week, or

(2) because the state week for which the benefit is paid includes one or more waiting period effective days, or

(3) because of an underpayment or overpayment of a previous State System Unemployment Benefit, the full amount of the State System Unemployment Benefit to which he otherwise would have been entitled for such state week shall be used in the calculation of "State Benefit and Other Compensation" for such state week.

(e) In the event that the State System Unemployment Benefit recieved by an applicant shall be for less than a full state week because the State System benefit year has expired within such state week, or because of a revision in the state law or procedures, the amount of the Weekly Supplemental Benefit payable for such state week shall be an amount which bears the same ratio to the Weekly Supplemental Benefit which would have been payable had a full weekly State System Unemployment Benefit been paid as the partial State System Unemployment Benefit received bears to a full weekly State System Unemployment Benefit.

(*f*) In the event the State System benefit period shall be shorter than a 7 day period due to commencement or termination of unemployment other than on the first or last day of his normally applicable state week, the period of the normally applicable state week shall be used in calculating "State Benefit and Other Compensation" for such state week.

SECTION 3. INSUFFICIENT CREDIT UNITS FOR FULL BENEFIT

If an applicant shall have available less than the full number of Credit Units required to be cancelled for the full amount of the Weekly Supplemental Benefit or Short Week Benefit (as set forth in Article VIII) for any Week for which he is otherwise eligible, he shall be paid the full amount of such Benefit and in such event all remaining Credit Units or fractions thereof shall be cancelled.)

SECTION 4. EFFECT OF LOW CREDIT UNIT CANCELLATION BASE

Notwithstanding any of the other provisions of the Plan, if, and as long as, the applicable Credit Unit Cancellation Base for any Week shall be Twelve Dollars and Eighty Cents ($12.80) or more, but less than Forty-one Dollars and Sixty Cents ($41.60), any Benefit for such week (other than a Short Week or a Special Benefit for a Scheduled Short Workweek) as computed under the preceding Section of this Article (or under Article IX or XIII) shall be reduced by 20%, but shall in no event be reduced to an amount less than Five Dollars ($5) by reason of such reduction; and if, and as long as, the applicable Credit Unit Cancellation Base for any Week shall be less than Twelve Dollars and Eighty Cents ($12.80), no Benefit (other than a Short Week or a Special Benefit for a Scheduled Short Workweek) for such Week shall be paid.

SECTION 5. WITHHOLDING TAX

The Trustee shall deduct from the amount of any Benefit (or Separation Payment) as computed under the Plan any amount required to be withheld by the Trustee or the Company by reason of any law or regulation, for payment of taxes or otherwise to any federal, state or municipal government.

ARTICLE VIII. DURATION OF BENEFITS

SECTION 1. CREDIT UNIT CANCELLATION BASE

There shall be a Credit Unit Cancellation Base which shall be determined for each calendar month after September, 1961. The Credit Unit Cancellation Base for any particular month shall be determined by dividing the current market value of the total assets in the Fund as certified by the Trustee as of the close of business on the Friday preceding the first Monday of such month (except as provided in Section 2 of Article IV), by the sum of (i) the number of Covered Employes on the Active Employment Rolls, and (ii) the number of persons laid off from work as Covered Employes who are not on the Active Employment Rolls but who have Credit Units; both numbers shall be determined by the Company as of the latest date for which they are available. The Credit Unit Cancellation Base for any particular month shall be applied to each of the Pay Periods beginning within such month; provided, however, that whenever the Credit Unit Cancellation Base for any particular month is less than Forty-one Dollars and Sixty Cents ($41.60), the Credit Unit Cancellation Base shall be applied only to the first Pay Period beginning within such month, and thereafter there shall be determined a Credit Unit Cancellation Base for each Pay Period until the Credit Unit Cancellation Base for a particular Pay Period equals or exceeds Forty-one Dollars and Sixty Cents ($41.60). When the Credit Unit Cancellation Base for a particular Pay Period equals or exceeds such amount, such Credit Unit Cancellation Base shall be applied to each Pay Period until a Credit Unit Cancellation Base for the following calendar month shall be applicable. The Credit Unit Cancellation Base for a particular Pay Period shall be determined on the basis of the current market value of the total assets in the Fund as certified by the Trustee as of the close of business on the Friday preceding such Pay Period (except as provided in Section 2 of Article IV).

SECTION 2. NUMBER OF WEEKS OF BENEFITS

The number of Weeks or Workweeks for which an eligible applicant shall receive a Weekly Supplemental Benefit or Short Week Benefit, or a combination thereof, (except as provided below) shall be determined on the basis of the number of his Credit Units and the Credit Unit Cancellation Base applicable to the Weeks for which such Benefits are paid to him. When all of an eligible applicant's Credit Units shall have been cancelled, he shall be entitled to no further Benefits until he shall have been credited with additional Credit Units.

SECTION 3. CREDIT UNITS TO BE CANCELLED ON PAYMENT OF A BENEFIT

The number of Credit Units to be cancelled for any Weekly Supplemental Benefit or Short Week Benefit shall be determined on the bases of the Seniority of the person to whom such Benefit is paid as of the last day of the Week for which such Benefit is paid and of the Credit Unit Cancellation Base applicable to the Week for which such Benefit is paid, in accordance with the table on the following page; provided, however, that one-half of the number of Credit Units required to be cancelled according to the table will be cancelled for an Unscheduled Short Week Benefit when with respect to such Week the Employe has earned from the Company an amount equal to or in excess of sixty-two (62%) per cent of his weekly straight-time Ford wage plus One Dollar and Fifty Cents ($1.50) for each of his Dependents up to a maximum of four (4); and no Credit Units shall be cancelled when an Employe receives (i) a Short Week or Special Benefit for a Scheduled Short Workweek or (ii) a Benefit for which he is eligible under Section 2 (b) (3) (v) of Article V, or (iii) a Short Week Benefit for an Unscheduled Short Workweek where such Benefit is payable for a period of less than three (3) hours.

If the Credit Unit Cancellation Base applicable to the Week for which such Benefit paid is:	And if the Seniority of the person to whom such Benefit is paid is:					
	1 to 5 Years	5 to 10 Years	10 to 15 Years	15 to 20 Years	20 to 25 Years	25 Years and Over
	The Credit Units cancelled for such Benefit shall be:					
$272 or More	1.00	1.00	1.00	1.00	1.00	1.00
243.20–$271.99	1.11	1.00	1.00	1.00	1.00	1.00
214.40– 243.19	1.25	1.11	1.00	1.00	1.00	1.00
185.60– 214.39	1.43	1.25	1.11	1.00	1.00	1.00
156.80– 185.59	1.67	1.43	1.25	1.11	1.00	1.00
128.00– 156.79	2.00	1.67	1.43	1.25	1.11	1.00
99.20– 127.99	2.50	2.00	1.67	1.43	1.25	1.11
70.40– 99.19	3.33	2.50	2.00	1.67	1.43	1.25
41.60– 70.39	5.00	3.33	2.50	2.00	1.67	1.43
12.80– 41.59	10.00	5.00	3.33	2.50	2.00	1.67
Under 12.80	No Benefit Payable					

ARTICLE XII. SEPARATION PAYMENT

SECTION 1. DEFINITIONS

As used in this Article "Separation Period" means a period when a person is not working in the Contract Unit due to:

(i) a layoff (other than a temporary layoff) of such person and which layoff commenced on or after September 1, 1958, or

(ii) such person having been actively at work on or after September 1, 1958 and having become totally and permanently disabled on or after such date, provided that he has been found eligible in all respects by the Board of Administration under the Retirement Plan (established by agreement between the Company and the Union) for a "disability retirement benefit" under Section 3 of Article IV of said Retirement Plan except that he does not have the requisite years of credited service, or

(iii) a combination of such layoff period and disability period, and which period is continuous through the date on which application for a Separation Payment is received by the Company; or

(iv) such person having been terminated on or after January 1, 1962 at or after age 60 for reasons other than a quit or discharge as defined in Article VIII, Section 5 of the Collective Bargaining Agreement or because of death, provided that he is ineligible for a retirement benefit under said Retirement Plan.

SECTION 2. ELIGIBILITY

An applicant shall be eligible for a Separation Payment if:

(a) he had two or more years of Seniority on the last day on which he was on the Active Employment Roll; and (*b*) (i) in the event he is age 60 or over on the first day of his Separation Period, he had, as of such date, less than ten years of creditable service under the Retirement Plan established by agreement between the Company and the Union; and

(ii) in the event he is under 60 on the first day of his Separation Period, he could not have been eligible at the end of 26 weeks for a "disability retirement benefit" under said Retirement Plan; and

(*c*) the layoff was not the result of any of the circumstances specified in Section 2 (*a*) (3) or Section 2 (*b*) (4) of Article V of the Plan; and

(*d*) there has been an interval of at least one year between the commencement of his Separation Period and the date of his application hereunder (provided, however, that the Company may determine on the basis of the applicant's prospects of re-employment by the Company to permit earlier application; and provided, further, that this Subsection (*d*) shall not be applicable to a person covered by Section 1 (iv) of this Article); and

(*e*) in accordance with procedures established by the Company under Article XI of the Plan, he has made application for a Separation Payment within eighteen (18) months from the commencement of his Separation Period; or, with respect to a Separation Period commencing after March 1, 1960, within twenty-four (24) months from the commencement of his Separation Period; and

(*f*) his application is received by the Company during a Pay Period when the Credit Unit Cancellation Base for such Pay Period is equal to or in excess of Forty-one Dollars and Sixty Cents ($41.60) (provided, however, that applications of otherwise eligible applicants received during a Pay Period in which the Credit Unit Cancellation Base is less than Forty-one Dollars and Sixty Cents ($41.60) shall become payable in order of dates of receipt by the Company if, but only during the period of time when the Credit Unit Cancellation Base becomes equal to or in excess of Forty-one Dollars and Sixty Cents ($41.60). When the Credit Unit Cancellation Base becomes equal to or in excess of Forty-one Dollars and Sixty Cents ($41.60), such Separation Payments shall have priority of payment over any other applications for Separation Payments; and if, in the opinion of the Board, assets in the Fund are or may become insufficient to pay Benefits and Separation Payments with respect to all applications then on file, the Company may take such action as it deems appropriate, including deferral of payment of Benefits otherwise payable, to facilitate the priority of payment of Separation Payments over Benefits. The amount of any Separation Payments or Benefits, or both, deferred in payment shall be deducted, for the purpose of calculating the Credit Unit Cancellation Base, from the amount of assets in the Fund. Nothing in this Subsection (*f*) shall be construed to alter in any respect the provisions of Section 1 of Article X); and

(*g*) he has not incurred a Break in Seniority, except as a consequence of a termination under the conditions specified in Section 1 (iv) of this Article, on or prior to the date on which application is made to the Company.

SECTION 3. EFFECT OF SEPARATION PAYMENT ON SENIORITY

The Seniority of an applicant who is issued and accepts a Separation Payment shall be deemed to have been broken as of the date his application for such Separation Payment was received by the Company.

SECTION 4. PAYMENT

(a) A Separation Payment shall be payable only from the Fund and in a lump sum.

(b) Determination of Amount

(1) Except as provided in paragraph (2) of this Subsection (b), the Separation Payment, effective with respect to payments made on or after January 1, 1962, shall be an amount determined by multiplying (i) the applicant's Base Hourly Rate (plus the cost-of-living allowance in effect on the last

SEPARATION PAYMENT TABLE

Years of seniority on last day on the active enrollment roll	Number of hours' pay
2 but less than 3	50
3 but less than 4	75
4 but less than 5	100
5 but less than 6	125
6 but less than 7	156
7 but less than 8	188
8 but less than 9	219
9 but less than 10	250
10 but less than 11	288
11 but less than 12	325
12 but less than 13	363
13 but less than 14	406
14 but less than 15	450
15 but less than 16	500
16 but less than 17	550
17 but less than 18	600
18 but less than 19	656
19 but less than 20	713
20 but less than 21	775
21 but less than 22	838
22 but less than 23	900
23 but less than 24	969
24 but less than 25	1,038
25 but less than 26	1,113
26 but less than 27	1,188
27 but less than 28	1,263
28 but less than 29	1,338
29 but less than 30	1,413
30 and over	1,500

day he worked in the Contract Unit but excluding all other premiums and bonuses of any kind) by (ii) the applicable Number of Hours' Pay as shown in the following table. If the Credit Unit Cancellation Base as of the date application is received by the Company is below $160.00, the amount of such Separation Payment shall be reduced by 1% for each full $1.60 by which the Credit Unit Cancellation Base is less than $160.00 as of such date; provided, however, that with respect to Separation Payments deferred under Section 2 (f) of this Article, the Credit Unit Cancellation Base in effect as of the date the draft in payment of the Separation Payment is issued shall be used in the above computation in lieu of such Credit Unit Cancellation Base on the date the application was received.

(2) The amount of a Separation Payment as initially computed shall be reduced by:

(i) the amount of any Benefits paid or payable to an applicant with respect to a Week occurring after the last day the applicant worked in the Contract Unit; and

(ii) the amount of any payment, financed in whole or in part by the Company, received or receivable, on or after the last day the applicant worked in the Contract Unit, with respect to any layoff or separation from the Company (other than a State System Unemployment Benefit or a benefit payable under the Federal Social Security Act), and

(iii) the amount of any Moving Allowance deductible under Article IX of the Collective Bargaining Agreement.

SECTION 5. REPAYMENT

If an applicant is re-employed by the Company after he has received a Separation Payment, no repayment (except as provided in Section 3 (b) of Article XI) by him of such Separation Payment shall be required or allowed and no Seniority cancelled in connection with such Separation Payment shall be reinstated.

SECTION 6. NOTICE OF APPLICATION TIME LIMITS

The Company shall provide written notice of the time limit for filing a Separation Payment application to all persons who may be eligible for such Payment. Such notice shall be mailed to the person's last known address according to the Company's records not later than thirty (30) days prior to both the earliest and the latest dates as of which he may apply pursuant to the provisions of Sections 2 (d) and (e) of this Article XII.

ARTICLE XIII. SHORT WEEK BENEFIT

SECTION 1. ELIGIBILITY

An Employe shall be eligible for a Short Week Benefit with respect to a Workweek commencing on or after January 1, 1962, only if

(a) he has at least one (1) year of Seniority as of the last day of such Workweek; and (*b*) during such Workweek he works for the Company but his Compensated or Available Hours, determined as provided in Section 2 of this Article, total less than forty (40) hours (excluding any Workweek for which holiday pay or pay for scheduled vacations is the only pay received from the Company); and

(*c*) during some part of such Workweek he was on layoff from the Contract Unit for one of the reasons set forth in Section 2 (*a*) (2) of Article V; and

(*d*) with respect to such Workweek, he satisfies all the conditions of eligibility set forth under Subsection 2 (*b*) of Article V, except Subsections (*b*) (1), (*b*) (2), (*b*) (3), (*b*) (9) and (*b*) (10); and

(*e*) with respect to such Workweek, he is ineligible to receive a State System Unemployment Benefit only (i) because his wages or remuneration from the Company are equal to or in excess of his Estimated State System Earnings Limit or (ii) because he has been employed by the Company for a period equal to or in excess of the period which would disqualify him for a State System Unemployment Benefit or waiting week credit, or (iii) because of circumstances described in (i) or (ii) above occurring in conjunction with one or more of the reasons set forth in Subsection 2 (*b*) (3) of Article V; and

(*f*) with respect to such Workweek, if an Unscheduled Short Workweek, the Credit Unit Cancellation Base applicable to the Fund was $12.80 or more; and

(*g*) the Employe does not have a period or periods of layoff in such Workweek and in the preceding or the following Workweek which occur in such sequence that the Employe has a "week of unemployment," as defined under the applicable State System, which includes some part of such Workweek; provided, however, that when an Employe has a period of seven or more consecutive days of layoff with respect to which he has established a "week of unemployment" under the applicable State System which starts on a day other than Sunday or Monday, he may apply for a partial Short Week Benefit for any hours of layoff on days within a Workweek which are not included within any established State System "week of unemployment." Such partial Short Week Benefit shall be calculated on the basis of the number of hours for which the Employe would regularly have been compensated for such days if he had not been laid off and of his Compensated or Available Hours for such days; and all of the eligibility requirements applicable to a Short Week Benefit for a Workweek shall apply to such days except the requirement of this Subsection (*g*).

SECTION 2. COMPENSATED OR AVAILABLE HOURS

For purposes of this Article XIII, Compensated or Available Hours for a Workweek shall include:

(*a*) all hours for which an Employe receives pay from the Company (including call-in pay and holiday pay and pay for scheduled vacations but excluding pay in lieu of vacation) with each hour paid at premium rates to be counted as one (1) hour; and

(*b*) all hours scheduled or made available by the Company but not worked by the Employe (including any period on leave of absence); and

(c) all hours not worked by the Employe because of any of the reasons specified in Subsection 2 (a) (3) of Article V; and

(d) all hours not worked by the Employe which are in accordance with a written agreement between the local management and the local union or which are attributable to absenteeism of other employes; and

(e) with respect to a Part Time Employe, or an Employe on a three-shift operation on which eight (8) hour shifts of work are not scheduled, or an Employe on any shift of work on which less than forty (40) hours of work per Week are regularly scheduled, the number of hours by which the number of hours for which such Employe is regularly compensated during a Workweek are less than forty (40).

SECTION 3. DETERMINATION OF AMOUNT

(a) The Short Week Benefit payable to any eligible Employe

(1) for a Scheduled Short Workweek shall be an amount equal to the product of (i) 65% of his Base Hourly Rate (plus 65% of any cost-of-living allowance then in effect but excluding all other premiums and bonuses of any kind) multiplied by (ii) the number by which forty (40) exceeds the number of his Compensated or Available Hours for such Week (with any fractional hour expressed as a decimal to the nearest tenth), determined as provided in Section 2 of this Article,

(2) for an Unscheduled Short Workweek shall be an amount equal to the product of (i) 50% of his Base Hourly Rate (plus 50% of any cost-of-living allowance then in effect but excluding all other premiums and bonuses of any kind) multiplied by (ii) the number by which forty (40) exceeds the number of his Compensated or Available Hours for such Week (with any fractional hour expressed as a decimal to the nearest tenth), determined as provided in Section 2 of this Article;

(b) For purposes of the Plan, a Scheduled Short Workweek with respect to an Employe is a Short Workweek which Management schedules in order to reduce the production of the Plant, department or other unit in which the Employe works, to a level at which the production of such Plant, department or unit would be for the Week were it not a Short Workweek, but only where such reduction of production is for the purpose of adjusting production to customer demand.

(c) For purposes of the Plan, an Unscheduled Short Workweek with respect to an Employe is any Short Workweek:

(i) which is not a Scheduled Short Workweek as defined in Article XIII, Section 3 (b); or

(ii) in which an Employe returns to work from layoff to replace a separated or absent Employe (including an Employe failing to respond or tardy in responding to recall), or returns to work after a full Week of layoff in connection with an increase in production, but only to the extent that the Short Workweek is attributable to such cause; or

(iii) in which an Employe last works at the beginning of, or in which he first works at the end of, a model change period as defined under Article VIII, Section 21 (*a*) of the Collective Bargaining Agreement.

(*d*) For any Short Workweek with respect to an Employe which results both from the circumstances set forth in Section 3 (*b*) as well as those in Section 3 (*c*) of this Article XIII, (i) the Benefit for the hours of the Short Workweek attributable to the circumstances set forth in Section 3 (*b*) shall be calculated on the basis that the hours attributable to the circumstances set forth in Section 3 (*c*) were Compensated or Available Hours and (ii) the Benefit for the hours of the Short Workweek attributable to the circumstances set forth in Section 3 (*c*) shall be calculated on the basis that the hours attributable to the circumstances set forth in Section 3 (*b*) were Compensated or Available Hours. The Benefit for such a Short Week shall be the sum of the Benefits calculated in both (i) and (ii), subject to the provisions of item (ii) of the introductory paragraph of Section 1 of Article VII.

(*e*) Any Short Week Benefit computed under the preceding Sections of this Article shall be subject to the provisions of Section 5 of Article VII and, if for an Unscheduled Short Workweek, shall be subject also to Sections 3 and 4 of Article VII.

SECTION 4. METHOD OF PAYMENT

A Short Week Benefit shall be paid from the Fund. No application for such Benefit shall be required of the Employe except as otherwise provided in Section 5 of this Article. Any Short Week Benefit payable for a Workweek under the provisions of this Article XIII shall be in lieu of any other Benefit payable under this Plan with respect to such Workweek except as otherwise provided under Section 1 (*g*) of this Article XIII.

SECTION 5. APPLICATION FOR DETERMINATION

If an Employe believes himself entitled to a Short Week Benefit for a Workweek under this Article XIII, which he does not receive on the date when Short Week benefits for such Workweek are paid, he may make written application therefor within 60 days in accordance with procedures established by the Company. The Company promptly shall determine the Employe's eligibility for a Short Week Benefit, and such Benefit shall be paid or denied in accordance with such determination. If the Company determines that an Employe is not entitled to a Short Week Benefit with respect to the Workweek for which application for such Benefit is made, it shall send prompt written notice thereof to him.

Sometimes workers seek job security through work rules which require a certain number of workers or certain types of workers for given functions, or which require that jobs be performed in certain ways—rules whose purpose is to protect the "rights" of present employees in their jobs. By cost-minded employers such rules are regarded as "restrictive" or "make-work" provisions. Their corporate security lies in efficient per-

formance in a competitive economy. Thus the security interests of work-
ers and managers clash.

THE MENACE OF RESTRICTIVE WORK PRACTICES

United States Chamber of Commerce, 1963, pp. 8–12

JURISDICTIONAL DISPUTES AND UNREASONABLE DEMANDS

What is the basic cause of the featherbedding problem? There is no single and simple answer. Jurisdictional disputes and unreasonable demands to control the work are principal causes.

A recent jurisdictional dispute involved plumbers and carpenters who disagreed on installation of sinks in bathrooms and kitchens. The month-long dispute was reported to have delayed completiion of 189 cooperative apartments being financed by the International Ladies Garment Workers Union. Each side in this dispute claimed the right to fit the sink tops into place. When agreement was finally reached, the carpenters put up sink tops with six to eight screws instead of the usual nails. The plumbers then unscrewed the tops, put in the sinks, connected the sinks to the pipes, and rescrewed the tops into position. Because of the delay caused by the dispute, new owners scheduled to move into the cooperative reportedly began receiving eviction notices from the apartments they were vacating.

Maintenance mechanics in some plants in Alabama reportedly refuse to perform simple electrical work, such as replacing bulbs or electrical fuses, claiming that this is work for an electrician.

An Ohio plant reported a real problem connected with its right to assign work. It said:

Our primary problem hinges upon the effort of certain employees declining to perform work which in their judgment is more properly work of others. This is particularly true in the areas of maintenance and craft work.

A small tools and parts manufacturing plant in Illinois, whose employees belong to several different unions, reported:

Various trades refuse to do any work which by any stretch of the imagination, might be considered as a part of another trade . . . Pegging production on certain incentive-rated jobs (by one of the plant unions) is obvious where earnings on such jobs level off and are non-varying.

A Connecticut firm, with a sheet-metal workers union in its plant, reported that sheet-metal workers in a large east-coast city will not install products unless they are at least partially fabricated in their own area by their own local union. An Illinois manufacturer, without a sheet-metal workers union in its plant, said sheet-metal workers in two large mid-western cities "will not install their (the manufacturer's) products in their jobs" because, while union-made they were not made by members of their own union.

A California firm reported that sales drivers are not allowed to use fork lifts to load trucks, since this work is exclusively granted to loaders who are also members of the same union.

Another California firm reports that both a maintenance electrician and an electronics maintenance man in its plant have to iron out work jurisdiction problems almost every time repairs are needed.

Several manufacturing plants reported restrictions on subcontracting maintenance and construction work which in-plant unions could perform even though subcontracting represented the cheapest and most efficient way of doing the work. One union was reported to have demanded that "(a) no outside help of any kind be permitted unless agreed to by the local union and (b) no work of any kind will be sent out unless agreed to by the local."

In many individual plants, it was reported to be common to forbid contracting out of maintenance or construction work where "such contracting appears to threaten security of employment."

A mid-western firm reported that a union in New York "assesses any truck deliveries made into New York State from out of state $20 per trip due to a requirement that a city driver must ride in the cab."

A Connecticut company, which exhibits at trade shows for promotions and advertising purposes, reported:

> We, along with other exhibitors at trade and consumer shows throughout the country, are compelled to employ local union labor to erect and dismantle the display. Our sales personnel is well able to do this work and must be on hand anyway to supervise . . . the rates are exorbitant.

An upstate New York firm quoted the following rates for display erection in New York City: "Carpenters—straight time, $7.15 an hour; overtime, $13.95; exposition workers, $4.90 an hour, overtime $7.25; decorators, $7.15 an hour, overtime, $13.95."

FEDERAL BANS ON FEATHERBEDDING

Several attempts have been made by Congress or the Executive Branch to control featherbedding. The first was the Sherman Act, which was intended to ban restraints or suppression of trade.

In 1937, Thurmond Arnold, then U.S. Assistant Attorney General, said he was going to prosecute labor unions under the Sherman Act for various featherbedding practices. However, an attempt in 1941 failed to indict the International Hod Carriers Union for stopping employers from using labor saving concrete truck mixers. Likewise, a prosecution of a San Francisco painters organization for restricting paint sprayers was unsuccessful, and an action against the American Federation of Musicians for allegedly forcing NBC to hire standby musicians in places where recorded music was used, was dismissed.

The question was then settled by the Supreme Court of the United States in exempting unions from liability under the Sherman Act, unless they colluded with management to restrain markets.

Later, because of adverse public reaction to featherbedding by the musicians union, Congress enacted a specific law aimed at the Federation of Musicians.

This was the Lea or "Anti-Petrillo" Act of 1946, forbidding use of force, coercion, or duress to induce employers in the broadcasting industry to employ more men than needed.

Although the U.S. Supreme Court said the Lea Act is constitutional, the only attempt ever made to enforce it—against the American Federation of Musicians' President, James C. Petrillo—was abandoned by the Justice Department after a lower federal court said the Lea Act required actual knowledge by a defendant that additional men were not needed by the employer. No further federal prosecutions have been attempted under the Act.

Congress again attempted to control featherbedding in the Taft-Hartley Act by making it an unfair labor practice. As finally passed in 1947, and unchanged in the statutes since, section 8 (b) (6) of the Act makes it an unfair labor practice:

> . . . to cause or attempt to cause an employer to pay or deliver or agree to pay or deliver any money or other thing of value in the nature of an exaction, for services which were not performed or are not to be performed.

However, the Supreme Court has made section 8 (b) (6) ineffective by construing it narrowly. Attempts by unions to obtain such payments by employers are not covered so long as employees perform actual services, even though they are trivial, unnecessary, or unwanted. The law is applied only to the rare cases where no work is performed, or services rendered or offered.

The Court held in *American Newspaper* that a union is not responsible for the commission of an unfair labor practice unless services are not performed or "not to be performed." Because "bogus" type for advertising was eventually set and services performed—even though unnecessarily, section 8 (b) (6) was not applicable.

Other narrow but significant congressional attempts to control featherbedding were the Copeland Act and its successor, the Hobbs Anti-Racketeering Act. Under the Hobbs Act, a union official may be held guilty of criminal extortion if he uses force or threats of violence to require an employer to use unneeded workers. Two court decisions under the Hobbs Act—The *Kemble* and *Green* cases—are significant.

In *Kemble*, a defendant business agent tried to get employment for one of his union members as a truck driver's helper unloading a truck. The driver was forcibly stopped from unloading, although he could have completed the job without help. The court convicted the defendant of violation of the Hobbs Act for use of violence and coercion to force use of superfluous and unneeded employees.

In *Green*, a defendant business agent sought employment for his union members as "swampers" (people who scout pitfalls for bulldozers in difficult areas) in a construction project. The employer refused to hire them, and the defendant threatened him, and later appeared with a large number of men who shouted such things as, "We ought to bash in his head," and "Throw his car in the canal." The U.S. Supreme Court held that the defendant had attempted by force, violence or fear to obtain "unwanted, superfluous or fictitious" jobs for union members, even though it appeared that the members actually intended to do the work.

The Court's decisions appear to mean that the Hobbs Act is applicable to situations where force or violence is used (*a*) to get jobs, or (*b*) to obtain wages without doing any work. The Court's opinions also suggest that the Hobbs Act applies independently of the Taft-Hartley Act's section 8 (*b*) (6).

In spite of the Hobbs Act and section 8 (*b*) (6) of Taft-Hartley Act, it appears that featherbedding practices are legal today if conducted free of compulsion, or where services are offered or are to be performed, even when unneeded.

FEATHERBEDDING

Statement of L. R. Boulware, Vice President, Employee Relations, General Electric Co., in National Labor Relations Act of 1949, hearings before a special subcommittee of the House Committee on Education and Labor, 81st Cong., 1st Sess., 1949, pp. 892–893, 889–890

Production is the secret of our ever-rising American standard of living. We have only what we produce. To be sure, we get practically all our advances in production from incentive-inspired and owner-provided technological improvements that lengthen man's arms. But to the exact degree that we let "make-believe" work limit the amount of production otherwise available from our national work force, just to that degree do the rest of us needlessly pay, feed, and encourage nonproducers, thus lowering the standard of living otherwise available to all. This is obviously unfair to the people who do work. "Featherbedding" is morally bad and economically feebleminded.

We have had considerable experience with the types of "featherbedding" practice which are not presently covered by the law, unless coupled with an illegal secondary boycott (and the difficulties of proof of threatened boycott are almost insurmountable). Here is just one example which occurred right here in Washington last year:

During 1948, the medical clinic of Drs. Croover, Christie, and Merritt, radiologists, purchased X-ray equipment for installation in their new additional quarters in the Columbia Medical Building Annex, Washington, D.C.

This equipment was purchased by them for a price which included installation. Other building renovations were being made at the time installation of the X-ray equipment was going on, and the union threatened to boycott and strike the entire job unless permitted to do the work of also installing the X-ray equipment. Because of pressure exerted on the company by the customer, to avoid a serious delay in installation and a boycott of the entire renovation job, and their unwillingness to assume the extra cost, the job was done by the union.

This procedure cost the purchasers approximately $4,000 more than they had contracted to pay. It was agreed in the purchase contract that in the event the manufacturer's personnel was not allowed to make the installation, the purchasers would defray the costs of hiring outside labor.

I urge you to permit me later to describe our Sherman Creek turbine case, for instance, and many others. Meanwhile I urge that the present law be strengthened to cover needless work as well as work not performed. Again, the reason for Federal legislation is to be found in the power of the unions present in such situations.

MR. BURKE: . . . You say, "We get practically all our advances in production from incentive-inspired and owner-provided technological improvements that lengthen man's arms."

I quite agree with the latter part of that statement, and probably most of it. In our process of industrial evolution the hand tool was the extension of the man's hand, and the machine tool was the extension of the hand tool.

Now, do I understand your statement here to mean that simply because increase in production through technological improvement is, first, incentive-inspired, and, next, the technological improvement is owner-provided, then any challenge that the worker might make to the production standard that the owner of the machine tool might desire would be in the nature of featherbedding?

MR. BOULWARE: Oh, no, indeed. We feel that the fair day's work as to the combination of skill, care, interest, and effort is something that should be going up all the time in the skill and care and interest, and should perhaps be going down as to physical effort, as we know how to take the work out of the work.

MR. BURKE: I understand. . . .

MR. BOULWARE: What we are saying here is that this is the way we can provide—I do not know, but maybe a 4-day week.

MR. BURKE: I understand that the theory of mass production is that the idea is to take the load off the man's back as much as possible.

Now, in writing a law, you would advocate, then, that that law provide that the setting of production standards shall not be subject to the process of collective bargaining?

MR. BOULWARE: Oh, no, indeed. What we are after here is this: You have a full day's work, by reasonable modern standards. That is the way we describe it, a full day's work content. And what we are after here is that you cannot come in and by force set up the situation where a fellow is going to do a half day's work just because of some power involved, when it is unfair, palpably unfair, to other people. There are plenty of irregularities in a day's work. You cannot regulate the machines that well.

MR. BURKE: But production standards can properly be subject to the processes of collective bargaining.

MR. BOULWARE: That is right.

WHAT IS FEATHERBEDDING?

Testimony of George W. Armstrong, Jr., Chairman, Industrial Relations Committee, National Association of Manufacturers, in Taft-Hartley Act Revisions, hearings before the Senate Committee on Labor and Public Welfare, 83d Cong., 1st Sess., 1953, part 1, pp. 257–258

MR. ARMSTRONG: It is recommended that the present featherbedding provision be strengthened by providing that it is an unfair labor practice to cause or attempt to cause an employer to pay for the hiring of employees who in his judgment are not required or for the performance of services which in his judgment need not be performed.

SENATOR TAFT: Mr. Armstrong, this matter, of course, was up particularly in the conference committee on the Taft-Hartley law in 1947. The difficulty we had was in determining who was going to determine whether this demand was a reasonable demand or not. We hesitated to give the Board power to go into every industry and decide how many men were needed and how many men were not needed. I see you put it entirely in the employer's judgment. That raises the question of the full-crew law. The union said, "To run a train safely we require five men." The employer said, "I want only four."

Are you going to be absolutely bound by the employer's decision on the question? You have the case of mine inspectors where the union says, "To be safe in this mine we insist on two inspectors." The employer said, "One is enough."

Do you propose that the union cannot demand two men under those cases, when the subject of making the demand or insisting upon it as a condition of the contract becomes an unfair labor practice? Do you think we should go that far?

MR. ARMSTRONG: I think the employer is about the only one who can judge as to the work to be performed and the people required to do that work.

SENATOR TAFT: In effect, what you say is that the union cannot say to the employer, "We want two mine inspectors," because if they do they are subjecting themselves to an unfair labor practice judgment.

That seems to be rather a radical position for us to take. If you do not do that, then you have to say somebody will determine, the Board presumably, whether it is a reasonable demand or not. Then you put the Board into the actual operation of a thousand industries about which they know very little and are hardly competent to decide.

MR. ARMSTRONG: I can see in cases where safety is involved, that there is considerable room for someone else aside from the employer to have a voice in that. But in these instances, there is no hazard here, no hazard question at all.

SENATOR TAFT: I mean the man might say, "We can't play decent music with 3 men, we have to have 5 in this theater. And we insist in order to show our proper professional capacity we must have 5 men."

Do you rule that out as an unfair labor practice if they demand 5 instead of 3 in the movie orchestras? I want to call your attention to the difficulties that we are up against as a method of trying to work up practical solutions to problems even if we agree on the principle.

LEAVE FEATHERBEDDING TO COLLECTIVE BARGAINING

Statement of Arthur J. Goldberg, General Counsel, Congress of Industrial Organizations, in Current Antitrust Problems, hearings before the House Antitrust Subcommittee, 84th Cong., 1st Sess., 1955, part 3, pp. 2149–2150

Union practices which employers denounce as featherbedding are the counterpart of employer practices which unions denounce as the "stretchout." If featherbedding may be defined as union insistence on pay for work that is not done, the stretchout may be defined as employer insistence that workers perform more work without corresponding additional pay.

If it is bad for a union to ask for pay for work which is not being done, it must be, from a balanced view, equally bad for an employer to require the union to agree to extra work without the employer paying for it. But we have not heard of anybody's recommending legislation which would make it an unfair labor practice for employers to require unions to agree to a stretchout provision.

Nor do we recommend such legislation. The issues involved in featherbedding and the stretchout are better left to collective bargaining.

Modern industry can have devastating consequences on the worker's livelihood and health unless the worker, through his union, makes some attempt to abate the impact so that the worker alone is not compelled to suffer the full consequences of the management drive for profit making. In the course of collective bargaining, therefore, management and labor have evolved working rules, which Professor Slichter, of Harvard, has put under the heading of industrial jurisprudence, to determine sensible ways of meeting the many problems of finding a mutually agreeable middle ground between workers being worked too hard and workers lying down on the job.

This is not to say that the stretchout or featherbedding is not in some situations carried to unsound extremes, but it is extremely doubtful whether a legislative rule can be devised which will automatically catch within its provisions only the unsound and leave undisturbed the sound practices.

In the summer of 1950 eighteen divinity students worked as laborers in Pittsburgh steel mills and factories while enrolled at the summer seminar of the Presbyterian Institute of Industrial Relations, of which Marshal Scott is dean. Students gathered to exchange and discuss experiences regularly over the three-month period.

WHAT MAKES A MAN WORK AND HOW HARD DO MEN WORK?

Excerpts from the Dean's Report on the results of this project

No subject was discussed more frequently from the evening of the first day on the job until Labor Day than that of efficiency on the job and the motivation to work. All the students appeared to go through the same cycles in their own experiences (possibly two of the men on one job did not follow the pattern closely).

On the first day or two of the job the going seemed rough. Quickly, however, the men got the impression that most men aren't working too hard and that there was plenty of opportunity for "goofing" on the job. At supper there was much joking about it. But as the summer wore on the grind got more and more wearisome and the men got more and more tired. There was little joking about goofing at work in the last month of the summer.

Toward the end of the summer one evening was spent in discussion of how men work and why. The experience of this group, recognizing its limitations (for instance, no man was on a mass production assembly line, no man had a skilled job), revealed several tendencies:

1. Not all idle time is loafing. Frequently the job of the man is to tend the machine and when his chore is done he must wait for the machine to act before he is needed again.

2. At some jobs the work pace is such that no man can keep it up for hours at a time and there must be rest periods on the job.

3. The supply of tools and its relation to work efficiency was one of the most surprising discoveries of the summer. In most of the mills and factories there was an inadequate supply of hand tools for laborers. In the steel mills it is common practice for one shift to hide the tools they have found so that the next two shifts can't find them. A lot of time is spent hunting tools. In one factory, which has an alert management, one student kept track of his time for a whole day. That day he spent more time hunting tools than in productive work. The tools needed could have been paid for by one man's pay check for one day.

4. Of much greater importance, however, in the mind of the students were two other factors. One is the attitude and the skill of the foreman. The foreman, it was found, needed to know his job but also must know how to handle men. In one plant there was a high level of work efficiency and the workers were happy. Yet the wage rate was lower than in most of the other plants. The reason seemed to lie with the management. The workers had a union and the management fully accepted it; the management had a foreman who was effective in dealing with men. If a worker had a rough job one day he was given an easier assignment another day. Thus men had a sense of being treated personally, and fairly. They had a sense of freedom from knowing that they could speak to the foreman or make suggestions and that they had the protection of the union, which would receive a fair hearing.

In other shops there were foremen who lacked the ability to plan work well and there were foremen who sought to boost their egos by taking every opportunity to deflate the men they supervised. In such shops it was sometimes almost a game for laborers to see how little they could do and get away with it.

The experience of the students of this project was that the foreman is the *most important* factor between good work and poor work—and his attitude toward persons is at least as important as his know-how about the productive process.

5. The other major factor is in some respects closely related. For many men—probably *most* men—the work motivation is not production of a product but is the desire to get the weekly pay check. If a man works only for a pay check then a minimum of effort and efficiency is sufficient. In many jobs there is little sense of importance to turning out a few more routine motions per hour or per day and opportunities for advancement by working harder are not very obvious to the worker. A lot of men feel and say "What's the use?" Again, the foreman, more than any other person, can give to the workers other satisfactions and other motives than the pay check—if he is skilled enough.

There was no evidence, within the experience of the group, that labor unions had curtailed the amount of work effort or work efficiency on the job. In the only shop where a union had been introduced recently it was reported that work efficiency had increased.

The group had very limited experience—too limited for drawing conclusions —with economic incentives, such as bonuses, but all had the impression that management greatly over-rates economic incentives and that much greater benefits could come from more attention to better human relations—attitudes and feelings.

A possible resolution of the divergent interests of employees in job security and managements in corporate efficiency lies in joint programs in which the two parties divide the benefits of improving productivity while guaranteeing that no employee will lose his job as a consequence. Such plans have a considerable history, but one of the most recent expressions has been at the Kaiser Steel Corporation.

LONG-RANGE SHARING PLAN FOR KAISER STEEL EMPLOYEES (JANUARY 11, 1963)

III. SCOPE OF PLAN

The plan shall cover all employees of Kaiser Steel Corp. at Fontana, Calif., who are represented by the United Steelworkers of America. The plan shall become effective March 1, 1963.

IV. EMPLOYMENT SECURITY

In order to achieve, through cooperative effort, the greatest possible increase in productivity as rapidly as improvements can be made, it is necessary not only to provide that the result of such increase in productivity will be shared appropriately between the company and the employees, but also to provide appropriate protection against the loss of employment or of income for individual employees which might otherwise result from such action. In order to achieve this objective, and thus to induce the greatest possible increase in productivity, the following measures are adopted. However, none of the following provisions shall be construed as requiring the company to hire new employees.

A. *Employment Guarantee*. 1. The purpose of this provision is to provide appropriate protection against the loss of opportunity for employment from the effective date of this plan because of technological change, new or improved work methods, or any other change in operations not resulting from a decrease in man-hour requirements caused by a decrease in finished steel production, or a change in product or production requirements. This protection shall be provided by the establishment of a plantwide employment reserve. No employee shall, however, be entitled to employment in the plantwide employment reserve, or to otherwise share in the protection provided in this section, until he has worked for the company in 26 weekly pay periods.

2. Any employee who, except for this section IV. A, would be laid off in any month as a result of a change in work practices resulting from installation of a technological improvement or new or improved work method shall be entitled to employment in the plantwide employment reserve. The right to such employment shall continue unless the employee is displaced under paragraph 6.

3. No employee shall hereafter be laid off if, at the time at which he would not be entitled to a job except for this section IV. A, the number of employes in the plantwide employment reserve is less than the maximum for that month. Such employee shall, instead of being laid off, be assigned to the plantwide employment reserve.

4. If, at the beginning of any month, there are employees who are laid off on or after the effective date of this plan and the number of employees in the employment reserve is less than maximum for that month, then employees who are on such layoff status will be recalled to work in order of KSC (Kaiser Steel Corp.) dates, to the employment reserve, up to the company's maximum obligation. No such recall shall, however, be made to any job to which any other employee has recall rights under existing seniority arrangements as modified in paragraphs 14 and 15.

5. If, at the beginning of any month, the number of employees in the employment reserve is more than the maximum, employees may be laid off from the employment reserve on the basis of KSC dates so as to reduce the reserve to maximum, except as provided in paragraph 2.

6. Whenever forces are reduced, layoffs will be made through the employment reserve on the basis of KSC dates, rather than from the lowest job in each respective line of progression. Employees will be demoted under existing seniority provisions but shall be entitled to displace employees in the employment reserve on the basis of their KSC dates. The total number of employees in the employment reserve shall, however, not exceed the maximum provided in paragraphs 10 and 11.

7. An employee in the employment reserve declining or failing to accept an opportunity to a permanent vacancy with a higher job class outside the employment reserve, which he has the ability to perform, shall release the company from any further obligation to provide him with employment in the employment reserve.

8. Employees in the plantwide employment reserve will be assigned, at the discretion of the company, to perform work functions throughout the plant. Such assignment shall not, however, be such as to result in the displacement of any other employee from his job, the avoidance of recall of employees on layoff, or reduction in the hours of work of any other employee below 40 hours per week. Employees assigned to the employment reserve shall be provided employment at 40 hours per week or the average hours worked per week in the plant, whichever is lower.

9. No employee shall be required to accept assignment to the employment reserve or be denied supplemental unemployment benefits (SUB) for failure to accept such assignment. An employee who refuses assignment to the employment reserve and who is denied State unemployment compensation for that reason shall, nevertheless, be entitled to SUB if otherwise eligible.

10. The maximum size of the employment reserve for any month shall be determined as follows:

(a) In the first month in which this plan is in operation, the maximum shall be deemed equal to the number of employees entitled to employment in the reserve under paragraph 2, hereof, who are not offered other employment by the company.

(b) In succeeding months, the maximum shall be the number of employees then entitled to employment under paragraph 2, hereof, who are not offered other employment by the company or the following, if higher: the difference, if positive, between the relevant standard man-hours for the second preceding month and the actual hours worked in that month (excluding hours worked by employees assigned to the employment reserve) divided by 173 or by the average hours worked per month in the plant, whichever is lower, and rounded to the nearest whole number.

11. (a) The relevant standard man-hours shall be related to the level of production and shall initially be determined on the basis of the actual weighted man-hours per ton of prime finished steel produced in 1961 as related to various levels of output, adjusted by the percentage improvement, if any, between 1961 and the month prior to the month in which the plan is placed in operation. The figures used in determining this standard shall be the same as those used in the calculation of gains to be shared, except that hours paid for but not worked shall be excluded.

(b) If in any month there are no employees on layoff status, the standard shall be revised by subtracting the actual man-hours worked in such month, plus any hours for which a short week benefit is payable under subsection C, hereof, from the relevant standard for that level of production. The remainder will be converted to a percentage of the weighted standard man-hours for that level of production. The standard for all levels of production shall then be adjusted by reducing it to that percentage. No adjustment in standard shall be made in any month in which there is an employee on layoff.

(c) Notwithstanding the above, the lesser of the following shall be used as the relevant standard man-hours if, for any month, it is greater than the relevant standard man-hours described in paragraphs (a) and (b) above:

(1) The average hours worked per month during 1961 minus 173 hours per KSC employee as of December 31, 1961, who has since terminated; or (2) The standard man-hours for that level of production based on 1961 (without the adjustment provided for in paragraph (b)) minus 173 hours per KSC employee as of December 31, 1961, who has since terminated.

12. If an employee entitled to employment in the plantwide employment reserve under paragraph 2 elects not to accept asssignment to the employment reserve, he shall, nevertheless, be deemed assigned to the employment reserve for purposes of calculating the company's maximum obligation.

13. The production and maintenance employees and the clerical and technical employees shall be considered two separate groups, and an employment reserve established for each insofar as application of this section IV. A is concerned.

14. Except as provided below, no change shall be required by the plan in existing lines of progression and seniority agreements. Permanent production and maintenance vacancies, including labor classifications, will be filled in the following manner (employees transferring from one line of progression to another must meet the requirements for the job to which transferred, such requirements to be determined in the first instance by the company, subject to the grievance procedure):

(a) First, by employees with callback rights under existing seniority agreements (including employees on layoff status).

(b) Second, by employees in the plantwide employment reserve with callback rights to any job in any line of progression above labor classification, based on KSC date.

(c) Third, by employees in the plantwide employment reserve having no callback rights above labor classification, based on KSC date.

(d) Fourth, by employees on layoff status having callback rights above labor classification, based on KSC date.

(e) Fifth, by employees on layoff status having no callback rights above labor classification, based on KSC date.

(f) Sixth, by new hires.

15. Except as provided below, no change shall be required by the plan in existing lines of progression and seniority agreements. Permanent clerical and technical vacancies will be filled in the following manner (employees transferring from one line of progression to another must meet the requirements for the job to which transferred, such requirements to be determined in the first instance by the company, subject to the grievance procedure):

(a) First, by employees with callback rights under existing seniority agreements (including employees on layoff status).

(b) Second, by employees in the plantwide employment reserve, based on KSC date.

(c) Third, by employees on layoff status, based on KSC date.

(d) Fourth, by new hires.

B. Displacement Differential. Any employee who, but for a change in work practices resulting from installation of a technological improvement or new or improved work methods, would have been entitled, under existing seniority arrangements, to a job of a higher job classification than the job he is assigned to, or whose job is lowered in job class as a result of such change, shall receive a displacement differential. Determination shall be made, at the time of the change, of the job to which each employee (including those with valid callback rights) would be entitled at the various operating levels. Such determination shall not, however, affect the timeliness of any subsequent grievance by an employee claiming a displacement differential.

1. *Amount.* (*a*) The displacement differential paid for each hour worked shall be an amount equal to the difference between the standard hourly rate of the job he would have been entitled to were it not for such change, minus the standard hourly rate of the job actually worked during the hour involved.

(*b*) The displacement differential shall be paid as additional earnings in the form of an "add on," and shall be part of the employee's regular rate of pay, but shall not be included in the calculation of incentive earnings.

2. *Duration.* (*a*) The payment of a displacement differential to an employee will be terminated after 52 weekly payments have been made to such employee or on the date: (1) on which the employee is assigned to fill a permanent vacancy with a job class equal to or greater than the one for which the differential is being paid, or (2) on which the employee declines or fails to accept a promotion to a permanent vacancy with a higher job class than the one working on, which he has the ability to perform.

(*b*) The payment of all displacement differentials based on a particular change shall be terminated after 3 years have elapsed from the date of such change.

3. *Eligibility.* (*a*) No employee who was not entitled to a displacement differential at the time of a change shall become entitled to a displacement differential because of the death, retirement, quit, or discharge of an employee in the line of progression in which the change occurs.

(*b*) No person shall become entitled to a displacement differential unless he was employed in, or had valid callback rights to, the line of progression in which the change occurs.

The displacement differential for an employee who is not working in that line of progression at the time the change occurs, but who is otherwise eligible, shall begin with the pay period in which written application is first made. Likewise, if the level of operation of said unit becomes lower than at the time the displacement differential was established, such displacement differential will be eliminated to the extent appropriate, on the basis of the crew size required for that level prior to installation of the change.

4. *Payment.* (*a*) The displacement differential shall be calculated and paid weekly, but the company may delay such payment for approximately 2 weeks to allow adequate time for payroll processes.

(*b*) All displacement differentials paid shall be deducted from the total dollar gains as computed under section V. B under the sharing plan.

C. *Short Weeks.* 1. Any employee who, as a result of a change in work practices resulting from installation of a technological improvement or new or improved work methods, is scheduled for a workweek of less than 40 hours, and who is available for 40 hours of work per week, shall be entitled to a short-week payment equal to his average hourly earnings times the number of hours less than 40 that he is paid for in any week in which he is so scheduled.

2. All short-week payments shall be deducted from the total dollar gains as computed under section V. B under the sharing plan.

V. SHARING OF GAINS

A. *Standards.* 1. All improvements in labor performance, material and supply usage, yield improvement, and utilization of technological changes shall be measured from the base point of the actual operations in the calendar year 1961. The standards and the improvements in manufacturing cost shall be in terms of appropriately weighted manufacturing cost per finished ton of iron and steel produced. Nonsteel byproducts will be handled as manufacturing credits. New standards will be established by the parties for any new products not heretofore produced by the company.

2. The standards (1961 performance) are in a separate document. Standards have been developed for the various products in each mill so as to permit adequate reflection of changes in product mix, as well as changes in the operating level. The standards are composed of a base, a labor standard, and a material and supply standard based on the various operating levels experienced during the year 1961; and each expressed in dollars. The standards are such that when applied as a composite to the calendar year 1961, the sharing plan standard cost equals the actual cost for the year 1961, assuming the actual hourly wage rates, payroll tax rates, and all benefits in January 1963 were in effect for the whole year of 1961.

3. The standards for material and supply costs as set forth in section V. A shall be increased or decreased by the percentage increase or decrease in the Wholesale Price Index for each appropriate steel mill products category of the Bureau of Labor Statistics from either the year 1961 or the latest month available as of the date the plan is installed, whichever is lower, to the latest month available as of the 10th day of the month following the month for which the calculation of gains is made.

4. The standards for labor costs as set forth in section V. A shall be increased or decreased by the percentage increase or decrease in the national Consumer Price Index of the Bureau of Labor Statistics from either the year 1961 or the latest month available as of the date the plan is installed, whichever is lower, to the latest month available as of the 10th day of the month following the month for which the calculation of gains is made.

5. The actual cost, in any month, of raw materials produced internally by the Kaiser Steel Corp. shall be calculated on the basis that the price of such materials is the same as the price used in the calculation of the standard, with appropriate adjustments for changes in quality. There shall be no loss or gain for such materials due to changes in the Wholesale Price Index for steel mill products. The cost of other materials consumed for which an inventory is main-

tained shall be calculated on the same basis as used in the calculation of the standards.

B. Calculation of Gains. 1. The measured gains each month, based on actual labor and material and supply usage per finished ton of steel produced, but excluding the cost of capital improvements, shall be calculated by comparison with the weighted standards as adjusted above, and expressed in dollars by:

(*a*) computing the difference from standard of material and supply costs per finished ton of steel produced, times the number of finished tons produced in that month, and adding to it

(*b*) the difference from standard of labor costs per finished ton of steel produced times the number of finished tons produced in that month. Labor cost figures shall be the actual labor cost in the month, excluding the effect of any payroll tax rate increases and wage rate or benefit increases which become effective after January 1963.

2. The total dollar gains shall then be adjusted by the cost of those capital expenditures made to reduce product cost on existing facilities; for example, the addition of oxygen to an existing open-hearth furnace. Capital expenditures for new processes or new equipment to increase capacity, to establish a new department or to install a new process as, for example, the installation of a new oxygen furnace, shall not be the basis of an adjustment from total dollar gains. The adjustment for capital expenditures of the former type shall be limited to those months in which a reduction in cost has been achieved on the process for which the investment was made, and shall be in an amount equal to the lesser of: one-third of the actual reduction in cost for which the capital expenditure was made, or one-sixtieth of the capital expenditure. Such adjustments shall continue only until an amount equal to the capital expenditure itself shall have been prorated.

3. In the measurement of total dollar gains in any month, individual repair and maintenance jobs of $300,000 and larger shall be prorated over a 12-month period.

4. (*a*) The payment of lump sums by the company to eliminate incentive plans and out-of-line differentials as set forth in section VI shall be translated into a current labor cost each month based on each month's unit hours paid, the percentage for the year 1961, and the hourly wage rates in effect in December 1961. For units covered by an incentive plan and out-of-line differentials established subsequent to 1961, the calculation will be based on the percentage used to determine the lump-sum payment as set forth in section VI.

(*b*) Such addition to current labor costs shall begin with the first full month after the month in which such lump-sum payment is made, and continue until such amounts equal the lump-sum payment.

(*c*) Thereafter, such amounts shall continue to be calculated as above and considered as a current labor cost but shall be accrued to the employee's gross share each month. Such accruals shall be suspended for any unit for any period during which performance is voluntarily maintained at a level appreciably below that experienced during the base period.

5. Calculations shall be made monthly and audited annually. The basic summary statistics of production, man-hours, employment, employment costs, and material and supply costs shall be supplied monthly by the company to the union on a confidential basis. The data from which the summary is made up shall be available to the designated union representatives for examination and verification.

C. *The Employees' Gross Share.* 1. One part of the employees' gross share shall consist of 32.5 percent of the total net dollar gains as calculated above.

2. (a) From this part of the employees' gross share, there shall be subtracted, in the first month in which this plan is in operation, one-fifth of 1 percent of the total employment cost for that month, in the second month two-fifths of 1 percent, in the third month three-fifths of 1 percent, the subtraction continuing on a month-to-month basis and being increased by one-fifth of 1 percent in each month, until adjusted as provided below.

(b) The company shall maintain an account to be known as the Wage and Benefit Reserve. There shall be added to this reserve for each month the total of the subtractions from the employees' gross share described above. There shall be subtracted from that reserve each month the total increase in employment costs occasioned by the installation of wage and benefit increases in accordance with the guarantee provision of section VII of this plan. As an exception to this provision, only one-half of the employment cost increase, occasioned by any industry wage or benefit increase effective within 6 months after the effective date of this plan, shall be deducted from the Wage and Benefit Reserve. As a further exception to this provision, if in any month the total of employment cost increases occasioned by industry wage or benefit increases is in excess of the employees' gross share, then the amount in excess shall be considered a cost to the company, shall not be deducted from the Wage and Benefit Reserve, and will not be considered a deficit against future employee sharing plan earnings.

(c) The parties will, every 6 months, adjust the progression in the subtractions from the employees' gross share. Such adjustment will be based on the principle that the subtraction should increase, on an evenly spaced basis, over a 12-month period in such amount that 6 months after the effective date of any increase in wages or benefits occasioned by industry adjustments, the net balance of the Wage and Benefit Reserve should be zero.

3. A second part of the employees' gross share shall consist of:

(a) The amounts provided for in subsection B, paragraph 4 (c) of this section; and

(b) The amounts provided for in subsections H and L of section VI.

D. *Distribution of Gains.* 1. The employees' gross share as computed in section V. C above, less any amount which, from time to time, as the parties may decide, is required for the improvement of an existing benefit or for a new benefit (other than those covered by section VII) such as, but not limited to holidays, vacations, insurance, pensions, SUB, reduced hours of work, shall be distributed to the employees as an addition to earnings on the basis of the following weights until group A earns 10 percent:

Group [1]		Factor
A	....	2. 0
B	....	3. 5
C	....	5. 0
D	....	6. 5
E	....	8. 0
F—Units remaining on incentive are excluded	..	. 0

[1] The specific group to which each individual unit is assigned is indicated in Exhibit "A," Group Assignments, based on the combination of historical and equitable earnings relationships.

(a) Multiply the total standard hourly wage rates of each group by its respective factor to obtain the factor units of each group.

(b) Divide each group's factor units by the total factor units to obtain each group's percent share of the total employees' share.

(c) Multiply each group's respective percent share times the total employees' share to obtain each group's dollar share.

(d) Divide each group's dollar share by the respective standard hourly wage rates to obtain each group's percent pay.

(e) Multiply each group's percent pay times each individual's standard hourly wage rate.

2. The amount remaining in the employees' share, after application of paragraph 1 above, shall be distributed to the employees as an addition to earnings in the following manner:

(a) Divide the amount remaining by the total standard hourly wage rates of all Long Range Sharing Plan employees participating in its distribution to obtain percent pay.

(b) Multiply each individual's standard hourly wage rate by the percent pay.

3. The employees' share shall be paid as additional earnings in the form of an "add on," and shall be part of the employees' regular rate of pay in the month for which it is paid, but shall not change the basis of calculation of existing incentive earnings.

4. When the employees' share, or any portion thereof, is allocated by the parties to a new or improved benefit, the cost of such benefit shall be estimated, prorated monthly, and adjusted yearly as may be appropriate.

5. Payments to production and maintenance employees for a given month will be made on the last Thursday of the following month, and to clerical and technical employees on the next payday thereafter. The payments for each month shall be based on the statistical method of best fit designed to avoid undue fluctuations from month to month using the most recent 6 months' figures.

VI. INCENTIVES

All incentive provisions of the collective bargaining agreement between the parties shall be continued in effect except:

A. The company shall not establish new incentives to cover new jobs or jobs not presently covered by incentive applications, nor apply existing incentives to employees not covered by such incentives as of the date this plan is installed. Such employees shall participate in the Long Range Sharing Plan.

B. Present temporary incentive installations shall be settled as permanent installations by agreement of the parties or, if necessary, by referral, at the request of either party, to final and binding arbitration after 60 days following the installation of this plan.

C. Employees in a unit covered by an incentive plan which resulted in incentive earnings during the 13-week period just prior to a company offer as described in this subsection C shall have an option (expressed through a majority vote of the employees on that unit), when offered by the company to either:

1. Accept an elimination of such incentive plan, subject to the following conditions:

(a) The money difference per hour between the total actual earnings paid each job under the incentive plan in effect, and the standard hourly wage rate for such job under the eliminated incentive plan for this period, will be calculated for each job.

(b) A lump-sum payment shall be made by the company to each incumbent employee, based on the money difference per hour previously calculated for each job and the hours paid during either of the following periods, whichever is the greater: (1) The most recent 13-week period just prior to the company offer, multiplied by 10, or (2) the 52-week period immediately following the elimination of such incentive plan.

(c) During the periods covered in paragraph (b), hours of authorized absence from such occupations due to illness and union business shall be considered as hours paid.

(d) The payment required by paragraph (b) (1) shall be made in a lump sum no later than 2 weeks following the elimination of the incentive plan. Any additional payments required by paragraph (b) (2) shall be made in a lump sum no later than 2 weeks following the end of the 52-week period.

(e) Employees on an incentive unit who accept a lump-sum payment for the elimination of their incentive plan, shall participate in the distribution of the employees' share to the extent of two factor groups less than their factor group assigned in Exhibit "A." This participation shall continue during the period the lump-sum payment is considered a current labor cost as set forth in paragraph 4 (b) of section V. B. Thereafter, such employees shall participate in the distribution of the employees' share based on their own respective factor group.

2. Decline to accept the elimination of such incentive plan as described in paragraph 1, in which case the following conditions will prevail:

(a) Employees receiving incentive on such units will not participate in sharing plan payments of the Long Range Sharing Plan. However, such employees shall participate in the Sharing Plan under the conditions indicated in subsections J and K.

(*b*) In order to permit subsequent offers to be made by the company separately under this subsection C and under subsection G, the company may adjust such incentive plans which continue, as follows: (1) The average hourly earnings of employees under the adjusted incentive plan during the same 13-week period as that used in determining that a lump-sum payment for plan elimination, as under section VI. C. 1 was in order, would have been no less than 135 percent. (2) The money difference per hour between the total actual earnings paid each job under the incentive plan in effect, and the total earnings calculated for such job under the adjusted incentive plan for this period, will be established as an individual hourly differential. (3) Upon calculation of such individual hourly differentials for each job, the adjusted incentive plan will be installed and incumbents of record entitled to such differentials will be established as of that date. (4) Concurrent with installation of the adjusted incentive plan, the appropriate individual hourly differentials will be paid by the company to the established incumbents for each hour worked on the incentive plan.

D. When employees on a direct incentive plan are offered a lump-sum payment for the elimination of their plan, employees covered by incentive plans which are dependent in whole or in part on said direct plan shall be offered a lump-sum payment at the same time for the elimination of that portion of their incentive plan. In the event that dependent plan employees vote to accept such offer of plan elimination, the provisions of section VI. C. 1 shall apply. If dependent plan employees vote to decline to accept the plan elimination, the following shall apply: that portion of their earnings in the 13-week period just prior to the company offer which was based upon the direct plan thus eliminated shall be translated to a dollar amount per direct incentive plan unit operating hour. Such amount shall be paid to the dependent plan incumbent employees thereafter until subsequent options are exercised.

E. Future general wage increases and increment increases shall be added to the standard hourly wage rates, but shall not change the basis for the calculation of incentive plans.

F. 1. The company shall first offer the options set forth in section VI. C and D to the incumbents of the first incentive unit within 30 days, and thereafter, as rapidly as practicable to incumbents of the remaining incentive units after installation of the Long Range Sharing Plan. The employees shall notify the company of their choice of options within the following 90 days.

2. In the event that such options are not offered to the incumbents of an incentive unit within 2 years after installation of the Long Range Sharing Plan, the incumbents shall thereafter participate with group A of this plan unless, in any consecutive 3-month period within such 2 years, the earnings paid to their respective factor groups for which they would be eligible under this plan exceed the incentive earnings of their respective group under the incentive plan. Such participation is in addition to the continued application of their incentive plan. However, participation with group A as outlined in this paragraph shall terminate when either of the following occur:

(*a*) Employees on the incentive plan are offered and advise the company of their choice of options set forth in subsections C and D.

(*b*) Payments to the respective factor group for which they are eligible under the Long Range Sharing Plan equal or exceed the earnings paid under the incentive plan for 3 consecutive months.

G. Employees in a unit covered by an incentive plan having out-of-line differentials resulting from any reason, including application of present paying wage rates, shall have an option (expressed by a separate majority vote of the employees on that unit having each type of differential) when offered by the company to:

1. Accept a lump-sum payment of such differentials within 60 days of their being offered, to be calculated on the actual amounts paid during the most recent 13-week period multiplied by 10. These monies will be paid in a lump-sum payment no later than 2 weeks following the acceptance of such offer to all employees who are incumbents of record; or

2. Decline to accept.

H. The sums which would have been payable to former employees under subsections C and G, if they were employed as of the date of the adjustment, shall be added to the employees' gross share described in subsection C of section V.

I. Lump-sum payments to eliminate incentive plans and out-of-line differentials shall be considered as earnings in calculating pension benefits. In the calculation of any other benefits due for a period after a lump-sum payment is made, earnings used in the determination of the lump-sum payment shall be excluded.

J. The company, at its discretion, may in the future reoffer lump-sum payments in lieu of out-of-line differentials or in order to eliminate incentive plans, subject to the same conditions set forth in this section VI. If such reoffers are made, the employees concerned shall notify the company of their decision within 60 days after such reoffers are made.

K. After this Long Range Sharing Plan has been in effect for 60 days, employees who are covered by an incentive plan may elect (expressed through a majority vote of employees on that unit) at any time, to withdraw from coverage of such incentive plan in favor of full participation under this plan and thereby receive the appropriate share as defined in section V. D. Such election will be effective in the second month following the month in which the election is made.

L. The sums payable to employees covered by incentive plans as of the date this plan is installed shall be transferred to the employees' gross share under the following conditions:

1. When employees who are covered by incentive plans elect to withdraw from coverage of such plan in favor of full participation under the Long Range Sharing Plan.

2. When employees covered by the Long Range Sharing Plan are assigned to jobs on units covered by incentive plans.

The amounts to be transferred shall be handled in the same manner as for those units that accept lump-sum payment.

M. For the purposes of this section, any employee having valid callback rights to a job covered by an incentive plan as of the effective date of this plan shall be deemed to be an employee covered by such incentive plan. If employees covered by an incentive plan are assigned to jobs not covered by an incentive plan, they shall participate in the Long Range Sharing Plan for the period of such assignment.

VII. MINIMUM GUARANTEE

A. An analysis shall be made on December 31, 1963, and at the end of every calendar year thereafter, of the actual labor cost and total actual labor and material and supply cost for each such period. If the results of such analyses reflect that total actual labor cost (including the employees' gross share) results in a smaller percentage of total labor and material and supply cost than standard labor cost was of the total standard cost for each such period (before application of BLS indices), the company will pay into the first part of the employees' gross share, an amount which, together with the actual labor cost (including the employees' gross share) results in a total labor cost (including this payment) that is the same percentage of total cost (including this payment) that standard labor cost was of the total standard cost (before application of BLS indices). One-twelfth of such amount will be paid monthly into the first part of the employees' gross share beginning no later than the second sharing plan pay period following this calculation until the entire amount has been paid into the employees' gross share. Such amounts shall not be included in determining the company's future obligation under the application of this subsection. This shall be a cost to the company and will not be considered as a deficit against future employee sharing plan earnings. However, application of this paragraph shall not result in total actual labor and material and supply cost for this period, including the employees' share, exceeding total standard costs for that production.

B. The provision in the supplemental memorandum of agreement, dated March 9, 1961, between the company and the union that any wage and benefit adjustments agreed to by the union and the major basic steel producers shall be put into effect by the company shall remain in effect.

C. The total increase in employment costs occasioned by subsection B, except for any industry wage or benefit increase effective within 6 months after the effective date of this plan, shall be subtracted from the Wage and Benefit Reserve for each month as set forth in section V. C. 2 (b). As set forth in that section, the net balance of the employees' share in any month shall never be a minus quantity. If the first part of the employees' gross share described in subsection V. C is less than the total amount resulting from application of industry general wage increases and additional fringe benefits not now provided, the company will make up the difference. In computing the cost of such individual wage increases, the incentive impact thereon as applicable at KSC as of the year 1961 shall be included. The amount of the incentive impact shall be distributed to the employees in the same manner as that used for distribution of the employees' shares. This shall be a cost to the company and will not be considered as a deficit against future employee sharing plan earnings.

VIII. RELATIONSHIP OF THE PLAN TO OTHER AGREEMENTS

A. Grievances involving the application of, or compliance with, the provisions of this plan shall be processed and settled under the grievance and arbitration provisions of the collective bargaining agreement between the company and the union; grievances involving the interpretation or meaning of this plan shall be referred for settlement to the procedure set forth in subsection B. If a grievance is referred to arbitration under the collective bargaining agreement, and the arbitrator finds that it involves a disagreement concerning the interpretation or meaning of the provisions of this plan, he shall, if either party so requests it, refer such grievance for settlement to the procedure set worth in subsection B.

B. In the event of a disagreement between the company and the union involving interpretation of the provisions of this plan, or as to whether any portion of the employees' share shall be used for the improvement of an existing benefit or for a new benefit, under section V. D. 1, or in the event of a disagreement concerning the employment cost of such benefit, or if the company and the union disagree concerning a revision of this plan under the provisions of section IX, the matter shall be referred to the Long Range Committee for disposition and, if necessary, to the public members of that committee for final and binding arbitration.

C. Unless changed or modified by the provisions herein, all existing agreements between the company and the union shall remain in full force and effect under their terms. It is understood that management's rights and responsibilities with respect to such matters as sales policies, purchasing policies, research projects, management compensation, expansion of capacity and other similar areas shall neither be enlarged nor diminished as a result of this plan.

IX. DURATION

A. This plan shall continue in effect, subject to review and revision by the company and the union annually in the 90-day period prior to each anniversary date.

B. For any sharing plan pay period during which there is no production of finished steel products for more than 24 consecutive hours, the base standard for labor and for material and supplies will be reduced proportionate to the period in which there was no finished steel production.

C. This plan may be terminated by either party upon 4 months' notice to the other party, served within the 12 months following the fourth anniversary date of this plan, and each 4 years thereafter.

D. In the event that either party gives notice of termination, the parties shall jointly determine what provisions shall be made for the period subsequent to such termination. Such determination shall give due consideration to the objectives outlined in the underlying facts and assumptions section of the Long Range Sharing Plan, the events which occurred under the plan, and the reasons assigned for its cancellation. If the parties are not able to agree within 60 days, the matter shall be referred to the public members of the Long Range Committee for their review.

E. Upon the basis of this review, the public members of the Long Range Committee shall then be authorized to take any one or all of the following steps:

1. Determine to take no action or to postpone action until there has been an opportunity for further discussions;

2. Engage in mediation efforts, including private consultation with representatives of each of the parties;

3. Convene a meeting of the Long Range Committee; and, finally,

4. Issue a report to the parties summarizing the positions of the parties, defining the issues in dispute, and making recommendations to the parties.

F. Upon termination of this plan, and in the absence of agreement to the contrary, either party may resort to strike or lockout, as the case may be, in support of its position, the provisions of any other agreement between the parties notwithstanding.

G. Upon termination of this plan, the entire amount in the Wage and Benefit Reserve shall be paid to the employees in the same manner as the employees' share was paid under the plan.

15: Combating Unemployment and Poverty

The problem of unemployment involves more than the reemployment of workers displaced from their jobs. It also requires making job opportunities available to millions of new workers who will be entering the labor force in the next decade. For both the displaced and the unplaced a crucial question is whether they possess the qualifications which employers are demanding. A question of equal or even greater importance is whether the economy as a whole is operating at a level of activity which induces employers to hire additional workers even if qualified.

Both these aspects of the unemployment question—personal qualifications and social dynamism—also determine the distribution of poverty.

MANPOWER NEEDS OF THE SIXTIES

Statement of Seymour Wolfbein, Deputy Assistant Secretary of Labor in Manpower Problems hearings before the Senate Committee on Labor and Public Welfare, 86th Cong., 2d Sess., 1960, pp. 24–26

Coming to the specific point that was raised, what do we see ahead during this decade in terms of occupations, we see the biggest growth in the professional and technical field—about a 40-percent increase. Anything above the 20-percent mark would be more than the national average and anything below the 20-percent mark less than the national average. These are based not only on the projection of past trends, but also on interviews with many people in industries and unions and professional societies.

As you know, we have an occupational outlook program in the Bureau of Labor Statistics going on for the past 15 years, whose major job is to make this kind of study and projection. Perhaps you are familiar with the Occupational Outlook Handbook which we get out every 2 years, which goes into this. It is very important because it indicates for the next decade the least employment opportunities are going to be for the unskilled person, who requires the least amount of education and training, and for people who work on the farm, where again you are getting a continuation of this long-term trend away from agriculture.

The last figure for last year is about 6½ million people on the average were employed in agriculture. In 1870 the figure was also 6½ million.

Senator CLARK. Would this be too broad a generalization: That by 1970 boys and girls who have not completed their high school education are going to have a lot of trouble finding a job?

Mr. WOLFBEIN. I would say that to use technical language, that the prognosis for employment for them would be negative. Yes.

We have said that the labor force of the United States, the number of workers coming in in the decade of the sixties, is going to change from about

	(Millions)
Number of workers in 1960...................	73.6
Subtract:	
Withdrawals—death, retirement, marriage, childbearing, etc.......	−15.5
1960 workers still in labor force in 1970........	58.1
Add:	
Young entrants..................	+26.0
Adult women returning to work....	+ 3.0
Number of workers in 1970...................	87.1

73½ million to 87 million. That is the first figure and the last figure. It is the net increase from 73.6 to 87.1. But it is very important to understand that there is a lot of in and out movement in any month or any year's period. There are a lot of people entering and a lot of people exiting from the labor force. If you look down to those who will be added, you will see that added to the labor force in the sixties are going to be 26 million new young workers. This we think is one of the major challenges, as well as opportunities for the 1960's.

Here is an enormous number of young people who will be coming into the American labor force looking for work. There it is portrayed so you see how it has been going in the 1950's. In the 1950's we had about 19 million coming in. There is going to be a 40 percent increase, or 26 million new young people coming in as workers in this country in the 1960's.

THE NEED FOR GOVERNMENT ACTION ON UNEMPLOYMENT

Statement of W. Willard Wirtz, Secretary of Labor, in Nation's Manpower Revolution, *hearings before the Senate Committee on Labor and Public Welfare, 88th Cong., 1st Sess., 1963, part I, pp. 5–10, 30, 32*

Full employment, and by that I mean full utilization of the Nation's current and expanding manpower potential, is the immediate and primary objective of economic policy. Although we have a very long way to go from our current much-too-high level of 4 million unemployed, it is my conviction that as a result in large measure of the efforts of this subcommittee, we have embarked on the development of a national manpower policy that will have historic results in achieving this end.

This will not be easy. The objective of full employment must be accomplished in the face of a virtual manpower revolution which over the next few years will be changing the profile of the Nation's labor force in a manner that can as yet be only partly foreseen. Automation and technological change, along with shifts in the nature of consumer and business demand for goods and services, are having profound effects upon our manpower needs.

Yet we must accomplish that end; and the recognition of that fact, the programs that have resulted from its recognition—the area redevelopment and manpower development and training programs, the annual manpower report —and these hearings, are all significant steps in the successful accomplishment of the task.

My testimony today proceeds from a brief restatement of the statistics of unemployment in the United States.

Last year, about 4 million persons on the average were unemployed each month—about 5½ percent of the civilian labor force. This was the fifth consecutive year in which the unemployment rate averaged at least 5½ percent. Another 2.7 million workers who wanted full-time employment could find only part-time work. The loss of worktime totaled a billion workdays—6.7 percent of the potential available worktime. This loss was equal to shutting the country down—with no production, no services, no pay—for over 3 weeks.

Despite some general improvement in the level of economic activity and an increase in nonfarm employment in recent months, the unemployment rate in April of this year was still slightly over this 5½ percent mark.

There is one element in these statistics which has not been sufficiently noticed. Emphasis on a monthly unemployment figure—5½ percent, or about 4 million people—does not reflect the full impact and pervasiveness of unemployment. Reliable estimates (based on projections of previous experience) indicate that approximately 14 million men and women were unemployed at some time during the year 1962. This means that one in every five people who were working or looking for work last year were out of work part of the time. Two million or more persons had two spells of unemployment and 2½ million additional suffered three or more spells. Over 4 million workers were unemployed 15 weeks or more counting all of their periods of unemployment; about 2 million for more than half a year.

So the facts, not suggested by the monthly figures, are (a) that unemployment is affecting a very large number of people, almost one-fifth of the work force, to some extent; and (b) that unemployment is becoming an all-too-permanent condition for a "hard core" group of men and women.

Most of these unemployment statistics have become almost monotonously familiar. I should like, however, to urge upon this subcommittee one set of implications of these figures which has received too little recognition.

Most of the thinking about unemployment has been of its consequences in terms of human distress, of its corrosive influence upon the skills and self-respect of workers, the hardship it imposes on their families. No one apologizes for this kind of thinking. It reflects the best in a society that recognizes human values as paramount.

This thinking, though, ignores the economic impact of today's unemployment, and encourages reliance upon the argument that since the unemployed in the U.S. work force can weather this condition without experiencing dire poverty we do not need to worry about the economic effects of unemployment.

This argument obviously understates the problem. Most unemployment does result in real hardship and acute want. Two-thirds of those who experienced unemployment last year were 25 and over. One-sixth of all family heads in the labor force suffered some unemployment, and more than a third of these were jobless for 15 weeks or longer.

Furthermore, what is involved here is not just freedom from want; it is freedom of opportunity.

Beyond this, and as the principal burden of this testimony, I want to emphasize the central point that unemployment represents a cost and loss item which the economy as a whole simply cannot afford. It represents a stunting of economic growth at a time when vigorous economic growth is critical to the continued good health of a free enterprise system.

The unemployment figures are not intended to be an index of poverty; they are the measure, rather, of the denial of individual opportunity and of the retardation of national economic growth—of national waste.

So when it is pointed out by those who would rather shrug their shoulders than roll up their sleeves, that many of the unemployed are young people—with no previous attachment to the work force, and with no mouths to feed—they miss the real point.

It is unquestionably true that the unemployment figures for last year were swollen by the fact that one-third of the young men in this country who were looking for work were unable to find it part of the time—over 30 percent of them for 15 weeks or longer. But the significance of this is not diminished or diluted by the fact that many of them could still eat and sleep at home. The economy still lost the growth their full productiveness would have meant. It cannot afford this loss. Nor can it afford the more permanent effect this kind of stumbling start has on a million young men, particular on their idea of what making a living—and the obligation as well as the right to work—means in America.

Unemployment and underemployment in the United States last year represented a loss to the economy of between $30 and $40 billion in additional goods and services.

It is urged, and properly, that full use must be made of automation to increase productivity, both in terms of improving efficiency and in terms of expanding the gross national product. We have no choice, if the economy is to grow at the rate it must, but to use every technological resource which is available. It is no less important to use every manpower resource. It is understandable that the operator of an individual business will see this in terms of which is cheaper, a man or machine. He has to make that choice in those terms. But from the standpoint of the economy and society as a whole, a man-hour of unemployment represents the same waste of potential for maximum growth as does the nonuse of a new method or machine.

One of the most serious consequences of not accepting this fact is that we are disregarding the waste and loss of underemployment, underutilization of the full manpower capacity.

It is only one illustration of what is involved here that the underutilization of male agricultural workers alone is estimated as being equivalent in effect to the full-time unemployment of a million workers.

The same thing happens when Negro workers are denied the opportunity to develop skills, and when those fortunate enough to secure the right training and education are barred from employment in which they could use what they have learned.

Another form of underemployment involves those people who are willing, and in many cases anxious, to work but who do not actively seek employment because job opportunities do not exist for them. This underemployment affects most prominently older workers at or near retirement age, married women and handicapped workers. The extent of this underutilization of manpower frequently becomes evident in periods of economic recovery when the rate of growth of the labor force increases sharply. Thus, in a period of recovery from high unemployment, substantial increases in employment frequently occur without concomitant reductions in unemployment as increased numbers of workers enter the labor market looking for work or to take jobs that have become available. This is going to make the reduction of unemployment more difficult in the current period of economic expansion.

I urge, therefore, that the unemployment problem in this country be recognized not only as involving the needs of unemployed workers and their families but in addition as involving an unused, and therefore wasted, capital asset which has to be put to full use if the economy is to grow at the rate which it must achieve. Full employment will be achieved faster if it is considered not as an end in itself but as a means to the end of full use of the nation's economic potential—with a consequent increase of everybody's well being and standard of living.

This does not answer, but rather only poses, the question of how this is to be accomplished.

It is increasingly clear that there are two parts to that answer.

That part which is most basic lies outside my competence as a witness. It involves that course of action which will, by maximizing consumer demand and the incentives for investment, invigorate the economy to the extent that there will be a call upon the full manpower asset. The proposal presently before the Congress for a major tax reduction and revision is designed to achieve this purpose.

There is, in addition, the necessity of assuring the readiness of the manpower force to meet the demands of the expanding economy. It is not enough that there is a sufficient volume of manpower. Unless the right skills are included in the right places at the right times there will be a drag on the expanding economy.

A significant aspect of the present, and even more of the prospective, situation is that two basic shifts are occurring in the manpower demands of the economy: There has been a speedup in the long-term movement away from employment in goods-producing industries and toward more services; and the rapid pace of automation and technological change is resulting in a shift in employment toward relatively more skilled occupations.

The proportion of all workers in goods-producing industries (agriculture, mining, manufacturing and construction) has fallen sharply—from 51 percent in 1947 to 46 percent in 1957, and to 42 percent in 1962; the rate of decline in the last 5 years was about two-thirds greater than in the previous decade. By contrast, the service section of the economy has increased its rate of employment growth because of expansion in State and local governments and the continued employment growth of the service sector.

The past decade and a half has seen an acceleration of the long-term trend of increase in professional, managerial, clerical and sales occupations at the expense of manual occupations. Employment of blue-collar or manual workers in 1962 was only slightly above (by 3 percent) the level of 15 years earlier, while the number of white-collar jobs has increased by almost 50 percent.

But, most significant, among both blue- and white-collar occupations, has been the shift away from unskilled jobs caused by rapid technological change. Among white-collar workers the fastest growing occupational group has been the most highly trained—professional, technical and kindred workers, whose number has more than doubled since 1947. Among blue-collar workers, almost all the increase in employment in the past decade occurred among skilled craftsmen, while the numbers of unskilled and semiskilled workers have shown little or no increase.

Thus, virtually all of the occupations providing expanding employment opportunities in recent years have been those requiring long periods of education and formal training. Our projections indicate that these are the occupations that will also be expanding in the future; little or no increase is expected among the semiskilled and unskilled occupations.

Many of the jobs requiring little or no training which were available in past decades to new workers and to unskilled or semiskilled workers who were dis-employed in contracting areas of the economy are disappearing. As a result, technological change and the dynamics of economic growth are tending to result in longer periods of unemployment and higher unemployment rates for workers who do not have the education and skills required by modern industry.

The picture of unemployment trends in recent years mirrors this situation dramatically. Among all groups with high unemployment rates, including young workers, older workers, and nonwhite workers, the absence of required occupational skills looms large in their employment difficulties. The highest unemployment rates among major nonfarm occupation groups are recorded by nonfarm laborers (12 percent); operatives, largely semiskilled production work-ers (7 percent); and service workers (6 percent)—all relatively unskilled groups.

At the other end of the scale, unemployment rates are extremely low (under 2 percent) among professional and technical workers and among managers, officials, and proprietors.

Thus, at the same time that large numbers of workers are unemployed, job openings have remained unfilled for lack of workers trained in required skills. Requirements for personnel have been strongest in professional and technical fields, but shortages exist in many occupations in other white-collar and in service and skilled production categories. And, within each of these broad occupational groups, the trend has been toward employment of workers at the top of the skill range of the occupation and less opportunity for workers with minimum qualifications.

This situation underlines the great need for additional emphasis on adequate education and vocational training. At the same time, programs are also needed to assist workers in making the necessary transitions—from declining to expand-ing industries, from contracting to growing occupations, and from labor market areas in which job openings are being reduced to those of rising job oppor-tunities.

Recognizing these needs, Congress last year passed the Manpower Develop-ment and Training Act. This legislation introduced the concept of federally supported retraining of the unemployed on a broad national scale. Equally important, it provided for a comprehensive unified manpower research and development program.

In the past, manpower and labor market programs have too frequently been justified on the basis of temporary, welfare considerations alone. Comprehensive manpower and labor market programs are essential in an expanding and chang-ing economy. If the rate of national economic growth is to be maximized it is critical that manpower be geared to changes in demand and developments in science and technology. Workers must be equipped with the basic mobility that comes only with the ability to reapply skills to changing demand situations.

Here, again, we have tended properly to concentrate on the values of educa-tion and training to the individual, as a matter personal to him—but have not emphasized sufficiently the broader importance of his education and training to the economy as a whole.

Recent studies have shown a close correlation between education and unemployment. Adult males (25 to 54) with less than an eighth grade education had an unemployment rate of 9 percent; while the rate for those who went on to high school, but didn't finish it, was nearly 7 percent; the rate for high school graduates well below 4 percent; and for those with some college education, about 2 percent.

If more education means less unemployment, it also means higher income when employed. A study of the income of men 25 years of age and older in 1961 shows a median income range from $2,275 a year for those with less than 8 years of school to $5,550 for high school graduates and $7,700 for college graduates. A Census Bureau study estimates the difference between the average total lifetime (age 25–64) income of men with less than 8 years of schooling and high school graduates at about $100,000; the difference in lifetime income between a high school graduate and a college graduate is close to $140,000.

These differentials undoubtedly reflect factors in addition to formal education, but it is certain that the difference in educational attainment is a prime reason for the income differences.

Important as these advantages are to the individual, they are no less important to the economy as a whole. The tendency to think of the untrained, unskilled worker as an underprivileged individual tends to cloud the realization that he is also an underproducer in an economy that depends on expanding production, an underconsumer in a market which controls production, a low taxpayer—and very possibly a debit rather than a credit item on the overall economic balance sheet.

There are presently about 700,000 young Americans out of school and out of work. Most of them are today unequipped for any jobs which there is reason to expect will be available to them during their work lives; they lack identifiable skills, and they are today developing nonwork habits which make it very likely that they will not be self-sustaining members of the work force even in unskilled jobs. It is a conservative estimate that this group of untrained young men and women represents a prospective loss of almost a billion dollars a year for the next 40 years in lifetime income.

Experience with the Manpower Development and Training Act permits a somewhat more precise illustration of the same point. The cost of training is averaging between $1,000 and $1,250 per trainee. If this training does no more than move the worker only one step up the occupational ladder, for example, from unskilled nonfarm laborer to semiskilled operative (a rough equivalent for women would be from operative or service worker to clerical worker), the increased income the trainee will receive on average in 1 year ($1,300) as a result of occupational upgrading would amount to more than the total cost of his training. In the course of a working lifetime, the trainee's increased income would total about $50,000.

Moreover, about one-third of the total cost of training would be recouped by the Government in a single year; about 20 percent as additional income tax revenues, and an additional 10 percent because of lower costs of unemployment compensation. These estimates do not include the savings accruing because of the lower costs of public and private assistance and savings in other welfare expenditures.

These estimates are conservative since they assume only a one-step rise in occupational level when in fact many trainees will move further up the occupational scale. No allowance has been made for the multiplier effects on income of the increased earnings of trainees or the increased productiveness of the economy resulting from the higher skill level of the trainees. Nor do these estimates include the savings in social costs which cannot be expressed in monetary terms—the broken homes and uncared for children of men who cannot earn enough to support a family, increased crime, and other costs that continue into the lives of the children of unemployed and underemployed workers.

It represents no disregard for human values, or the central importance of individual lives, to emphasize the economic importance of manpower as the economy's greatest capital asset and its most creative element. Unemployment and underemployment represent a costly dissipation of this resource, a waste as sure as if a factory were burned down. Investment in manpower is not merely a desirable objective of welfare, but an essential element in economic growth. We are still somewhat backward in our system of national accounting in that we have so far been able to translate only in the crudest way the value of our investment in manpower. The economic yield of our expenditures for training which I cited earlier are only rough estimates of the first generation of return and they do not take account of a multitude of factors which influence our national output and national wealth.

Among other positive contributions of programs which match and fill job vacancies with unemployed workers through training and retraining, through provision of information on vacancies and occupational needs, through assistance in mobility and through adequate placement service is this significant stimulus to economic growth. The "multiplier" effects of these programs, in addition to those stemming from the income directly produced, include among others, the generation of vacancies for supporting positions, and the effects on manpower requirements for raw materials, for processing and distribution of products, and for investment in equipment. In addition, of course, the aim of training programs is to make available to employers the workers with required skills, when they are needed, where they are needed, so that manpower scarcity need never be a drag on economic growth. Our program of manpower research is aimed in part at anticipating changes in requirements so as to avoid these bottlenecks to expansion in the economy.

The value of programs that minimize manpower dislocations associated with economic growth and thereby make possible the most efficient economic adjustments to change may not be precisely measurable, but is certainly substantial.

Surely this emphasis on the overall economic importance of a comprehensive manpower policy will not be taken as reflecting any disregard of the essential individual values which are equally involved. We are dealing with people— with individuals who, when they are unemployed for long periods, feel acutely a loss of status in their community and in their homes and begin also to lose faith in their ability ever again to play a useful role in the economy. When these individuals, through guidance and testing are given new assurance of their basic abilities, and through training are given marketable skills, they are brought back from an economic twilight world into a position of full parity in our society. Although possibly unmeasurable in terms of dollars and cents, these are very real and very valuable contributions of manpower programs.

One of the most important dividends of training is its contribution to rebuilding the pride of workmanship and the sense of creativity that accompanies the possession of a useful skill. The deterioration of this sense of contribution has been one of the most tragic aspects of industrialization. We have been more fortunate than deserving in the past in that those who have been chronically unemployed have not developed a greater lack of confidence in the institutions which failed to provide them with opportunities to gain a livelihood and a disrespect for the standards of society which tolerated such a situation. The opportunity offered to workers by the Manpower Development and Training Act program, through training and retraining, to acquire the pride of skill, or to those whose skills have obsolesced to regain a respected place among employed craftsmen, can hardly be overvalued.

Throughout this presentation I have emphasized the value of a comprehensive labor market policy. Recognition of the components of such a policy is not new. Briefly, it would contain:

A current labor market information service providing information on job vacancies, occupational needs and availability of workers;

An early warning system of impending changes in employment, especially layoffs, so that action can be taken immediately to place workers or put them into training;

An effective vocational guidance and counseling program beginning in the elementary school;

A program of research and its implementation to the educational system fully responsive to manpower needs, current and prospective;

A nationally oriented placement service;

A program of training and retraining for unemployed and underemployed workers; and

A program for aiding the mobility of workers, responsive to the changing geography of employment opportunities.

Some of these programs exist but need strengthening.

Replies by the Secretary of Labor to questions by the Subcommittee on Employment and Manpower, U.S. Senate Committee on Labor and Public Welfare

QUESTIONS BY SENATOR CLARK

. . . *Question No. 2.* If technological displacement and shift in demand patterns accelerate, isn't it likely that jobs for which people have been retrained will also disappear? Isn't there a likelihood that the same person will be displaced not once but several times in his life? If so, won't we have to assure a basic education for everyone adequate to create a flexible labor force capable of adjusting to any change which may occur in the future?

Answer: Studies by the Department of Labor confirm the conclusion that the rapid pace of technological developments and shifts in demand patterns may well necessitate the retraining of some people more than once during the course of their working lives; also that it is very important for all young people to receive as good an education as possible, in order to provide a basis for their training and retraining and give them occupational flexibility. Determined, nationwide efforts must be made to reduce the proportion of boys and girls dropping out of school before high school graduation (from the current figure of around 30 percent), and also to make available to the millions of adults who are totally or functionally illiterate the basic education they need to qualify for occupations offering prospect of employment opportunities. . . .

Question No. 5. Are we likely to be faced with the need for a national manpower policy enabling us to face problems as or before they arise rather than after they reach crisis proportions?

Answer: The need for a broad manpower policy aimed at maximizing the use of the Nation's manpower potential has emerged clearly in recent years. These hearings have acted to focus attention on the very substantial manpower problems we now face and will be facing in the next decade, and the critical need for active programs to anticipate and avoid these problems.

With the enactment of the Manpower Development and Training Act of 1962, Congress recognized that an effective policy aimed at achieving high employment and growth also requires a major national effort to improve the functioning of the labor market and the quality and adaptability of the labor force. Included in this legislation was the request for an annual Presidential report on "manpower requirements, resources, utilization, and training." Together with the program for training of the unemployed and underemployed, these provisions mark the emergence of manpower programs as a specific instrument of national policy.

Under the provisions of the Manpower Development and Training Act, the Department of Labor is harnessing the research facilities, not only of its own agencies, but also of those elsewhere in Government and outside, to study and anticipate the nature and extent of manpower problems that will be facing us during future decades. These programs also supplement research, underway to develop approaches to solving our major economic problems—inadequate growth in employment opportunities. In our dynamic economy, with constantly changing demands for labor, both in nature and extent, a national manpower policy enabling us to anticipate manpower problems is essential if we are to minimize unemployment and manpower dislocations as well as create the manpower basis for a high rate of economic growth

Statement of Thomas F. Morris, Vice President SKF Industries, Inc., Philadel-
phia, in Retraining of the Unemployed, *hearings before the Senate Committee*
on Labor and Public Welfare, 87th Cong., 1st Sess., 1961, pp. 102–104

As businessmen, we welcome these timely hearings by the Subcommittee on
Employment and Manpower of the Senate Committee on Labor and Public
Welfare and appreciate the opportunity to present our views on the proposed
Vocational Retraining Act of 1961.

This chamber * took an early interest in the basic problem of technological
unemployment and we are proud of our initiative in helping to organize the
Conference on Jobs and Business Climate in Pennsylvania, sponsored jointly
by leaders in labor and business management, which was held in Philadelphia
on March 12, 1959.

On the problem of unemployment, we hope that all Members of the Congress
will subscribe to, and be motivated by, the truly American concept expressed
by the distinguished Governor of Pennsylvania, Hon. David L. Lawrence, who
stated in part in his address before that conference:

"What we do want, what we must have, is a program of public action which
will be the catalyst, the energizer, the necessary ingredient, that will stimulate
the private economy to put our people back to work."

According to the most recently available statistics, unemployment in Greater
Philadelphia is currently 7.7 percent of the work force or exactly the same as
the national average. We are rated as an area of "substantial labor surplus."
Unemployment is just as high as it was 3 years ago—at roughly 150,000—due
to a major expansion in the labor force. Teenagers born in great numbers in the
early 1940's are now entering the labor market and are finding it difficult to get
the high-pay type jobs which were plentiful in the postwar years up to 1957.

The current business recession in the eight counties of Greater Philadelphia
is primarily in manufacturing which is down by 20,000 jobs since this time
last year. During these same 12 months, there has been an increase of 20,000
workers in construction, marketing, finance, most service trades and Government employment. Two recent blows to the area's economy have been the loss
of 1,500 jobs through the permanent closing of the Ford Motor Co's assembly
plant at Chester, Pa., and the announcement of the layoff of 5,000 workers at
the Camden, N.J., yards of the New York Shipbuilding Corp.

There exists in the Greater Philadelphia industrial community a paradoxical,

---

* The Chamber of Commerce of Greater Philadelphia represents business and
industry in the Philadelphia standard metropolitan area which comprises Bucks,
Chester, Delaware, Montgomery, and Philadelphia Counties of Pennsylvania and
Burlington, Camden, Gloucester Counties of New Jersey. Greater Philadelphia has
over 90 percent of the types of industries classified by the U.S. Bureau of Census,
as one of the Nation's largest space and naval arsenals, the second largest petroleum
refining center in the country, the No. 1 port in total tonnage in foreign trade, and a
great research and development center with a dollar volume of projects in hand which
is larger than that of the research clusters around Boston-Cambridge in Massachusetts,
Chicago in the Great Lakes area, or Palo Alto and Pasadena in California.

serious condition. We have chronic unemployment of the unskilled and semi-skilled workers and a rising and continuing demand for skilled workers and technicians.

This demand is unsatisfied and the situation will worsen.

Temporary business dislocations aside, local manufacturing will continue to be embarrassed for the shortage of skilled workers. A study of the help-wanted ads in the Philadelphia Inquirer and the Evening Bulletin of Philadelphia for a month will demonstrate the needs. The Pennsylvania State Employment Service has thousands of unfilled orders for skilled employees that it cannot fill. Exhibit A [not included here] shows some 15 areas of manufacturing in Philadelphia where the need for trained people cannot be met.

The apparel industry, the largest single employer of labor in Greater Philadelphia, is an example. It estimates that several thousand semiskilled workers could be developed from those presently unskilled and put to work in the immediate future. In addition, there is a pressing demand for hundreds of skilled hand sewers. In the knitted goods section of the industry, a seasonal trade, there is a continuing demand for workers as well as a need to provide training for those workers already in the trade to give them an alternate skill so that they may find employment during the slack seasons.

Not only are our manufacturing industries being impoverished for the want of qualified workers, our business and service industries need thousands of people they cannot readily hire—auto mechanics, service station attendants, nursing aids, stenographic and clerical help, are examples. . . .

Today people have to be trained to get and hold jobs. They need training in skills and they need to learn the meaning of work so they will appreciate and uphold the dignity and responsibility of a job. We don't just need workers; we need good workers.

Back to the basic problem. We have jobs going begging, we have men and women who want to work. Training is the catalyst that will bring these jobs and people together. As industries change to meet the demands of technological advancement, there exists an increasing need for retraining employed as well as the unemployed people whose skills have been obsolete.

To meet this serious need, Philadelphia must establish an industrial training school. The community's public schools and other facilities cannot do the job.

This statement seeks to first point up the community need for skill training and secondly to recommend such a program.

The need is manifest for—
  1. Apprenticeship training.
  2. Industrial upgrading.
  3. Vocational training.
  4. Unemployment retraining.
  5. Occupational training.

While these areas are not exclusive, each or all can be programed through one central facility without serious overlapping.

There are five groups of people who would most advantageously benefit from industrial training and contribute to increasing and stabilizing the labor market.

1. Present industrial employees requiring skill upgrading or vocational retraining.

2. Youths 16 to 21 years of age.

3. Older workers, men over 45 and women over 35.

4. Minority groups, principally Negroes and Puerto Ricans. Cubans may possibly become a third classification.

5. Technically displaced and unskilled.

It is estimated there are 10,000 people in Philadelphia alone now on relief who want to work but need some training to make them employable. Ten thousand trained people added to the labor force would be a significant contribution to business and industry.

To achieve the objective of training to meet job vacancies in an industrial economy continually changing because of technological advances and shifts in market demands, the chamber has proposed the creation of a centrally located vocational and technical training school. This proposal has been approved and endorsed by the Departments of Labor and Industry, Commerce and Public Instruction of the Commonwealth of Pennsylvania, by the board of public education, and by labor and industrial leaders of Greater Philadelphia.

The school would be operated by the Board of Public Education of the city of Philadelphia. It would have sufficient flexibility to meet the changing needs of governmental, institutional, commercial and industrial employers in the volume of semiskilled and skilled workers required.

In addition to the professional vocational teachers supplied by the board of public education to staff the school, Greater Philadelphia industry could be counted upon for full cooperation and assistance from its training departments. Furthermore, the School of Vocational Teacher Training of the University of Pennsylvania and the Drexel Institute of Technology have offered to cooperate when necessary in the development of accelerated training techniques and methods.

The groundwork for this community effort has been well laid. We have reached the point at which financial assistance is urgently required from Federal sources to launch this training project which could serve as a national pattern. With the requisite financial support, we believe that the proposed school will be a working "laboratory" in which solutions will be found for many aspects of national problems of unemployment and of training and retraining. If this Nation is to compete with its friends in world markets, if we are to meet the gauntlet thrown down by the leaders of the Sino-Russian bloc in the economic hot war in which we are engaged, then we must continually upgrade the skills of our workers. This can be done only by providing vocational and technical training facilities such as Philadelphia's proposed school.

Therefore, the Chamber of Commerce of Greater Philadelphia gives its wholehearted support to S. 987—the Vocational Retraining Act of 1961—and urges the early approval of this bill by the Congress. We would, however, like to propose that section 8 (*b*) be amended by the deletion of the words "or rental" (p. 10, lines 1 and 2 of the printed document).

The chamber makes this proposal because of the immediate need for space for expanded training and retraining facilities, space which is not readily available in existing public school buildings. Communities cannot meet this national emergency in worker training without a breakdown in normal educational operations. By this suggested amendment in the bill, funds could be made available to the public school authorities so that they could rent much-needed space for establishment of temporary training facilities until such time as permanent facilities can be developed. It is impracticable at this time to forecast the ultimate requirements in buildings and training equipment. Such a forecast will be possible only after experience has been gained in our industrial communities in the operation of accelerated vocational and technical training programs such as we contemplate in Philadelphia.

By passage of this bill, with the proposed amendment, the Congress will be launching a program which will permit major strides toward the solution of a great national problem—providing full employment in a dynamic private economy flexible enough to meet and benefit from technological advances.

MANPOWER DEVELOPMENT AND TRAINING ACT

Selected clauses from the act of March 15, 1962, as amended December 19, 1963,* designed "to require the Federal Government to appraise the manpower requirements and resources of the Nation, and to develop and apply the information and methods needed to deal with the problems of unemployment resulting from automation and technological changes and other types of persistent unemployment"

TITLE I—MANPOWER REQUIREMENTS, DEVELOPMENT, AND UTILIZATION
STATEMENT OF FINDINGS AND PURPOSE

SEC. 101. The Congress finds that there is critical need for more and better trained personnel in many vital occupational categories, including professional, scientific, technical, and apprenticeable categories; that even in periods of high unemployment, many employment opportunities remain unfilled because of the shortages of qualified personnel; and that it is in the national interest that current and prospective manpower shortages be identified and that persons who can be qualified for these positions through education and training be sought out and trained [as quickly as is reasonably possible] in order that the Nation may meet the staffing requirements of the struggle for freedom. The Congress further finds that the skills of many persons have been rendered obsolete by dislocations in the economy arising from automation or other technological developments, foreign competition, relocation of industry, shifts in market demands, and other changes in the structure of the economy; that Government leadership is necessary to insure that the benefits of automation do not become burdens of widespread unemployment; that the problem of assuring sufficient employment opportunities will be compounded by the extraordinarily rapid growth of the labor force in the next decade, particularly by the entrance of

* Portions which were added then are enclosed in brackets.

young people into the labor force, that improved planning and expanded efforts will be required to assure that men, women, and young people will be trained and available to meet shifting employment needs; that many persons now unemployed or underemployed, in order to become qualified for reemployment or full employment must be assisted in providing themselves with skills which are or will be in demand in the labor market; that the skills of many persons now employed are inadequate to enable them to make their maximum contribution to the Nation's economy; and that it is in the national interest that the opportunity to acquire new skills be afforded to these people [with the least delay] in order to alleviate the hardships of unemployment, reduce the costs of unemployment compensation and public assistance, and to increase the Nation's productivity and its capacity to meet the requirements of the space age. It is therefore the purpose of this Act to require the Federal Government to appraise the manpower requirements and resources of the Nation, and to develop and apply the information and methods needed to deal with the problems of unemployment resulting from automation and technological changes and other types of persistent unemployment.

EVALUATION, INFORMATION, AND RESEARCH

SEC. 102. To assist the Nation in accomplishing the objectives of technological progress while avoiding or minimizing individual hardship and widespread unemployment, the Secretary of Labor shall—

(1) evaluate the impact of, and benefits and problems created by automation, technological progress, and other changes in the structure of production and demand on the use of the Nation's human resources; establish techniques and methods for detecting in advance the potential impact of such developments; develop solutions to these problems, and publish findings pertaining thereto;

(2) establish a program of factual studies of practices of employers and unions which tend to impede the mobility of workers or which facilitate mobility, including but not limited to early retirement and vesting provisions and practices under private compensation plans; the extension of health, welfare, and insurance benefits to laid-off workers; the operation of severance pay plans; and the use of extended leave plans for education and training purposes. A report on these studies shall be included as a part of the Secretary's report required under section 104.

(3) appraise the adequacy of the Nation's manpower development efforts to meet foreseeable manpower needs and recommend needed adjustments, including methods for promoting the most effective occupational utilization of and providing useful work experience and training opportunities for untrained and inexperienced youth;

(4) promote, encourage, or directly engage in programs of information and communication concerning manpower requirements, development, and utilization, including prevention and amelioration of undesirable manpower effects from automation and other technological developments and improvement of the mobility of workers; and

(5) arrange for the conduct of such research and investigations as give promise of furthering the objectives of this Act.

SKILL AND TRAINING REQUIREMENTS

SEC. 103. The Secretary of Labor shall develop, compile, and make available, in such manner as he deems appropriate, information regarding skill requirements, occupational outlook, job opportunities, labor supply in various skills, and employment trends on a National, State, area, or other appropriate basis which shall be used in the educational, training, counseling, and placement activities performed under this Act.

MANPOWER REPORT

SEC. 104. The Secretary of Labor shall make such reports and recommendations to the President as he deems appropriate pertaining to manpower requirements, resources, use, and training; and the President shall transmit to the Congress within sixty days after the beginning of each regular session (commencing with the year 1963) a report pertaining to manpower requirements, resources, utilization, and training.

TITLE II—TRAINING AND SKILL DEVELOPMENT PROGRAMS

PART A—DUTIES OF THE SECRETARY OF LABOR

GENERAL RESPONSIBILITY

SEC. 201. In carrying out the purposes of this Act, the Secretary of Labor shall determine the skill requirements of the economy, develop policies for the adequate occupational development and maximum utilization of the skills of the Nation's workers, promote and encourage the development of broad and diversified training programs, including on-the-job training, designed to qualify for employment the many persons who cannot reasonably be expected to secure full-time employment without such training, and to equip the Nation's workers with the new and improved skills that are or will be required.

SELECTION OF TRAINEES

SEC. 202. (a) The Secretary of Labor shall provide a program for testing, counseling, and selecting for occupational training under this Act those unemployed or underemployed persons who cannot reasonably be expected to secure appropriate full-time employment without training. Workers in farm families with less than $1,200 annual net family income shall be considered unemployed for the purpose of this Act.

[(b) Whenever appropriate the Secretary shall provide a special program for the testing, counseling, selection, and referral of youths, sixteen years of age or older, for occupational training and further schooling, who because of inadequate educational background and work preparation are unable to qualify for and obtain employment without such training and schooling.]

(c) Although priority in referral for training shall be extended to unemployed persons, the Secretary of Labor shall, to the maximum extent possible, also refer other persons qualified for training programs which will enable them to acquire needed skills. Priority in referral for training shall also be extended to persons to be trained for skills needed within, first, the labor market area in which they reside and, second, within the State of their residence.

(d) The Secretary of Labor shall determine the occupational training needs of referred persons, provide for their orderly selection and referral for training under this Act, and provide counseling and placement services to persons who have completed their training, as well as follow-up studies to determine whether the programs provided meet the occupational training needs of the persons referred.

(e) Before selecting a person for training [other than for training under subsection (i)], the Secretary shall determine that there is a reasonable expectation of employment in the occupation for which the person is to be trained. If such employment is not available in the area in which the person resides, the Secretary shall obtain reasonable assurance of such person's willingness to accept employment outside his area of residence.

(f) The Secretary shall not refer persons for training in an occupation which requires less than two weeks training, unless there are immediate employment opportunities in such occupation.

(g) The duration of any training program to which a person is referred shall be reasonable and consistent with the occupation for which the person is being trained.

(h) Upon certification by the responsible training agency that a person who has been referred for training does not have a satisfactory attendance record or is not making satisfactory progress in such training absent good cause, the Secretary shall forthwith terminate his training and subsistence allowances, and his transportation allowances except such as may be necessary to enable him to return to his regular place of residence after termination of training, and withdraw his referral. Such person shall not be eligible for such allowances for one year thereafter.

[(i) Whenever appropriate, the Secretary of Labor may also refer for the attainment of basic education skills those eligible persons who indicate their intention to, and will thereby be able to, pursue courses of occupational training of a type for which there appears to be reasonable expectation of employment. Such referrals shall be considered a referral for training within the meaning of this Act, and such persons shall be eligible for training allowances for not to exceed an additional twenty weeks.]

TRAINING ALLOWANCES

Sec. 203. (a) The Secretary of Labor may, on behalf of the United States, enter into agreements with States under which the Secretary of Labor shall make payments to such States either in advance or by way of reimbursement for the purpose of enabling such States, as agents for the United States, to make payment of weekly training allowances to unemployed persons selected for training pursuant to the provisions of section 202 and undergoing such training in a program operated pursuant to the provisions of this Act. Such payments shall be made for a period not exceeding fifty-two weeks [except where authorized for individuals referred for training under section 202 (*i*)] and the amount of any such payment in any week for persons undergoing training, including uncompensated employer-provided training, shall not exceed $10 more than the amount of the average weekly unemployment compensation payment (including allowances for dependants) for a week of total unemployment in the State making such payments during the most recent quarter for which such data are available: *Provided however,* That in any week an individual who, but for his training, would be entitled to unemployment compensation in excess of such allowance, shall receive an allowance increased by the amount of such excess. With respect to Guam and the Virgin Islands the Secretary shall by regulation determine the amount of the training allowance to be paid any eligible person taking training under this Act.

With respect to any week for which a person receives unemployment compensation under title XV of the Social Security Act or any other Federal or State unemployment compensation law which is less than [$10 more than] the average weekly unemployment compensation payment (including allowances for dependents) for a week of total unemployment in the State making such payment during the most recent quarter for which such data are available, a supplemental training allowance may be paid to a person eligible for a training allowance under this Act. This supplemental training allowance shall not exceed the difference between his unemployment compensation and [$10 more than] the average weekly unemployment compensation payment referred to above.

For persons undergoing on-the-job training, the amount of any payment which would otherwise be made by the Secretary of Labor under this section shall be reduced by an amount which bears the same ratio to that payment as the number of compensated hours per week bears to forty hours.

[The training allowance of a person engaged in full-time training under section 231 shall not be reduced on account of his part-time employment which does not exceed twenty hours per week, but shall be reduced in an amount equal to his full earnings for hours worked in excess of twenty hours per week.]

(*b*) The Secretary of Labor is authorized to pay to any person engaged in training under this title, including compensated full-time on-the-job training, such sums as he may determine to be necessary to defray transportation and subsistence expenses for separate maintenance of such persons when such training is provided in facilities which are not within commuting distance of their regular place of residence: *Provided,* That the Secretary in defraying such subsistence expenses shall not afford any individual an allowance exceeding $35 per week, at the rate of $5 per day; nor shall the Secretary authorize any transportation expenditure exceeding the rate of 10 cents per mile. . . .

(*h*) If State unemployment compensation payments are paid to a person taking training under this Act and eligible for a training allowance, the State making such payments shall be reimbursed from funds herein appropriated.

The amount of such reimbursement shall be determined by the Secretary of Labor on the basis of reports furnished to him by the States and such amount shall then be placed in the State's unemployment trust fund account.

(*i*) A person who, in connection with an occupational training program, has received a training allowance or whose unemployment compensation payments were reimbursed under the provisions of this Act or any other Federal Act shall not be entitled to training allowances under this Act for one year after the completion or other termination (for other than good cause) of the training with respect to which such allowance or payment was made.

(*j*) No training allowance shall be paid to any person who is receiving training for an occupation which requires a training period of less than six days.

ON-THE-JOB TRAINING

SEC. 204. (*a*) The Secretary of Labor shall encourage, develop, and secure the adoption of programs for on-the-job training needed to equip persons selected for training with the appropriate skills. The Secretary shall, to the maximum extent possible, secure the adoption by the States and by private and public agencies, employers, trade associations, labor organizations and other industrial and community groups which he determines are qualified to conduct effective training programs under this title of such programs as he approves, and for this purpose he is authorized to enter into appropriate agreements with them.

(*b*) In adopting or approving any training program under this part, and as a condition to the expenditure of funds for any such program, the Secretary shall make such arrangements as he deems necessary to insure adherence to appropriate training standards, including assurances—

(1) that the training content of the program is adequate, involves reasonable progression, and will result in the qualification of trainees for suitable employment;

(2) that the training period is reasonable and consistent with periods customarily required for comparable training;

(3) that adequate and safe facilities, and adequate personnel and records of attendance and progress are provided; and

(4) that the trainees are compensated by the employer at such rates, including periodic increases, as may be deemed reasonable under regulations hereinafter authorized, considering such factors as industry, geographical region, and trainee proficiency.

(*c*) Where on-the-job training programs under this part require supplementary classroom instruction, appropriate arrangements for such instruction shall be agreed to by the Secretary of Health, Education, and Welfare and the Secretary of Labor.

[LABOR MOBILITY DEMONSTRATION PROJECTS]

[SEC. 208. During the period ending June 30, 1965, the Secretary of Labor shall develop and carry out, in a limited number of geographical areas, pilot projects designed to assess or demonstrate the effectiveness in reducing unemployment of programs to increase the mobility of unemployed workers by providing assistance to meet their relocation expenses. In carrying out such projects the Secretary may provide such assistance, in the form of grants or loans, or both, only to involuntarily unemployed individuals who cannot reasonably be expected to secure full-time employment in the community in which they reside, have bona fide offers of employment (other than temporary or seasonal employment), and are deemed qualified to perform the work for which they are being employed. Where such assistance is provided in the form of grants, such grants may not exceed 50 per centum of the expenses incurred reasonably necessary to the transportation of the person who is relocating, and his family, and their household effects. Where such assistance is provided in the form of loans, or a combination of loans and grants, the total amount thereof may not exceed 100 per centum of such expenses and shall be made subject to such terms and conditions as the Secretary may prescribe. Of the funds appropriated for a fiscal year to carry out this title, not more than 2 per centum thereof, or $4,000,000, whichever is the lesser, may be used for the purposes of this section.]

PRESIDENT JOHNSON'S DECLARATION OF WAR ON POVERTY

From the State of the Union Message, January 8, 1964

This budget, and this year's legislative program, are designed to help each and every American citizen fulfill his basic hopes:

His hopes for a fair chance to make good.

His hopes for fair play from the law.

His hopes for a full-time job on full-time pay.

His hopes for a decent home for his family in a decent community.

His hopes for a good school for his children with good teachers.

And his hopes for security when faced with sickness, or unemployment or old age.

Unfortunately, many Americans live on the outskirts of hope, some because of their poverty and some because of their color, and all too many because of both.

Our task is to help replace their despair with opportunity.

And this Administration today, here and now, declares unconditional war on poverty in America, and I urge this Congress and all Americans to join with me in that effort.

It will not be a short or easy struggle, no single weapon or strategy will suffice, but we shall not rest until that war is won.

The richest nation on earth can afford to win it.

We cannot afford to lose it.

One thousand dollars invested in salvaging an unemployable youth today can return $40,000 or more in his lifetime.

Poverty is a national problem, requiring improved national organization and support. But this attack, to be effective, must also be organized at the state and the local level, and must be supported and directed by state and local efforts.

For the war against poverty will not be won here in Washington. It must be won in the field, in every private home, in every public office, from the court-house to the White House.

The program I shall propose will emphasize this cooperative approach. To help that one-fifth of all American families with income too small to even meet their basic needs, our chief weapons in a more pinpointed attack will be better schools and better health and better homes and better training and better job opportunities to help more Americans, especially young Americans, escape from squalor and misery and unemployment rolls, where other citizens help to carry them.

Very often a lack of jobs and money is not the cause of poverty, but the symptom.

The cause may lie deeper in our failure to give our fellow citizens a fair chance to develop their own capacities, in a lack of education and training, in a lack of medical care and housing, in a lack of decent communities in which to live and bring up their children. But whatever the cause, our joint Federal-local effort must pursue poverty, pursue it wherever it exists. In city slums, in small towns, in sharecroppers' shacks or in migrant worker camps, on Indian reservations, among whites as well as Negroes, among the young as well as the aged, in the boom-towns and in the depressed areas.

Our aim is not only to relieve the symptom of poverty, but to cure it, and, above all, to prevent it.

No single piece of legislation, however, is going to suffice:

We will launch a special effort in the chronically distressed areas of Appalachia.

We must expand our small but our successful area redevelopment program.

We must enact youth employment legislation to put jobless, aimless, hope-less youngsters to work on useful projects.

We must distribute more food to the needy through a broader food stamp program.

We must create a National Service Corps to help the economically handi-capped of our own country, as the Peace Corps now helps those abroad.

We must modernize our unemployment insurance and establish a high-level commission on automation. If we have the brain power to invent these ma-chines, we have the brain power to make certain that they are a boon and not a bane to humanity.

We must extend the coverage of our minimum wage laws to more than 2 million workers now lacking this basic protection of purchasing power.

We must, by including special school aid funds as part of our education program, improve the quality of teaching and training and counseling in our hardest-hit areas.

We must build more libraries in every area, and more hospitals and nursing homes under the Hill-Burton Act, and train more nurses to staff them.

We must provide hospital insurance for our older citizens, financed by every worker and his employer under Social Security contributing no more than $1 a month during the employe's working career to protect him in his old age in a dignified manner. without cost to the Treasury, against the devastating hardship of prolonged or repeated illness.

We must, as a part of a revised housing and urban renewal program, give more help to those displaced by slum clearance; provide more housing for our poor and our elderly, and seek as our ultimate goal in our free enterprise system a decent home for every American family.

We must help obtain more modern mass transit within our communities as well as low-cost transportation between them.

Above all, we must release $11 billion of tax reduction into the private spending stream to create new jobs and new markets in every area of this land.

These programs are obviously not for the poor or the underprivileged alone.

Every American will benefit by the extension of Social Security to cover the hospital costs of their aged parents.

Every American community will benefit from the construction or modernization of schools and libraries and hospitals and nursing homes, from the training of more nurses, and from the improvement of urban renewal and public transit.

And every individual American taxpayer, and every corporate taxpayer, will benefit from the earliest possible passage of the pending tax bill, from both the new investment it will bring and the new jobs that it will create.

SENATOR GOLDWATER ON POVERTY

From an address by Senator Barry Goldwater before the Economic Club of New York, January 15, 1964

It is my chore to ask you to consider the toughest proposition ever faced by believers in the free enterprise system: the need for a frontal attack against Santa Claus—not the Santa Claus of the holiday season, of course, but the Santa Claus of the free lunch, the Government handout, the Santa Claus of something-for-nothing and something-for-everyone.

In short, the Santa Claus promises of the State of the Union Message to which we recently have listened.

If this sounds like I am against good works and good goals, let me ask your patience while I explain. I am not against good works or even against all forms of Government activity. I am certainly not against restraint in Government spending or a true understanding of what really makes our economy tick and how it can enrich the lives of everyone in this nation.

I am not against those things. I am against:

. . . The direction of a Government establishment that confuses local need with national necessity, trying to buy off today's problems with tomorrow's bankruptcy.

The direction of a nation being led to believe that relief programs can end poverty rather than only institutionalize poverty.

The direction of a nation that has built the greatest prosperity ever known, by individual initiative, but which now is tempted to forsake that initiative for the illusory comforts of Government guardianship. . . .

This Administration is a child of depression-born theories and its current family chieftain is a captive of them right down the line or, rather, right down the breadline.

The facts are there for anyone to see. This Administration is aiming a double-barreled shotgun of Federal spending at our heads.

Now, answer these questions; you must answer these questions: has Federal spending of this sort really created jobs upon which working men and women can depend; has it created a rise in the standard of living; has it modernized our industrial plant to make it more competitive with overseas producers; has it? Can it?

Or must they be done in the market place, by working men and women, by investors willing to risk and with the capital to do it, by scientists and engineers building the new tools, techniques, and products? You cannot be on both sides of the question or the answers. The current Administration cannot either.

Let me make this clear: I have no disagreement with the statement that our economy demands a tax reduction. It most surely does.

My point is that this needed tax reduction should be earned by the real kind of economizing in Federal spending that would be possible if the effort were sincere.

Many of the new programs with which we are to be faced, however, are said to be part of a war on poverty. And who can be against that?

America, for most of its years, has waged a war on poverty. And wherever it has waged that war in factories, in laboratories, in shops, over counters and under the enterprise system, it has won that war. It has won it, is winning it more surely than any nation on earth.

And I say that this war on poverty can only be won that way. I say that when we work our way to wealth, we win that war. I say that when Government tries to spend its way to wealth, we lose that war. Santa Claus dreams, or rolled-up sleeves! We have to make a choice! . . .

The first question, of course, is how many Americans are poor? Franklin Roosevelt said that a third of the nation was impoverished and you can still hear the same figure cited, although the certified, pasteurized, homogenized, officialized figure is now one-fifth.

Also, a few years ago, some called a family poor if its income was below $1,500. Now it is $3,000. Others say that any family is poor if it can't afford what the Department of Labor computes to be the standard of living of the average urban worker.

In a country as wealthy as ours, it is implied, everyone should be above the average! An interesting statistical exercise!

The fact is, of course, that these income levels are regarded as true wealth in the rest of the world. Workers in many other countries cannot earn as much as our welfare clients receive!

As our production and income levels have moved up over a hundred years, our concepts of what is poor have moved up also—and they always will! It is like greyhounds chasing a mechanical hare. You can never catch up. There will always be a lowest one-third or one-fifth.

Under the governmental policies of the Big Government Party over the past three decades we have reduced rewards for good work and also reduced the penalties for laziness or waste.

If somebody set out deliberately to slow down economic growth he could not do better than to reduce the incentives for enterprise and abolish the consequences of inertia.

I strongly believe that all people are entitled to an opportunity—let me stress that—to an opportunity to get an education and to earn a living in keeping with the value of their work.

I also believe that those in trouble through no fault of their own must be helped by society. I believe that those in trouble through their own fault should always have an opportunity to work themselves out of it. But I do not believe that the mere fact of having little money entitles everybody, regardless of circumstance, to be permanently maintained by the taxpayers at an average or comfortable standard of living. . . .

Many unskilled jobs have disappeared simply because the wages that have to be paid for them exceed the value of the work. Relief has not helped solve this but has compounded it.

This, it seems to me, raises the question of an essential safeguard we should place on public welfare programs: those who are physically able to work should be put to work to earn their benefits at a specified rate per hour.

We are told, however, that many people lack skills and cannot find jobs because they did not have an education. That's like saying that people have big feet because they wear big shoes. The fact is that most people who have no skill, have had no education for the same reason—low intelligence or low ambition.

We have talked of many details in this over-all problem. But we are not talking about many principles. Only two, basically, are involved. Enterprise versus regimentation, a society fluid in its opportunity, or a society hardened into a Government mold.

Specifically, in a society where the vast majority of people live on a standard that is envied by all other nations, it must be appropriate to inquire whether the attitude or action of the small group not participating in the general prosperity has anything to do with the situation.

I would call a conference with participation from all of the states to study this problem of poverty and jobs, to pin down the figures, to survey all the solutions and not seek to impose the Federal one.

I would, also, seek to find for the Federal Government more of a role in removing restrictions than in imposing new ones—at every level of the economy.

In higher education, I have already offered, in the Senate, an example of what I consider to be the proper Federal role. I have proposed, and have been pleased to see even some outstanding Democrat legislators similarly propose, that the Federal Government permit certain tax credits to those who pay tuitions and fees for their children or others at colleges and universities.

No matter the detail, I stand on the side of such principles. There is, as one of your colleagues so neatly puts it, no such thing as a free lunch.

Industrious Americans have made this the wealthiest nation on earth. Concerned Americans have kept it a free nation.

We have only to make the choice: will we use the energy and revitalize the heart, or will we abandon both for false securities?

In this choice we will either build tomorrow or write our epitaph.

16: Political Activity

Unions and managements bargain not only across the table, over the terms of a collective agreement, but across the ballot box, over the terms of legislation. Both groups are concerned with the basic labor legislation, to be sure, but both are also concerned with many other types of laws which Congress and the states may consider—laws dealing with taxation, housing, education, social security, minimum wage, and so on.

As each group seeks to influence the terms of such legislation by putting into office friendly legislators and administrators and by keeping the pressure on such legislators and administrators once elected, they inevitably find themselves engaged in highly organized political activity. In recent years public attention has been more fastened on union political action, but businesses have been no less active in their own way.

RESTRICTION ON POLITICAL CONTRIBUTIONS

From the Labor Management Relations Act of 1947, Sec. 304

It is unlawful for any national bank, or any corporation organized by authority of any law of Congress, to make a contribution or expenditure in connection with any election to any political office, or in connection with any primary election or political convention or caucus held to select candidates for any political office, or for any corporation whatever, or any labor organization to make a contribution or expenditure in connection with any election at which Presidential and Vice Presidential electors or a Senator or Representative in, or a Delegate or Resident Commissioner to Congress are to be voted for, or in connection with any primary election or political convention or caucus held to select candidates for any of the foregoing offices, or for any candidate, political committee, or other person to accept or receive any contribution prohibited by this section. Every corporation or labor organization which makes any contribution or expenditure in violation of this section shall be fined not more than $5,000; and every officer or director of any corporation, or officer of any labor organization, who consents to any contribution or expenditure by the corporation or labor organization, as the case may be, in violation of this section shall be fined not more than $1,000 or imprisoned for not more than one year, or both. For the purposes of this section "labor organization" means any organization of any kind, or any agency or employee representation committee or plan, in which employees participate and which exists for the purpose, in whole or in part, of dealing with employers concerning grievances, labor disputes, wages, rates of pay, hours of employment, or conditions of work.

AFL-CIO COMMITTEE ON POLITICAL EDUCATION

Testimony of Jack Kroll and James L. McDevitt, Codirectors, AFL-CIO Committee on Political Education, in 1956 Presidential and Senatorial Campaign Contributions and Practices, hearings before a subcommittee of the Senate Committee on Rules and Administration, 84th Cong., 2d Sess., part 1, pp. 48–63

. . . the Committee on Political Education was formed on December 5, 1955, by action of the first convention of the American Federation of Labor and Congress of Industrial Organizations.

That convention also adopted a resolution, which we submit here for the record, outlining our tasks and our goals.

The committee chairman is George Meany. Its secretary-treasurer is William Schnitzler. It consists of the 27 vice presidents of the AFL-CIO plus 27 other officials of affiliated unions. The day-to-day operations of the committee are carried on by the codirectors, James L. McDevitt and Jack Kroll, and their staff. The staff consist of 41 persons at the headquarters in Washintgon plus 13 people who devote their time and attention to the field activities of our organization.

The work of our committee falls into three general catgories.

We have it as our first responsibility, as we have indicated, the education of our own membership on the issues which we conceive to be of prime concern. We believe they should be as fully informed regarding these questions, and the stands of those they elect to positions of responsibility and trust in government, as possible.

We therefore publish a wide variety of literature which ranges from methods of political organization to discussion of such subjects as the Taft-Hartley Act, social security, and welfare legislation.

We have undertaken this year to provide each member of our organization with a voting record of his Senators and his Representative dealing with about 20 labor, general welfare, domestic policy, and foreign aid issues over the years so that the member can form his own judgment as to the character of his representation.

The AFL-CIO has appeared before the platform committees of both major parties and presented its views on the major public questions.

We have held meetings in various parts of the country at which men and women have gathered to talk about the problems which confront them and the country. Our field representatives are meeting constantly with local union organizations assisting them in discussing issues and in formulating programs.

Our State conventions and other large bodies have gone out of their way to invite candidates from both parties to address them and give them the benefit of their views.

And we would like to emphasize that the program and policies we are concerned with are not narrow, partisan, group-interest issues. They are issues which affect every American, whether or not he or she is a member of our organization and whether or not he or she is engaged in industry, agriculture, or a profession.

We do not believe that we control any votes. We would not want that power were it within our grasp because such power in the hands of any individual can only run counter to the interests of democratic government. Nor are we so arrogant or naive as to believe that any American citizen would surrender his conscience and his judgment to anyone.

We have faith in the good sense and judgment of the American people and we are willing, at all times, to abide by the will of the majority however distasteful that decision, at any given moment, may be to us.

What is important, however, is that as many citizens as possible participate in our elections and this is the area in which the second category of our activities falls.

We are currently engaged in a registration campaign that will raise the level of political participation to what we hope will be its highest peak. We want to be content, after election day, that no member of our organization failed to understand the privileges available to him through any fault of ours.

We have designated appropriate weeks in the various States "R Week" during which time we will seek to utilize all the channels of communication open to us to inform our members of where they can register, when they can register, and what the registration procedures are.

We are proud that we have succeeded as well as we have in making the Nation registration-conscious. It is a campaign we have been conducting for the last three national elections and throughout all the intervening State and local elections.

Today there are many organizations engaged in this activity. We are proud of the contribution we have made in being among the first to call attention to this problem.

In this connection you will note that among the resolutions adopted by the convention of the AFL-CIO is one which calls for a uniform registration system throughout the States which will eliminate the many unnecessary and cumbersome rules and regulations which now prevail in many places.

The third category of our activities deals with the support of candidates for public office. As we have indicated the first deals with information respecting the issues while the second concerns itself with voter participation.

We should like to make it clear that our organization, the Committee on Political Education, does not and will not recommend candidates for senatorial, congressional, State, or local offices. That is not our job. It is the job of the local and State organizations and the local voters, and they would and properly do resent any attempt to have an outside judgment imposed upon them.

We do not, therefore, as we have many times stated, have any purge list either public or secret and all attempts to concoct one are the mere products of a political campaign.

That does not mean that we do not consult with our local and State organizations or that we do not make available to them such facts and materials as we may have in our possession which would assist them in forming their own opinions. On the contrary, we believe one of our important functions is to keep them as fully informed as possible.

The recommendations with regard to candidates for the President and Vice President are the province of the general board of the AFL-CIO which will be meeting in Chicago on September 12 for the purpose of considering such action.

There is one additional phase of our activity that may be of some interest.

We have made, and we will make, modest contributions to candidates for public office who have been commended to us by the local and State organizations.

We have filed a statement of such contributions, as well as the other details of our finances as the law requires, with the proper authorities.

It will be apparent to you as you examine this statement that our treasury and financial resources hardly merit the attention which has been paid them by certain opponents of labor. Our total expenses this year were just about matched by the political contributions of just four families in the 1954 congressional elections. We assume these families will not be less interested this year.

We do not believe that the power of money can or should win elections. We believe that it is the power of ideas which can and does win elections. It is ideas, not money, which generate the kind of enthusiasm and willingness to participate that you gentlemen know is the essential ingredient of successful elections. It is a program, a record of promises made and kept, a devotion to public service and public service alone that moves people to the kind of activity which results in election victories.

If we have been successful in our program it has not been because of our financial resources. It has been because of the kind of activity we engage in. We believe it has been wholesome and beneficial and it has won adherents on that account and on that account alone. . . .

SENATOR GORE: The committee would like to know the exact amount of funds which the organization you represent, AFL-CIO Committee on Political Education had on hand as of September 1. . . .

MR. MCDEVITT: $215,360.60. In the educational fund we have $117,754.41.

SENATOR GORE: How do you differentiate between the educational fund and the campaign fund or the funds of the Committee on Political Education?

MR. MCDEVITT: The explanation for those two funds, Mr. Chairman, are that the political fund is raised through voluntary contributions for political purposes only.

The educational funds are for educational activities only and do not become a part of any expenditures in behalf or in opposition to any candidate.

SENATOR GORE: Now, I failed to make note of the educational fund of $100,000-some, you said?

MR. MCDEVITT: That's right. To be exact again, Mr. Chairman, $117,754.41.

SENATOR GORE: Do I correctly understand you to testify that at no time do you plan to use for purposes of a political contribution any funds derived from your ordinary membership dues?

MR. MCDEVITT: That's right.

MR. KROLL: That is quite correct.

SENATOR GORE: Are these funds maintained separately in a bank account or are they commingled?

MR. MCDEVITT: They are maintained as separate accounts, Mr. Chairman.

SENATOR GORE: What is your budget for the political year 1956?

MR. MCDEVITT: Are you referring to a budget involving the political fund?

SENATOR GORE: I would like that, please, sir.

MR. MCDEVITT: There is no budget for the political funds, Mr. Chairman.

SENATOR GORE: There is no budget for the political fund?

MR. MCDEVITT: No. That is a voluntary fund. That is what we call the voluntary dollar, and we are necessarily guided in our expenditures by the amount of dollars we receive, and therefore there isn't any way in establishing a budget for that approach. . . .

SENATOR GORE: Well, if you do not have a specific budget, is it reasonable to presume that you do have some plans, some estimates of the amount of funds that you will have for political activity?

MR. KROLL: May I answer that, Jim. We cannot do it because we never know from day to day how many voluntary or political dollars we will be getting in. And we do it this way. If we think a candidate merits our support because of the action of the State or local code, then we give them a partial payment and if the rest of the money comes in we send them the balance that is recommended by the State. Do you follow me?

SENATOR GORE: Yes; I follow you.

MR. KROLL: Do I make myself clear? We make no commitments until we have the money. We can't spend the money until it comes in, and we have no way of knowing how much money comes in.

SENATOR GORE: You have no estimate of the amount of funds you may raise? How much did you raise by this method in 1952?

MR. KROLL: Well, 1952 we were not merged. I think between the 2 organizations we made about $700,000. I think that was about what it was.

SENATOR GORE: The two organizations?

MR. KROLL: Combined.

MR. MCDEVITT: Ours averaged out at less than 3 cents per member for all of the membership of the American Federation of Labor in the year of 1952.

SENATOR GORE: Do you think you will do as well in 1956?

MR. KROLL: We certainly hope so.

SENATOR GORE: Do you expect to do so?

MR. KROLL: We are trying to do better.

SENATOR GORE: What is your goal?

MR. KROLL: Our goal, as Mr. McDevitt has said, our goal is every member 25 cents.

SENATOR GORE: Do you think you will reach as much as $1 million?

MR. KROLL: I doubt it.

MR. MCDEVITT: I doubt it. . . .

MR. KROLL: Mr. Chairman, if I may add this up, as a trade-union movement it is traditional with us that when we are solicited for help by any organization in any State in the Union that are in difficulties, the trade-union membership is more than anxious to help, and that is traditional. We carry that into the political field when an organization in a given State needs help to elect, financial help to elect a good candidate or defeat a bad candidate, the organizations are more than willing to help. As I said, it is traditional.

SENATOR GORE: Are you not willing to leave, Mr. Kroll, to the judgment of the people of a given State or a given congressional district the exercise of their judgment as to who is a bad or who is a good candidate?

MR. KROLL: Oh, sure, sure, we are. But Mr. Chairman, these Senators or Congressmen who come here vote for good or bad legislation affecting the trade-union movement, not of just the one State. They legislate for the entire 48 States, and a bad Congressman from 1 State can affect the membership in New York State just as effectively as if he comes from New York State alone.

These Senators don't legislate for one State alone. They legislate for the Nation as a whole.

SENATOR GORE: Well, would not that be equally true with respect to a corporate interest?

MR. KROLL: I don't know if corporate interests wait for solicitation from the members in their State. We wait until that State asks us for help.

SENATOR GORE: Is that the only distinction you draw?

MR. KROLL: At the moment. . . .

SENATOR CURTIS: The point is your whole educational expenditure is for political purposes now; isn't it?

MR. KROLL: That is not true.

MR. MCDEVITT: Definitely not true.

SENATOR CURTIS: What is it for?

MR. MCDEVITT: Educational purposes. Everything that the word implies, educational.

SENATOR CURTIS: Don't the political parties carry on that?

MR. MCDEVITT: What's this?

SENATOR CURTIS: The Republican Party carries on a tremendous educational program. They tell people about the President, they tell the people about what it has accomplished. That is education.

MR. MCDEVITT: Is it?

SENATOR CURTIS: I think it is.

MR. MCDEVITT: I'm inclined to think, Senator, I think that is designed by the Republican National Committee in its behalf.

MR. KROLL: Senator, we talk about no candidate. We talk about issues as those issues affect our people. We talk about no candidate at all. When we talk about a candidate, we use voluntary money. Now, let's understand that clearly. We talk about issues, no President. . . .

SENATOR MANSFIELD: Now, just to reiterate one particular point again, because the question has been raised in this committee and elsewhere, the contributions made to COPE are all on a voluntary basis and there is no coercion used.

MR. MCDEVITT: As far as for political purposes, that is either in behalf of or in opposition to a candidate, that's right.

Now, we accept contributions to our educational fund, but that is not used at any time under any circumstances in connection with anyone's campaign.

SENATOR MANSFIELD: Is the purpose of the educational fund indirectly connected with campaigns to the extent that records of Members of Congress, analysis of bills and things of that sort are put down on paper and distributed?

MR. MCDEVITT: We pay out of the educational fund the cost of distributing that voting record. That is for information, and there is nothing in the voting record, Senator, if you will wait just a second, there is nothing in the voting record—this is the set here that was put out for 48 States, there is nothing in that record that suggests that you vote for Jones or Smith or not vote for Jones or Smith. We make no recommendations. We simply take the bills that we had an interest in, where the AFL-CIO took a position, and we announce to the State, to our membership, just how the Congressman and the Senators voted on that particular measure or that series of measures.

MR. KROLL: I'd like to add to that. We also use the educational money for urging registration, urging the memberships to register.

MR. MCDEVITT: And also on forum discussions in classes and instructing them on legislation and how to operate their unions insofar as our interests are concerned.

SENATOR MANSFIELD: The educational fund is used strictly for educational and public-service functions.

MR. KROLL: Right.

MR. MCDEVITT: Exactly.

UNION POLITICAL DOMINATION—REALITY OR NIGHTMARE?

An address by Cola G. Parker, President, National Association of Manufacturers, and Director, Kimberly-Clark Corporation, before the Economic Club of Detroit, October 15, 1956

A TIME FOR PLAIN SPEAKING

This could be a decisive year in the history of America.

It is the year in which organized labor leadership has proclaimed an all-out effort to elect a Congress, and if possible an Administration, which will do the bidding of the handful of men who have the effrontery to claim the American working man as their chattel and possession—who have the gall to say that they, and they alone, speak for American working people. Even many of their own members are unwilling captives, and their total enrollment represents only about one-quarter of the nation's work force.

What I'm telling you is not news. There has been no effort to conceal this power-grab from the nation. Heady with the power they already possess by virtue of holding millions of American working people within the iron grasp of compulsory unionism, the leaders of organized labor boldly announce their intention of seizing political control of the country.

As I say, this is not news to this audience. Nor is it news to anyone who reads the papers. But what appalls me is the stark indifference—and indifference which is alarming—which prevails all over the country. As I read the situation, the people are relying on business and professional men to meet and turn back this challenge to their political traditions. But, I speak for businessmen. And so my remarks will be confined to them.

The businessmen of America sit like rabbits hypnotized by a snake, seemingly helpless to organize a program to defend the American political and economic system, which is essential to the welfare of the American people and to their own welfare. Worse still, they seem too indifferent, or lethargic, or paralyzed by a feeling of hopelessness to seize upon and use the weapons of defense which are available to them.

I should tell you at the outset that NAM does not deny the right of employees to form or join unions and to bargain collectively. We are not out to "bust" unions. But we are opposed to monopoly power in the hands of either business or unions. We are against illegal and unethical practices in the operation of unions. And we are against the use of union funds and union organizations for partisan political purposes. . . .

The intentions, and the program of action, of organized labor in this political campaign are amply documented. Like Hitler when he wrote "Mein Kampf," and like Karl Marx when he wrote "Das Kapital" and the "Communist Manifesto," the leaders of the AFL-CIO have proclaimed in writing and in public statements exactly what they intend to do.

George Meany said last November: "The scene of the battle is no longer the company plant or the picket line. It has moved into legislative halls of Congress and the state legislatures."

The use of the term "battle" is revealing as to the mental attitude and processes of organized labor's leadership.

The union objective, according to their spokesmen, is to elect their own definition of liberal representatives at all levels of government and, if possible, a President and state governors, mayors and other local officials, who will be pliable to the demands of Mr. Meany and his associates.

Now, how are they going about it? What are they actually doing in this campaign, today, to gain their objectives?

They are pouring money and manpower in the election drive at a rate which makes previous efforts seem strictly bush league.

They are diverting to political activity the services of more than 60,000 full-time paid union officers—men and women who are well versed in and capable of applying to electioneering the same tactics of misrepresentation and intimidation which have been used so frequently in industrial disputes.

They have organized election workers from their ranks in as many of the nation's 140,000 voting precincts as possible.

They have turned more than 1,000 union newspapers, with circulation in the millions, into outright propaganda sheets for favored candidates.

They have stepped up the political voltage and the slant of their two regular nationwide network broadcasts as well as union-controlled sectional radio and TV programs.

They are buying time on radio and television for their candidates to appear before the public.

As they did with one of the great political parties here in Michigan, they are taking over political organizations where they are weak at state as well as local levels.

They are infiltrating community organizations of all kinds, from Parent-Teacher Associations, to school boards and social service agencies.

They are wooing the votes of everyone—farmers, white collar people and non-union as well as union members—with the pocketbook approach, promising lower taxes, higher wages, greater social security, less work hours, and larger unemployment and workmen's compensation payments.

They are preparing and distributing every conceivable type of campaign aid for the candidates who have their endorsement.

And, perhaps most effective of all, they are enlisting some 2,000,000 campaign workers with the proclaimed objective of calling at every home in the land they can reach. . . .

But, this is only the beginning. The union political organization will grow and be perfected. And the union leaders will try and keep trying, until they win. In 1958, they will be more effective than in 1956, and in 1960 they will know better what to do and how to do it than in 1958. Unless halted, organized labor eventually will dominate the American political scene. Our history will become the history of Socialist England all over again. . . .

Laws are made by politicians, and politicians want to be elected and re-elected. We cannot rely on the politicians of either party to take forthright action against the political machine the unions already have built up, and which they are putting through its paces in this election. As time goes on and the machine grows stronger, the chances of their doing so will become less and less.

The only effective action is to create a countervailing force—an organization which gets down to the people in every state, and every county, and every precinct—an organization which can carry the truth to the people in their homes. . . .

The preservation of what we call the American way of life transcends the personal or corporate interest of every one of us. No sacrifice is too great, no task too onerous, no foe too fearsome—Walter Reuther or Dave McDonald or anyone else—in this struggle to keep America a nation of all the people.

It is a time for plain speaking, and—as one American—I have tried to speak plainly.

On October 17, 1956, the AFL-CIO News Service released a story carrying a reply to Mr. Parker by George Meany, AFL-CIO president. It included the following paragraphs.

When Parker "wakes up from his nightmare," Meany retorted, he will find "that the former head of General Motors runs the Defense Dept. and that other big business leaders occupy virtually every key post in our national government."

If Parker "thinks labor would like to change this situation, he is right," Meany said. "But our political activities are being conducted by democratic and legal methods" and "every citizen has the right to vote and speak his mind on politics."

Political activity may involve more than bargains with candidates and efforts to get people to vote for the right man. In recent years the unions have been countering business charges that huge political machines have been formed out of the labor movement with the charge that business has its more subtle instruments for molding public sentiment in support of its programs. Again it is the politically conscious UAW which authored the article.

THE SECRET STRUGGLE TO CHANGE YOUR IDEAS

From Ammunition, published by the United Automobile Workers, September, 1955, pp. 6–10

"During the past two decades, top management slowly awoke to the fact that what employees thought, and how they subsequently voted, were vitally important factors—and that these factors had a direct and telling effect on the climate in which business had to operate," a recent article declared in the *Public Relations Journal.*

Increasingly, industry is trying to change the way its workers and members of their families have been thinking. It's pulling the strings and paying the bills for this super-expensive campaign, and not just because the way its workers vote can affect the "climate" in which corporations operate.

Equally, it's trying to coax workers into accepting management policies and decisions they normally would oppose through their unions, along with political policies which would bring the same reaction.

The task of manipulating such policies and decisions to make them more palatable to the public is being taken over now on a larger scale than ever before by so-called public relations men, a new injection in the top management structure.

Once upon a time, they were known as press agents. Their only function then was to get publicity for the company, its product and its officers.

Now, however, they're striving—with management help—to become one of the most powerful opinion-swaying groups in the country. Their big push toward that objective moved forward rapidly after the 1952 election which might be said to have been aided more by the gimmicks of Madison avenue advertising agencies than by Republican doorbell ringers.

How important their function is considered by top management was summarized by *Time* magazine which, in an article on industry's use of public relations, declared:

"Public relations is a long and continuous campaign, aimed at molding public opinion on a broad basis for the benefit of a corporation."

And you're the target!

You're the target, and management's ideas are being aimed at you in every possible way, shape and form all through the day. Daily newspapers, radio and television programs, reading racks, house organs, movie shorts—all these and other methods of reaching vast numbers of people are being used intensively in industry's unending efforts to get people to accept its ideas as their own.

These efforts, of course, take place behind the scenes. They couldn't be effective otherwise. Propaganda loses its value when it's recognized for what it is. Newspapers particularly are aware of this.

Almost all slant the labor, political and economic news they print to favor management and the political policies and candidates management supports. But the papers also attempt to give this respectability by tying it to a news source or event or occasionally by printing "the other side."

Newspapers particularly are susceptible to industry's propaganda campaigns. For the most part, industry pays their bills. The papers depend on industry-bought advertising for the bulk of their income. The majority, therefore, have listened willingly to the siren song of the corporation Loreleis.

Additionally, newspapers themselves are big business. They operate, as other companies do, to make a profit. They hire and fire, buy and sell, depreciate buildings and machinery, turn out products, meet payrolls—and don't stay in business very long if they lose money.

The radio and television industry is in somewhat the same position. It, too, depends on advertisers for its income. Instead of buying space on the printed page, the advertisers dealing with radio and TV stations buy time.

Often, however, they use that time to sell the corporation's ideas more than its products. Many huge corporations, which sell only to other companies and not to the public, now sponsor lengthy, expensive programs as well as those featuring news analyses or commentaries. It is not surprising that the corporation's economic, labor and political ideas turn up on these broadcasts in the form of "comments" or commercials.

They also turn up in pamphlets on factory reading racks and in company house organs. Management has been using both increasingly in the campaign to get its views across to workers and their families.

The house organs—a trade name for company magazines—are an obvious setup for industry propaganda. They're where readers would expect to find management's point of view. They're financed by the plant to tell its own story. It's expected that what a company magazine prints will be written to emphasize management's ideas.

This, however, is vastly different from the hypocritical appearance of "impartiality" that industry tries to tack on to its propaganda in other forms of reaching people.

Aside from newspapers and radio and television, reading racks are a strong example of this. About 4,000 corporations now are estimated to have reading racks in their plants. The *Wall Street Journal* has estimated that in-plant pickups of reading rack pamphlets total more than 30 million individual copies a year.

Many of these contain the names of apparently disinterested organizations as their publishers. Actually, they're put out by companies financed by industry or busines organizations. These are paid to prepare the reading rack material to tell a particular story so it can be used in management's propaganda campaign. The Foundation for Economic Education, the Good Reading Rack Service, the Advertising Council, Inc., the American Economic Foundation, and the Committee for Constitutional Government are among the industry-financed propaganda groups preparing and supplying these pamphlets.

One purpose of this multi-million-dollar-a-year industry is to "lessen employee resistance to information considered to be a management story," the *Wall Street Journal* declared. General Motors Corp. alone spends a half-million dollars a year on its plant rack program, *Fortune* magazine has disclosed.

Additionally, company magazines now are published regularly by more than 8,000 corporations, the *Journal* reported earlier this year. Each issue of these magazines combines to total some 19 million copies, and about 80 million people read them, the newspaper added.

The companies mail them to their workers' homes or hand them out at plant gates; they're put on dealers' counters, given to salesmen to distribute, sent to customers.

"Managements around the country think enough of these publications to spend about $140 million annually on them," the *Journal* stated. And, it added, companies are "getting their money back many times over."

Increasingly, the public relations experts are taking over supervision of these company-financed publications and programs, and representing management in dealing with the others. In the past, they talked in terms of these operations as methods to boost morale and production and to "help the worker appreciate the company."

But now, their field is becoming broader by their own action. They not only want to stimulate but also to manipulate how workers think and react. They believe they're developing the tools to accomplish that.

And one way in which some public relations specialists themselves see their new role was stated by Kieber R. Miller, public relations director for the Hawaii Employers Council. He said:

"Through the adroit application of psychology and social physics, it should be possible for the public relations man to transform left-wing union leadership into an enthusiastic corps of Christians and ideological caiptalists."

To the employers Miller represents, all union leadership is left-wing, and only those who conform to management's ideas and programs can be saved.

Industry's campaign to win the minds of its workers and their families has been under way for many years. From time to time, its methods change but its objective remains the same. As recently as the 1930s many bosses still tried to dictate how workers were to vote. And wage earners in many instances were fired just for expressing an idea with which the boss disagreed.

Although such tactics still take place in some shops, they generally have been replaced by more subtle and hidden efforts to sway workers' thinking. Policies which companies sponsor and advocate strongly are passed along to workers increasingly in the form of publications or messages from sources which appear to have no direct connection with management.

Striving to speed up the headway made through this approach, however, the public relations and advertising men have been plugging the development of improved methods for influencing people. One they've been working on involves adapting the gimmicks which persuade people to buy particular products so they can be used to coax them into "buying" particular ideas.

Still in its formative stage, the new technique is a combination of advertising and psychology. The advertising and public relations specialists call it "motivation research." It's based on what they find out in "depth interviews" which plumb your innermost feelings—or those of others like you.

The idea is when the researchers know why you go for certain products or ideas—when they know what factors cause you to react as you do—they'll know how to aim their advertising and messages to get the biggest response. . . .

Some researchers now are hard at work trying to speed the development of these techniques so they can be used to sell company programs and ideas on a large scale as well as company products.

One such study recently recommended that management use two different programs to influence the attitudes of the people on its payrolls. Supervisors ought to be given both sides of an issue, according to this report, while rank-and-file workers should get only a one-sided propaganda campaign.

The recommendation was based on the researchers' theory that supervisors are better educated than workers. The fact that supervisors generally come from the ranks of workers seems not to have been considered in forming either the theory or the recommendation.

Nor was the tradition that all people have the right to know both sides of a question so they can make up their own minds about it. . . .

Both in factories and communities where workers and citizens have widely-varied interests and loyalties, the public relations campaigns to shape the acceptance of corporation thinking could have only one result if it were not being met by opposing forces—and that would be to build conformity, to turn back progress, to weaken workers' job security, to stifle union gains and ultimately to patternize the thinking of individuals.

The struggle to get one's ideas and policies generally accepted is natural in democracy. Ideas are offered; they compete; when they come to be believed, they are acted on.

The apprehension and concern over industry's public relations programs for spreading acceptance of its ideas and policies doesn't involve this process as such.

Instead, it's aimed at the fact that issues are not put squarely before the people. Rather, efforts are made to "sell" them through the use of laboratory-developed hidden methods, guinea-pig-tested techniques, deliberately misleading impressions, and scientifically-prepared propaganda devices.

How can people guard against these usually-secret efforts to influence their ideas?

Propaganda appeals can be recognized. They can be looked into. They can be analyzed.

You should decide whether the source is reliable or not.

You should know whether the appeal is emotional or factual.

You should see whether you're being told the whole truth or just part of it—or if you're not being told the truth at all.

When you look at the source, you know whether it can be trusted to tell you the truth or not.

You know if it's fought for you in the past or against you.

If its name doesn't give you any indication of this, see if what it says sounds as if it comes from a source you do know.

If the appeal is made to your emotions instead of your ability to think and analyze, ask yourself why. Are the emotional appeals put there because there aren't facts to support the appeal? Are they trying to play up to emotional drives, such as the desire of many people to feel important? If they are, will it benefit you or them?

Do they use words which can mean different things to different people? If your boss or a newspaper editorial talks about security, do they mean the kind of security that would benefit the many or the few? If the company or a reading rack pamphlet or an editorial or a Republican politician talks about reduced taxes, does that mean your own taxes have been reduced? Can a law which reduces taxes just send them down for industry but not for you? Can it give people with big incomes much more of a tax cut than you?

Are you being told the whole story by what you read or hear or see? Not in every detail, perhaps, but so you get a full picture of what's going on? Are you being given both sides or not? Is the appeal only a mixture of opinions and a few facts put together to get you thinking in a certain specific line?

Finally, what results are being sought by those trying to influence the way you think? Who'll benefit—you or they?

For that's the key to why the appeal was made to start with.

BUSINESS—AND THE MANY

From General Electric Public & Employee Relations News, January 28, 1957

This is the time when public servants at the national, state and local level are trying to decide what to do in the best interests of the public. This is no easy task.

People have been told too long that government can solve all problems and make all dreams come true. It is, therefore, no wonder that more and more people are looking to government for painless solutions and effortless gains —in the mistaken idea that all this is available.

Faithful public officials are distressed because they know that no government representative can deliver up to any such false expectations. Yet too many feel they must try—and believe they must convince their constituents they are trying.

The public's expectations can be brought into line with sober reality only when misinformation has been corrected. Public servants can be freed to act on the merits of proposals only when they are relieved from the pressure of the misinformation in the minds of the folks back home. Otherwise, the electorate's representatives will be forced or permitted to embark on unrealistic adventures that can result only in costly consequences.

Too largely missing at the moment is the necessary "something-for-something" realization by the public—and by some public servants—that government can give only what it first takes, and that what the government promises cannot be taken from any *few* but must be taken from the *many* through:

—Indirect taxes that have to be included in prices everyone pays; or
—The brutal tax of inflation that also shows up in prices; or
—Through the lessened investment toward the faster future rise in the level of living.

There is even confusion as to who's the *few* and who's the *many*.

For instance, here in the United States there are 4 million businesses and there are 160 million citizens. We businessmen have been so lacking in alertness that we have let the demagogs successfully promote the political fallacy that "business" is the few and "people" is the many. Whereas, business *is* people— is simply a *gathering* of people, a gathering of the *many*.

A business brings people together and makes it possible for them to do more for each other than they otherwise could. Unless it does this, the business expires.

For *customers, employees, savers, suppliers, distribution folks*—and these and others as *citizens*—are all brought together in a business to make their contributions and claim their just rewards.

If the particular business does not provide each contributor-claimant with the opportunity to get more for what he contributes than would be the case without the aid of that business—or if some other business offers material or nonmaterial rewards he thinks he will like better—he and his fellow contributor-claimants will start pulling out and the gathering will fall apart.

The free competition among businesses to be effective in pleasing free people—with the spur of extra rewards to those contributor-claimants who are most diligent and efficient within those businesses—is the best technique ever evolved by mankind for that steady rise in attractiveness and that steady reduction in relative cost which make desirable things obtainable in ever greater quantities by an ever greater *many*.

Here's a place where each local General Electric manager and his associates in other local businesses can publicly supply specific information that will, in the public interest, help clear up misinformation. Here's a place where they can provide their public representatives with specific information as to how their businesses serve the interests of not the few but the *many*.

Every conscientious public servant at local, state or national level, for instance, sincerely tries to judge each issue or proposal on the basis of how it is likely to affect the jobs and businesses of his constituents. He wants to make his decisions contribute to what is best for the many and not just any few.

These public representatives will be aided in this purpose by any local help they can get in generating among their constituents the kind of understanding, approval and support in their community that will permit and enable them to vote in the way that is sound and really for the common good of all.

Whether a Governor of a State or a Congressman, for example, has ever thought of it in quite this way before, he and General Electric have a uniquely common interest in jobs and the flow of business within his state or in his district. The local General Electric manager—or *any one* of his professional or other associates—can succeed in *his* job only if he helps many, many others there succeed in *their* jobs. Many of these he helps will be inside—but *most outside*—the General Electric plant or office walls.

This interest in jobs and the flow of business is one all businessmen and all public representatives have in common. But we businessmen simply have not made known in warm, specific, and intimate detail—the only way that is persuasive and meaningful—how each business serves the many and how there is no such thing as a program helping or injuring only a given business without likewise helping or injuring all those dependent on or affected by that business. . . .

There is *no* reason why *any* local manager shouldn't be anxious to put in the hands of his community neighbors and in the hands of their various public representatives the [above] kind of facts * as they may apply specifically to a particular locality or state or as they may apply to all the constituents in whom a particular official is certain to be interested. In fact, there are *many* reasons why *every* effort should be made to show the public and the public's representatives how General Electric—as only one example of the millions of responsible American businesses—is not only trying to serve the *many*, rather than the mere *few*, but also how the evidence indicates we are *doing pretty well at it* all things considered, even though we are *trying* all the time to do *still* better.

The public and the public's various representatives, whether local, state or national, should be aware of local management's efforts to explain the direct

* As to jobs and payrolls: number of suppliers, retailers, and owners; local tax contributions, etc.—Ed.

interest of the many in business; they should be aware of the wide support which awaits those who in public life are trying to do the things that are genuinely in the short and long term best interests of all who are dependent on or are affected by business—which is obviously just about everybody.

Our public servants and community neighbors should have adequate *background* information concerning the business of General Electric and how it is that whatever seriously affects that business will likewise affect *persons*—persons who are well-known not only for their general usefulness and significance in the particular community but also as General Electric customers, employees, suppliers, retailers, wholesalers, and shareowners.

Such background information—not only as to General Electric, but as to other business as well—would seem essential for any sound two-way communication between public officials and those they represent.

There is no reason why such information should not be made available whenever the opportunity presents itself. There is no reason why such background information should not be volunteered to interested public officials as essential factual data highly relevant to the innumerable official decisions they are required to make on almost a daily basis.

Finally, the reason for the suggestion that such background information be based upon the jobs and other opportunities our Company provides locally—and inferentially that any other business should thus prepare its own information rather than have an association try to speak for all—is that totals or averages can hardly be more than cold business statistics. They fail to portray a given business clearly as a gathering together of free and independent *people*. They simply cannot present as intimate, meaningful and significant a picture as do the individual company examples to the public and to the public's servants.

Catalog

If you are interested in a list of fine Paperback
books, covering a wide range of subjects
and interests, send your name and address,
requesting your free catalog, to:

McGraw-Hill Paperbacks
330 West 42nd Street
New York, New York 10036